THE POLITICAL
FOUNDATIONS OF
INTERNATIONAL LAW

JOHN WILEY & SONS, INC.

NEW YORK · LONDON · SYDNEY

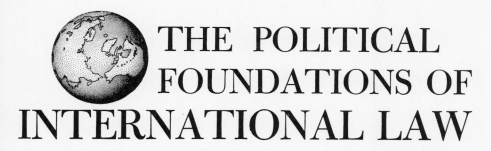

THE POLITICAL
FOUNDATIONS OF
INTERNATIONAL LAW

MORTON A. KAPLAN   and   **NICHOLAS DeB. KATZENBACH**

BOOKS BY M. A. KAPLAN
AND N. KATZENBACH

The Political Foundations
of International Law

BY M. A. KAPLAN

System and Process
in International Politics

The Revolution in World Politics

Library of Congress Catalog Card Number: 61-11520

Printed in the United States of America

FOURTH PRINTING, JULY, 1967

PREFACE

In this book, the major contours of which concern the interlocking patterns of international politics and law, we make use of a systems theory of international politics. We hope such an approach relates the norms of international law to their political foundations from an illuminating theoretical perspective. We trust also that it explains and delineates more clearly than other approaches the differences between international law in a nineteenth-century "balance of power" system and in the contemporary loose bipolar system, and provides fresh insights into the ways in which international law might change in the future.

Such an approach also permits us to investigate the constraints that serve to maintain the normative structure of international law. An approach that emphasizes the extent to which international behavior is normatively oriented—even the extent to which it is both wise and desirable for such behavior to be normatively oriented—may help to disabuse some of the notion that all state behavior is or ought to be oriented primarily toward considerations of power. Although the international society is one that depends upon a considerable amount of self-help, it cannot properly be understood without recognition of the fact that it is also a system in which there is law and order. To clarify how and why this normative order functions is a major purpose of the present volume.

We agree with other authors in seeing nineteenth-century international law as a broad and effective pattern of universal law, even though, in another sense, it was the international law of Europe. However, in that century international politics was largely the product of European international relations. Contemporary international law also has its universal elements, and these are, in one sense at least, more pervasive than the norms of the nineteenth century, since virtually all nations of the world help to produce these norms. The universally applicable norms of contemporary international law, however, are different in many important respects from those of the nineteenth century; there is also less stability and less applicability of prior norms. Many aspects of interbloc relations, for instance, are not effectively regulated by norms sustained by enduring community interest, but, rather, they are regulated by a too-tenuous "balance" of military capabilities.

On the other hand—and perhaps this is not yet appreciated sufficiently—an extremely wide range of activities is coming under normative rule within blocs. Obvious examples are available in NATO and in the Communist bloc. But other blocs (such as the Asian and the Arab) exist, and there are many overlappings. Extremely wide ranges of activity are being brought within the area of supranational regulation, national "sovereignty" to the contrary notwithstanding. The development of supranational institutions constitutes one of the most important and revolutionary features of the present age.

Interest in the problems mentioned earlier is, or at least should be, widespread. The scholar needs to understand these problems in order to understand both the substantive constraints on international law and the normative constraints on, political behavior. Statesmen and the public in general need to understand these problems if they are to play intelligent and constructive political roles. The concern of the student is obvious. We hope that this book will aid each of the three audiences in understanding the role of international law in international politics and the political constraints on the scope and substance of international law.

It is not easy to write a scholarly monograph, a book for the public, and a textbook, all at the same time. The requirements are not the same, and the effort to satisfy perhaps conflicting requirements runs the danger of producing a volume that satisfies none. If we have not failed in our endeavor, this is not so much a consequence of any particular virtues we possess as of the accidental fact that the requirements of the three objectives did not, in this particular instance, differ as much as we might have believed before making the effort. If we have not succeeded as well as we had intended, we hope that the difficulty of the endeavor will be taken into account.

In the best of circumstances, however, some particular objectives must be sacrificed to others. We could not place the relationship of international politics to international law in proper perspective and at the same time work out in detail the precise way in which doctrine needs to be adapted to cases. To have attempted this latter task in addition to the former would have obscured both. In choosing the former—that of the relationship of international law to its political foundations—as our major concern, we do not intend to imply that close doctrinal analysis is less important; but we do believe that the approach we have chosen has theoretical priority.

We recognize that those unfamiliar with doctrine may find it difficult to work out for themselves the application of doctrine to particular cases. The layman, however, would not have substantial interest in detailed applications. And the student can be aided in this effort by his teacher, particularly if he uses a good case book.

We have also been forced to compromise on the precision of our vocabulary—and occasionally of our theorizing—in the effort to communicate with a varied audience. We do not think the loss has been serious; the reader who is concerned professionally has access to writings by the present authors in which greater technical precision has been employed. We have not, however, attempted to write this book in a highly popular style. Works that read too easily are usually quite imprecise or superficial, and often both. We are aware, on the other hand, that convoluted styles and jargon are often used where the thoughts involved could have been expressed more simply in everyday vocabulary. Although we have attempted to avoid such lapses, we may not have been entirely successful. However, too simple a style and vocabulary sometimes increases the grace of expression at the price of adequacy of analysis.

With respect to the general recognition of political constraints on law, and to the importance of the normative regulation of international and national activities, we are indeed indebted to the pioneering efforts of Harold Lasswell and Myres McDougal. No one has done more than these two scholars to rescue international law from the realm of disembodied legal essences and to relate it to the world we live in. They have amply demonstrated that a political science indifferent to values and political purposes is an arid and ineffective discipline.

This book is a joint effort in the best sense of that term. We have not divided subject matter according to discipline; indeed, we could not have done so and still have remained true to the approach we took. Some chapters are more the work of one of us than of the other; this is inevitable. The reader will note stylistic differences between and within chapters that, despite our best efforts, we have not been able to eliminate entirely. Yet each of us has worked on every page of the manuscript—writing, rewriting, editing. Each of us takes responsibility for the whole.

This book was written and had gone into proof before Mr. Katzenbach was offered and had accepted his present position as Assistant Attorney General of the United States. Nothing in this book was written as, or is to be interpreted as, an expression of official policy or as an official recommendation concerning future policy.

M. A. K.
N. deB. K.

Chicago, Illinois
March, 1961

ACKNOWLEDGMENTS

W<small>E</small> wish to thank Professors William T. R. Fox of Columbia University and Leon Lipson of Yale University for careful reading of the manuscript and much helpful advice. Professor Soia Mentschikoff of the University of Chicago gave us considerable help with respect to selected portions of the manuscript, and the unknown reader chosen by John Wiley and Sons was quite perspicacious in his comments. Dean Carl Spaeth of the Stanford Law School extended facilities to one of the authors during the summer of 1958 at which time work on the manuscript was in progress. For this, we are both grateful. Mrs. Roslyn K. Schiller typed portions of the manuscript and performed other useful services for the authors. We wish to thank the Social Science Research Committee of the Division of Social Sciences of the University of Chicago for funds used for typing and mimeographing the manuscript.

CONTENTS

part  I

INTRODUCTION

1

LAW IN THE INTERNATIONAL COMMUNITY

PERHAPS the purest analytical concept of "law" is that in which an impartial judge objectively applies a pre-established rule to decide a controversy. And perhaps the purest analytical concept of "politics" is that in which the stronger influence or interest regulates the social distribution of values. In the real world, however, judges cannot avoid exercising at least some political discretion in the decision of cases. And in any stable political system, the political process is also subject to normative constraints.

Law exists, and legal institutions operate, only in particular political contexts. Contexts vary through time and space, and are influenced by many social, economic and cultural factors. We can and do legitimately separate "law" from "politics" in particular contexts for particular purposes. In educational institutions, for example, the study of law is largely the study of the judicial process, the application of rules by judges to the resolution of disputes arising from given factual situations. Political scientists, on the other hand, focus primarily on the process through which various policies are transmuted into effective community prescriptions. Yet both lawyers and political scientists are conscious of the fact that judicial institutions are meaningfully related to other processes of law-government which exist in a given community at a given time; that is, to the larger context in which authoritative community decisions are made.

If law is associated with a body of principles, or rules, claimed by someone to be authoritative, then it is relevant to ask who prescribes these principles, who invokes them, in what arenas, and with what results. How, and by whom, are they formulated, applied, and enforced, and what are their effects? If law is associated exclusively with courts composed of impartial judges, then it is important to realize that the impartiality of these courts, the kinds of disputes they can effectively resolve, and their techniques of judicial decision making are closely related to and dependent upon the other institutions of government within the relevant community.

Perhaps the point is most readily illustrated by our domestic institutions of law-government. When we speak of the "rule of law" or of a "government of laws," we clearly do not mean the rule of judges or a government of judges. We are talking about the larger, formal process, through which members of the society pursue and realize values in an orderly way. It scarcely requires argument that "law," viewed as a body of authoritative rules, pervades all the institutions of modern democratic government and is no monopoly of judges. We have a constitutional allocation of functions, supplemented by custom, experience, and ways of doing business within government, which gives to these processes a "legal" character. Legislators, administrators, and judges are all parts of a related process; all are subject to legal rules, and all invoke legal rules in the performance of their official tasks. They play different roles, and the role of each is related in important ways to the existence of, and the role played by, the others. Expectations of the community are generally structured in accordance with going conceptions of role performance.

An examination of the function of legal rules in the Congress would show these rules to be both similar to, yet strikingly different from, those of the Executive or the Judiciary. There are important distinctions between what the Congress does, and how it conceives its role, and what judges do and how they conceive their role. Not all disputes within society will be or should be resolved by judges employing the methods and techniques we associate with the judicial process. These techniques are primarily designed to insure impartiality between litigants and, in modern times, subservience to policies laid down by other governmental organs. It is possible rigorously to insulate our judiciary from partisan politics precisely because there are other institutional means for formulating and prescribing rules which adjust broader disputes as to community policy.

In the international system, the processes of law-government are far less highly developed than comparable processes within nations. Political organization is largely decentralized in the nation states which are the principal participants in the process. Political and legal institutions—institutions for prescribing, applying, and enforcing formal community policies—are not well differentiated. A world court exists, but no world executive or world legislature (at least, none with extensive authority). Their absence quite apparently affects the role which the International Court can successfully play. Similarly, assertions about law in the United Nations General Assembly or in diplomatic correspondence perform important functions contributing to international order, and capable of observation and analysis. But it is clear that these are not the same functions which such assertions would play in the context of impartial adjudication by a court.

No one can observe the international political system without being aware of the fact that order does exist, and that this order is related in important ways to formal and authoritative rules, that is, to a body of law and to a process of law-government. These rules are sustained by the genuine interests which nations have in restraining certain forms of international conduct, even though these constraints must apply to their own conduct as well as to that of other states. To understand the substance and limits of such constraining rules, it is necessary to examine the interests which support them in the international system, the means by which they are made effective, and the functions they perform. Only in this way is it possible to predict the areas in which rules operate, the limits of rules as effective constraints, and the factors which underlie normative change. It is in this sense, then, that we shall be studying the political foundations of international law in this book.

INTERNATIONAL LAW AS "LAW"

Sometimes international law is viewed as a rather strange breed of law to which the term "law" is applied only by courtesy if at all. A number of great legal philosophers—Hobbes, Pufendorf, Bentham, and Austin are examples—have all doubted the legal character of international law, and the charges and counter charges which pervade the international community today seem to provide empirical support for their view. Clearly some definitions of law would exclude international law. Disputes, for example, are not routinely decided by an international judiciary, and there exists no coercive agency of formal international status which can effectively enforce the law. Rules do not emanate from any single "sovereign." Indeed, the legal order is not primarily vertical, or hierarchical, as it normally is in domestic government. Rather it is structured horizontally, composed predominantly of formally equal centers of legal authority called "states." We have only the beginnings of supranational authority in the United Nations and in various regional organizations.

It is possible, of course, to define law in such a way as to require a hierarchical structure. Austin did this in his theory that rules become authoritative and binding because they are sovereign commands. If law is defined in this way, then it is accurate to say that there is little in the international community.

In addition, and perhaps of more importance, is the fact that the present posture of world politics is scarcely favorable to the development of, or reliance upon, universal legal rules. All systems of law tend to break down in crisis situations. In such situations, there is major provocation to act politically with little deference to pre-existing rules. Revolutionary justice following the collapse of the Vichy Regime in France, and the Gaullist accession to power following the May 13, 1959 uprising in Algeria, even though technically constitutional, are examples. The importance of force in contrast to constitutional procedures is greatly emphasized when the existing institutional structure is endangered—when, for example, a ruling elite finds itself threatened by a counter-elite advocating a coup or a new form of government. Government by decree and the suspension of normal legal processes are common phenomena in such a situation.

Thus emphasis upon force as a means of controlling the decisions of others is usually a function of crisis, often presaging major readjustments in the system of law-government. The nineteenth century saw a series of democratic revolutions. The recurring crises of this century, both in terms of a changing domestic social order and in the international "balance of power," have had noticeable consequences for the international legal order. Violence and the threat of violence mark international politics today.

A realistic study of law must, as has already been noted, see law in relation to its institutional support, examining the larger process through which rules are created, applied, and administered. There is a difference between the institutions which accomplish this within a domestic system and within the international community. This makes it necessary to examine international law within its particular political context. Disputes between states as to what international law requires or permits in a given situation are seldom referred to an

international judiciary for decision. In the absence of judicial resolution, controversy may continue as to whether or not a particular act
is "lawful." For example, in 1956, President Nasser nationalized the
company operating the Suez Canal over the strong protests of the
United Kingdom, France, the United States, and others. Those opposed claimed the nationalization was in violation of international
law; on the other hand, Nasser, with considerable Afro-Asian support, contended it to be a legitimate exercise of national authority.
The latter contention prevailed and effectively disposed of the dispute; the company has remained Egyptian. But those unwilling to
accept the rule applied were unwilling to concede the legality of
Nasser's decision. To do so would have been to abandon a rule
which they hope may be effective as a deterrent to similar acts of
nationalization elsewhere. Therefore, they continue to characterize
it as "unlawful," and to deplore the lack of effective enforcement of
international law.

In domestic society, controversy is rarely carried on in these terms
because we have in the courts an institution whose judgment we
accept as final. Generally, once a case is definitively decided, we,
as observers, may criticize the decision as "good" or "bad" according
to a variety of relevant criteria ranging from the technical competence of the court to our own ethical and policy preferences; we
may castigate the court for overstepping institutional limitations by
being guilty of "judicial legislation"; or we may accuse it of being
wilfully blind to social consequences, of being either too literal or
too liberal in its reasoning, and so forth. We may seek through political channels to reverse or mitigate the rationale of the decision as a
norm for similar future situations; and where, as in the American
Constitutional system, we find it occasionally beyond the reach of
legislative reversal, we may employ a variety of techniques, ranging
from scholarly criticism to thinly veiled political pressure (President
Franklin Roosevelt's proposal for packing the Supreme Court is the
obvious illustration) to limit its future application.

Now, in spite of the differences in terminology and the fact that a
critic may get considerable political mileage from invoking the ac-
cusation that international law has been flaunted, processes in the
international and domestic arenas are in some respects comparable.
The particular decision disposes of the case and enters into the body
of available precedent, whether that decision is persuasive or not.
The focus of critical attention is to undercut its status as a norm to
be invoked by others in similar circumstances, and it is to this end

that some continue to call it a violation of international law. The more arbitrary it can be made to appear, the more radical the innovation, the more it can be related to selfish objectives of a particular state, and the more it offends widely shared and deeply felt values, the less persuasive it will be as precedent for others.

We cannot ignore the fact that in this process the same official may combine legislative and adjudicative functions, with emphasis, indeed, upon the former. Although national officials talk as if they were concerned only with what the law is, they are in fact equally concerned with promoting rules for the future which support policies they favor. The range of legislative creativity is limited by the interstitial nature of disputes, by the need to state principles that are widely acceptable and that are unobjectionable if invoked by others in like circumstances, and by the political cost of too flagrant a disregard of the expectations of other states based on past practices. In the absence of developed supranational legislative institutions, rules are prescribed, amended, adjusted, and applied by a time-consuming process of agreement or by unilateral state decisions. As a result rules are often quite fluid until formalized in treaties, and are subjected to political strain in their interpretation and application. Considerations of policy, customarily denominated "political," which would be largely irrelevant in predicting decision by a domestic court because clearly beyond its function, may well be relevant, often controlling, when we examine invocations of law in the international process.

But to say this is not to concede the naive criticisms which plague intelligent discussion about international law. Often it is said that, since a state may decide for itself what constitutes international law, how it should be interpreted, and how it should be applied to a fact situation, it can decide cases arbitrarily. Obviously this argument is but a rephrasing of the thought that an independent judiciary is essential to impartial decision, and, hence, to law. If this argument is meant to imply that states do in fact act without regard to international prescriptions, it is descriptively inaccurate. If it implies that they are "free" to do so, it is wrong on both theoretical and practical grounds. If it implies that upon occasion, and particularly in times of crisis, states act without regard to what is generally accepted as controlling doctrine, it is quite right.

This argument is close cousin to the old saw that the Constitution means what the Supreme Court says it means—a formulation that, without qualification, would imply judicial autocracy. It ignores the institutional framework in which the Supreme Court sits, works, and decides. Similarly, each state has a stake in preserving the general structure of international law—the existence of a system of order effected through compliance with recognized norms—even though particular norms may be distasteful to a particular state. Each state will seek to influence and change those norms which it dislikes, since there is always temptation to evade adverse consequences in particular fact situations. However, the general interest in preserving the system is a force both for self-limitation as a means of inducing others to a similar response, and for the use of a variety of political pressures when others overstep the bounds of what is tolerable. Quite a bit has to be at stake, and a state has to be quite sure of its ability to "get away with it," before it will overtly violate norms which are generally accepted. Radical innovation which offends other decision makers may be worth it, but such innovations have political costs as well as profits.

Another appeal of the enforcement argument relates to the uncertainty, or flexibility, of the legal norms themselves, and to the degree to which different formulations and applications legitimately can be put forward. As we have noted, debate (in the absence of adjudication by an impartial judiciary) tends to be carried on in terms of accusations about non-compliance with the law. If, of course, one accepts as correct one's own formulation, that rule, so interpreted and applied, is not always adhered to by others. This fact creates the illusion of either no law or no enforcement of the law. A limited choice of rules and a limited discretion in their interpretation is, however, a far cry from no rules at all. Most of us would like to have the rule as we interpret and apply it enforced internationally, though we might be more sceptical of a norm formulated and enforced by others. Few of our domestic political leaders are enthusiasts for world government, though they are loud critics of weak international law enforcement.

Doubts about a law-system which lacks judge and sheriff have, we think misleadingly, been frequently expressed as a theory of international law which describes it as a "voluntary" system based on the "consent" of "sovereign" states. It does not require much insight into law-politics to see a parallel between this theory and the consent theory of domestic government. Whatever the moral appeal of the consent theory at both levels (it represents a dislike for coercion), states "consent" to international prescriptions in the same sense that individuals "consent" to existing laws. They recognize the general need for a system of order, they regard the bulk of existing regulation as either desirable or at least tolerable, and they accept what remains because they have to—because they lack the ability to change it. The more intolerable a regulation is, the more pressure there is to seek a change by any means possible.

The point is not, of course, that legal institutions in the international community are adequate to contemporary affairs. Obviously they are not. But these institutions, such as they are, exist and contribute to international order. They will continue until some political combination has the capability to create new institutions more consonant with order and, we can at least hope, with a decent regard for human values. This creative process is presently taking place, on both a universal scale (the United Nations complex) and, perhaps more successfully, in a variety of regional and functional organizations such as NATO and the European Communities.

The authors recognize the merits of criticisms that distinguished observers such as George Kennan have made regarding too great a reliance upon legal processes. American foreign policy has often been formulated without sufficient attention to the role of force and of national interests. We do not wish to encourage naiveté of the sort he describes as "legal idealism," a reliance upon abstract rules that are institutionally unsupported. We concede that nations often do act in partisan ways in support of immediate political objectives. But we contend that much of international conduct is doctrinally consonant with normative standards, even though inconsistent with particular immediate interests, and that long-term self-interest can and does provide political support for internationally lawful conduct.

Furthermore, the terminology employed affects attitudes toward the institution described, and, if it becomes popular terminology, the institution itself. If judges were consistently called "politicians," and their decisions described as political, it would not be surprising if judges eventually behaved in a way appropriate to political or legislative and not to judicial institutions. Similarly, if the process of international decision making is described as wholly political, others are encouraged to focus exclusively upon its political aspects and to develop, in turn, attitudes that legitimize conduct commonly ascribed to political institutions, thus destroying to some degree the moderating influence that legal norms have. Perhaps a brief inquiry into the nature of legal and political processes and the content of law systems will enable us to return to this theme and to stress more clearly toward the end of the chapter the legal aspects of the process of international norm formulation.

THE JUDICIAL ROLE AND THE LEGAL PROCESS

The popular conception of the judicial role and of the legal process is dominated by—indeed, abstracted from—the political institutions of modern western government. It takes for granted a separation of legislative and judicial functions and the existence of an independent judiciary with, at most, a limited policy-making role. The focus of legal scholarship has long been upon the judicial process, and the interaction of legislature and courts in their mutual adjustment to social processes has been glossed over, save, perhaps, at the constitutional level. The mythology of impartial adjudication overlooks the political role of judges as well as the impact of existing legal norms upon the legislative process, and seeks an unrealistic dichotomy between judicial and legislative processes. Our purpose here in stressing this interaction is not to obliterate valid analytical distinctions between the adjudicating and policy making roles of officials, considered conceptually, but merely to stress the relationship and interdependence of the legal and political processes—to give emphasis to the political context in which doctrine is operative in helping to shape effective decisions.

It is not necessary to reach far into the political past of England to find functions of policy prescription and adjudication unsegregated. The gradual separation of judicial and legislative functions and the growth of an independent judiciary accompanied the rise of democratic institutions and the fight for parliamentary supremacy on the one hand, and the growing functional inadequacy of rules based purely on custom on the other. In a relatively stable, uncomplicated society it is possible to resolve disputes by reference to customary rules. This is accepted because of the expectations built upon traditional ways of doing things. Although this mode of decision continues to play a role, it becomes far less adequate when a society becomes increasingly complex and interdependent, when government is conceived as a conscious instrument for achieving community policies, and when the society itself is in a process of dynamic change. As democratic industrialism replaced feudal agrarianism, the role of the judiciary changed, as did the role of other governmental institutions, by a process of mutual adjustment to new social and political facts.

In a tradition-oriented society, judges can and do play important legislative roles, for, in the settlement of disputes, they clarify the traditional rules that compose the formal law as they apply them. This was the method of the common law, and it has had its place in other systems as well. But, with the breakdown of tradition, the growth of popular politics and the power of Parliament, this function of the judiciary changed. Judges became independent, thus protecting against autocracy. They could no longer be directly and literally administering the King's justice in a society where the King was to be limited by Parliament; and they, like the King, had to be subservient to whatever rules Parliament formally enacted. Judges could still employ customary rules to decide some cases, but legislation became the dominant source of judicial standards.

A good deal of jurisprudential writing has been concerned with the nature of the judicial process and the extent to which judicial discretion can be limited. It has been popular to conceive the task of judges as the mechanical application of rule to fact. Law is seen as a closed, deductive system, which judges are to apply without any important element of choice. This theory, popularized in the jurisprudence of Austin, reflects a desire for a system of law-government in which judges are given extremely limited and narrow policymaking functions. It is, of course, an overstatement, for it is impossible to remove all discretion and all choice from judicial decision-making. Judges must select from a number of rules urged to be applicable, they must subsume particular facts under general rules, and they must exercise judgment in determining from conflicting evidence what the facts are and what facts are relevant.

In short, extra-doctrinal standards cannot be eliminated from the judicial process if it is to perform its function in society. Thus, there is such a phenomenon as judicial lawmaking. But it is important that judicial lawmaking be firmly constrained within institutionally understood limits. The adjudicating institution—with its prescribed function of impartial application of doctrine to cases—is itself a functionally necessary institution of the social system. Society, therefore, has an interest in maintaining it as a system that, in general, acts according to relatively clear and determinate standards, that is not responsive to local or temporary pressures, and that is insulated from immediate political considerations.

The unique aspect of the judicial process derives from the fact that litigants go to a tribunal that is, in general, unresponsive to them as individuals, a tribunal that treats them anonymously except for the legally relevant facts, hears the matter according to certain established procedures, and decides the case within the constraint of rules that have been established in advance. A legislature may be inhibited from making a radical change in existing law by a desire not to shock existing expectations, by a desire to maintain social peace, or by fear of political reprisal; but that legislature would be acting within its formally limited role in making that kind of radical change. A court may be influenced by any or all of these considerations, but that court is required to relate its decision to existing norms. The technique is different. Some rationales would so clearly violate those norms that a court is very unlikely to use them. The court is limited in its capacity to create new rules; the appeal by both counsel and court is to a justification in terms of rules which already exist, or which can be inferred from pre-existing rules or custom.

The distinction between the legal and political processes is not that matters of political importance lack clear standards for decision, other than counting supporters, and that matters of law are settled according to such standards. The distinction is best made in terms of the different functions and different techniques of separate institutions. The complexity of modern society, and the rapidity of change within it, require an abstract and generalized legal structure permitting judges some freedom in their choice of premises and some freedom in the fitting of premises to facts. What rules are applicable? And what rules determine the subsumption of the factual situations under the rules? These questions require interpretation and leave some freedom of choice to the judge. But the judge must do more than merely justify both determinations in the light of existing standards. He must also recognize that he is establishing a rule for subsequent cases, for even in a system that does not give formal status to decisions as precedent, consistency is a condition of maintaining impartiality among particular disputants.

The range and scope of judicial creativity depend upon the law institutions and traditions of the particular community. Generally, limits are related to a number of variables. Among these may be listed the status (in terms both of official position and, often, of personal reputation) of the particular judge; the considerations, or evidence, he is permitted to evaluate; the existence or non-existence of other forums better equipped to deal with innovations; the extent to which there has been detrimental reliance by a party, or by influential groups generally, upon a rule widely thought to be applicable; the extent to which the new norm will be acceptable to political elites, and therefore has political durability. In particular, the judicial policy maker is limited by the interstitial nature of the judicial process and the consequent haphazard and piecemeal modification of rules pronounced only in relation to particular facts arising in particular dispute contexts. Judicial rule making is always *ex post facto* with respect to the controversy at hand, and, therefore, to be acceptable to the community, it ought not to depart radically from expectations conditioned by norms previously pronounced and by customs widely shared and relied upon. Furthermore, changing one aspect of a rule may require adjusting other relevant doctrine to make it fit into a viable body of law, and judicial ingenuity may be unequal, or the information available to a court inadequate, to so large a task of law revision.

Apart from listing the considerations that must be balanced, no set formula can be offered to determine the limits of judicial law-making. In the final analysis the test is political—the tolerance accorded by the political system and the need to maintain sufficient norm stability to perform the role of impartial adjudication. Laymen are often shocked by the extent to which securing such acceptance is a matter of technique; the skill with which a judge formulates issues, determines relevant facts, and selects applicable norms. But the existence of an informed professional bar makes acceptance more than a matter of mere verbal consistency; the argument must convince on its merits, if not as to its result, at least as to its being within the limits of tolerance.

The role of the judge as impartial arbiter negates open political partisanship. The fact that he is subservient to political officials in matters of policy determination also requires him to be cautious in creating new doctrine which is hotly controversial. He lacks the means to test his proposals in any extensive forum, though, to some extent, he may look to proposals made in the political forum, or by scholars and other influential groups. But both myth and technique make rapid, radical innovation difficult, and the need to be impartial puts a premium upon consistency. For the judge, the past is a safer guide to the future than are orgiastic visions of a new society. But he can exercise choice; some of the possible choices have stabilizing effects on the institutions and values of the society, or may even help to implement values and institutional developments thought to be desirable or just. Even though tempered by a proper caution, the role of the judge can be a creative one in which there is individual intervention and action.

NATURE OF THE POLITICAL PROCESS

The political lawmaker is more likely than the judge to be identified in a partisan role as the representative of certain interests, which he attempts to promote by establishing rules favorable to them. His influence and his tenure in office depend upon the support of identifiable groups. The political lawmaker may attempt to disguise his partisanship by referring to wider community interests, or he may subordinate the immediate interests of the groups he represents to longer-term interests of the body politic on the basis of values he holds or asserts. But he is under no obligation to derive his decision from prevailing norms.

Like the judge, the lawmaker will use prior experience, or precedent, as a means of legitimizing his proposals. But, unlike the judge, the political law maker is not formally required to relate his position to the past and the range of policy considerations open to him is therefore more extensive. Not being confined to the facts of a particular case or controversy and the need to do justice according to existing norms as well as to formulate prospective norms, he may adjust the scope of his proposals to political considerations.

Part of the political process is a contest to determine what values and what conceptions of the public interest will prevail. Part of the political process involves a contest to determine Constitutional norms, jurisdictional competences, and allocational authorities. Part of the process is a contest to determine who gets what. One of the legitimate functions of the political lawmaker is to influence the distribution of rewards and penalties in the society. For these reasons, the political role is, in part at least, a partisan role. However, other considerations modify and constrain the partisan aspects of the political role. It may be a generally accepted value of a political system that existing values and expectations should not be treated too harshly. Apart from this possible consideration, any political act, whether by vote or force (except under conditions of despotism), establishes a precedent for like situations. Moreover, the political lawmaker will take into account the need to conciliate opponents and to refrain from radical changes that will incite radical reactions should the political pendulum swing. The prudent politician, therefore, in a stable political environment is partisan but moderate. His "fairness" gains assent because it is moderate, not because it is impartial. But the role is conceptually different from the judicial role.

A political leader strong enough to change the structure of government over political opposition is unlikely to tolerate judicial frustration of his political objectives. Even in the American system, where the self-proclaimed Constitutional supremacy of courts is accepted, it is difficult to point to decisions that have thwarted a strong Executive from carrying out popular policies. The Supreme Court is most courageous in its policy role when the storm is past. Indeed, how could it be otherwise?

This conclusion may come hard to many who, with reason, regard the Judiciary as the guardian of the Constitution and particularly of those liberties guaranteed to individuals by the Bill of Rights. The authors do not belittle these functions or the moderating influence imposed on other branches of government by the consciousness of judicial review. But even the Supreme Court exercises its Constitutional prerogative sparingly, and influences policy at the margin only through techniques of interpretation. Courts do play extremely important roles in policing the police, in curbing tendencies toward petty tyranny by minor officials, and, thus, in insuring that in their daily work public officials do not exercise the public power capriciously or beyond the expressed public purpose. It would be dangerous and misleading to underestimate the importance of these functions for the protection of basic human values, or in preserving norms of decency and justice from gradual attrition at the hands of opportunists. But rarely can courts intrude into areas of political importance. Given a genuine political crisis, courts are likely to capitulate or to be bypassed. This may be different in important degree from the situation in the international sphere, but the similarities are nonetheless worthy of attention. Treaties are not the only formal covenants that have been treated as "scraps of paper."

The authors will have more to say about the interdependence of legal and political institutions, and the importance of role and function. For the moment it is sufficient to emphasize that the role customarily ascribed to judges is dependent upon and closely related to contemporaneous political institutions; that the relationship of legal processes to political processes is largely a function of these institutional arrangements; and, finally, that the institutional arrangements themselves can survive only as long as they are politically tolerable. To the extent these institutions can be adapted to orderly change a durable system of law-government exists. To the extent they cannot be so adapted, we may expect change by less orderly means, by the use of violence in varying degrees.

THE CONTENT OF THE LAW

Some observers say that only rules consistent with fundamental principles of justice can properly be regarded as law. They thus posit a "higher" law, the principles of which are universal and eternal, against which one can test so-called positive law. Sometimes this higher law has a divine origin, or at least a religious one, and most of its principles in this secular age are referred to as rules of "natural law." Communists, too, resort occasionally to a somewhat similar technique of criticism of existing law by pointing out that in bourgeois countries law is the instrument by which the bourgeoisie dominates the proletarian masses, an instrument of class warfare, and therefore not true law at all.

In all political systems, formal authority must be legitimized in some way. The rules formally prescribed and enforced constitute the law for all those subject to them. The authors have defined law simply as formal authority coupled with authoritative doctrine. We have sought to distinguish it from pure force by requiring that the exercise of force be subjected to the test of authority, to rules of law known and adhered to.

The authors take no position regarding the substantive contents of the rules other than that these contents exist, can be discovered by observers, and, within unspecified limits of tolerance, are operative as standards governing official action. By putting no limits on the substance of law, we offend all adherents of natural law—although, in terms of personal preferences, we would agree with the values natural law usually embodies, and believe that a good case can be made for the fact that many of these, internationally as well as domestically, are parts of the positive law as it exists. We do not incorporate these rules into our conception simply because it is not necessary to our analysis.

What we do wish to emphasize in this connection is that law is more than a system of order in the sense that any legal system also embodies values other than order. Thus the law prevents A from doing something he desires to do; it punishes B for something he has done; it transfers C's wealth to D, or declares that E rather than F is the owner of some land or chattels; and so forth. Every decision, every official act, and every norm that authorizes such an act, reflects some system of values, some ethical or moral judgment.

As participants in the political processes of government we all seek to influence official action so that it accords as nearly as possible with our preferences, with the kind of society (local, national, global) that we want, and that supports a distribution of values of which we approve. We seek at every level to persuade, cajole, and coerce the officials who set policy, to make them enact rules that will distribute rewards and penalties in accordance with our desires. We are successful to the extent to which we command political influence, which is variously measured in various societies, and which ranges from rational argument to the threat of violence. Order itself may be high on the scale of values—today violence in the international community may mean annihilation—but history indicates that other values may be more important to various participants.

Thus, in all legal systems, there is a direct connection between the rules prescribed and the prevailing ethics and morality, and throughout the politico-legal process a constant interaction of "ought" and "is." One technique of argument is to identify the two, to persuade the relevant decision maker that the law is so-and-so because that is what it ought to be. To some decision makers, precepts of natural law may be persuasive in this task of convincing. In addition, some values are regarded as more important than others, and often these are, or can be, identified with fundamental natural law doctrine. For example, the American Bill of Rights incorporates what are thought to be fundamental liberties of individuals against constituted authority, and although American judges need go no further than the positive prescription to find these particularly favored rights, others may find these in an "unwritten" constitution.

Through space and time, different polities are likely to give different emphasis to different values—to make different choices when "freedom" of individual action conflicts with the requirements of "order," when "private property" conflicts with some conception of "social welfare." However, the cultural heritage of western civilization has in fact given us a common core of basic human rights which are widely shared, and which, within the limits of judicial creativity, undoubtedly influence the interpretation of legislation and the choice of applicable norms by judges. It is these principles, in various formulations and interpretations, which many natural lawyers, like the authors of the American Declaration of Independence, regard as inviolable and beyond the reach of politics, legislative majorities, charismatic leaders, military juntas, or secular priests. Particular laws that violate these norms are themselves "illegal" because they violate principles of law which are universal, valid for all people, in all times, in all political contexts.

Now it may well be true that nature—human, social, psychological, or physical—does impose some requirements upon individuals and does set constraints upon what can wisely and profitably be regulated through official action. It may be that the true essence of law can only be found in the true nature of man. The authors leave that problem, along with the diversity of standards and their correct application to particular situations, to philosophers. Our task is less ambitious. We are concerned only with the actual practices of states and the norms enacted, promulgated, and enforced by formal governmental institutions. To reflect upon whether or not these practices accord with natural law directs attention to a wholly different question. Even if decision makers decide according to their conception of natural law, its actual existence (save as positive law) is irrelevant to our analysis. For our purposes we can learn more from studying actual decisions, the conceptions which in fact prevail, than we can from attempting to discover what natural law truly is. Of course, a belief in natural law may be operative in decision making, and this belief may be a relevant datum, particularly in the interstices where there is room for judicial creativity. But it is relevant to our analysis because of its influence upon the legal process, not because of its inherent rightness.

This is not to say that there is no connection between law and the prevailing ideas of ethics and morality; or that whatever is, is right; or that legal systems at war with the nature of man are good and will endure. We simply emphasize the role of law as a system of formal authority in effecting a distribution of basic human values, in enforcing social policies, within the relevant society. We are concerned with understanding the norms that are enforced as law within society. Whether these norms accord with a higher or eternal "law" is a different question.

Nature of the International Law System

Let us turn to a more specific examination of the international system, its peculiarities and its compass. In the first place, the sys-

of other states to act, or a duty to refrain from acting, in the same way in like circumstances. To the extent that such claims can be related to existing rules or can be reasonably inferred from past experience and past conduct of others in similar situations, the standing of the claims as legitimate and persuasive formulations of principle is enhanced. If, over a period of time, such claims are acknowledged and acquiesced in by other states, they become part of the body of doctrine applicable to all.

This process is similar to the judicial process of gradual modification of rules through interpretation and reformulation in the light of changed factual conditions. The same techniques are employed. Just as the domestic judge rationalizes his decision by verbally identifying it with the law as it "is," rather than acknowledging his choice among doctrinal alternatives as an "ought" or preferential one, so too the international decision maker will identify his view as the correct one required by existing doctrine. Verbally, at least, he will be reluctant to flaunt international law and to rely upon an argument based merely upon his power to do as he prefers. His argument may be accepted by other participants because they accept the statement in justification as being consistent with the existing body of doctrine; because they find it a desirable formulation of law; or because it is moderate and backed by sanctions strong enough to make acquiescence a wise political act. Grounds for conceding the claim are seldom differentiated in practice, and would, indeed, be difficult to differentiate in view of the mixture of motivation, encouraged by the technique, normally present. Only the very abrupt break from the past, unsupported by substantial argument based on accepted norms, is clearly a political act, and even this may be widely accepted by others on its policy merits. The point was made earlier in this chapter that the incentive to act politically is greatly enhanced by crisis. If its basic institutions and values are threatened, a state is likely to act to the full extent of its capacity, whether that capacity is measured in terms of political or of economic capabilities, or even of force; this is true, too, of a domestic government threatened by revolution.

We speak of such unilateral claims as being acknowledged or acquiesced in over a period of time in order to describe one aspect of the process by which authoritative doctrine is created. From the perspective of predicting future conduct, such acquiescence is essential to accurate prediction of how specified officials are likely to act on particular issues. The greater the acquiescence with regard to a rule—the greater the consensus—the more useful it is as a tool to prediction. But even if not acquiesced in—even if protested, rejected, or deplored by other states—an effective act enters into the stream of decisions which make up the total body of law. Like dissenting opinions of the United States Supreme Court, or frustrated legislative proposals in the Congress, such a decision is a potential factor to be reckoned with. It may, like most dissents and unenacted bills, wither away and cease to be operative in future decisions. There is, however, always the possibility that it may be resurrected as the correct and proper statement of the law on some future occasion.

In addition to this process of claims and concessions, or "customary law," rules may be made more explicit in formal agreements, or treaties. Where agreement on a mutually satisfactory basis can be negotiated, treaties have several advantages. In the first place, the explicit language of treaties, even if quite general, tends to limit the discretion of national officials rather more than do several formulations over a period of time by several decision makers. Frequently, treaties are codifications of past practices, and as such perform the useful function of making rules both more certain and more stable. In this respect codification of international rules resembles codification of domestic rules, a practice that has been going on in the United States and England, and elsewhere, for the last century or more. Diversity of interpretation of treaty provisions may still exist in the absence of joint institutions to determine their application, but it tends to be reduced to marginal applications rather than more basic policy—provided that the basic policy continues genuinely to be supported by the signatories.

A treaty, for these reasons, is an effective means for implementing international law nationally; in a modern bureaucracy it is more likely to insure that officials not charged with important policy functions do not, through inadvertence or ignorance, create foreign policy complications. Critics often focus so exclusively upon the crisis situations that they ignore the extent to which international agreements are faithfully executed. This is accomplished through the simple device of giving treaties (either through implementing legislation or regulation, or through a principle which makes them directly effective) the same status as domestic legislation. As a result, national judges and administrators carry out treaty provisions as a matter of course, and it requires a major political decision to vary their terms.

Finally, treaties are a method of securing policy goals in matters previously unrestrained and unregulated by international rules, or of consolidating support for a particular view where conflicting assertions of "customary" law are so numerous as to raise serious questions about what the operative rules may be in any given situation.

Quite often treaties are cast in a general language that permits signatories considerable latitude in their implementation through domestic governmental processes. In the absence of a built-in dispute-resolving mechanism, some differences may arise with respect to the interpretation and application of an agreement in specific situations. In general, such differences are tolerated, or resolved through diplomatic consultation. If serious, however, they may be invoked to suspend or terminate the provisions of the treaty generally. Usually pressures for consonance and toleration exist, and in the absence of major shifts in political power, adjustment is possible. Even agreements which cease to have the reciprocal advantages perceived at the time of signature may be scrupulously adhered to, or, alternatively, voluntarily modified. There are usually enough other objectives requiring cooperation to make either compliance or amendment preferable to treaty violation.

Frequently treaties have provisions for termination on relatively short notice, and such provisions increase the likelihood of continual appraisal and revision. Where this is not the case, and where the period specified is a long one, the necessary job of appraisal and reformation in the light of new conditions is far more difficult to accomplish. In extreme cases, the pressure for strained unilateral interpretation, or even termination, may be irresistible. There is a doctrine occasionally invoked (*rebus sic stantibus*) that holds that treaties do not endure when conditions have so changed as to frustrate their basic purpose. But this may be easier for one party to perceive than the other, and it is never a mutually satisfactory basis for termination; if it were, it would not need to be invoked unilaterally. Often the only conditions which have changed are the political ones; one party has greatly increased its bargaining power.

Unilateral termination is not generally acknowledged as legally proper, but it may be politically feasible if there is support for the contention that the treaty is "unfair" or "unjust." Usually termination is sought to be legitimized by talk of prior violations, implied conditions, or through strained interpretation which makes it less burdensome. It may be tempered, too, by a stated willingness to abide by certain principles in the future. When President Nasser of Egypt nationalized the Suez Canal, he was quick to acknowledge the binding obligations of the Treaty of 1888, which guaranteed free and non-discriminatory passage to foreign ships, and to acknowledge the interests, but not the formal authority or control, of user states in the efficient operation of the canal.

No state is prepared to abandon the principle that agreements must be performed (*pacta sunt servanda*) any more than, in domestic matters, it is willing to abandon the idea that laws must be obeyed. But at the same time it is abundantly clear that whenever the "bargain" concept is projected too far into the future, whenever an agreement is felt to have been unfairly imposed or coerced (as at Versailles), or whenever one of the parties strongly feels that there is no longer any reasonable relationship between benefits and burdens, it runs into difficulty—doctrine to the contrary notwithstanding. The conditions—predispositional as well as environmental—that led to the original agreement do, of course, change, and not necessarily in the same direction and at the same rate among signatories. If changed circumstances lead a party to a treaty to challenge the fairness of applying the treaty's provisions without modification, a refusal by the other party to the treaty to renegotiate may persuade the first nation that it can protect its interests only by violation or abrogation of the treaty.

This problem cannot be solved by doctrine concerning the sanctity of agreements. The difficulties of settling such problems lie not in some doctrinal deficiency but in clumsy political processes for appraisal, recommendation, and modification of treaty provisions. The appropriate analogy for disputes of this kind is not that of contract law but rather that of legislative reform and amendment. Comparison with domestic procedures makes this clear. In domestic law-government, the political organs of government have the responsibility for resolving political disputes by enacting new laws or by changing old laws. For this reason, in domestic law-government there are judicial institutions that can resolve disputes as to the application of legal rules but not differences as to the desirability or direction of major change in the law. Laws must be faithfully observed (with some inevitable latitude in their interpretation), but the possibility of amendment or repeal by the political organs of government is always present.

International disputes that revolve around the interpretation of formal treaty obligations are only partly, and often peripherally, related to genuine disputes as to the meaning or application of the norms. Genuine interpretation problems are soluble through diplomatic discussion, or, indeed, may be voluntarily referred to third-party resolution. The difficult disputes are those in which one of the parties really wants to change the agreement—to amend, repeal, extend, or supplement its provisions—in a way that the other does not support. This desire may be masked as interpretation of existing terms, or reference may be made to "implied conditions," and the issue paraded as a legal question. The dispute could be decided by a court; all disputes can. In domestic law-government, such a dispute would probably be amenable to *both* judicial and legislative resolution. In a sense, this is true internationally because of refusal to submit to adjudication as the exclusive mechanism, thereby looking to resolution through a diplomacy in which judicial and political techniques are intermingled.

What has been said with regard to disputes based on treaties is even more likely to be true in the more fluid process of invocation of "customary" law and general principles of jurisprudence. Here norms are less refined, in a more or less constant process of change, and capable of more broadly divergent application. Nonetheless they do serve as a force for stability, for they act as deterrent to extreme decisions and encourage a moderate approach.

General principles and "customary" rules of international law are said to be universally applicable to state conduct, whereas treaties are viewed as special legal regimes which are obligations of signatories only. However, the distinction is not quite so clear in practice. A great many treaties codify and restate what the signatories believe to be "customary" law adjusted to contemporary conditions. The greater the number of signatories, the more persuasive the codification and the more likely it will be invoked by or against non-signatories, not as a treaty obligation, but as persuasive evidence of a "customary" rule which binds them as well. Indeed, even where there is no contention that a rule is based on past practice and "custom," its incorporation in a number of treaties, or in a single multilateral treaty, may make it the measure of what is "reasonable" or even "lawful" under general standards, and thus arguably binding on non-signatories as well. There is a persistent tendency toward universalizing, or at least projecting as far as possible, rules frequently found in treaties. One reason is simply that it is administratively desirable to have the greatest amount of uniformity with regard to international problems, and it is complicated to administer a number of special legal regimes dealing with substantially the same subject matter.

The other side of the coin is equally interesting. Rules based on "custom" or derived from general principles of law are claimed to be universally applicable, even though it is clear that, in fact, there are often a number of divergent statements as to what the law is and how it should be administered. Some areas approach universality, particularly those where reciprocal advantages and interests are general and obvious; diplomatic immunity would be an example, though even here some rules (for example, asylum in an embassy) are quite variant. In other areas (for example, expropriation of private property owned by foreign nationals) doctrinal divergencies are clear and fundamental. Accurate description would, as in the case of treaties, find in reality a number of legal regimes, rather than a single universal one, among states that share more or less similar views as to what the rule is and how it should be interpreted.

Why are rules that, descriptively, are not universal claimed nonetheless to be so? The answer, of course, is that, in the absence of joint legislative institutions with continuing formal power to prescribe the law, the claim to universality of unilateral formulations is a technique whereby state officials promote rules which serve policies in the international community which these officials support. They wish to make these rules obligatory for others, and the claim that all states are so bound permits them to push their contentions. Reciprocal doctrine to the effect that each state determines international law for itself, and that no state can be bound by a rule unless it consents (but it may consent impliedly), serve the opposite purpose of preserving oneself as a formally coequal legislator.

Conflicting interpretations of treaties and conflicting formulations or applications of "customary" law may lead to disputes. These may be settled by mutual agreement, arrived at through direct diplomatic negotiation, or through third-party intervention in the form of good offices, mediation, conciliation, arbitration, or adjudication. In all these processes legal rules play roles, for they are appealed to by the disputing parties and by third parties seeking to resolve the dispute. Since state officials, unlike private parties in a domestic dispute, do have a legislative role, and have therefore to be prepared in the future to abide by the contentions they urge in particular disputes, the use of legal rules and legal arguments may narrow issues in dispute and assist in promoting moderate approaches. So, too, does the possibility of sanctions of varying degrees of coercive effect. Here the role of legal norms is to justify and legitimize acts of coercion which would otherwise be unlawful.

It is this flow of effective decisions by officials invoking international norms that is the substance of international law. We cannot categorically state its content. Like all legal systems it is in a process of change, and as peoples grow more dependent upon one another for the realization of common values, matters previously unregulated become appropriate subjects for formal regulation. There is a predisposition on the part of national decision makers to be cautious in promulgating norms too detailed and too rigid to permit adjustments to the contingencies of a politically fluid society, or, alternatively, to be cautious in delegating to supranational officials (whether judges or legislators) very much formal authority to prescribe such adjustments. It may be easier to adapt national laws to international facts without attempting to state a binding international standard. After all, an international norm is self-limiting as well as being a potential limitation on others. Political leaders still have great reluctance to limit their own political freedom beyond what is absolutely necessary to secure immediate objectives.

The historian can trace the problems of the last century in the international law-doctrine that grew out of them. Britain's dominant sea power gave her a capacity to "enact," almost by herself, an international law of the sea—a law that, although it undoubtedly served her purposes well, also served those of the larger community. Emigration from Europe led to new problems about the granting of citizenship, as the various national laws failed to mesh in the conflicting interests of new and old. Popular revolutions led to new practices and new doctrine about recognition and interference in internal affairs. Dominant theories of laissez-faire economics, and the pound sterling as an international currency, led European nations to back up their merchants, their businessmen and their money lenders with a series of norms concerning the obligation of debtor states, the sanctity of money, and the protection of commercial property. In addition to colonial governments, the developed countries established a number of regimes in non-European countries for the protection of Europeans from the unfamiliar and harsh requirements of alien legal systems. Technologically backward countries were held accountable for damage to the person or property of foreigners where local law and order was not preserved, and for this purpose, as well as for the collection of debts, doctrine supported creditor self-help. Protests by smaller nations were seldom effective. The Latin American countries, for example, attempted to legislate again the use of force in collecting debts (the so-called Drago doctrine) and against the use of diplomacy in backing up private business. They found, however, that even with the political protection provided by the Monroe Doctrine, they were still unable to make these new laws effective against their European creditors.

In this century we have seen the outbreak of violence on a tremendous scale, and much of our effort has gone into efforts to modernize the laws of war, to prevent, control, limit, and mitigate the consequences of violence. From disarmament, through the punishment of war crimes, to contemporary problems of nuclear energy and space missiles, this problem has dominated the period since the First World War. In addition, we are plagued with the problems of the end of colonialism, of an emergent nationalism which asks for Afro-Asians not merely freedom and independence, but "social justice" as well. The slogans of domestic politics have been internationalized as problems once national in scope have become international. Human problems pass across territorial boundaries with ease and transform themselves into problems for the international community to solve.

Older political solutions became transformed, as political solutions do, into legal norms through treaties, practices, and customs. Many such solutions are not adequate for international problems as they are no longer adequate for comparable domestic ones. The distribution of political influence in the hands of competing national political elites offering competing solutions makes some problems more difficult to resolve. The international community is going through a period of crisis and the preservation of order will depend on the strength, the political ingenuity, and the skill of Western leaders in creating new law and new institutions of law-government if the international community of the future is to reflect the system of values held by the West rather than that held by the Soviet Union. The task of international lawyers and statesmen alike is to weed, to prune, to create—not to cling to outmoded solutions of another era and bemoan the passing of international law as they do so.

2

THE PATTERN
OF INTERNATIONAL
POLITICS

THE principal purpose of the present chapter is to relate the normative structure of international law to the underlying patterns of political behavior that have characterized the modern state system. The political constraint upon the normative structure of law is only one of many; there are also economic, technological, social, and ethical constraints. Nonetheless, investigation of the political constraint provides many insights with respect to the changing substantive content of law and also illustrates the way in which theory helps to provide an understanding of subject matter.

A systematic study of the structure of the international society has been attempted elsewhere by one of the authors. Two different models of international systems employed in that attempt have particular relevance to the present problem. These are the "balance of power" model of the international system, which has as its counterpart the international politics of the eighteenth and nineteenth centuries, and the loose bipolar model of the international system, which has as its counterpart the international politics of the present. The two models, are less complex than the actual patterns of action, but they permit us to explore, hypothetically, important differences in system structure and behavior that can be related to normative standards.

A model of the international society, like the model of any kind of system, attempts to relate some of the variables of the system in some systematic way. In a social system, one may look at the kinds of members, at the role functions which they perform, at the conditions under which they perform them, and at the conditions that are necessary for the stability of the system.

THE "BALANCE OF POWER" INTERNATIONAL SYSTEM

If one turns to a model of the "balance of power" international system, certain striking characteristics become evident immediately. In the first place, the members of the international society are nation-states, unlike the situation in the loose bipolar system, in which there are also blocs, like NATO and the Communist bloc, and universal organizations like the United Nations.

In this system the nation is the focus of solidary sentiments for the members of the nation. The nation is the ultimate protector of the values, of the economic prospects, of the health, and of the physical safety of the individual. Within the nation the individual *belongs,* and outside of it he is an alien. But the nation-state itself must depend largely upon its own ability to survive. This is not unrestrictedly true for all nation-states, as further modifications will demonstrate; yet it is a central assumption upon which the behavior of important participants in the "balance of power" system model depends.

If one turns from the model to the historic system, illustrative applications are readily available. The failure of Spain, toward the close of the period of colonial conquests, had a devastating effect upon Spain's internal life. The demise of the Austro-Hungarian Empire shattered Austrian national life and threatened Austrian viability. The present decline of Britain and France has had an easily traced effect upon their internal societies and upon their ability to protect themselves. On the other hand, the unification of Germany in the nineteenth century, except for the political misuse of German power, turned Germany into a flourishing and prosperous country. Americans are aware that, whether American destiny were manifest or not, the policy of national expansion was essential to the present importance and prosperity of the United States. Today the European Common Market rests upon the belief that only a new supranational organization can bring back past glories. But, in the eighteenth and nineteenth centuries, the nation was the essential unit. If one nation did not pursue its possible gains in the international system, another nation would, to the advantage of its citizens and often to the detriment of the citizens of the first nation.

According to the model of the "balance of power" system, the relationships of nations to one another must be competitive, suspicious, and primarily instrumental. Considerations of interest and expediency must be paramount. The first rule of conduct for each nation must be to seek security for itself. A nation will be ready to move from one alliance to another whenever such a move promises to provide more security.

Since changes in national productivity of an unexpected nature might disturb the "balance," each nation will strive to gain a margin of security for itself and to prevent any other nation from becoming so strong that it becomes a serious threat. For these reasons, nations will enter coalitions to gain prizes of some sort or another, such as territory, resources, shipping facilities, and so forth.

Coalitions in a "balance of power" system will tend to become fragile when they become too strong. If too successful, such a coalition might eliminate defeated nations and thus threaten the interests of the weaker members of the successful coalition, whose security would then become precarious. Also, a weak coalition might make large offers to a powerful nation that was not aligned with other nations or even to a member of the opposed coalition, not for gain but to protect itself against loss. Moreover, different issues might give rise to different alignments. Therefore it is characteristic of the "balance of power" international system that previously uncommitted nations, or even members of an established coalition, swing into the "balance" against the predominant coalition. We may remember the process through which the Russian-British-French entente was consolidated by 1907 or the process through which Italy was split off from the Triple Alliance.

Restraint in victory is also a characteristic of the "balance of power" international system, not necessarily for any reasons of altruism, but because restraint protects the interests of the members of the international society. Each strong nation has an interest in maintaining the existence of other strong nations in order to be confident of future allies in case of disagreements or clashes with its present allies. The restoration of France after the defeat of Napoleon was at least partly responsive to this need. Even the support given to German and Italian unification had some relationship to this aim.

The "balance of power" system was dependent among other things, upon the maintenance of a minimum number of large and strong nations. A system of three large nations would probably have been inherently unstable. It might still be possible in a three-nation system for the nation defeated in a war to combine with the weaker of the victorious nations against the stronger victor. But the risks would be great and the opportunities to undo mistakes would be minimal. Such a system would place a high premium on striking first, on taking advantage of opportunity, on forming combinations, and on betraying allies. In a three-nation system, under conditions of conventional capabilities, turmoil and strife would be the rule; and the number would soon be reduced.

On the other hand, with a greater number of large and important nations, there is a greater opportunity to counter any individual alliance. Numbers of uncommitted nations would be available to redress the "balance." The opportunity to attract a member of an alliance to a different alliance would be relatively great. With a large number of great nations, there would be a premium upon delay and moderation. Whereas with three nations, it would be better to eliminate the opponents before they could combine against oneself, with a larger number it would be better to preserve them so that they could combine with oneself in the future. With a large number of major nations, it would be easier to find a coalition to prevent major change. In the First World War, for instance, America was available to restore the "balance" of Europe. Numbers give time for thought and time for action and provide the nations that must carry out the actions.

In such a system, every nation may have an interest in conquering other nations. But there will be more nations—provided there is a minimally large number of them—to whose interest it will be to prevent this. It would hardly be surprising, therefore, to discover in such a system that national "sovereignty" has become an enforceable norm of the system, for national sovereignty reflects essential needs of the "balance of power" system, and is compatible with the organization of domestic politics around the unifying concept of the nation. Each nation is an independent unit, not subject to conquest, amalgamation, or other forms of political domination by other nations; each nation preserves for itself optimal flexibility with regard to alignments; each nation is organized territorially on the basis of existing culture groups. Any permanent international organization, or, indeed, any joint institutional arrangements such as we have today would have been an unwarranted and undesirable drag on the flexible diplomacy that maintained political stability among the great nations in the "balance of power" system. The nations belonging to the "balance of power" system have a joint or cooperative interest in maintaining the norms of this system. And, although in one sense each is "free" to violate the norms, each has an interest in protecting the norms from violations by other nations.

A number of other factors tended historically to support this state of equilibrium postulated by the model. One factor already emphasized in this book is nationalism. The growth of solidary sentiments of loyalty toward the nation gave the nation-state a strength and coherence that other forms of political organization lacked. The struggle for national independence did not, of course, interfere with the suppression of minorities, as in Hungary, where they existed as isolated islands within a larger geographical area. These minority problems, however, did create domestic instabilities that affected the roles of such nations internationally, and, as a result, produced international instability; the recurrence of the Balkan problem is the prime example. But where nationalism was effective domestically it tended to limit expansive international objectives. It is difficult for politicians to preach the values of national independence for themselves without according it to others. Nationalism tends to differentiate beyond the area which it can unify, increasing the difficulties of conquest by force. Hitler's pan-Germanism had little appeal to non-Germans. One may limit national independence of minorities to "civilized" countries; one may accept the suppression of minorities within a nation; one need not refine or stereotype the qualities of the nation-state so far as to insist upon cultural self-determination of a Wilsonian sort. But the existence of national identity as the focal point for sentiments of loyalty at home is bound to legitimize it for others on principle, and, in fact, will increase the problems of conquest and annexation of all save border areas of mixed cultural content, as occurred in the Sudetenland.

Another factor contributing to preserving the "balance of power" system stemmed from the difficulty, increased by the ideology of nationalism, of any attempt by one nation to extend control over another. Consider the situation at the end of the Franco-Prussian War. Suppose that Bismarck had desired to establish German hegemony over France; how successful would he have been? Even apart from direct intervention by other nations on behalf of France, many considerations would have militated against a German attempt at hegemony. Given the state of technology of the period Bismarck would have found it very difficult to carry out this attempt. Factories in the remote provinces of France would have been capable of producing weapons quite comparable in fire power to those used in the Prussian Army. Garrisoning major portions of France would have immobilized the Prussian Army in case of military problems elsewhere in the world and would have placed a great strain upon the Prussian economy. Communication and transportation were not efficient enough to permit the central stationing of an occupation force for use in the provinces whenever disturbances broke out. To occupy a colonial area was one thing; to occupy metropolitan France was distinctly different. In addition, the attempt to occupy France permanently would have weakened Prussia with relation to other potential enemies, and a seemingly successful conquest would also have stimulated others to enmity as a consequence of fear.

All the factors enumerated above tended to reinforce a social system in which the nation as an independent and sovereign entity played a key role. Still another factor, however, was to give particular support to a society of formally equal and sovereign nation-states. The "balance of power" international system operated upon the basis of alliances designed to adjust immediate and short-term interests of the major nations. As already indicated, a key feature of this system was the formation of a counter-alliance whenever a predominant alliance seemed to be in the process of formation. This required the maintenance of a minimum number of major nations. But it also required a willingness to consider any nation an acceptable role partner under appropriate circumstances and to consider alliances as transitory and short-term arrangements.

Many of the questions at the time of the Congress of Vienna become clearer when interpreted in light of this principle. The quick acceptance of France as a full member of the Congress after the defeat of Napoleon is illustrative. (This may be contrasted with the treatment of Germany at Versailles.) But the difficulties over the fate of Napoleon reflected a genuine dilemma of the European statesmen of the time. If the nations had refused to deal with Napoleon, as some advocated, this would have reflected a degree of interference in the internal affairs of the nation-state inconsistent with the state system of the time. On the other hand, the revolutionary character of the Napoleonic system and the refusal of Napoleon to limit his objectives made it virtually impossible to enter into short-term alignments and to restrict alignments to short-term interests, regardless of form of government or emotional sympathies. Napoleon challenged the flexibility of the system of alignments and therefore the character of the state system itself. Flexibility of alignment is difficult in a revolutionary period when state regimes become unstable and when considerable foreign popular support is available to the revolutionary nation.

Flexibility of alignment—or the acceptance of any nation as an acceptable role partner under the appropriate circumstances—was an essential characteristic of the "balance of power" international system, because, if this principle did not operate, the process of forming counter-alliances would have been impeded, and the system would have developed rigidities making for instability. The "feud" between Germany and France after the forced cession of Alsace-Lorraine, for example, was one of the major circumstances leading to the breakdown of the historic "balance of power" system and the eruption of virtually total war in 1914.

If hostility between nations would impede the operation of the principle of flexibility of alignment so necessary to the security of the member states, so would control of one nation by another. Independence of the nation, therefore, was a prerequisite of this system. And, although each individual nation might have an interest in violating this principle, each nation had an even stronger interest in supporting it against the encroachments of all other nations. Moreover, the appeal to other nations to prevent an encroachment would necessarily be phrased in terms of the legitimate value of national independence. In short, this was necessarily a guiding norm, which the existing political circumstances supported against violation, and which almost automatically guaranteed the outraged resentment of the community of nations against any violator. This principle was a key to the legal code of the international society of the late nineteenth century. Fear of the revolutionary character of democracy and perhaps a desire to maintain the social order did lead the Holy Alliance to proclaim a doctrine of collective intervention against democracy. Had the cases of application proved highly exceptional, this limitation might have been maintained. However, in the nineteenth century world, such an effort was inconsistent with more basic needs of the "balance of power" system. And this exception to the rule proved potentially so dangerous that it was abandoned, despite the fact that the collective element of the intervention was designed to minimize the unstabilizing effects of the intervention.

Non-interference in the internal affairs of another nation characterized the historic "balance of power" international system and accords with the requirements of the model. The aims of war must stop short of such interference except when nations were confronted with the kind of dilemma Napoleon posed. Influence upon minor principalities, which often could not be avoided, represented such violations of the code that they were disguised lest the general principle be called into question. Even the troubles within the Ottoman Empire were treated with relative restraint. And British and French interference in Egypt—which was not at the heart of the European world—at least maintained the legal formalities. American "dollar diplomacy" restricted intervention to certain definite and limited objectives. Even so, it was difficult to accommodate these actions within the norms of the "balance of power" international system, and the fiction of the dependent state had to be adopted to square the circle.

At least with respect to the major nations, the legal norms conformed fairly well with the facts. No nation had such predominance that it interfered with the internal life of other nations in any substantial way. Although most actions having any influence upon citizens were settled within the territorial state by the government of that state, the concept of sovereignty as unlimited and indivisible jurisdiction was a fiction. The logical difficulties of this fiction did not affect its practical adequacy in explaining what took place; it was a fiction that each nation had an interest in maintaining and fostering. The absurdity of auto-limitation as an explanation of international law should not obscure the fact that the concept reflected the real needs that the community of nations had in protecting the myth of sovereignty.

Now, the doctrine spawned from the basic idea of a sovereign state was fundamentally more applicable to large states than to smaller ones, for it is the former which make or redress the "balance of power," whose independence is essential to maintenance of the minimal number of nations necessary to "balance," and whose equality within that system comes moderately close to accurate description —not, of course, on a one-to-one basis, but on the ability of each to equalize the "balance." Its extension to a number of smaller states within Europe and Latin America (after the Monroe Doctrine) served essentially the same purpose of preserving the status quo. The admission of smaller states on terms of formal equality was not, as in the case of the great nations, primarily related to their utility as military allies or even to their direct impact on the political or military capabilities of the important states. In effect, their "sovereign" status was guaranteed by the major nations for two reasons: (1) In a system of flexible alliances it was not possible to agree upon any workable or viable division of smaller European countries. (2) The difficulty of acquisition by military force was considerable because of difficulties of assimilation into different national cultures, and scarcely worth the effort if others could be persuaded not to do so. Under such circumstances the best common policy usually was to neutralize the smaller states, and extending the doctrine that was applicable to major nations was well suited to this purpose. Statesmen of minor European nations were quite aware that their independence was the product of a "balance" they could not directly influence, but which it was to their advantage to preserve. They could best accomplish this by avoiding domination by any particular nation, and by insisting upon their rights as "sovereign" entities while scrupulously, for their own part, adhering to the code. The stalemate among the great nations gave the minor nations considerable freedom of action so long as they invoked standards that were impartial. Their interest in preserving their independence and neutrality coincided with that of the great nations, and was converted into a force for law and order. In Europe, at least, the "balance" was at all times sufficiently fragile to make minor statesmen "responsible."

Although the "sovereignty" of these smaller states had, as in the case of the great nations, an obvious relation to "nationalism," it had little to do with any universalized self determination—at least in Europe—until a much later period. Until Wilsonian idealism coincided with the breakup of the "balance of power" system, there was no inconsistency acknowledged between the sovereignty and independence of states and the existence of colonies and other forms of "dependent" states. The hegemony of the great nations over much of the world was simply taken for granted and remained undisturbed. Equality of rights and freedom from intervention were necessities only where they affected the political positions of the great nations, principally, therefore, in Europe. Military intervention or even lesser forms of interference in the administration of other states could not be tolerated where they had a direct effect on military capability. In other parts of the world intervention could be tolerated, and might, indeed, be indispensable to the pursuit of other objectives. The great nations had no hesitation in imposing their system of values and culture, and in forwarding the interests of their nationals in those parts of the world in which intervention was tolerable to other great nations. Colonial claims were recognized and conceded on a status quo basis; further intervention was tolerated and incorporated into a doctrine of dependent statehood to minimize the potentially unfortunate feedback of intervention as a precedent invalidating the general rule in areas where is was necessary for the general rule against intervention to apply.

Doctrine with regard to the rights and duties of states became a matter of defining what constituted a "state," and here there was no reference to national self-determination as a principle. Inevitably the definition was tautological, for it included, as one essential, a capacity to enter into relations with other states—a capacity which depended upon its being a state—that is, upon the ability to act independently of any of the great nations. A new state came into being only with the acquiescence of the great nations, an aquiescence which might come from agreement among them not to intervene or from a geographical location which meant that intervention by a single nation would be opposed forcibly by others. An analogous situation occurred with regard to the recognition of new governments of old states whenever crowned heads fell before popular revolutions. Although the notion of popular sovereignty was anathema to various governmental elites, and although there was a common interest in suppressing radical ideas, intervention constituted an even greater danger. Other nations could support an existing government in various indirect ways, but such assistance had to stop short of measures which would threaten its independence.

Now it is clear that doctrine authorizing or inhibiting forcible intervention or direct control of the political institutions of another entity, whatever the justification of such intervention, is a limitation. only upon the great nations. All states may be equally governed by the same general rule, but the rule's bite is against only those who have the capacity to intervene. Similarly the appeal of those intervened against must be to those who have the capacity to protect them. Small states do not intervene against large states, whatever the provocation, and no rule of law is necessary to prevent it. Because the "balance of power" depended upon the large nations, these large nations occupied a special social position in the family of nations. The position of small nations depended upon how specific applications of policy affected the competitive position of the great nations. The great nations were, so to speak, the informal office holders in the "balance of power" system. They would intervene, but would not be intervened against. Legal norms were those norms that they promulgated or acquiesced in.

The special position of the great nations in establishing and enforcing international law meant that the law established could not run contrary to their interests or—to the extent a pluralistic system permitted—to the capabilities of each. To say this is not to say that the norms established were incompatible with the interests of small nations or, indeed, with the interests of individuals who were not citizens of one of the great nations. Undoubtedly there were advantages to being born an Englishman just as there are advantages to being born of a wealthy family. But the rules that the great nations promulgated at least had the merits of formal generality and equality. Englishmen did not have formal privileges internationally because they were Englishmen, any more than they did domestically because they were rich. True, such rules might have the defects suggested by Anatole France's sardonic comment about the law equally forbidding rich and poor to sleep on park benches. But formal equality, however unequal in fact, is preferable—at least to the small states—to formal inequality. Nor were the great nations, in theory or in fact, outside or above the rules they put forward as binding on all nations. They put forward, as rules governing the international community, what they regarded as desirable for the world community and what they were willing to abide by themselves—provided others did likewise. Like all law, it was subject to change where conditions changed.

During the nineteenth century the great nations came to share a similar economic philosophy, a similar regard for the individual, and similar views as to domestic politics. That is to say, the great nations shared the principal values of a common civilization, of a common legal heritage, and of a common faith in laissez-faire economics. They were quite willing to impose the essentials of this system on the world at large wherever it touched their interests, or the interests of their nationals. Among themselves there was little need to insist on such standards because each was committed to the belief that these principles served its national interest. There was—despite some notable exceptions—little desire to bring the benefits of European civilization to the non-European world; administration was the white man's burden. But the great European nations did desire to make the non-European world a safe place for Europeans to trade wherever trade was profitable. This involved various degrees of intervention in less technologically developed parts of the world—intervention to insist upon the payment of debts, to protect nationals and their property, to insure for nationals minimum standards of Western justice. Depending on the circumstance (the willingness and capacity of local governments to insure these objectives), the forms of intervention varied from an *ad hoc* landing of troops (or the threat of a British gunboat) to various continuing forms of control: colonies, dominions, dependencies, protectorates, mandates, trusteeships, and so forth. Intervention was possible only where it did not affect to an important degree immediate interests of other great nations—but for much of the nineteenth century this included much of the world. Since it was almost always justified by economic objectives widely shared as "right," since in general the areas administered were open to all for purposes of trade on equal terms, and since it did not appear to endanger the security of other major nations, intervention was tolerated. Since the intervention was justified on principle, the law was enforced. It was enforceable because it did not threaten the security of other major nations and did not appear to adversely affect their political positions.

Thus, despite the conflicts between the great nations, which could be analyzed in terms of a competitive game, these conflicts were moderated by a non-zero-sum cooperative supergame.[1] This supergame established norms that bounded the play of the competitive game. The nations of the "balance of power" system thus had interests in maintaining the integrity of the great nations; there was an interest in maintaining the integrity of the nation's sovereign jurisdiction over its internal affairs, since a nation subject to interference in its internal affairs would not be a free agent in its international dealings. Such a lack of freedom would interfere with the flexibility of alignment necessary for the stable operation of the "balance of power" international system. Even the nations at war with one another were bound by common interests, for they might be allies at some later date. Thus, they had an interest in behaving in ways that made such future cooperation possible. At least minimal confidence that such future cooperation might be possible was required. Declarations of war, limitations of objectives in war, and rules governing the conduct of war all played roles in maintaining confidence—that is, in maintaining a social structure within which the stable "balancing" of the system could be effected. The alternative would have been an unlimited and unstable war of all against all, in which all would have lost and in which all would have contemplated precarious and dangerous futures.

BREAKDOWN OF THE "BALANCE OF POWER" SYSTEM

For reasons which cannot be discussed in full here, the historic "balance of power" international system fell into unstable equilibrium

---

[1] A non-zero-sum game is a game in which the sums and losses of all the players do not add up to zero. A cooperative game is one in which players can increase their gains by coordinating with other players on choice of strategy.

toward the latter part of the nineteenth century and was replaced by a loose bipolar system after the Second World War. Perhaps one of the most important events making the "balance of power" system unstable was the cession of Alsace-Lorraine after the Franco-Prussian War. The inflammation of national sentiment produced by this event made it impossible for France and Germany, during the next eighty years, to enter into alignment with each other, and the hostility and suspicion between the two nations made necessary strong alliances directed by each against the other. But these alliance systems were too rigid for the almost automatic "balancing," and "counter-balancing" of a stable "balance of power" system. Thus the flexibility of alignment required for stability of the system was precluded by the hostility between Germany and France.

Since neither nation was a potential alliance partner of the other, the interest of either nation in preserving the other as a major nation or in limiting its objectives in war was also vitiated. The mechanisms making for equilibrium were thus additionally weakened. The range of special treaties and arbitration agreements, and the establishment of the Hague tribunal may be viewed as vague responses to the need for some other sort of mediatory mechanism to protect the interests of the nations. In the absence of the almost automatic operation of the alignment process, treaties and special agencies were designed to fill the old international role of the shifting of alignments.

After the First World War, the League of Nations was brought into being. This development was in itself evidence of the growing rigidity and rapid decline of the "balance of power" international system. In the eyes of its sponsors and under the influence of Wilsonian idealism, the League of Nations was viewed as a break with the "power politics" of the past. Collective security was to replace the insecurity of the system of national alliances. War was not yet renounced as an instrument of national policy. But the old diplomacy, viewed as insidious because it was secret and as selfish because it was generated by a class-bound diplomatic service, was renounced. National self-determination was the order of the day, and every nation was to be the legal equal of every other nation. The crystallizing force for peace was to be found in the democratic sentiments of the free citizens of independent nation-states, whose interests were harmonious and whose energies for constructive peace would be mobilized by national independence and democratic political processes.

Not all nations subscribed to this new and fanciful view of the world. France begged vainly for security guarantees from England and the United States and, in desperation, constructed an ineffective *cordon sanitaire* around the defeated Reich. Attempts to enforce collective security via the projected Geneva Protocols were transmuted into the ambiguous Locarno Pact. The 1920's saw a ridiculous and potentially disastrous series of disarmament conventions; the United States sank its fleet and agreed to naval limitations that made little sense from the standpoint of security. Meanwhile, efforts to outlaw war eventuated in the supreme monument to human futility, the Kellogg-Briand Pact.

If the efforts following the First World War to compensate for the rigidities of the dying "balance of power" system were in response to a genuine need of the international community, the means employed were in utter conflict with the requirements of the situation. If the rigidity of the system of alliances before the war increased the possibilities of a war to the finish, the system of alliances at least encouraged effective action. The genius of collective security, however, lay in its ability to fragment opposition to an expanding nation. It placed an emphasis on collective action within a formal organization when it was to the advantage of some not to act at all and to others to rely upon still others to act for them. Unlike the situation in Korea in 1950, when the United States was forced to act because no other nation had the capability, the relative equality of the great nations in the interwar period prevented the focussing of responsibility upon a single great nation. Therefore, in the absence of an alliance upon which responsibility automatically would have fallen, every nation looked to some other nation to act. In the absence of formal agreement in advance, it was difficult to arrange effective action when trouble broke out. In the absence of clearly delineated aims related to some national interest, reasons for procrastination seemed stronger than reasons for action. Collective security turned into collective insecurity.

The complete roster does not need to be called, but it includes Ethiopia, the Rhineland, Manchuria, Austria, the Sudetenland, and so on. If the failure of the League cannot justly be ascribed to a single cause, it would nevertheless be a serious mistake to underestimate the degree to which the fragmentation resulting from collective security played a role in this failure. But other factors also entered in. The refusal of Britain and France, until too late, to cooperate with the Soviet Union (assuming there was a possibility of

Soviet cooperation) violated a cardinal rule of the "balance of power" system, namely, flexibility of alignment. The failure of French and British leaders to recognize the need to move against expansive nations was also important. And so was the pacifism that regarded war as an inherent evil and alliances as the prelude to war. The actions of the British Labour Party in calling for a halt to Nazi aggression at the same time its members opposed increased arms budgets in the House of Commons illustrates the inconsistent thinking of the period.

During the period from the First World War to the close of the Second World War, the transition from the "balance of power" to the loose bipolar system did not produce any variations with reasonable prospects for stability. Nor did the period produce standards of international law which had reasonable prospects for acceptance. The instability and transitional character of the international social structure in this period were directly responsible for the confusion and instability in the standards of law. There is no law without support; no support without a social structure that can provide support. But law is usually ineffective within nations during periods of rapid and revolutionary change. Law, by its very nature, conserves the values of a social system. And when the values are themselves in transition, the system of law gives way to political or quasi-legal activity. Revolutionary Communist tribunals were produced by the efforts to build a new social system, not by the conservators of an existing social system. What was legal in Hungary during October 1956? The answer necessarily depended on who won. But, even so, both sides found it difficult if not impossible to abide by the procedures of any established legal system. When the direction of change is visible, we may discover the seeds of new law in the innovations of the legal process. But when the transitions fluctuate in several directions in rapid succession, order appears lacking.

Thus, the period from 1870 to 1945, with brief interludes, was a period in which conflicting standards of law were asserted by nations acting within a changing and transitory social structure. There was inconsistency between geographic regions and lack of regularity within regions, at least with respect to the more important political aspects of international law. Some of the norms that depended upon economic values fared better. Nor can it be said that the period of transition came to an end with the conclusion of the Second World War in 1945. The structure of international action still lacked the consistency that permits, if it does not guarantee, social stability.

Many of the beliefs and activities of the time were founded on premises divorced from political reality and therefore divorced from the means whereby legal norms gain support from the community of nations.

The Nuernberg trials could have been justified on the assumption that the use of force for aggressive purposes was really outlawed, that the nations of the world had no conflicting interests of a scope great enough to prevent agreement upon a standard outlawing aggressive war, and that sufficient consensus existed to make the trials of aggressive leaders an objective and impartial process not dependent merely upon the wills of the victorious parties. These were doubtful assumptions.

The old concept of "just" wars had been rejected in the age of the modern nation-state, precisely because this concept was incompatible with effective limitation of war. The only way to regulate war effectively was to ignore a standard which necessitated direct intervention in the internal affairs of the defeated nation by an arbiter who represented the victorious nation. This very effort would have involved a control over the defeated nation that would have jeopardized the interests of third nations and that would also have led to rigidity in the system by giving rise to a desire for revenge. The state system of the seventeenth century gave rise to a need to regulate the conduct and conclusion of wars, rather than the motives of the warring states. Moreover—because of the difficulties of getting warring parties to agree as to who had a just motive—the attempt to impose such a standard would have interfered with the limitation and regulation of the war process. Each nation would have asserted the justice of its cause and insisted on its right to use the means necessary to bring the war to a favorable conclusion. The "balance of power" system required, for its stability, standards that limited war and that were independent of any consideration of justice of cause, and the members of the system had an interest in endorsing such standards.

The Nuernberg trials are incomprehensible, apart from their function in satisfying world opinion by the punishment of the fascist leaders, if the *ad hoc* tribunals employed to hear the cases were expected to function as the standard method for trying such cases in the future rather than as an expedient designed to meet immediate needs; in short they were comprehensible only if the reasons that led to the demise of the concept of the just war no longer operated. To make sense, these tribunals had to represent a development toward an ordered world community in which the use of force by national authorities without sanction from some international body was outlawed and in which effective tribunals for punishing transgressors were established (or, alternatively, a world in which nations had no joint or cooperative interests—a world represented by a zero-sum game).[2] Such an ordered world community did not exist and could not exist under the conditions then prevailing and had not existed at the time of the offense.

The United Nations represented the effort to create such a world. The United Nations represented a concession, in the minds of its authors, to the realities of international politics. It was recognized that the military capabilities of the world would be monopolized by the United States, the Soviet Union, and Great Britain. It would take military force to keep the peace. Therefore, a major responsibility was given to the new superpowers to keep the peace. The United Nations rested upon the hypothesis that the great nations would unite to keep the peace and, therefore, upon the corollary that the peace was to be kept against the encroachments of the smaller nations while the defeated fascist nations would be prevented from ever again building military machines with which to threaten the peace of the world.

There is much to be said for the view that at least the European aspects of the Second World War were a direct consequence of the aggressive and even insane ambitions of Adolf Hitler. There is somewhat less to be said for the view that dictatorships are naturally aggressive and even less for the view that the disarmament of Germany and Japan would eliminate the local points of world danger. But the view that international conflicts of interest stem primarily from the psychologies of national leaders and from the cultures of particular nations is a great oversimplification of the situation, even when this view contains elements of truth.

Specific conflicts of interest may stem from any of the aforementioned sources. But it must be recognized that the international society is, in part at least, a competitive—and not necessarily peacefully competitive—society. The lives of individuals and the existence of social institutions are bound primarily to the largest unit of effective and inclusive organization. Within this organization, hopes

---

[2] On the other hand, the norms supporting neutrality and the norms restricting world community interests to the conduct of war, rather than its origin, no longer are as strongly supported as was the case in the "balance of power" system. This subject will be explained further in Chapter 8.

are satisfied, values fulfilled, and lives lived. Within it, loyalties are organized and to it loyalties are pledged. For most of modern times, this largest and most effectively inclusive organization has been the nation. The greatest danger to any nation must stem from some other nation, and the greatest deprivation most individuals can sustain must follow from the defeat of their nation by an enemy nation.

The United Nations was founded upon the hypothesis that the great nations would cooperate in keeping the peace through the machinery of international organization. But two great nations, Germany and Japan, were eliminated by defeat and disarmament. China was not a great nation, although it may some day become one under Communist rule. France had lost its greatness in defeat. And a few years were to demonstrate the reduction of England to second-class status. In effect, two superpowers remained: the United States and the Soviet Union. But each of these two nations constituted the greatest potential danger to the other. No substantial political or economic change could occur anywhere in the world without affecting the relative positions of these two great nations. Nor could any barrier to change be maintained without influencing their relative positions. In short, these two nations were placed in positions of one of the greatest conflicts of interest the world had ever known. Almost any dispute would range them on opposite sides. Yet the peace of the world was supposed to rest upon their harmonious cooperation. Perhaps the expansive goals of Stalin worsened this condition. But one must come to the conclusion that the organizing concept of the United Nations was hopelessly inadequate.

In effect, two gravitational poles for world political organization came into being. They were in necessary conflict with respect to many important problems. Moreover, other nations inevitably must be attracted to one or another of the poles, for many would find their greatest safety against the encroachments of one of the poles in the protective shelter of the other. It took a long time to recognize this, for all were not as prescient as Winston Churchill in his Fulton speech. Nor did the awakening come all at once, and perhaps it came at all only for extraneous or not quite relevant reasons.

The story can only briefly be sketched here and these limited details are already well known. Developments in Eastern Europe led to great anger in the West. When the rebellion in Greece and the threat against Turkey appeared to endanger the strategic position of the United States, the Truman doctrine was enunciated. A major objective of the Marshall Plan was to reduce the danger of Communism in Western Europe and, in accordance with this objective, the steel capacity of Western-occupied Germany was increased greatly. By the end of 1947, and perhaps partly in response to this increase, the Cominform was organized, ambitious economic plans for Poland and Czechoslovakia were promulgated, and, early in 1948, the coup took place in Czechoslovakia.

The process may be viewed as one of successive responses and counter-responses. Russian control of Eastern Europe and the war in Greece constituted a threat to the West. The Truman Doctrine looked like a military threat to the Communist bloc and the Marshall Plan threatened the unity of the Communist Nations. The Cominform and the Czechoslovakian coup seemed to herald the threat of imminent war, although there is now considerable evidence that war was the last thing Stalin wanted.

It was not the threat of war that endangered the West—at least until 1955. It was the attractive power of the Communist bloc. It was not the visible Cominform, which probably never undertook any major activity, but the organizational character of Communism that constituted the great danger. Once a nation joined the Communist bloc, that nation would find it difficult to leave, the example of Yugoslavia to the contrary notwithstanding. Such nations would be attached by party controls. That is, they would be joined to the Soviet Union by the power of Moscow to intervene between competing national Communist factions to maintain control and also by the fact that a national Communist regime would find it difficult if not impossible to remain in power without the support of the Soviet Union. In this way the external unity of the Communist nations is maintained.

On the other hand, if the Western nations were to behave as they appropriately had in the "balance of power" period, on the basis of immediate interest, they would be fragmented, and the Communist bloc would gain a decisive influence in international affairs. Only a unity based upon long-term rather than upon short-term advantage could suffice to maintain the interests of the Western nations. If this unity was purchased by a false belief in the threat of imminent war, it nevertheless constituted a response to a real need in the new loose bipolar international system.

NATO, the Western response to the Soviet bloc, was an unprecedented organization in the modern world inasmuch as it established a supranational command and joint military facilities during a time of peace. Although efforts were made to relate NATO to the United Nations, NATO clearly represented a break with previous conceptions of the role of the United Nations in the world community. Perhaps for reasons of public opinion, or perhaps because the formulators of policy did not themselves clearly see the revolutionary consequences of their actions, efforts were made to mute or to camouflage indications of the change. But it represented a necessary step toward a potentially stable structure of international relations.

The loose bipolar system, during its early stages, reflected the development of the new supranational blocs. There was a sharp gravitation toward the two poles of international influence. This development was aided and affected by the devastation of the world after the Second World War, the economic impoverishment of large areas of the world, the economic power of the United States, Soviet conventional military capabilities and American monopoly of atomic weapons, disorganization in newly independent ex-colonial areas, and the Korean War. With economic recovery in Western Europe, continued colonial unrest, growth of governmental experience in the new nations, the stalemate in Korea, Soviet nuclear parity, and the consolidation of Communist control in China, the situation achieved relative stability, and some stresses in the opposite direction began to appear. The position of the uncommitted nations was strengthened, and the members of the blocs of the United States and of the Soviet Union began to exercise somewhat greater independence in policy.

The legal norms that characterized the "balance of power" system could hardly be expected to survive unchanged during this system's period of instability and failure. The Hague tribunals and the League of Nations had provided sufficient evidence that the old system was collapsing. It was not really possible to keep in their fullness the rules governing non-interference in the internal affairs of other nations, limitations on objectives, rules governing declarations of war and practices in occupied territory, and so forth, for these rules were too directly related to a system in which flexibility of alignment was a major characteristic. Nations observed these rules in dealing with opponents who might soon be allies. Even the rules governing the treatment of prisoners of war, so recently sanctified in treaty, no longer had as much support as earlier. However, they would still be observed when national and cultural values supported them or when the other side could take measures in reprisal and one still wanted to protect one's own nationals. These changes in international law, as the political changes that gave rise to them, prepared the way for the new bipolar system.

THE LOOSE BIPOLAR INTERNATIONAL SYSTEM

The loose bipolar international system is composed of two major blocs, a large number of uncommitted nations, and a universal organization like the United Nations. This system came into being as a consequence of the events recounted in the previous section. This system is different from the "balance of power" international system in many important respects that have consequences for the operation of international law. In the first place, the blocs are more than alliances; they have supranational characteristics. In the second place, the system is not stabilized by the almost automatic operation of immediate interest which leads to the formation of alliance and counter-alliance. In the loose bipolar system, alignment must be on the basis of long-term interest and the blocs become relatively stable patterns of alignment within which conflicts of short-term interest tend to be ignored. Since the members of the blocs lack an interest in maintaining the independence of the members of the opposing bloc in order to maintain the possibility of future combinations or coalitions, the particular motives for limitation of objectives and non-interference in the internal affairs of other nations that operated in the "balance of power" system do not operate in the loose bipolar system. Indeed, apart from the positive motivations to intervene, the negative factor of the concentration of capabilities in the leading members of the blocs makes it difficult not to intervene. Almost any decision of the United States or the Soviet Union must have important consequences for the other members of their blocs and for uncommitted nations.

Interdependence is especially great in the modern world. The United States cannot ship wheat to Yugoslavia without affecting the Canadian wheat farmer. Nor can it ship arms to Pakistan without effect upon the Indian budget and Indian politics. American aid programs affect the internal politics of the country to which they are addressed, regardless of the terms of the program. The absence of aid also has its effects. Interference does not have to be overt, for the knowledge that the activities of a nation will affect the judgment of the American Congress in voting funds will itself have an influence. There is no way to avoid this influence with the best will in the world, for no government can vote funds without considering the possible consequences of the loan. Soviet loans, even when technically free from "all strings," have important political repercussions within the countries to which they are made.

Soviet intervention in the internal affairs of Hungary is brutal and in Poland obvious. But can the United States avoid all such interference? Has not the situation in Algeria necessitated efforts to influence French governmental policy? Obviously it has, but there are so many internal constraints that the influence has been exercised in a halting and ineffective manner. And, if governmental changes may influence the viability of NATO, can the United States remain indifferent? Interference may not be as obvious as in the Italian elections of 1948 but we must be conscious of the effect of policy upon friendly political parties within allied bloc countries.

In the "balance of power" system, intervention usually occurred in colonial, dependent, or minor areas. In the loose bipolar system, positive intervention is more likely to occur within major allied bloc nations than in uncommitted areas. The competition between the two leading bloc nations will be effective in reducing direct intervention by the two blocs in the ex-colonial areas, as will the proud, new nationalism of these nations. The organic forms of union among the bloc nations will reduce barriers between members of the blocs and lead to greater sharing of jurisdiction, while the most zealous guarding of the nation's "sovereign powers" will occur within the new nations.

The fact that the loose bipolar system has two blocs is of direct consequence for the operation of the system. In the "balance of power" system a minimum number of five major nations probably was necessary for stability. Increasing the number of major nations reduced the directness of rivalry between nations and reduced the need to strike first. Simultaneously it made it more desirable to limit objectives in order to maintain the possibility of future combinations. The two blocs of the bipolar system, however, are in direct competiton. Neither has an incentive to maintain the other. Rivalry is direct and is limited primarily by the horrors of thermonuclear war. Alignment is not flexible. Communist nations necessarily tend toward the Soviet bloc. Communist China, for instance, although in many respects physically capable of asserting its independence of Moscow, takes great pains, at least for the time being, to maintain the priority of the Soviet Union as the leading member of the bloc. Within the free world there is a natural proclivity, except among those whose memories of colonial control remain active, to associate in some way with the United States.

Mediation, thus, is not a general role of all nations of the loose bipolar system, but is a specialized role. Uncommitted nations may exercise the same kind of role as that of the uncommitted parties who are often so useful in mediating industrial disputes. The process of accommodation is a difficult one, and the blocs would be in considerably greater trouble with each other if they did not have to appeal to uncommitted nations or if they could not turn to such uncommitted nations to mediate a compromise. Withdrawal from an announced position may be both difficult and painful if not eased by moral pressure and suasion from independent and neutral bystanders who are able to invoke larger principles as well as their own independent judgment. Sometimes the most difficult step is to get contending parties to talk to each other. The uncommitted nations often perform yeoman work here. This job may be done irresponsibly as well as responsibly, and it is possible that the greater responsiveness of the democratic nations to world public opinion may yet weigh heavily and negatively in the race for survival. The mediatory function of the uncommitted nations is nonetheless, in principle at least, an important one for the stability of the loose bipolar system.

The uncommitted nations are protected in their position both by their usefulness to the blocs from a mediatory point of view and by the desire of each bloc to keep these areas out of the grasp of the other. Although the uncommitted nations themselves lack important military capabilities, they are often, for political, economic, or geographic reasons, of considerable importance in the contest between the two blocs. The accession to the Soviet bloc of Southeast Asia, the Near East, or North Africa would be serious for NATO. Thermonuclear stalemate increases considerably the bargaining power of the uncommitted nations.

Another important agency that performs mediatory functions is the United Nations. The removal of the United Nations from its role as the keeper of peace—a role performed more adequately by the two blocs and the condition of thermonuclear equilibrium—enables this organization to function more effectively, in the loose bipolar international system, as a mediator and as a forum. In these roles it helps to reduce tension between the blocs. The United Nations may also, under exceptional circumstances, and with the aid of one of the blocs, mobilize the international community against a bloc whose activities threaten to undermine world peace. Here, the organization will play a supporting role to the bloc, as in the case of Korea, where the United Nations supported the United States.

It is in the nature of the loose bipolar system that a bloc will attempt to subordinate the interests of the United Nations to its own interests. This happens because, in the final analysis, the bloc must depend, for survival, upon its own political and military resources. However, a bloc is also motivated to subordinate the interests of the other bloc to those of the United Nations, for, in this fashion, it can mobilize support against the other bloc. In this way, a bloc can best appeal not only to the uncommitted but also to its own bloc governments and to citizens within the bloc. And the uncommitted nations, of course, have particularly strong motivations to subordinate the interests of the blocs to those of the United Nations, for it is by this means that these uncommitted nations can best compensate for their own weaknesses and strengthen their positions in the international system.

Unlike the major nations in the "balance of power" international system, the participants in the loose bipolar system do not have similar reasons for fostering or not fostering given principles of international law. Instead their situational interest varies with the positions they occupy in the system. The uncommitted nations should have the strongest motivation to maintain the normative rules without distinction as to roles or sizes of nations, for the degree to which these rules are observed corresponds best with the requirements for their safety. Non-interference, sovereignty, absence of force, and similar norms correspond best to the needs of the uncommitted nations, although, even here, some questions might be raised. Reliance upon voting in the General Assembly of the United Nations for the settlement of issues gives greatest importance to their numbers and formal voting equality. The blocs must pay some attention to these principles to attract support from uncommitted nations and to be able to use them against the opposing bloc when conditions so warrant. However, it is not possible for the blocs to consign their vital interests to the keeping of the General Assembly, whose voting processes may depend upon substantively irrelevant considerations and whose formally equal members do not have to take responsibility for the consequences of their decisions. The United States and the Soviet Union may try to prevent others from resorting to force but they cannot themselves abstain from the use of force under conditions necessary to protect their vital interests. Nor can they always refrain from internal interference with other nations. (This interference, except within the Soviet bloc, is seldom likely to be as direct as it was during the Suez crisis of 1956.) For these reasons, the law of war and the right of reprisal may not have changed as much as the authors of the Charter of the United Nations intended.

In the relationship between the structure of the international political system and some broad and important elements of international law, some important differences between the "balance of power" international system and the loose bipolar international system have appeared. In the "balance of power" system, each major nation had a vital interest in preventing other major nations from interfering in the internal politics of any major nation. This prescription was self-reinforcing because the other members of the international community could always combine against the transgressor.

In the loose bipolar system, on the other hand, each leading bloc member has a direct interest in interference. And the competitive bloc actor has an interest in permitting this interference when applied within the bloc itself as was so fully demonstrated at the time of the Hungarian uprising. The withdrawal of Hungary from the Soviet bloc would have constituted a deadly threat to the entire satellite empire, and the loss of the empire would have threatened the parity of the Soviet bloc. The very considerations which forced Soviet intervention acted to secure American non-intervention. Under these circumstances, resort to thermonuclear war made greater sense for the Soviet Union than for the United States (if one assumes —perhaps incorrectly—that the Soviet Union had nuclear parity with the United States at the time), because the loss of the empire would have constituted a vital threat to the Soviet Union while the failure to exploit the loss was not a serious threat to the security of the United States.

For political and strategic reasons, the United States cannot intervene in England or France, for instance, by means of military force. It is almost necessarily constrained, therefore, to use subtler but not necessarily less effective measures of political and economic intervention. However, this permits the Soviet Union also to intervene, and, since the intervention is not military, it can be accomplished without the consequences that American intervention might have had during the Hungarian uprising.

Non-intervention, therefore, applies to the minor uncommitted areas rather than to the major areas of the world. And even in the uncommitted areas, non-intervention by the blocs is supported primarily by a very tenuous "balance" between the United States and the Soviet Union. The uncommitted states are not committed to non-intervention, although they often use this slogan to cloak their resistance to bloc pressures. The revolutionary and subversive appeals and campaigns initiated against other uncommitted states by leaders like Nasser, Kassem, Castro, and Nkrumah bear striking witness to this fact. Consequently, the legal values associated with non-intervention and those associated with sovereignty meet far less support under current international conditions than they did during the "balance of power" period. Moreover, the strong stands taken by the new nations and by many influential groups within older, more established nations against the vestiges of colonialism have the function of further reducing the insulation of the nation-state from the application of external and international pressures. With the decline in the importance of the lone nation, with the miracles of transportation and communication, and with the spread of American-Soviet rivalry to all areas of the world, almost every situation is vested with an international interest. It is ironic that the writers of the United Nations Charter were more conservative than the authors of the League of Nations Covenant in attempting to insulate national jurisdiction from external intervention. Their "realism" has not prevailed, however, against the requirements that inevitably flow from the new structure of international politics. Neither will the restrictions against the use of force and against reprisal be likely to have the same importance which the Charter writers intended, for reasons to be analyzed in a subsequent chapter.

3

THE THEORETICAL
FRAMEWORK
OF INTERNATIONAL
LAW

CONTEMPORARY theory and doctrine of international law are the product of the emergence of the European secular nation-state and its evolution over the past four centuries. One conceptual cornerstone, the myth of state sovereignty, had its beginnings in the struggle against the mediaeval order, and correctly reflected the power of the new national entities to reject external arbitration by the politico-religious institutions against which they revolted. The agreement, for example, of Spain and Portugal that disagreements with respect to colonization could not be appealed to the Papacy gave evidence to both the temper and the growing independence of the new political units.

We can view this development in three reasonably distinct phases: First, the period from the Renaissance to the Congress of Vienna, a period in which philosophers searched for a unifying theory of human relations to replace the unifying theory and institutions of Christendom, and variously found it a universal law of nature. Second, the period from 1815 to the First World War, during which "positivism" tended to replace natural law and the conceptually universalistic "law of nations" became international law with a strong European orientation. Third, the period from the First World War to the present, characterized by the breakup of the European system and the universalization of world politics within a loose bipolar system. Like all historical classifications, this one is both general and arbitrary; history is a continuous process in which past, present, and future merge without abrupt demarcation.

THEORY BEFORE 1815: NATURAL LAW AND THE LAW OF NATIONS

The easiest way to view the development of international law prior to the nineteenth century is to keep in mind three important considerations which influenced its theoretical development. In the first place, international law tended to be regarded as a part of a universal law of nature. There was no very systematic creation of an international legal order as distinct from national legal orders. Nor was there any very clear definition of the subject matter of such a legal order. As the old religiously oriented political system broke down, philosophers sought to legitimize and order the new developments that pressed one upon another for rationalization and status. By what right and authority did monarchs rule? What obligations did they owe the Church, or God, or their subjects? And what of their relations with one another? These were conceived as related subjects, and ideas were transposed from one context to another. Language and thought were increasingly secularized, religious wars became national wars, other-worldly values became worldly values, and the *a priori* reasoning which characterized Church philosophy gave way to empirical observation—but always within the universalistic ideological heritage of its religious origin.

Philosophers of the late Renaissance and of the still later Age of Reason sought universally valid principles on which to base not merely international relations but all law. Understandably, in view of its religious origins, jurisprudence continued to associate quite explicitly morality and law, and to see the foundations of legal rules in conceptions of reason and justice—universal principles equally applicable to everyone everywhere and thus part of a universal law of nature. Every schoolboy is familiar with the early controversies that were carried on in religious terminology with regard to the duty of Kings to subject themselves to the Will of God, and to what was done about Kings who did not. The absolute duty to obey became, in the hands of the Scottish Protestant, John Knox, an absolute duty to revolt, a notion later secularized, under consent theories of government, into the "right of revolution." So, too, in international matters we find with Grotius the applicable parallels of the duty to obey versus the right of revolution in his conceptions of the "just war" versus the "unjust war." Whether we are talking about municipal law or international law we find monarchs subjected to a higher law which imposed upon them various duties variously phrased. Even with respect to foreigners, sovereigns were subject to the obligation to abide by the law of nature and the law of nations, to do justice.

We can get the flavor of this ethical jurisprudence from almost any of the early writers despite differences among them as to particular rules. The basic tenet of the Spanish School of the sixteenth century—Vittoria, Vasquez de Menchada, Ayala, and Suarez—was simply that relations among nations were governed by principles of Justice, and that such principles, according to Suarez, for example, were perpetual, immutable, universal principles of natural law. Gentili, the great Italian who taught civil law at Oxford, had the same idea when he envisioned the Law of Nations as that "which is in use among all the nations of men, which native reason has established among all human beings, and which is equally observed by all mankind. Such a law is natural law." With Grotius, perhaps the greatest and certainly the most systematic and comprehensive of the early writers, there is a slight shift of emphasis toward modern positivism when he sees the law of nations as deriving its obligatory character "from the will of all nations or many nations." (We can see as early as 1625 the emergence of the great European nations and the deference Grotius pays their power.) But Grotius adds that "outside the sphere of the law of nature, which is also frequently called the law of nations, there is hardly any law common to all nations." And, with his predecessors, Grotius posits the essential principles of the law of nations as "universal and immutable."

The second major point to keep in mind is simply that the great bulk of domestic law was based upon custom and common conceptions of morality. The concern here is not so much with method, the style of opinions of judges or commentators, or the sources of law; rather, the authors, wish merely to emphasize the absence of any conception of law as a creation of government, consciously designed to implement community values. Law processes were not highly formalized, rationalized, and bureaucratic, and they were not to become so until the nineteenth century and after. There was almost nothing in the way of "national laws" as that term is interpreted today, and relatively little in the way of national policy, save as it concerned itself with maintaining the monarch on his throne and free from too much foreign interference in local matters. Virtually the only national law and the only national policies which touched the people were those concerned with taxes. Standing armies were becoming the fashion, and it is not surprising that much of the writing on international law dealt with rules of warfare.

Finally, we must remember the institutional context of law when one reads jurisprudence before (very roughly) the French Revolution. In the realm of foreign affairs, policy was exclusively for the monarch, and politics was the avocation of the few, not the many. Distinctions between law and policy—between the "is" and the "ought"—so important to modern governmental institutions, were a later development and could not have mattered less. Such distinctions had nothing to do with the distribution of political power or with the method of making effective international decisions. Law and morality were closely tied together. Just as legislatures had not developed to give explicit form and content to government policy as law, neither had treaties developed as a comparable phenomena in the relations of nations. The sovereign did not distinguish between what he was obligated to do by law and what he was free to do as a matter of policy; rather he asked in all cases what was required by law, justice, reason, and morality. These terms were more or less interchangeable. The law required that the sovereign always act justly, reasonably, and morally.

In a very real sense, scholars played what we would call today a legislative role. That is to say, it was they who discovered custom; it was they who derived principles from past practice, from analogy, from Reason; it was they who put these forward for the instruction of kings and judges as applicable law. In international affairs, particularly, the scholars sought to influence governmental action, and often they occupied important positions in State Councils. They were, in a sense, the secular priests who used their learning to persuade monarchs to particular action and who rationalized the action taken. In this task they employed all the techniques of legal scholarship of their time; they drew upon ancient history, Roman law, and Canon law, as well as upon various precepts that they identified with the law of nature. They made extensive use of analogy, and, increasingly, they drew upon past diplomatic practice and past decisions of local courts where the cases had had foreign elements. And, it is important to remember, they attempted to formulate the rules they posited in universal terms, binding upon everyone, related to morality and justice and not (save coincidentally) to particular national advantage. Much of that conceptual heritage (strained through nineteenth century positivism) remains with us today.

Thus, in viewing the law of nations as part of the law of nature, writers simply based its existence upon necessity and reason. If states were to exist in anything but a constant condition of warfare, in which none could survive, there must be rules to govern their relations one with another. For the same reason that individuals must have rules in order to live together, so, too, must states. Nature itself, it was said, imposes on all mankind a legal order as a condition of survival. By the use of reason, with which all men are endowed, and by diligent study of history, it was thought that men could not merely perceive the necessity of law generally, but could discover the specific rules that would enable them to live together in harmony. In theory, the use of force and the waging of war were avoidable, but these could not always be avoided, for there was the constant possibility that some might transgress the law; hence the "just war," as distinguished from the "unjust"—a conception often very close to the modern parallel of self-defense as distinguished from aggression.

Those rules prescribed by nature could be determined in various ways. The earlier philosophers tended toward the method of postulating certain general principles, or deriving them from Church teachings and from philosophy, or Canon Law, and argued from these to lesser principles as derivatives. This was the method largely used by the Spanish Jesuits. Grotius, however, combined *a priori* reasoning with empirical observation. Grotius gave more emphasis, than did his predecessors, to the actual practices of states in their foreign relations, and to the decisions of courts throughout Europe. These he regarded as persuasive evidence of the existence of the rules of natural law that he was urging; the fact that there was widespread agreement as to a given rule was in itself indicative that it was a rule of the law of nature, and, hence, of the law of nations. The rule found its source in Nature, as evidenced by common agreement, and was binding because it expressed the will of nations.

The method Grotius used, with its empirical bias, was followed by many writers and foreshadowed positivism. More and more writers made use of actual "cases," of statements by foreign office officials and courts, and of comparative techniques to discover the particular rules of the law of nations. Some, notably Bynkershoeck, relied exclusively on such evidence, abandoning entirely *a priori* reasoning. Others, of whom Pufendorf is the best known, maintained a purer (or at least older) approach, depending upon reason rather than upon practice as the foundation for natural law. Most remained

"Grotians" in maintaining an intermediate position. But, despite divergencies of view, Lauterpacht is undoubtedly correct when he states that international law until the close of the eighteenth century was "part not only of a general system of jurisprudence but also of a universal moral code."

A good deal of natural-law theory has survived, even among those who would not describe themselves as "natural" lawyers. Certainly it is common to find writers stating that international law has its origin and basis in the need for order in the international community —that it exists simply because we cannot get along without it. In an age of atoms and missiles there are many who pose the choice of mankind as one between law and total destruction, and who, like Grotius, urge governments to follow the path of reason before we blow ourselves up. Nor, on the other hand, can anyone seriously doubt the existence of norms, from the simplest to the most complex, in all communities, including the international community. In this respect, modern sociological jurisprudents have much in common with early writers who knew that norms do and must exist wherever there are human relationships; *ubi societas ibi lex.* From the family to the United Nations we can observe methods for settling disputes and maintaining order even though they may break down in crisis situations, even though they are in a constant state of evolution.

But to say this is not to say very much. Legal systems are always particular legal systems, related to particular communities and to particular social and political structures, and composed of particular norms determined and enforced through particular institutions. It is a long jump from the general necessity for a legal system to a particular one, from the abstract necessity of norms to particular rules, and from the ideal rule of law to workable law-rules. The need for order is at most one consideration tending to produce order, and the particular order that exists may always be viewed by some participants in the political processes as more deprivational in character than alternatives, even when those alternatives envision war or revolution. Whether norms can be modified or created which will make those alternatives less attractive than adherence to the system depends on the ingenuity of politicians. Furthermore, in a system where the participants (or some of them) are capable of large-scale violence, there is always the danger of political miscalculation. It is relatively easy to get a consensus as to the desirability of law as opposed to chaos, to peace as opposed to war. It is true that major wars and revolution—at least in the twentieth century—have involved deprivation for the victor as well as for the vanquished, and it seems as a consequence that reasonable men ought to settle their differences peacefully. It is somewhat harder to work out law-norms and law-institutions to which all will voluntarily agree or to which all can be forced to acquiesce.

FROM THE CONGRESS OF VIENNA TO THE SECOND WORLD WAR: POSITIVISM

In the century from 1815 to 1914 the law of nations became international law. Several factors contributed to this change.

The Congress of Vienna is a convenient starting point because it both epitomized and symbolized what was to follow. Here in 1815 the great nations assembled to legislate not merely for Europe, but for the world. Thus the Congress marks a formal recognition of the political system that was central to world politics for a century. International law had to fit the conditions of Europe, and nothing that could not fit this system, or the interests of the great European nations collectively, could possibly emerge as law in any meaningful sense. Essentially this imposed two conditions: First, international law had to recognize and be compatible with an international political system in which a number of states were competitive, suspicious, and opportunistic in their political alignments with one another; second, it had to be compatible with the value system that they shared. In both respects, international law was Europeanized.

It was not always easy to develop theory and doctrine which would square the two conditions. On the one hand, the major European nations had to maintain vis-a-vis each other an emphasis upon sovereignty, independence, formal equality—thus insuring for themselves individually an optimal freedom of action to maintain the "flexibility of alignment" that the system required and to avoid anything approaching a repetition of the disastrous Napoleonic experience. But there was no pressing need to maintain these same standards with regard to most of the rest of the world. Thus, theory and doctrine applicable among the great nations and the smaller European states did not really comfortably fit less developed and less powerful societies elsewhere. Political interference in Africa and Asia and even in Latin America (though limited in Latin America by the special interest of the United States as expressed in the Monroe Doctrine, itself from the outset related to European politics and long dependent upon the "balance of power" system in Europe) was necessary in order to preserve both common economic values and the European "balance" itself. A nation such as Switzerland could be neutralized by agreement and could be relied upon to protect its neutrality; more doubtful, but possible, (with an assist from the North) was the neutralization of the Latin American countries; out of the question was the neutralization of Asia and Africa.

This Europeanization of the law was made explicit by a number of 19th century scholars. More emphasis was put upon the fact that international law was the law of "civilized nations"; Kent and Story, the great early American scholars, repeatedly made use of this phrase, or of "Christian nations," which is a substantial equivalent. Wheaton stated that the public law was essentially "limited to the civilized and Christian peoples of Europe or to those of European origin." Of course it had always been of European origin in fact, but it had maintained a universal outlook under the natural law theory. Now, with virtually every writer, not only was the European origin of public law acknowledged as a historical phenomenon, but the rules thus established by the advanced civilizations of Europe were to be imposed on others. The European customs on which international law was based were to become, by force and fiat, the customs that others were to accept as law if they were to join this community as sovereign states. Hall, for example, was quite explicit on this point when he said "states outside European civilization must formally enter into the circle of law-governed countries. They must do something with the acquiescence of the latter, or some of them, which amounts to an acceptance of the law in its entirety beyond all possibility of misconstruction." During the nineteenth century these views were protested by virtually all the Latin American writers, though ineffectively, just as the new nations of Africa and Asia protest them, with more effect, today.

A number of other nineteenth-century developments contributed to the transmutation of the law of nations into international law; that is, from aspects of a universal system of Justice into particular rules governing the relations of sovereign states. The difference is important, for although the older law of nations did cover relationships among sovereigns, this was by no means its exclusive domain. The law of nature governed sovereigns in their relationship to their own citizens, to foreigners, and to each other in a conceptually unified system. The theory of international law, which in the nineteenth century became common to virtually all writers in Europe and

America, broke this unity and this universality. It lost sight of the individual almost entirely and confined itself to rules limiting the exercise of state power for reasons essentially unconnected with justice or morality save as these values might affect international relations. No longer did the sovereign look to the law of nations to determine what he ought to do; his search was merely for rules that might limit his freedom of action.

To appreciate this development, we must relate it to other aspects of nineteenth-century philosophy. First, and most obvious, was the growing nationalism and the tendency to regard the state, and the individual's identification with the state, as transcending other ties of social solidarity. National identification was not new, but it was accelerating in intensity and scope throughout Europe as new unifications occurred. It reached its ultimate philosophical statement in notions of "state will" put forward by the Germans, especially by Hegel, although political philosophers will recognize its origins in the rejected doctrines of Hobbes. National identification was reflected jurisprudentially in law theories which incorporated this Hegelian abstraction and saw law, domestic and international, simply as its formal reflection. In the international community this reduced law to Jellinek's auto-limitation. A state, the highest form of human organization in fact and theory, could be subjected to Law only by a manifestation of self-will, or consent. According to the new theories, the nineteenth century corporate sovereign was "sovereign" in a quite new and different sense from his historical predecessors. He no longer sought to find the law; he made it; he could be subjected to law only because he agreed to be. There was no law, domestic or international, except that willed by, acknowledged by, or consented to by states.

Hidden behind Hegelian abstractions were more practical reasons for a changing jurisprudence. Related to, but distinguishable from, nationalism was the growth of democracy in one form or another. Increased participation in politics and the demands of various groups for status and recognition had dramatic effects upon law institutions. The efforts of various interest groups to control or influence governmental decisions, particularly when taken in conjunction with the impact of industralization, led to a concentration of attention on the legislative power and the means whereby policy could be formulated and enforced as law through bureaucratic institutions. Law became a conscious process, something more than simply doing justice and looking to local customs and a common morality for applicable norms.

Particularly was this true when the norms previously applied were no longer satisfactory to many, when customs were rapidly changing as the forces of the new productivity were harnessed. The old way of doing things, which depended on a relatively stable community with stable ideas dealing with familiar situations, was no longer adequate to the task. First was the period of codification of existing law: the Code Napoleon in France and the peculiar codification that, in fact, resulted from Austin's restatement and ordering of the Common Law in England. Codification was followed in all countries by a growing amount of legislation, some changing and adjusting the older law, much dealing with entirely new situations. The legislative mills have been grinding ever since, and when its cumbersome processes were no longer adequate to the task, a limited legislative authority was delegated in one form or another, to the executive. Whereas the eighteenth century had been a time in which man sought justice, the nineteenth and twentieth have been centuries in which men are satisfied with law. Indeed, with developed positivism, the separation of law from justice, or from morality generally, became quite specific.

In municipal systems we tend to view what is called positivism as fundamentally a movement to democratize policy by increasing the power of parliament—the elected representatives—at the expense of the more conservative judiciary. When the power of the latter was made both limited and explicit—when norms were clarified and made more precise and the creation of new norms was placed exclusively in parliamentary hands—two purposes were served: Government was made subservient to an institutionalized popular will, and law became a rational system for implementing that will, for serving conscious goals, for embodying the "public policy." It is true that, initially, the task was to remove restrictions that, it was thought, inhibited the free flow of money, goods, and labor; but even laissez-faire was a conscious policy. Law was seen as an emanation of the "sovereign will." However, the sovereign was not Hobbes' absolute monarch but rather the parliamentary sovereign of Austin. It was, too, an optimistic philosophy, and, though it separated law from morality, it was by no means an immoral or amoral one. Man, through democratic institutions of government and economic freedom, was master of his destiny. The theory did not require, though it unfortunately might acquire, a Hegelian mystique. It was merely a rationalization and ordering of new institutions of popular government. It was not opposed to either justice or morality; it merely wished to minimize subjective views of officials who wielded public authority.

Particularly was this true as laissez-faire capitalism became the dominant credo of Western society. To free the factors of production was a major objective of the rising bourgeoisie, and this objective required that governmental authority—administrative officials and judges—be limited as precisely and explicitly as possible; that old customs which inhibited trade be abrogated; that business be free from governmental supervision and notions of morality which might clog the automatic adjustments of the free market; that obligations of status that were inconsistent with the new politics and the new economics be done away with. Contract—conceived as the free bargain of formal equals—replaced the implied obligations of a more static and status-conscious society. Indeed, contract was the dominant legal theme of the century, the touchstone of the free society. Government itself was based upon contract; business organization—the corporation—was analyzed in contractual terms; trade was based on freedom of contract, and money was lent and borrowed on contractual terms; even marriage and the family was seen as a contractual arrangement. It is not surprising that the international obligations of states were also viewed in terms of contract. In fact, some—Anzilotti is the principle example—went so far as to say that all international law could be traced to the single legal norm, *Pacta sunt Servanda.*

The displacement (at least to a considerable extent) of the ethical jurisprudence of the seventeenth and eighteenth centuries by positivism reshaped both international law theory and doctrine. In the first place the new doctrine brought a formal separation of international from municipal law, rejecting the earlier view that both were parts of a universal legal system. One result was to nationalize much that had been regarded as the law of nations. Admiralty law, the law merchant, and the host of problems which arise in private litigation because of some contact with a foreign country were all severed from the older Law of Nations and made dependent on the several national laws. Private international law (which Americans call the "conflict of laws") was thus segregated from international law proper, or, as it is often called, public international law. States were free to enact, within broad though (perhaps) determinate limits, their own rules as to the application of foreign law by their courts, to vary the law merchant, and to enact legislation with regard to many claims arising on the high seas. The change was not quite so dramatic as it sounds because in fact common norms continued to be invoked by municipal courts and were only gradually changed by legislation, and then largely in marginal situations. But there was no dispute after the middle of the nineteenth century that such issues of "private law," unless incorporated in treaties, were outside the scope of international law and could be varied by national legislation. This distinction, like all law, had its roots in the past. Earlier writers had suggested a distinction between *jus gentium* and *jus inter gens*, but it was really with Bentham and his successors that the distinction became formalized, accepted, and the latter called international law.

The second important result of Positivist theory and method was to narrow further the amount of international practice which it was willing to call law. As we have already noted there had been increasing use by the so-called pre-positivists of empirical methods. This trend was both accelerated and formalized by rejection of an ethical jurisprudence. In addition, although positivists did not reject custom as a source of law norms, they insisted that, to be obligatory upon states, custom must reflect an acknowledgment that it is based on a binding legal norm. Thus the mere fact that states had acted in a certain way in the past, however uniformly and consistently, did not create an international obligation to act in the same way subsequently. Furthermore—as the Permanent Court later put it in the famous case of *The Lotus*—limitations upon states' freedom of action could not be presumed from mere custom. Needless to say, this requirement, conceptually related to consent and contract, makes it extremely difficult to know, in the absence of a treaty, what customs reflect international law and what customs do not. Some observers will state a rule as law; others, on identical evidence, will posit it as mere "comity," customarily adhered to but not obligatory.

Partly for this reason and partly because positivist theory and domestic law institutions required, or were thought to require, more formal and precise norms, the 19th century, and particularly its latter half, saw the beginnings of an ever-increasing complex of formal international arrangements, or "international legislation." The conduct of foreign affairs itself was formalized to a far greater degree by the exchange of written memoranda and aides-memoire, as well as by explicit treaty arrangements. The great bulk of treaties dealt simply with matters long recognized as appropriate for international agreement as a matter of foreign relations: general arrangements governing friendship, commerce and navigation; rights, privileges, immunities, of Consuls; Consular jurisdiction; extradition of criminals; naturalization (a newer problem); trademarks and copyrights. In addition, of course, a few dealt with the solution to *ad hoc* disputes, arranging for the arbitration of claims or similar matters. Although there were some efforts at multilateral arrangements—The Congress of Vienna itself is an example—by and large a multilateral approach is a twentieth century development. Exceptions were predominantly matters that necessarily involved more than two states, such as international waterways: the Rhine, the Bosporus, and the Suez Canal.

The net impact of this activity was to make much of international law simply a matter of treaty interpretation, just as much domestic law became a matter of code, legislation, and regulation. Not all matters, of course, were subjected to formal arrangements among all states, a problem complicated by the entry of new states into the international community. In a society in which states wish to maintain optimal freedom of action, it is often easier to act consistently with existing norms while refraining from acknowledging these as obligatory, than to create a rule which, once acknowledged, cannot be unilaterally terminated save at a relatively high political cost.

Nothing in nineteenth-century positivism really took issue with any of the basic contentions of natural law theory. Positivists did not deny the need for or even the existence of international norms governing the conduct of states. They simply asked, "But are they law?" and answered, in considerable measure, "No." To a great extent this was a matter of definition. Austin himself could not see the possibility of a pluralistic legal system except in pluralistic terms; international law was simply international politics or international morality, but certainly not law. Others compromised by importing into international law a contractual analysis, despite its inherent conceptual and practical difficulties.

As is usually the case, governments carried water on both shoulders. A mild positivism fitted international politics pretty well, though no state was prepared to deny the existence of international law, or to deny that treaties were "binding legal obligations," or even to abandon the use of other sources to support the claims it saw fit to make for reasons of both policy and politics. There was some conceptual difficulty with the contractual notion, and it was not very satisfactorily solved by claiming that others must accept the norms worked out by civilized Europe. In point of fact, as might be expected, no major nation has ever really accepted the idea that lesser states had to consent to the rules of international law espoused by major nations in order to make them obligatory. Despite consent theories, the citizen must take municipal law as he finds it; so, too, the new state must take international law as it finds it. The less certain international law is, the less onerous is it for new states to accept existing norms of international law. And much international law doctrine is, to say the least, flexible.

In addition, the basic premise of positivism that law is a matter of formal political consensus and not universal moral principles fitted the international arena perfectly. Morality was not irrelevant; it simply became subservient to common sense. However deplorable the principles espoused by a foreign government in domestic matters seemed, other nations did not regard it as their business. In a world political system in which peace depended upon flexibility of alignment, nations could scarcely afford to have their political judgment subservient to moral criteria. The system assumed that politics would make strange bedfellows, as indeed it did. Lloyd George and Clemenceau never could comprehend Wilson's failure to understand this simple fact, or what they regarded as his reckless introduction of political morality into the affairs of Europe.

Thus, the developed international law which we inherit today was the product of this nineteenth-century European development. In summary, it ran—and still runs—something like this:

International law is conceived by most observers as a body of rules binding upon nation-states in their relationships with one another. All states are subject to these rules, which embody correlative rights and duties. Presumably these rules can be changed only by concordant action of all (or almost all) states, though particular states may modify, supplement, or abrogate them as among themselves as long as they do so in a manner which does not affect the rights of others not party to the agreement, or who do not acquiesce in the change. These rules are said to have their origin in the needs of the international community and the consent of (or recognition of these needs by) the various participants. This consent, or recognition, is made evident in a variety of ways, predominantly in the practices that have prevailed in the past and in the prescriptions acknowledged as legally binding, explicitly or implicitly, by the formal participants. Since a great deal of doctrine has been formally codified or incorporated in treaties, most disputes today center around treaty provisions. What is unregulated by general doctrine applicable to all or by specific agreement as among particular states is left to the realm of the several national laws, to unilateral decision by national authorities.

This concept of states as the exclusive "subjects" of international law presumably differentiates international law from other legal systems which regulate individuals, groups of persons, and lesser political entities. Individuals, it is said, are not subjects of international law, though they may be "objects." It is conceded that the rules in question may be for the benefit of individuals or lesser entities than states, and the objective of many rules is the protection of private rights. The individual, however, usually has no international forum in which he can directly invoke these rules. Although the individual may plead them in municipal courts, he does so on the theory that such rules have become part of the relevant national law. He has no appeal to an international tribunal, nor, in general, is he subjected directly to any international rules save through the mechanism of "reception" or "incorporation" into municipal law. He must look to government both for punishment and for vindication of his rights through diplomatic channels, or if possible, in an international tribunal. If the state decides to espouse the citizen's claim it will adopt the claim as its own, and assert that its right (not that of its citizen) has been violated, that the state "in the person of its citizen" has been injured. The state will then seek an appropriate remedy.

THEORY SINCE 1914

The formal theory of international law has changed far less dramatically since the First World War than has international politics. We still think formally in terms of rules governing sovereign states who have acquiesced in their obligatory character, and who, in the absence of such rules, may act independently. Many of the norms are in a state of doubt, and there are many new formal participants, but the international community is still said to be composed of theoretically equal, independent, sovereign states.

Yet to leave matters thus would be grossly to understate what is in fact taking place, though, as yet events and institutions have outdistanced theory. It would be strange if two world wars, the Communist movement, the horrors of Belsen, the explosion at Hiroshima, and the conquest of space, could all be comfortably fitted into a nineteenth-century frame without major readjustments all the way along the line. Actually, the efforts of the last forty years have been toward devising new institutional arrangements to solve problems that cannot be satisfactorily dealt with through uncoordinated national law administrations. Perhaps our failure to create, as yet, institutions that will insure a minimum of violence, and the fact that our efforts are often groping, uncertain, and reserved, has disguised the considerable progress that has been realized with regard to a number of lesser problems. We have a variety of international bodies, both subnational and supranational, dealing with a number of specific problems. Some, such as the League of Nations, the United Nations, the World Court, the International Labor Organization, and the World Health Organization, aspire to universality. Others, such as the Organization of American States, NATO, the European Community, and the Warsaw Pact, are both regional and functional. Still others, such as the International Chamber of Commerce, and the International Red Cross, are both subnational and transnational. We scarcely invite argument in saying that a theory which views the international community as the exclusive domain of nation-states no longer reflects the facts of international life, and has already been passed by history.

President Wilson's Fourteen Points epitomize the development which international law has taken since the First World War. One is conscious already of the re-emergence of strong moral convictions about human rights, and of the idea that the problems of humanity are world problems. There was revulsion at the notion of "power politics"; a strong humanitarianism, which struck deep responsive chords among people (though not politicians) the world over and made Wilson an international popular idol; and an eighteenth-century faith in reason (public opinion) and democratic processes. In addition, there was awareness that Europe was no longer the exclusive focal point of world politics, and that problems of peace and law have once again to be thought of in broader terms.

The League, therefore, was not conceived as a revitalization of the Concert of Europe, broadened to take account of new-world nations, but rather a world version of parliamentary government thrust onto the international scene. There is here a curious mixture of eighteenth-century reason with nineteenth-century democratic political institutions. The struggle of nineteenth-century statesmen to achieve security through flexible alliances was seen less as the reason for almost a century of peace than as the cause of world war. American dislike for colonialism on moral, ethical, and economic grounds joined with confidence in "the people" to manifest itself in a new system that looked to national independence, self-determination under democratic political institutions, and peace built not on power relations but on the unreasonableness of war. There was a belief that modern warfare was a problem for the whole community, that neutrality for major nations (witness the American experience) or for minor nations strategically or tactically important to major nations was difficult if not impossible. Security had to be collective, universal; wars had to be renounced, peoples had to be freed (colonialism is seen as a "cause" of war) and the whole diplomatic and political process policed and secured by public opinion. It was an exciting vision, and it has affected much thinking since.

Of course, the failure to work out an effective security system, the effort of America to remain aloof to Wilson's League, and the futile attempts to solve international problems by the traditional form of treaty development, did not prevent the world from becoming increasingly interdependent as to all values. The full extent of this interdependence began to become obvious in 1929–30 when the United States exported the Great Depression. It became more obvious later, when Franklin Roosevelt, his eyes firmly fixed on American problems, devalued the dollar—although this resulted in the export of domestic unemployment as well. The international economy, based on laissez-faire policies common to most of the world in the nineteenth century, had already been subjected to severe public and private restraints; with the Depression it virtually disappeared. Economic salvation was thought to lie in a system of national controls, without international restraint. The expedients consequently adopted actually resulted in spiralling efforts by national politicians to transfer domestic problems to other countries. In the face of overwhelming empirical evidence that the world economy was interdependent, states solemnly agreed that economic regulation was a matter of "internal affairs." Economic nationalism was practiced to a degree by all, and foreigners were discriminated against in a variety of ways wherever temporary advantage could be achieved. Tariffs, quotas, exchange regulations, discriminatory exchange rates, barter, expropriation, and subsidy to national enterprises—all the paraphernalia of discriminatory regulation—marked the pre-war period. Much that had been international in practice ceased to be so regarded. The eyes of politicians were turned inward to their own domestic problems, not outward to the similar problems of their neighbors.

Yet even these national developments had their positive impact upon international law, for all involved, in various degrees, conceptions of law as positive instruments of public policy. A number of these national developments—the Communist experiment, Marxist and Fabian socialism in Europe, the New Deal in America—helped bring about a re-evaluation of legal doctrine in terms of human values. Law began to be thought of as social engineering, conscious choices among policies, methods of distributing and redistributing access to wealth, to health, and to other human values. In most countries it was an evolution of earlier Positivism; from customary rules to an ordered system to evaluation of order in terms of goals.

There is a common tendency to regard the nineteenth century as the age of "individualism," as opposed to modern "collectivism," carried to its extremes in the Communist and Fascist communities. In some senses this thesis is accurate enough and seems an unavoidable concomitant of specialization and of large-scale organization. But a good argument can be made that nineteenth-century ideology required the individual to subordinate his welfare to the common good—that the state had no obligation to relieve individual suffering, that, in fact, it was dangerous to tinker with the economy in an effort to achieve "social justice" for all. The twentieth century, on the other hand, has in some respects and some places seen a return to individual values, for the movement toward the "welfare state" can be conceived in terms of the obligation of society to its individual members, rather than their obligations to the collective whole. One phenomenon common to many societies has been the evaluation of legal doctrine in terms of its distribution of assets and liabilities, rewards and penalties, an analysis which seeks to examine consequences and evaluates function in terms of underlying community policy with regard to the distribution of values. Much of the growth of governmental function, with its concurrent growth of public law, has been aimed at improving the lot of the individual citizen through redistribution of values, and has explicitly demonstrated a far greater conscious concern for individual welfare than the laissez-faire economic theory demanded or, indeed, permitted.

Three related features of law-government are worth special mention for they have been transferred into the international arena by a substantial number of writers. All are associated with the intellectual *potpourri* which is usually lumped together as "legal realism" and is predominantly an American view. First, the notion that law is always an expression of "public policy," and therefore doctrine can be evaluated in terms of its contributions to goal values. Although such evaluation is normally the job of legislatures, it is also appropriate for judges to make evaluations within the areas of choice left open to them. Both judges and legislators should, therefore, according to this view, supplement doctrine with data from outside the formal system to assist in an informed policy determination. Those with the greatest faith in the capacities of social science techniques to assist this task regard law as a "policy science."

Second, to analyze law institutions in terms of achievement, judges or legislators must posit preferences about the kind of social structure they feel obligated by their role in society to support, and must then make competing choices about values. Many philosophers have taken democracy seriously by making the welfare of all persons in the community as individuals a matter of public concern and responsibility. They have tended to favor the widest possible sharing of all values among members of the community. Consequently, they have also tended to favor measures that increased opportunities for those who, comparatively speaking, lacked them. In this sense, at least, there was a return to both humanism and individualism, though there remains a great deal of disagreement on the best methods of achieving common objectives, and the proper hierarchy of values.

Third, the new jurisprudence saw law as a process rather than a body of formal rules. The lawyers of new school were quick to see and appreciate the limitations of doctrine (often overstating them) and the need for new institutional arrangements, conceived in less formal terms, to cope with new governmental responsibilities they posited as proper. Agencies were to be given broad charters to operate relatively unrestricted by formality, by precedent, by legal technicalities; they were to combine, within limitations, legislative-executive-judicial powers; they were to be free to experiment with new ideas. It is no coincidence that American realists were almost all New Dealers, active in setting up the "alphabet agencies," such as NRA, AAA, WPA, PWA, etc., with their new techniques and broad powers, although the curious melange of contradictions which marked the New Deal eventually separated them again. And it is no exaggeration to say that all lawyers, whatever their jurisprudential label (if any), have been affected by these developments; that all are more sceptical of doctrine and doctrinal solutions; that few feel so intensely the importance of doctrinal consistency when it seems to lead to undesirable results. The old adage of the late nineteenth century that "hard cases make good law" would be subscribed to by relatively few today. By losing its exclusive concern with legal logic and the problems of adjudication and by taking a broader view of the legal process, the legal process has moved much closer to policy and thus to politics, ethics, morals, and justice.

Realism is less a theory than an approach that insists that processes of law-government cannot accurately be described or analyzed except in their appropriate contextual framework. It has, therefore, the effect of broadening the focus of scholarly attention by seeking to clarify the goals sought, the methods whereby they can be achieved, and assumptions about human and institutional behavior. The major objection of realists to positivism as developed by Austin and his followers was simply that courts did not behave and could not behave in accordance with its theory, and that it was probably a good thing that they did not. It is this effort to re-examine assumptions against experience and knowledge about individual and group behaviour that makes realism "realistic." But realism does not yet offer a definitive theory to replace those it has questioned.

We emphasize realism not because it is an international movement (though an argument could be made for this proposition) but because it is symptomatic of a prevalent scepticism and anxiety. As a result of the rapid political and social change of the last two generations, both domestically and internationally, we are still in the process of re-examination and re-evaluation of our ideas about social and political institutions generally. There has been a resurgence of national law philosophy, of interest in the relation of law and ethics. Others have seen in a comparative approach the possibility of creating a common law of mankind—a close relative of natural law but, as in the Grotian tradition, depending on experience and positive law. Certainly international politics is full of reference to universals, to the aspirations of mankind rather than the rights and duties of states. There is a growing interest in the individual as the focus of international attention; witness the Declaration on Human Rights, the Genocide Convention, the Nuernburg trials, proposals for an international writ of *habeas corpus,* and so forth. Underdeveloped countries insist that those who are better off are obligated to assist them in their development, an obligation which in practice, though not always in principle, is very nearly accepted. And a whole new body of international administrative law is growing up as new institutions of a supranational character are launched into world politics.

We are living with a number of makeshift expedients and cautious experiments that do not fit into the old theory, but neither do they allow us with confidence to propose a new theory. At best, certain trends are clear, and a few generalizations can be essayed.

NEW PERSPECTIVES ON OLD PROBLEMS

In the nineteenth century, most observers tacitly assumed three major conditions of world politics: (1) that the nation-state was the only participant of importance in world politics; (2) that it was important to the stability of the system that states remain independent and solitary; (3) that economic interdependence, owing to increasing specialization in the means of production, was not a matter of major concern because, domestically and internationally, economics were outside the domain of politics. None of these conditions exists today.

Several factors account for the decline of the importance of the nation-state—at least in Europe. Some of these have already been mentioned. The most important, of course, is the rise of a huge Communist state and the relative decline of the European states after the close of the Second World War. France and Italy were defeated, Germany was defeated and divided, and Great Britain was impoverished and shorn of its Empire as a consequence of the magnitude of its contribution to ultimate victory. Europe, thrust out of Asia and Africa, was reduced to a peripheral land mass on the edge of the Eurasian continent; it still possessed important resources in trained manpower and technical facilities but was tired and divided. Within the Communist sphere, organizational party ties permitted a degree of unity and consistency denied the democratic nations within which political parties received support from electors whose demands focussed attention on local rather than general or supranational considerations. Without specifically supranational forms of organization, these wider interests could not secure recognition, and even with supranational organization it would be difficult to offset the pulls of national politics.

Still other factors militated against the division of Europe into isolated nation-states. Economically, this division made no sense and had harmful effects upon the economies of the individual nations. Moreover, modern technological warfare meant that the small independent nation-state could not play a major or even an important secondary role in world politics. Not only was it necessary for Europe to unite, but also required was the addition of the United

States to offset Soviet armed capabilities. Europe, even if armed with thermonuclear weapons, had not sufficient space to be fully defensible in the jet age and the age of rapid tank corps against either Soviet conventional capabilities or Soviet nuclear capabilities, unless the weight of the United States was thrown into the "balance."

Regardless, however, of the reasons for this development at the midpoint of the twentieth century, the fact of its occurrence merits attention. From the formal standpoint of international law, the supranational entity may constitute simply an additional "subject." But the existence of this new subject is bound to influence both its procedures and substance. It is not enough to repeat the phrase "the sovereign nation has bound its will for certain limited purposes with respect to rights delegated to these new supranational entities." The supranational entities exist, and it is their very existence that constitutes the relevant datum to which international law must be accommodated.

The task of achieving an orderly development of resources within the bloc has been complicated, for the democratic West at least, by the extent to which laissez-faire economic theory has been modified in all countries and virtually abandoned in some. States have undertaken considerable responsibility for allocation of income, natural resources, employment, social security, fiscal stability, and the like, in response both to economic theory and, more importantly, the political demands of organized groups for a greater share of the material benefits of society than the market would allocate. Agrarian reform movements and labor movements have demanded "social justice," and the use of the public power to ease their lot. Rightly, wrongly, or just unavoidably, domestic political elites have acquiesced in the politicization of economics on both sides of the iron curtain. As we noted earlier, more often than not this resulted in discrimination against foreigners, by creating barriers to trade and competition. But after the Second World War economic nationalism was a luxury no European state could afford.

The increase in governmental sectors of the economy in industrialized nations has greatly complicated the task of restoring a favorable climate for private trade and investment. Differences which would previously have been left to Adam Smith's invisible hand now require extensive negotiation, collaboration, and coordination of national policies. In Europe this has resulted in the growth of supranational institutions with power to deal importantly with economic matters. Elsewhere, through the World Bank, the Monetary Fund, the General Agreement on Trade and Tariffs and other agencies, similar progress toward consonance in national policies has been achieved.

In the less developed Afro-Asian countries local political leaders have made extravagant promises of economic progress and seek subsidy from one or another of the blocs. Their position vis-a-vis Europe and the West is not unlike the status of our South; and the United States has adopted an international version of the old Agricultural Administration Act to assist them. The AAA was a response to political demands of southern senators whose votes were important to the achievement of other New Deal policies. It would not be cynical to suggest an international parallel. More important, of course, is the fear of the West that a failure of non-Communist governments to provide results will lead to Soviet domination of an area of strategic importance to the West.

A political system that is based significantly on the old adage about hanging together lest all hang separately produces very strong pressures for cooperative decisions by national governments. It has become necessary to develop new institutions for recommending common policy, for fitting together different national legal systems, in many important aspects; chief among these are military policy, economic development, fiscal policy, conservation and exploitation of natural resources, and other areas of economic planning. With some notable exceptions in Europe, and a few United Nations agencies dealing primarily with international administration, we can still say that reducing common policies to common law remains a formal responsibility of national decision makers. Thus we can fit new developments, albeit a bit self-consciously, into traditional theory. But to do so is to sacrifice substance to form, and to miss the essential point.

In point of fact national decision makers are formulating policy recommendations for formal implementation in collaboration with others, sometimes through formal channels—as with NATO or GATT —and sometimes less formally through meetings of foreign ministers, economic experts, and even unofficial diplomats; the latter is most dramatically illustrated by scientific conferences resulting in the International Geophysical Year, by the pressure (possibly ill-advised) from domestic scientists for a halt to atomic testing, by the activities of such transnational groups as the International Chamber of Commerce, affiliated banking groups, labor unions, and others, whose recommendations must be and are considered by the several national governments. Even where formal consultation has not preceded national action, the effect upon other friendly states of unilateral national policy, and recommendations by both private and public groups, weigh heavily in the policy adopted.

It is a wholly impolitic and inadequate answer to the other members or affiliates of the bloc for a state to say that national policy with important transnational effects is unregulated by formal international prescriptions and that therefore such national policy is a matter exclusively for national decision. Even were this position accepted "as a matter of law" by interested states—and the point might not be readily conceded—it would be largely irrelevant. Political allies expect, indeed demand, sympathetic consideration of their views, an opportunity to present these views if they are not readily perceived, and an assurance that every effort will be made to avoid or at least mitigate any adverse impact upon their economies.

In the effort to work out consonant policies and consonant laws, to justify national decisions on their merits, there is a good deal of research into foreign law for the purpose of seeing how similar problems *as national problems* have been handled by national governments. Comparative research often yields common principles which can be extracted from the experience of many states and used as bases for agreements or, more modestly, as guides to what other decision makers will tolerate as being within the limits of national discretion. The obligation to act "reasonably" with regard to many matters is often embodied in formal international law doctrine contained in treaties or customary practice, and the usual method of giving substantive content to such a term is to examine how others have acted in similar situations. This in turn requires giving an operative content to the word "similar" and bringing in other data from economics and social science. If we can regard these not as problems of nation-state relationships but as problems, for example, of military policy or economic development, the analysis will be in functional terms rather than jurisdictional allocation. The Free World necessarily becomes a community with a common interest in individual welfare—human dignity—rather than a system of minimal restraints on unilateral acts of competitive, solitary, suspicious nation-states. This assumption is consistent, and is the only one that is consistent, with the ideology constantly urged upon the world by the United States.

The process of making effective decisions governing transnational events is the essence of international law. Today this process is increasingly subjected to effective restraints which limit the freedom of action of national officials and which promote policy choices which are compatible with an international political system of associated states which share (for the most part) a belief in human dignity for all persons. The United States by reason of its power and resources (and Europe to a lesser extent) plays a leadership role in promoting compatible national policies through the resolution of disputes within the Free World, usually by a process of suggestion coupled with subsidy. In these circumstances the law-job is, in the fashion of the Grotians, to distill from common experience and shared values general principles of law which, if adopted, make for consonant official decisions.

As we move from norms governing decisions affecting others within the Free World to the relationships of the two major blocs, we find a different situation. Here, pressures for consonance are minimal; negotiations are at arm's length and are largely related to the avoidance of violence. The members of the two blocs regard each other as competitive, and hostile, and decisions are arrived at only when the bargain is mutually advantageous in terms related to instrumental bargaining positions. Enduring solutions are simply not envisioned, and there is, as yet, a premium upon seizing every opportunity for political advantage.

part  II

THE
DOCTRINAL
FRAMEWORK

4

THE "STATE" SYSTEM: ORTHODOXY AND CHANGE

Two familiar, everyday concepts are those of "state" and "government." Generally there is no difficulty in distinguishing a "state" from other forms of social organization, or in perceiving the difference between the continuing entity (state) and the body of officials (government) who at any given time can speak formally and authoritatively for it. A state endures through changes of government, territory, and population, even though these changes are far-reaching and of major consequence. We would be hard put to say in what respects the United States of today is similar to the United States of 1789; yet there would be agreement that it is the "same" state. France will remain France after Algerian independence, despite a major loss of territory and population. And Cuba remains Cuba despite the Castro revolution with its potentially farflung changes of government, social and economic organization, and political orientation.

Despite the familiarity of common usage and conception, difficulties sometimes exist and distinctions become blurred. Existing states do pass out of existence and new states come into being. The process is not always orderly, and it may be difficult to pinpoint any single time of death or birth. Is Lithuania still a state? Are there two Germanies and two Chinas, or a single Germany and a single China with two governments each? What is their relationship with pre-Second World War Germany and China? Did Austria exist in 1941? Did France? If so, what group of officials composed its government?

Questions such as these may be asked in a variety of contexts, and cannot be intelligently answered unless the purpose of the inquiry is known.   Because international law is phrased so generally in terms of state obligations, difficulties occur whenever factual situations differ from the model, or ideal, on which the abstraction "state" or "government" is based.   A single definition may be satisfactory for a variety of purposes, and, undoubtedly, communication and analysis are improved if the terms used in legal doctrine reflect popular conceptions and usages.   But, if a definition or rule becomes increasingly inadequate in applications to real world situations, it may become necessary to consider alternative rules or definitions.   A state by definition has a single government; in actuality there may be two or more groups of officials claiming that status.   The decision maker does not have to decide in one jump that there are two states, or which government is the lawful government.   He may move to a number of lesser decisions closer to the facts by saying for one purpose he will treat the facts as though there were two states; for another purpose he will treat government A as the government; for another purpose he will treat government B as the constituted official authority; and so forth. In each case the effort is to measure the facts against both the rule and its purpose.   There is little sense in applying a rule in a way that defeats the purpose it is meant to serve, or in being blind to the consequences of a decision.

In the process of law-government the label that is attached may determine, in important ways, the consequences which follow.   The philosopher may be interested in the true essence of a state.   The governmental decision maker is not concerned with such an inquiry, but rather with what consequences follow from what factual conditions, and why.   He is seeking to formulate or administer rules that are phrased in terms of abstract categories: "state," "government," "property," "contract," and so forth.   Legal norms marry facts to policies, and the decision maker must always, to determine the operative scope and application of legal norms, look to both factual conditions and purposes served.   For the decision maker, the issue is, does this rule as applied to these facts serve the objectives that the rule was designed to implement and upon which it rests?   This process requires a discriminating judgment with regard to facts, norms, and policies.   In essence the decision maker, when he refers to an entity as a state, is simply saying that for the purposes at hand a given entity should be treated as a state because to do so serves the policies underlying the norm in question.   He may arrive at this conclusion by saying that the entity in question seems enough like others treated the same way to justify his conclusion; or he may say that, despite differences that clearly distinguish it, the particular rule should be extended to cover it; or he may say that, despite factual similarities with entities usually treated as states, in this instance the differences are more important because to treat this entity as a state would not serve the purposes of the rule invoked.

The point to be kept in mind is the general one that legal rules prescribe consequences to be attached by decision makers to specified factual conditions in order to promote policies. Therefore, the decision maker must always inquire as to whether or not the particular facts are those envisioned by the rule; one measure of this inquiry is whether or not the policy encompassed by the rule will be served by its application or by its rejection. In addition, as factual conditions change, the rule itself may become outmoded and may no longer be suited to the policy envisioned and served when the rule was first formulated.

Conceptions of state and government are fundamental to a great deal of international law theory and doctrine. International law is, after all, usually conceived as a body of rules governing the relations of states. But it was pointed out in Chapter 2 that most rules were formulated during a "balance of power" political system that made enduring supranational or intergovernmental institutions politically impossible, a system the stability of which was reinforced by a norm entailing the equality, independence, and sovereignty of states. We should not be surprised if the changes in the political structure of international relations of this century require overhauling and reformulation of much of the basic doctrine, and, indeed, of the theory itself insofar as it confines international law-government to state relations.

THE STATE AS THE SUBJECT OF INTERNATIONAL LAW

It is usually said that the state is the exclusive "subject" of international law, although individuals or other associations may be "objects." By this statement is meant simply that rules bind only states, though these rules may have as their purpose the securing of individual rights and duties, and that rules become operative in governing individual relations only through the mechanism of national laws and national law administration. There is no forum in which an individual can complain that international law is being violated. In a domestic court he can raise international law in support of his claim, but he does so (it is generally said) only on the theory that the rule he urges has been incorporated into national law. If the issue is raised in diplomatic channels, it is raised as a claim by one state against another for violation of its right (not the individual's) under international law.

The reasons for attaching a pre-eminent importance to the role of state have already been detailed in the preceding chapters, and need not be repeated here. The emergence of the nation-state required a theory compatible with its existence, with its practices, and with the juridical claims it made. The authority of rules, whether derived from the will of God or of the people, was not derived from higher worldly authority. Without any institutional framework apart from that provided by the several nation-states, efforts which posited individual rights and duties as the basis for international law fell before the ideology of nationalism, and the breakdown of the Medieval Church doomed political limitations justified by natural law, at least as administered from Rome. Like other institutions, law (together with legal scholarship) was secularized, nationalized, and positivized. Theory began with the nation-state and its sovereignty because nation-states were the effective actors in the international arena. There could be no law in the international community save as it was promulgated, acquiesced in, and enforced by states.

The conception of state was central to international law simply because the nation-state was central to the international political system. The political power of the nation-state lay in the capacity of its political elites to create and nourish group identification with and loyalty to impersonal and abstract symbols, and to merge these identifications and loyalties into a system of territorial administration. In the "balance of power" system, the distinguishing features of the state lay in its ideological isolation and its freedom from formal control by external and transcending bodies politic. The requirements of the "balance of power" international political system for flexible alliances among the great nations and the common interest in preventing each other from indiscriminate plunder of weaker states argued against enduring arrangements that solidified relationships among political elites. Freedom from external authority was an essential characteristic. States were formally equal in the sense that they possessed the same formal rights, were subject to the same formal duties—although in the formulation, interpretation, and enforcement of these norms the major nations played a major role. A state ceased to be a state when it was subjected to the formal control of another entity. It might still possess several of the common characteristics of statehood—population, considerable local autonomy, and a fixed area of administrative responsibility—but it was not a state if it was not formally independent of other states. Various degrees of autonomy were recognized—but the common feature of dependencies, mandates, protectorates, territories, colonies, and so forth, which distinguished them, internationally, from states was the formal relationship between such entities and the external bodies politic that exercised at least some measure of control.

The prototype for the concept "state" is, of course, the European nation-state as it developed over two or more centuries. It is a system organized according to geography rather than kinship, and possessing a governmental subsystem. It came into being when, taking a lead from the Church, the loyalty of persons within a geographical area was transposed from fealty to local chieftains to abstract symbols that, in turn, could be utilized and manipulated by a ruling elite. The population in an age of low mobility obtained social solidarity through their common identification with the symbols of national membership supplemented by common culture, language, tradition, and experience. Outsiders were foreigners who threatened the group, and the group, accordingly, looked to the national elite to organize protective measures. Except for the Church, there were no important social organizations that transcended national boundaries, and for this reason, Church-state relationships have always presented a peculiarly delicate problem. To the extent that other identifications existed they formed the raw material for further national unifications; the concepts of Italy and Germany existed before they emerged as integrated states in the political sense. The ruling elites within a geographical area insisted upon loyalty; they used various techniques to instill this loyalty among the populace, or they made use of the loyalties the situations provided. In the governmental organization—the hierarchy of authority within the geographical area —the ruling monarch (or otherwise-appointed head of state) insisted upon acknowledgement by individuals and subgroups of the sovereignty of the national government. This was made more effective by nationalizing the army and by the extension of a national bureaucracy and court system for applying national norms. There continued to be considerable competition for control of the apparatus of government, but one consequence of abstract loyalty and abstract symbols as the focus of national sentiment was that the society could survive dramatic changes in the governmental subsystem.

The state, as a geographically based society, is a useful concept because the invariance of activity gives it an identity. It has social existence and therefore can engage in activity and be held accountable for that activity. Individuals who act for the state act differently from the way they act in their private capacities. Within institutions individuals are selected who are appropriate for given roles and quite often, in filling the roles, their personalities, as well as behavior, became subject to role-appropriate modifications. This is equally true today as new institutions come into existence. The difference between the Joint Chiefs and the various United Nations Commanders during the Korean War[1] were so striking that they cannot be accounted for on the sole basis of personality or past military experience; they must be understood primarily by reference to the role requirements which the respective individuals filled. Major invariances in institutional behavior continue while various individuals filter through different roles. Observers would find striking similarities between the behavior of the House of Representatives and the United States Senate for 1935 and 1955 although major turnovers in personnel have occurred.

The state has a social existence, which continues throughout changes of government personnel and of governments themselves. Government is simply one aspect, although a most important one, of the state. As a social actor the state can be the subject of rights and obligations just as the individual within the society, as a social actor, can have rights and obligations that flow from his particular roles in the social system. As the most important actor in the international system, indeed, as the virtually exclusive actor during long periods of time, the state plays a central role in international legal doctrine.

The state was the exclusive actor or subject of international law simply because there could not be any enforcible law norms save those enforced by states within their own territory or forcibly imposed upon one state by others acting alone or in conjunction. This was so primarily because national governments claimed a monopoly of law enforcement institutions within their territories and were prepared to resist forcibly any institutional arrangement that weakened that authority. The struggle with the transnational Church hierarchy and the difficulty of that experience constituted an object lesson in the

---

[1] The Joint Chiefs, with global responsibilities, tended to argue for limiting the Korean War and, after Chinese intervention, for compromising on terms in order to end it. The United Nations Commanders tended to argue for inflicting a massive defeat upon the Communist forces.

danger of permitting any other political entity to exercise authority within its domain. To have permitted another national political entity, or combination of other nations, to do so would have been to weaken and diffuse the authority which was felt (quite rightly) essential to the existence of the state.

Definitions of state, for purposes of international law, still reflect these historic conditions. For example, the Montevideo Convention of 1933 asserts in Article I: "The State as a person of international law should possess the following qualifications: (*a*) a permanent population; (*b*) a defined territory; (*c*) a Government; and (*d*) a capacity to enter relations with other States."

Not all entities that, at least for some purposes, have been classified as states meet these requirements rigorously. Yemen, represented in the United Nations whose membership is confined to states, lacks a secular government and any very developed system of law. Israel's immigrant population was not very "permanent" at the time of its admission to statehood. Does Nationalist China have a defined territory? And are ByeloRussia and the Ukraine able (in any meaningful sense) to enter relations with other states?

The first three conditions of being a state under the quoted definition are factual. Apparently it is not necessary to have a "defined" territory, so long as there is at least some territory as to which control is generally acknowledged; a "permanent" population, similarly, means at least a core of people who acknowledge citizenship; and by "government" is meant a body of officials who may act in the name of the entity, although, where more than one group claims that authority, there may be conflict as to which body is the government.

The fourth condition, however, is normative rather than factual, for it posits a legal rather than a factual prerequisite to statehood. In addition, the condition is tautological. Does an entity satisfying the factual conditions of statehood have capacity to enter foreign relations because it is a state, or is it a state because it has such capacity? Obviously the condition is included in the definition in order to exclude those entities who would otherwise meet the factual criteria, but whose foreign relations are in the hands of another body; for example, the states of the United States, the Canadian provinces, or the various protectorates, mandates, and other dependent-state categories. Where a body politic meeting the factual criteria claims to be able to conduct its own foreign relations and no other state contests this by an opposing claim, no problem arises. But if the claim is contested, the definition suggests no criterion for judgment.   Such problems usually arise as questions of "recognition" and are discussed in the next Chapter.   What is important to note here is simply that the crucial question of what constitutes a state cannot be answered without reference to normative criteria not specified in the legal doctrine itself.

But this is by no means the only shortcoming of orthodox theory. In the nineteenth century, public organizations of a supranational character did not and could not exist.   Hence theory and doctrine could legitimately ignore them.   Today such organizations are no longer inconsistent with the security requirements of states in the international political system, and do in fact exist on both a global and regional level.   As entities such organizations must possess certain legal capacities, and their officials cannot perform their supranational functions if they are regarded as national officials or simply private citizens—neither of which is descriptive of their role. Within the area of their prescribed competence such organizations, acting through organization officials, perform functions analogous to those usually performed by political bodies.   They make contracts, agreements, administer property and personnel, and are assigned a modest decision-making capacity.

Orthodox theory classifies what is not international law, which it defines as indicated above, as national law, or one of the latter's subsystems.   One could scarcely maintain that supranational organizations were administering or were subject to national law; there would be no meaning left to their supranational character.   The alternative —and the only alternative which exists—is international law, or perhaps, to create an entirely new category of law.   Whether we have today a "supranational law" that is being slowly created, or whether international law has been conceptually broadened to take account of these developments, will depend on how people in the future interpret what is going on today.   At the moment, the classification does not seem terribly important except insofar as it is clear that such organizations and their officials are not generally subject to national laws.

A major inroad into orthodoxy took place when the UN Secretary General requested an Advisory Opinion of the International Court of Justice as to the capacity of the United Nations Organization to assert an international claim for the assassination of Count Bernadotte in 1947 while he was serving in the Middle East as a UN official. Theretofore the capacity to press international claims had been considered a right and function of states exclusively.   The Court, in affirming the capacity of the UN, did not conclude that the UN was a state, but did say that the extension of such capacity to it was consistent with its international political status and with the purpose of the rule; that the UN could be regarded as a "subject" of international law at least for certain purposes. Other examples of the same sort of reasoning are the extension of diplomatic immunity to officials of international agencies, and the capacity of international agencies to make international agreements binding under international law. This does not make such agencies into states, but it does recognize their political functions in the contemporary world.

Enduring alliances between nation-states with each other were impossible in the "balance of power" system. Extensive commitments would have impeded flexibility of alliance, and supranational, or even permanent intergovernmental arrangements, were unknown. For one state to enter into such relations with another would have suggested a form of domination of one by the other, or a federal state, and would have been thought to jeopardize the independence of the states involved.

In Europe, in particular, in the present bipolar period, states have conferred quite extensive formal decision-making powers on supranational authorities. By virtue of the Coal and Steel treaty, the Atomic Energy treaty, and the Common Market treaty, the European Community of "the Six" (France, Germany, Italy, Belgium, Netherlands, and Luxembourg) share common judicial, executive, and legislative institutions with formal power to make decisions, within limited areas, that are binding upon the states involved and upon their citizens. The functions so delegated, designed to promote economic integration, are quite far reaching and constitute a long step towards European political integration, or a United States of Europe. For example, any private person or business enterprise, member state, or the Community Commission may get a final determination from the European Court of Justice as to the interpretation of any of the three treaties, or as to the lawfulness of Community or state action under the treaties. With regard to all such questions, states have given up their rights of independent action.

No one seriously suggests that the Six, having delegated extensive economic powers to the Community, have ceased thereby to be states under international law and that the Community has itself become a state. Yet in fact the Six are becoming heavily federalized, and in some respects—for example, tariff negotiations under GATT—the Community negotiates with other states as an entity binding its members. Whether or not it is a state, the Community clearly is a "subject" of international law.

Perhaps, indeed, the Community is something more than a state, for, in one sense at least, it could be said that the Community institutions are directly administering a form of international law. Certainly they are dealing with the relationships of states and interpreting treaty provisions—traditional subject matter of international law. But they also directly regulate individuals and private enterprise, and orthodoxy claims this to be a function of states, because individuals are "objects" not "subjects" of international law. Officials within the Community fudge this question by saying that Community institutions formulate, administer and enforce "Community Law." Undoubtedly this is true, and it brings to mind the history of American federalism. Before 1865 (and the 14th Amendment) a good many Constitutional decisions resolving disputes between American States were decided by the Supreme Court on the basis of the Law of Nations, and even today, with regard to matters such as water rights on the Colorado River, the Court employs international law precedent to decide the relative rights of the fifty States. Since the precedent invoked is international, and may be used by other states to support their positions, it might be called "international law." But because it is invoked and administered by a national court it might be called, in a sense, merely "national law." So, too, are decisions by Community institutions appropriately called "Community Law."

A considerable part of France's (for example) control over her international relations has been delegated to the Community, for the Community may speak finally and authoritatively for France internationally on a variety of economic matters: customs duties, tariffs, exchange controls, and so forth. Does France still have the requisite "capacity to enter relations with other states"? Does she remain "independent" and "sovereign"—orthodox tests of statehood for purposes of international law? The answer is clearly yes, because today no one will question that independence. Yet there is high authority which would seem to lean the other way. In 1931 the Permanent Court was asked whether the proposed Austro-German Customs Union was in violation of the provisions of the Peace Treaty of 1919 whereby Austria agreed not to alienate her "independence" without the consent of the League of Nations Council. By a vote of 8-7 the Court held that the Customs Union (a far less extensive union than the Community of today) was incompatible with Austrian inde-

THE "STATE" SYSTEM: ORTHODOXY AND CHANGE

pendence. Even the dissenters conceded that independence would be lost if a state deprived itself of its organic powers, if "it lost the right to exercise its own judgment in coming to the decisions which the government of its territory entails," or if it alienated any of its sovereign powers "to another State or group of States." Apart from the point of Treaty interpretation, and the not unreasonable fear of too close a link between Germany and Austria, the inference from the Court's reasoning, and even that of the dissenters, is that membership in an institution such as the Community would be inconsistent with being a state. Times have changed.

The point, of course, is that theory and doctrine adjust to contemporary political conditions. The Community is not an anomaly; it merely represents the most extensive intrabloc arrangements yet implemented. In more narrowly defined functional areas, there are similar phenomena, some of which even transcend the two blocs. The United Nations itself, through the Security Council, can make decisions, and the Charter provides that "Members of the United Nations agree to accept and carry out the decisions of the Security Council in accordance with the present Charter." The area in which the Council may act is very limited; there exists the veto, and, in addition, there is the possibility of contending that the decision taken was not "in accordance with" the Charter. But, nonetheless, the growth of supranational decision making illustrates the general trend. So, too, decisions of the International Monetary Fund within the scope of the Breton Woods Treaty are binding on Members; and similar delegations of limited functional competence have been made to a number of other agencies: NATO, WHO, ILO, and others. In most instances, participating states have reserved a power of final formal decision to themselves, accepting or rejecting the "recommendations" of the international organization. But such recommendations are usually effective in fact if not in formal terms.

All these developments strain orthodox theory and doctrine. It would be surprising if they did not. The rule makers of the nineteenth century simply did not have to contemplate regularized intergovernmental and supranational arrangements. Either such arrangements are part of a contemporary international law (they cannot be national law), or we are badly in need of new labels: United Nations Law, Community Law, NATO Law, and so forth.

Further problems are raised if we consider comparable developments behind the Iron Curtain. The West has approached its interdependence in the loose bipolar political system through formal treaty arrangements creating functional areas of joint administration with degrees of supranationalism. The Communist bloc has adapted the Party as its primary tool of integration. Thus Communist states remain formally independent of Moscow while in fact subject to comprehensive and rigorous control. Today ByeloRussia and the Ukraine —to take the most extreme examples—are regarded as states for the purpose of membership in the United Nations. Formally they meet the classical definition, perhaps better than the European Six. In fact, however, they are no more independent than Texas or California, which, because formally forbidden by the American Constitution to enter into foreign relations, cannot qualify as states on the international plane.

We need not jettison orthodox doctrine in its entirety, for it still has operational scope and meaning. In the loose bipolar system the independent sovereign state remains important, though less independent and sovereign, but it is no longer the exclusive actor or center of the political system. Doctrine must be adjusted to these changes as they take place.

RIGHTS AND DUTIES OF STATES

The Treaty of Montevideo, mentioned in the previous section, proceeded, after defining state, to express the rights and duties of states. If we define international law as the rules governing state relations, it seems to make sense to proceed to a statement of what, in general, these rules are. The International Law Commission, as one of its first assignments from the General Assembly, undertook a similar task. So, too, a section on this subject is customary in treatises.

The most important rights are usually stated to be those of independence, equality, territorial jurisdiction or sovereignty, and self-preservation or self-defense. The most important duties are usually stated to be the renunciation of war, the carrying out of treaty obligations, and refraining from interfering in the internal affairs of other states. Obviously, these are principles of considerable generality.

Chapter 2 discusses the relationship of independent, equal, sovereign states to the nineteenth-century "balance of power" international political system, and there is no need to review those observations here at any length. The conditions asserted by the great nations for themselves were extended by common consent—sometimes formalized, as with the unilateral Monroe Doctrine or the multilateral creation of Switzerland and other European countries as parts of a general political settlement—to others. Although each great nation was interested in extending its own hegemony it had a greater interest in preventing others from doing likewise, and was reluctant to create an undesirable political precedent. Each great nation, to preserve its own political position, wished to preserve the status quo, particularly in Europe, against the designs of other nations, even at the cost of doing so for itself. No state was willing to give up voluntarily any area it controlled, but it was quite willing to tolerate any number of other states that could be relied upon to remain responsibly independent and that could maintain systems of local law administration adequate to the purposes of an expanding industrial society in Europe.

There was, then, an international political system in which major nations asserted certain "rights" that could be maintained effectively by the society of major nations. No nation was likely to attempt to acquire a large portion of the territory of a major nation during the "balance of power" period, partly because the attacked nation would fight back effectively and partly because maintenance of major nations was an important interest of the society of major nations—so important that action by other nations to sustain the viability of major nations could be expected, and so important that the independence of major nations was imbedded in one way or another in the norms of the system. With respect to minor nations in Europe, the great nations had a joint interest in protecting any of their number from indiscriminate plunder by any other great nation, even though a particular nation might have an immediate interest to the contrary. But the areas of Asia, the Middle East, and Africa had to be assigned an inferior status in the international system for a number of reasons. Marxist histories have already stressed the imperialistic aspect. Certainly economic gain was one element. The increase of national capabilities—an important element of the "balance of power" system—was another. Because such areas were not capable of participating responsibly in international politics and because they lacked modern political systems, they constituted a source of danger and difficulty. Placing them under protectorate was one method of preventing anyone else from conquering them. And regularization of their regimes eliminated—at least for a time—potential sources of instability in international politics.

Moreover the world of the great European nations depended upon industralization, and industrialization, in turn, depended upon regular access to raw materials and the means for trade. Many of the states, although technically not new, were not encompassed within the international community and did not have the form of political structure that would facilitate and protect the outward flow of raw materials or give adequate protection to foreign businessmen and industrialists carrying on trade and commerce. The municipal systems of law were inadequate by European standards. The finances were precarious. Political conditions, especially as economic change led to political change, were tumultuous. And, in general, these states were festering sores that boded ill for the peace and stability of the international society.

It is an interesting aside to note that Vittoria justified Spanish conquests in the new world on the ground that the Indians refused to trade. Suspicious as this argument was from the point of view of the moral thesis Vittoria defended, it was related to the realistic consideration that social institutions are the foundations of legal systems. The world of the "balance of power" period was the world of the inception and development of modern industry. It was the world of technological advance, of miracles in communications and transportation, and it was a world with an insatiable appetite for growth and development, an appetite that inevitably extended to those areas of the world which were not able to join as equals. That this development eventually produced the present contraction of European control by creating the conditions for nationhood and the aspiration for nationhood among the controlled is irrelevant to the functioning of the international legal system during the "balance of power" period.

From the facts of the political structure flowed the general legal standards states had to observe to function as full members of the community of nations. The state needed more than population, territory, and local government. It had to be able to assert its independence from control by other states in a way that would be effective with regard to any existing hegemony—to win its freedom—and to demonstrate its flexibility of alignment with regard to other nations. Once independence was achieved, it could usually rely on the guaranties inherent in the political system to prevent reconquest. Furthermore, it had to be capable of entering into commercial relationships and of carrying on the kind of trade necessary to the expanding European capitalistic system. Governments had to be sympathetic to this development and capable of maintaining political and financial stability under conditions of rapid economic and social change. When these capabilities were lacking, dependency or outright colonialism was usually the consequence. Dependency meant specifically that some other state(s) would intervene to assure that the society of nations (i.e., Europe) would have access to the resources of the area. Some measure of internal autonomy was left to the latter, however. Under conditions of colonialism, on the other hand, even internal autonomy was largely lacking, and the area was administered by a local agent of the controlling state.

Thus, areas that lacked any real possibilities of becoming full members in the international society of states were subjected to specific forms of controls governing both internal and external activities. These controls ranged from the exercise of virtually complete powers of government, in the case of colonies; through "dependent states" in which foreign affairs, finance, and some police powers were exercised; to the intermittent exercise of pressure from outside to force financial reform as in the case of Egypt during the latter part of the nineteenth century, and the Latin American countries during the period of "dollar diplomacy." Although the Latin American countries resented this interference, and tried to invent legal doctrines to prevent it, the surest mode of prevention was to achieve that degree of financial stability that secured the safety of foreign investments.

All these measures, from the most permanent and far-reaching to the most intermittent and slight, involved the direct and formally acknowledged administration by one state of governmental powers within the territory of another nation or area. In all cases the measures were addressed to states or areas which were not competent to play a full role in the international system. There were other cases, as we have seen, of states which played minor roles. Although not formally distinguished or classified, the minor state was generally given only a peripheral role, as in the drafting of the treaties at the Congress of Vienna ending the state of war. It was subjected to territorial change, and even to amalgamation with other states under certain conditions. Outside of Europe the inviolability of the minor state was only a conditional norm of the "balance of power" system, subordinate to norms maintaining the stability of the major state system—on which, after all, every nation's security depended.

There was a desire to spread European standards in the nineteenth century, and international law formally became the law of "civilized nations." But intervention, almost a political impossibility in Europe except under collective European sanction, was generally confined elsewhere to what was necessary to serve the cause of stability, commerce, and trade. In large areas of Africa, primitive conditions required colonial government; in other cases, a lesser control sufficed. For example, in some countries, systems of consular courts to deal with disputes among Europeans or between Europeans and natives were adopted without otherwise interfering in domestic standards of justice. When England intervened in Egypt—the breakup of the Turkish Empire was a constant source of difficulty—England was at pains to limit its objectives. After all, in the absence of collective institutions, someone had to intervene to protect the common interest of the major nations, and intervention was coupled with assurances of good intent. England claimed no sovereignty over Egypt, but the Suez Canal was important to all, and vital to England. The Treaty of 1888, in the best liberal tradition, opened the canal to ships of all nations, in peace and in war, without discrimination.

Doctrine regarding "hostile measures short of war" was resurrected and expanded to justify intervention vindicating treaty, property, or contract rights. Although force in appropriate measure was used, in those areas in which state systems existed, it was often declared by the user not to be against the "territorial integrity," or independence, of the adversary—a formulation calculated to reassure the great nations that conquest was not intended, even if it provided small comfort to the state attacked. Once the particular dispute was settled, the *status quo ante* would be reinstated. Objections were almost wholly those raised by debtor states, who claimed their sovereignty was being infringed upon—as, indeed, it was. But, to the major nations, preserving the sanctity of contract and the mechanisms of the international economy were far more important objectives than calming the sensibilities of, for instance, Latin American governments.

The nineteenth-century legal system classified certain political entities as states primarily to preserve the "balance" among major nations. Minor states, despite formal equality, did not play an important policy-making role in formulating relevant standards. Equality had little to do with democratic ideas of self-determination, or "home rule," and had nothing whatsoever to do with any "inherent rights" of states. A sense of national identification might and usually did exist wherever local elites were permitted to cultivate it. Major nations did not wish to encourage the colonial revolt to which nationalism led, but, at the same time, nationalism was desirable in minor states for it tended to preserve them from conquest by others.

Unfortunately it was not always possible to carve viable entities along national cultural lines, and the existence of minority national groups was often, as in Eastern Europe,[2] a source of potential subversion and instability.

In the present bipolar political system, talk about states' rights is likely to increase in volume and intensity, as are the extremes (such as Suez) in which it is invoked, although decreasing in real importance. In the loose bipolar system, independence born of states' rights is inconsistent with the objectives of the Soviet Union and of the United States who are trying to solidify and expand their blocs. Talk of states' rights continues to perform its traditional function only insofar as it helps to insulate uncommitted areas from involuntary commitment to the opposing bloc, or insofar as it serves the subsidiary purpose of creating problems within the other bloc by playing upon national sentiments of satellite populations.

The past few years have seen the creation of a very large number of new states in Afro-Asia as an incident of declining European power. Both Russia and the United States have supported the claims of former dependent nations for independent status and admission as formal equals to arenas of political interaction. Afro-Asian leaders, carried away with their new nationalism and access to world politics, have made quite extravagant claims about states' rights and sovereignty. In view of their past experience—particularly as it is colored by a Marxist vocabulary and claims of "exploitation"—talk of sovereignty and sensitivity to interference by outsiders generally, and former colonial nations particularly, is understandable. They tend to see themselves as victims of "power politics" rather than as victims of the operation of an impartial market mechanism, and American public opinion, long opposed to colonialism, seems sympathetic to this view. The leaders of these new nations picture economic development as a right and often appear to demand economic subsidy as a measure of social justice and repentance for past sins. Despite their talk about independence these Afro-Asian leaders are acutely aware of their continued dependence upon the developed countries of either East or West; they resent this dependence, but cannot avoid it. Their attitude is analogous to that of the small farmer who needs the bank to finance his crops and the farm machinery company to sell him equipment, but who resents interest

[2] Christian minorities in the Ottoman Empire were major sources of trouble in the nineteenth century. Minority problems in the Balkans produced the two Balkan Wars and finally touched off the First World War.

rates, prices, and refusal to extend credit. They behave politically in the same way; from radicalism and general cussedness to a demand for subsidy effective through political voting blocs. Their revolutionary attitudes, however, and their tendencies to intervene in each other's affairs, may in the end help to undermine the norms necessary for their own development as modern nations.

There are many obvious reasons why both the United States and Russia cannot absorb or reduce to a formally dependent status either bloc partners or uncommitted nations. Both the political organization of the United States, and the national values of its population prevent this course from becoming American policy. The Soviet Union is not deterred by either of these considerations and has at its disposal a political organization that would make incorporation of bloc partners feasible. However, the resistance of the satellite populations (already a headache) would likely increase, and, more importantly, uncommitted nations would be unnecessarily alarmed. Therefore it is unlikely that states will disappear in this way, and their formal status is thus likely to be maintained. As dividends, there are the voting advantages based on equality which accrue in the United Nations and other multilateral forums.

At the same time, leading bloc nations are interested in strengthening ties of bloc committment wherever possible. The United States has had some success in the creation and encouragement of supranational organizations. This method does not require that formal independent statehood be abandoned any more than control through the Communist Party required nations of Eastern Europe to give up formal sovereignty. To date supranational institutions, sponsored by United States policy, have been highly successful in Europe, less successful in Latin America and the Far East, and wholly unsuccessful in the Middle East. In part, American failure in the Middle East has been related to comparable success in Europe. NATO partners have been a drag on American policies in the Middle East and, to a lesser extent, in Asia. Perhaps, too, the transcending importance of security problems in the eyes of domestic American leaders, success with NATO, and the consequent military orientation of much of United States foreign policy, has led to the use of inapposite precedent.

The plethora of small states, and the difficulty of overcoming the principle of formal voting equality in the United Nations and elsewhere, will doubtless plague international society with representational problems for some time. Nonetheless states will continue to be treated as the formal policy-making entities, and reliance will be principally upon the informal delegation of responsibilities to supranational agencies as a substitute for, or preliminary to, the formal delegation of limited decision-making powers. Particularly where one can create a core of experts as a permanent staff, and create viable notions of role even in national-oriented officials, recommendations with no formal binding effect can be binding in fact and can pave the way for formal delegation of authority. But even such formal delegation of authority is not likely to affect the status of participants as states.

Doctrine about rights of territorial integrity, independence, noninterference in internal affairs, and other similar matters, was too general, and therefore never very helpful to the solution of particular problems. When identified with democratic revolutions and internal rights of self-determination, it got turned upside down. Independence, at most, meant independence from the formal claims of another state (which might have nothing to do with political participation in affairs for most of the population). Today we accept the committed hard core of the two blocs as "independent" even when their real independence is as illusory as that, for example, of ByeloRussia. How far a state may delegate its powers formally to a supranational institution, or be controlled by a transnational political party, without losing its status as a state is uncertain and is probably unimportant. The pressure to maintain votes in the UN and preserve local sensitivities and pride will no doubt prevail in the immediate future (the example of the United Arab Republic to the contrary notwithstanding), and blocs will continue to support and maintain the fiction of state sovereignty.

Similarly, freedom from interference in one's internal affairs has never meant more than freedom from dictatorial interference, backed by coercive measures aimed at impairing political independence. In the past, coercive intervention under a claim of right has been tolerated for limited purposes; reprisal, collection of debts, and protection of nationals and their property are examples. Today the formal norms vis-a-vis violence are expressed in the UN Charter (more of this later), but the important point may be that action by supranational authorities, or by states acting under such auspices, may, under some circumstances, be regarded as legitimate. More importantly, much law has always been related to efforts toward maintaining stability and toward avoiding major conflagration, and should be analyzed from this viewpoint.

Certainly non-intervention is not a general characteristic of the loose bipolar system—and subtler means of influence are repeatedly resorted to by nearly all states—although uncommitted states may be able to resist intervention by playing one bloc against the other. As a corollary, however, the blocs, in some circumstances, may not be able to protect some uncommitted states from revolutionary intervention or interference by other uncommitted states. Nasser, Castro, and others are presently sponsoring and supporting revolutionary movements directed against existing governments. Yugoslavia is smuggling arms to revolutionaries in the Cameroons. And it is possible that the Ghanaian and Guinean forces operating under UN auspices in the Congo may be used to promote the policies of their governments in favor of Mr. Lumumba.

The extent to which committed states will be permitted to change political orientation is doubtful. Hungary is a case in point, and we may be dubious whether, faced with a Communist revolution in France or Italy, the United States (probably acting *qua* NATO) would not react in the same way. Communist victory in a free election in France or Italy, or a shift in Poland's international position, would pose more difficult problems; moderation, however, may be met with moderation, if the break with past political orientation is not too decisive.

Legal norms of the past will not be abruptly abandoned, for they have some political functions in calming fears or legitimizing activities that would probably be taken in any event, but that might have more alarming interpretations if not related at least formally to the framework of law and expectations. Russia referred to the Hungarian "government's" request for assistance during the 1956 revolt, and the United States relied on President Chamoun's request, with much more substance factually, in Lebanon in 1958. But the point is that the United States withdrew quickly from Lebanon and the Russians stayed in Hungary. Both Lebanon and Hungary remained formally independent states. The relevant difference lay in the committed status of Hungary, and its relation to the Soviet security system, as against the uncommitted status of Lebanon and the consequent effect on other uncommitted countries of a refusal to withdraw. For similar reasons, the Baghdad Pact and the so-called Eisenhower Doctrine have been as great failures as the Truman Doctrine and NATO were successes.

Today a world conflagration can be avoided only by maintaining an inherently unstable bipolarity, and neither the United States nor the Soviet Union is likely to tolerate an abrupt change affecting its military posture. Members of NATO probably cannot go Communist— at least not by means of violence or coup, and possibly not even by popular vote—without provoking the United States to some sort of action. In all such cases, forcible intervention, if necessary, can be anticipated and might be tolerated whether or not some legal pretext for the action could be found. As we consider in turn less strategically significant committed states, uncommitted states of strategic significance, and uncommitted states of little strategic significance, we believe that forcible intervention by the United States or the Soviet Union becomes progressively less likely. Should intervention occur, it is more likely to be in strict factual and legal compliance with formal prerequisites (as in Lebanon) under proclaimed limited objectives, which, in traditional fashion, are designed to reassure sceptics that the *status quo ante* will not be changed. One feature of a non-hierarchical bloc like NATO is that a nation may be propelled to an uncommitted status before an overt Communist move is attempted. Thus by slurring and ambiguity, the United States may have less opportunity to use force than the Soviet Union, even though it may have greater need. This indeed might give the United States more interest in attempting to sustain the principle of the non-use of force than the U.S.S.R.

This appraisal does not belittle as worthless the values implied in local autonomy over internal affairs—values long cherished by the United States with its federal system. Western democracy is dedicated to the proposition that government should remain close to the people, that power should be widely shared, that policy should be prescribed and administered at the lowest feasible level that still permits the realization of other values, and that officials should remain responsive to the will of the governed. But these objectives are not necessarily realized by broad guarantees of states' rights unaccompanied by substantial qualification. And it is clear from history that restraints inherent in local autonomy over matters in which real interdependence exists—the tyranny of the minority—can result in loss of faith and confidence in the capacity of the democratic process to accomplish an adequate distribution of values other than power. The history of the Communist Party, with its relative success in backward areas, is the history of an educated and dedicated elite transmuting itself into a militant political tyranny in order to achieve forced industrial development.

States' rights is an old and unresolved internal problem for Americans. John Calhoun's clumsy union of sovereign States was beset with centrifugal forces that made it unable to deal with the intricate problems of an interdependent society, or cope with the threat of foreign intervention. But it did not require eliminating all sovereign powers of the States in order to resolve the apparent dilemma. Americans have developed and continue to develop at home (as they now seek to develop abroad) institutions of law-government capable of dealing effectively with particulars without need to resort to hopeless generalities, and thus achieve in a variety of ways a system of adequately consonant decision making by different officials of different "sovereignties."

It is difficult for many to imagine a viable political system without provision for final determinations of the limits of local autonomy. As Justice Story once said when rejecting an assertion of absolute States' rights against resolution by the Supreme Court: "From the very nature of things, the absolute right of decision in the last resort, must rest somewhere." In domestic American affairs it rests formally with the Supreme Court, backed by national power, but all save a few questions are resolved through political institutions. In international affairs, at least until recently, it has rested, with the same qualifications, in the major nations which could invoke force where necessary.

Finally, the loose bipolar system is not one in which individual states can often play the role of the "balancer" of the balance of power" system. New universal organizations like the United Nations and the International Court fill important mediatory roles which preserve the flexibility necessary even to the loose bipolar system. These universal organizations have become subjects of international law, as have other supranational organizations that maintain important relationships within blocs. Thus many different kinds of international persons with rights and obligations supported by the international community, or significant elements of it, are beginning to play important roles in the international system. This is also true to some extent of private associations and finally affects the role of the individual.

The Individual and International Law

In orthodox theory, individuals and private associations, unlike states and (today) international organizations assimilated for certain purposes to states, are mere objects rather than subjects of international law. In recent years, however, this conclusion has been questioned by a number of distinguished writers who suggest that the individual is, or ought to be, regarded as a subject.

Differences are largely jurisprudential, the issue being whether or not the individual derives rights and duties directly from international law or only mediately through the incorporation of international law-rules into national laws and practices. If a treaty provides that foreign nationals are entitled to certain rights in the territory of the signatory states, do persons derive these rights directly from the treaty or simply from national legislation that carries out treaty provisions? Are rules derived from treaties and customary law simply formal obligations of states to insure that they are enforced locally, or do they of their own force bestow rights and duties on the private beneficiaries? And does it make any difference which answer is given?

In general, those who say the individual derives his rights directly from international law are, to a degree, adopting a natural-law approach. Positivists on the other hand, see rights as the creation of the sovereign who enforces them, and refuse to acknowledge the existence of rights not found in the provisions of state law. The former support their view by expressly invoking natural-law theory and references to "inalienable rights"; by pointing to precedent and practice under the earlier Law of Nations approach; by noting that the bulk of treaties in fact deal with individual rights of one kind or another directly and not directly with state relations; by pointing to the fact that certain crimes (piracy is the principal example) are said to be crimes against the Law of Nations, and this older precedent is coupled with statements at Nuernburg that war criminals were punishable for violating international law against aggressive war; and, finally, the numerous instances of special tribunals, such as claims commissions, where the individual has directly pleaded claims based on violations of international guaranties is cited to show that the rights are directly those of the individual although he is usually without an equally direct remedy.

Orthodox positivism acknowledges all these facts but interprets them differently. It is said that precedent based on Law of Nations practices is outmoded and ignores the development over three centuries of existing theory based on the existence of sovereign states; the fact that treaties speak of individual rights only makes individuals objects, but the legal obligation of the treaty runs only to the other state or states involved; in most states treaty provisions do not become operative until local legislation, or executive decree, makes them effective, and even where they do (for example, in the United States, if the treaty is self-executing, or in Germany) they become effective by virtue of a local rule or practice that makes them effective and not because of international custom or obligation; there are innumerable statements to the effect that national courts apply only national law, even where a rule of customary international law, or a treaty provision, is the doctrinal guide to decision, and in most countries subsequent national legislation will be used by courts to decide cases even if contrary to treaty obligations; Nuernburg is regarded as a special case, and any remarks inconsistent with the Positivist approach are usually stigmatized as mere "dictum;" and, finally, it is pointed out that only as exceptions can individuals press claims based on international law in international tribunals, and when they do, this right (like the rules themselves) is one derived from state agreement to that effect. In sum, positivists see the rule as related to the decision maker who is administering it (national officials administer only national law), and law as derived from government. The individual can, therefore, be a subject only where states agree that he can invoke international law directly in international tribunals.

Except for differences arising from opposing conceptions and definitions of law, there is no disagreement as to the actual process. Those who say individuals derive rights and duties directly from international law do not dispute the fact that there are no forums, except those created by the several states, where these rights can be vindicated. Nor would they deny that the great majority of national decision makers do not presently accept their view as correct, though they would insist that certain past practices can be explained adequately only by admitting their premise. At the same time orthodox positivism does not dispute the obligation of states to enact rules consonant with international law and to enforce customary and treaty provisions within the territory of each state. They concede that individuals do raise international law doctrine directly in many national courts, but insist this is done because these rules are part of the national law created by the sovereign in fulfillment of his international obligations. Since they also acknowledge that individuals may derive rights and duties directly from international law if states so prescribe and create international or supranational agencies to administer them, practical consequences of theoretical differences would seem to be minimal.

The reasons underlying orthodox theory have already been discussed. Except where supranational institutions can be created, the reasons remain valid today. The orthodox approach reflects political aspects of the international law process both externally and internally. The impact of general acceptance of a theory that, like the older Law of Nations, held that individuals derived rights and duties directly from treaties and customary law, would principally be to modify the capacity of states to innovate and bargain. It might also tend to increase somewhat the role of national judiciaries at the expense of political departments of the government, because a right directly vested in an individual by international law could not, with theoretical consistency, be divested by subsequent national legislation. Although its exponents undoubtedly see as a virtue any idea that would cut down the scope of political maneuver, what is needed today for this purpose is not theory but supranational institutions that, within the areas of their competence, can improve upon the larger decision-making process. The job today is far too big to be accomplished by a process of gradual adjustment by judicial decision makers.

Yet orthodox theory is misleading in that it appears to understate the role of individuals and private associations in the international process by reducing them to objects. The growth of supranational institutions does in fact mean the existence of a number of arenas in which private persons may press their causes. Private groups are affiliated with UNESCO, and may directly urge for international consideration their views, though these will have to be implemented by government agreements. Specialized agencies of the United Nations also provide access to private groups; the most extensive participation is guaranteed by the International Labor Organization, where unions participate directly with governmental representatives in formulating agreements for national approval. In the European Community, individuals have access directly to the Court of Justice to challenge acts of the Community Commission and member states alike when incompatible with the constitutive treaties. All this suggests a political structure radically different from that implicit in the idea that states are the exclusive subjects of international law.

Other European developments point equally strongly in the same direction. In 1950, members of the Council of Europe signed a Convention for the Protection of Human Rights and Fundamental Freedoms, and created a European Commission on Human Rights with power to hear complaints of Member States, and of individuals within such states, where the state agreed in advance to such jurisdiction. Several have done so. The Commission may investigate facts and mediate or conciliate differences. If settlement fails, the Commission is bound to express its opinion as to whether or not a state has failed in its obligations under the treaty. By a two-thirds majority, the Council of Ministers may then make a binding decision. The Convention also provides for a European Court of Human Rights, finally established in 1959. Cases may be brought by any state that has itself accepted the Court's jurisdiction, and may also be brought by the Commission on behalf of meritorious individual claims that the Commission has investigated.

Undoubtedly these trends will continue, and, to the extent that they do, it will be hard to maintain that the individual is not a subject. New functional agencies on supranational lines will play increasingly important roles in building up new rules and new standards for regulating transnational events and putting them beyond unilateral state decision. As these institutions grow and amalgamate their functions, as in Europe, adjudicative organs will become more important in settling disputes. In all likelihood individuals will have direct access to such tribunals, as they increasingly have access to other agencies. Special areas of law-government institutions will thus come into being, and, within these areas, even the orthodox theorists will concede the role of the individual as a subject of the specialized legal system. But there will remain areas where, as before, agreements and custom operate without the interposition of supranational decision makers.

We are already running into problems of nomenclature where our choice must be between international law traditionally conceived and national law. Possibly, in these circumstances, international law will be reserved for areas where the system is more traditional in its concern for state relations. Already we have noted the existence of "Community Law" in Europe, and references in books to "United Nations Law." There is, too, a growing body of law regulating international administrative personnel, and this is becoming known as "international administrative law." If this reclassification continues the orthodox view can safely be preserved, for international law will represent nothing more than the rules governing the relations of states and we will have other categories of law to describe other governmental schemes.

Whether we begin to reclassify or not, it is clear that individuals are playing important roles in international political processes, and that they are increasingly being recognized as competent to press their contentions in special tribunals, or before intergovernmental boards. Decisions governing transnational events in the future will have to take account of these developments in one way or another.

5

RECOGNITION

THE term "recognition" means a formal acknowledgment or declaration by the government of an existing state that it intends to attach certain customary legal consequences to an existing set of facts which, in its view, justify it (and other states) in doing so. The usual examples are recognition of a new state or a new government of an existing state; governments also "recognize" neutral status, the existence of a state of war, belligerent rights for insurgent groups, the legality of a blockade, and so forth. Normally there is a claimant for the particular status urged, and difficulties arise because that claim is opposed by others. For this reason the act of recognition takes on some of the aspects associated with adjudication between conflicting claims and doctrinal justifications are urged in support of the decision made.

Two theories of recognition are currently urged, each having its scholarly adherents. The first, which numbers Lauterpacht and Kelsen among its supporters, takes the view that recognition is "constitutive;" that is, it is the act of recognition that endows a claimant with statehood or a government with capacity in international relations. Lauterpacht modifies orthodox constitutive theory by positing a legal duty to recognize a state or government fulfilling prescribed factual prerequisites. In his view, recognition is not (or, at least should not be) a "political" act.

The other theory is the "declaratory" or "evidentiary" theory, which says that statehood or governmental authority exist quite independent of recognition by other states since they depend merely on facts. Recognition is simply the formal acknowledgment of the preexisting factual condition. As Lauterpacht has observed, declaratory theory is a reaction to the idea that recognition is *both* constitutive and political, and seeks to bypass the latter by denying that the former is true.

The difference between the theories is largely that they begin the same circle at opposite sides and then chase each other around. Controversy over whether a state acquires legal status by virtue of recognition or by virtue of certain facts resembles a 6-day bicycle race. A right cannot flow from facts save as prescribed by some legal system that declares those facts to be determinative and finds them to be true; conversely, all legal doctrine relates to specified fact situations. We have the same problem in domestic jurisprudence: Does a person have a specified right because certain facts are true, or because the judge says he has such a right? Do his rights stem from the judicial finding or did he have them all the time? Constitutive theory says that these rights derive from the judicial pronouncement, although (with Lauterpacht) the court itself may have been obligated to pronounce them upon finding the existence of certain facts, and the decision (like recognition) is retroactive to the date of the occurrence of the relevant events. Declaratory theory simply views the process of recognition as one of confirming pre-existing rights; the man had the rights all the time, although the court might have found that he did not, in which event he would never have had the rights at all.

There is somewhat more substance to the question as to whether standards of recognition are "legal" or "political," although this is an unfortunate way of stating the problem. Lauterpacht joins adherents of a declaratory theory in urging the desirability of determinative rather than discretionary standards. For quite obvious reasons this is a view put forward in the past by smaller states that feared intervention by the larger nations and that desired as much local autonomy as they could achieve. To be recognized as a state helped to consolidate independence; to have a government actually in control recognized as the legal spokesman gave a maximum of freedom from intervention in internal affairs.

There is little doubt that, in practice, major nations have exercised considerable discretion—in the traditional language, they have made political judgments—in recognizing states and governments. Yet normative standards have operated to restrain extremes. States have been motivated by the same considerations which influenced the concept of "state" and by the consonance of this concept with the common objectives of the major nations. Whether new states adhered to standards of the international community was a matter of concern to the major nations; so, too, was the stability and behavior of revolutionary governments. Older states were often unable to exercise as much control over revolutionary regimes as they desired, because intervention would have brought them into conflict with each other. The problems of the Ottoman Empire, and the French Revolution and Napoleonic behavior are examples. But where they could exercise influence without getting into disputes among themselves, states sought to do so.

Confusion about recognition doctrine stems in large measure from the fact that recognition itself—that is, the ceremony or formal acknowledgment of the status claimed—is collateral to more specific claims. Recognition of a state (or a government) is normally an acknowledgment by the recognizing state that it will *for all purposes* treat the recognized state (or government) as being entitled to the rights and privileges normally attached to that status under both international and domestic law. The new entity thus, at the moment of recognition, is endowed, insofar as the recognizing state is concerned, with a whole bundle of customary rights, the most important of which is that its independence is supported against adverse claimants. Non-recognition—a failure to acknowledge this status— does not carry converse inferences. States refusing formal recognition do not say that none of the rights ordinarily attached to the status of statehood or government will be accorded to the claimant. They say nothing, but may in practice accord some rights and refuse others.

It is by no means self-evident that a "lump" approach best serves the interests of the international community, or even that the same criteria are or should be invoked by all decision makers for all purposes. Nor does a more selective approach require a new classification of "unrecognized governments" or "unrecognized states" with consistent treatment within each group. Facts are likely to be variant. Indeed, one cannot examine past and present practice without being aware of these variances—usually summed up by saying that the decision is a political or discretionary one.

Claimants have further confused recognition policies by their anxiety over obtaining full and unqualified status. They are quick to insist that certain acts "imply" recognition, or that, given certain factual conditions, there is a duty to recognize. On the other hand, most established states have insisted there can be no recognition without intention to recognize, that there can be "acts short of recognition," and that recognition can be qualified in various ways. Efforts to distinguish legal consequences of *de jure* and *de facto* status are crude attempts to express some divisibility among the consequences that attach to the status granted.

Focusing attention on the ceremonial aspect of recognition is to confuse sign with substance. If we look directly to the particular facts and claims in context we can get a better picture of the problems and the extent to which doctrinal criteria limit discretion.

ADMISSION (RECOGNITION) OF NEW STATES

The number and identity of the formal participants in the international political process are by no means constant. Yet the creation of new states and the disappearance of old states are of obvious concern to existing participants. Doctrine about recognition of states is concerned with the problems and process of admitting new entities to the various arenas of formal interaction. In the nineteenth century, when there were no important multilateral organizations, this meant establishing diplomatic and consular relations with new entities, and this type of admission thus became associated with the ceremony of recognition. Often this was made evident by receiving an ambassador or granting an *exequatur* to a consular official.

Legal distinctions between states and governments have a basis in popular concept and social function. The concept of "state" was derived from the nation-state prototype, and such entities typically had a genuine social existence and durability. Not all entities recognized as states, however, were able to focus sufficiently intense sentiments of national loyalty to insure durability and avoid either foreign control or secession. Thus wide differences of fact within the same legal classification existed, although, despite such differences, classification as a state served a common purpose; that is, to insulate from foreign control and to serve as a focal point for continuing responsibility. The corporate analogy is illustrative, for the social observer would find far more differences than similarities between General Motors and the local department store, though both may be classified for legal purposes as corporations.

The state became the focus of legal obligations because typically it did have durability and could provide the continuity that a system of order requires. Internally and internationally, law-norms must be able to outlast the vicissitudes of changing personnel, and must, therefore, often rest on a theoretical and doctrinal framework that permits role substitution among governing national elites. The rules of international law must bind all—new governments and new states, recognized or unrecognized, so long as they claim the status—whatever the consent theory of international obligation may logically seem to require. For similar reasons, individuals and governments must be able to make agreements that bind their "heirs, successors and assigns." As long as crowned heads ruled with fixed rights of succession, a monarch could be bound in much the same way as individuals might be bound.

The concept "state" becomes more important when there is no family tie of governmental inheritance, yet the need for continuity persists. In point of fact, continuity became more important because expanding trade and commerce demanded security for long-term financial and commercial arrangements. Money cannot be borrowed or lent, trade cannot thrive, unless means of insuring obligations over a period of years can be devised. Thus the state, as a continuing entity, and the capacity of one government to bind its successors are, among other considerations, necessary rules for stable monetary and trade relations. The legal purpose of the distinction between states and governments is precisely to make the obligations of the former independent of, and insulated from, changes in the latter.

The importance of this doctrine to the international system is further demonstrated by rules of "state succession." A change in the formal participants—disappearance of an existing state through merger or conquest, or the creation of a new state through partition, amalgamation, or independence of a dependent area—raises questions about the continuity of existing treaties, indebtedness, property rights, and so forth. Obligations, in the manner of corporate reorganization, merger or disolution, must be satisfied and assets distributed. The law of state succession is aimed at these problems. If state Y merges into state X, whatever the method, X must assume Y's obligations.

In general, we have no conceptual difficulty distinguishing a change of state from a change of government. Recognition of governments usually involves deciding between two claimants making identical claims to represent the same territory and population. Whichever is recognized, it assumes the obligations of its predecessor.

Recognition of states poses different problems. Here there are usually two governmental claimants without identical claims. One says it represents a territory and population not previously recognized as a state; the other claimant, the government of an existing state, claims it still has sovereignty over the territory in question. A similar problem occurs when an existing state swallows up another in its entirety; can the conquering state succeed to the assets and speak for the people of the former entity? Ghost states abound in the international community at times. The United States, for example, has refused to recognize Soviet Russian conquest of the former Baltic states of Lithuania, Latvia, and Esthonia.

Two important reasons for resting international law doctrine upon the conception of a "state" as it developed in the "balance of power" period were: (1) insulating from others an area and a population able to maintain an internal order consonant with European trade objectives in a time of expanding laissez-faire economic ideas; and (2) providing a conceptual focus for the continuity of legal obligations through imposing general standards for all states, governmental responsibility for state obligations, and rules of state succession to cover the situation whenever a participant disappeared. The great nations had a common interest in preserving the doctrine for both reasons. The first reason, since it also involved shifts in the basis of existing relations in terms of national capabilities—control over resources—was primary. Any new territorial claim by a major nation was likely to be opposed simply because it affected the "balance" itself, particularly if it occurred within or on the periphery of Europe.

Changes involving a shift of territory and population involve relations with existing states as well as relations with those who claim independence. Recognition indicates acquiescence in a permanent change in the political status quo, support for the new status claimed, and abandonment of support for the claims of other states to the area and population. As long as an existing state maintains its right to govern people claiming independent status, it may react to recognition of this claim by other states as an intervention in its internal affairs in favor of insurgents. In the "balance of power" system, third states were hesitant to take such action independently, and they usually sought, through consultation with others, to get the assurance inherent in joint action. If joint action were assured, there was a common interest in the viability of the new entity and its capacity without outside assistance to maintain forcefully and successfully its independence from a prior claimant.

Several situations can be distinguished. If an area previously under the control of an existing state sought through revolution to assert its national independence, it would in general have to assert it effectively before other states were willing to support it, particu-

larly if the prior claimant were a major nation. The obvious reason
is that no state wished to be involved in hostilities from which it
could gain no important advantage in a "balance of power" system,
operating according to the principle of flexibility of alignment. If
the action were in Europe, states were particularly hesitant about
any action that was not neutral with regard to the struggle. The
danger of extensive violence sometimes led to a collective effort to
settle the dispute and thus to stabilize the situation.

The revolt of several Latin American colonies against Spain provides one set of actual instances. Spain was unable to control the
rebellions; maintaining effective internal order is a condition of
maintaining sovereignty. Despite its political and ideological sympathy with the rebels—whose action was ridding the continent of
European nations—the United States took care to withhold unilateral
recognition or formal support and sought rather, by direct representa-
tions and through counseling with other European nations, to induce
Spain itself to recognize the independence of these colonies. Under
the collective pressure of states with trading interests in Latin America, and the hopelessness of reconquest without the outside assistance
that was not forthcoming, Spain eventually agreed to perform this
act. The new states were, after all, able to fulfill the general requirements of the "balance of power" system, and it is interesting to
note that our Minister to Spain, whose good offices were used to
bring about settlement, was instructed (in the case of Mexican,
Argentinian, and Colombian independence) to make sure that Spain
retained no "peculiar advantages in trade, or some extraordinary
privileges for her citizens, to the prejudice of other friendly nations."

The consent of Spain to the independence of her colonies was desirable because abandonment of her claims removed any immediate
threat to their independence, and also because it reduced friction
among existing major nations, thus making easier the "friendly relations" so essential to flexibility of alignment, and to expanding trade.
It was not a doctrinal *sine qua non* of recognition, but typically
states in the "balance of power" system sought to press a former
claimant to abandon its claims, wherever possible, prior to their
recognition. If the former claimant were stubborn and insisted on
legal rights it could not forcibly maintain—if the fighting was over
and there was no prospect of successful counter-measures—other nations usually recognized the new entity without acquiescence by the
former claimant. At this point their interest in insulating the new
state from claims of other states as a consequence of a deal with the

former claimant, and of maintaining trade relations with the new state, were more important than deference to claims of a nation unable to maintain effective control in an area over which it had formerly had authority.

Nations of the "balance of power" system had a substantial interest in the creation of new states that had promise of becoming great nations able to redress and contribute to the "balance" itself. Thus amalgamation of smaller entities through voluntary annexation coupled with judicious use of violence could be regarded as a substantial contribution to the system itself and to the security of all. Unification movements in Germany and Italy were generally supported by the great nations and the territorial adjustments quickly recognized. These movements (except for a few border problems) did not involve efforts by major nations to dominate and extend their hegemony at the expense of others in the Napoleonic way, but by adding to the number of major nations contributed to the stability and security of all.

Other instances of the recognition of new states in the nineteenth century frequently stemmed from a general European settlement arranged by the great nations. The map of Europe was redrawn at the Congress of Vienna in 1815, and new states were created (simultaneously with the abandonment of old claims to the territory) by multilateral agreement. Not all such settlements were able to avoid compromises that affected the viability of the arrangement. Belgium, for example, declared its independence of the Netherlands a few years later, and was able to maintain it against Dutch claims. The major nations quickly intervened to bring about a settlement which neutralized Belgium among themselves, and jointly recognized its independence in 1832, though the Dutch did not formally relinquish their claims for some 7 years. The real danger was not, of course, the Dutch threat, but the possibility that older European claims would be renewed by major nations who would take this opportunity to annex Belgium.

The effort of Hungary to gain national independence from Austria presented different problems. Other states maintained a typically neutral attitude, except for Russia, which intervened to assist Austria. Although Hungary was very nearly successful in its struggle, it failed because it could gain no major outside support for its new status. The dangers of intervention by others on the side of the insurgents were obvious, and there was, in general, no interest in changing the status quo by weakening substantially a major nation that was, as always, an important potential ally in its existing form but less important in a truncated form.

The most difficult recognition problems of the nineteenth century were those which resulted from the break-up of the Ottoman Empire. The backward and "uncivilized" character of Turkey had kept it in effect outside the community of civilized nations. It was recognized as "sovereign" but not, until midcentury, as a qualified participant. European nations had no love for Turkey, but the danger of the plunder of Turkey by one or more of the European nations was a collective concern. Forms of collective intervention and settlement in favor of insurgents were necessary to prevent this contingency. Thus the Greek war for independence (which promised more in the way of government by civilized standards) was supported by the guaranteeing powers who quickly recognized Greece in 1827. Understandably Turkey did not renounce its claims for 5 years, but it could not hope to make them effective. The efforts by Russia, on the other hand, to annex parts of Turkey—exactly what other European nations feared—were opposed by Britain and France in the Crimea. Yet the inability of Turkey to maintain order, and particularly an order consonant with European standards and needs, resulted in a number of British and French protectorates over parts of the Empire. Again collective territorial arrangements were necessary, and the independent status of Roumania, Serbia, and Montenegro resulted from the Berlin Congress of 1878.

Thus in Europe itself the "balance of power" system led through Versailles to collective property settlements and the abandonment of various claims by major nations through joint agreement to insulate various areas from amalgamation with other great nations through the device of independent statehood. These arrangements were primarily in the interests of the great nations and followed national cultural lines only as a measure of insuring increased internal order and resistance to change imposed from the outside. Exchange of diplomats followed formal or informal agreement among many to accord the status demanded, and thus assured the claimant of the support of others in making the arrangement effective. There was no predisposition to encourage revolt against any state which could maintain internal order, but merely to insulate areas from the claims of others and thus to stabilize the system.

In the "balance of power" system there was no "duty" to recognize. There was an accepted and enforceable norm against intervention on the side of insurgents (save where the revolt was against "uncivilized" Turkey), and generally there was no desire to help another nation maintain internal order in any area where it could not do so unassisted. Recognition that was "premature" was characterized as intervention. By the same token, a state could not, after the new entity had the support of a number of states, safely intervene forcibly to support older claims of the previous sovereign. But this obligation to oppose forcible intervention had nothing to do with an obligation to support claims of the new state; it rested on great nation interests in maintaining the "balance of power" system.

Obviously revolutionary claimants sought recognition by major nations, for their support in the changed status of territorial claims was important to the preservation of their independence and to their entry into commercial relations. The general interest of the major nations, once collective support assured that the new entity could maintain internal order and resist forcible claims by its former sovereign, was also in the establishment of relations for mutual benefit. Normally the new state gave formal assurances that it would respect existing rights and abide by the general norms of the international community; whether it gave such assurances or not, it would be made to act consonantly in fact.

Although it is clear that the ceremonial exchange associated with recognition was related to existing claims, it should be equally clear that a refusal to recognize might not have any direct relationship. Refusal by a prior claimant indicated it wished to keep its claims alive, and thus was a potential source of danger. Refusal by others with no claims of their own was dangerous only if it meant that these others were likely to support the prior claimant, and this was rarely done in the "balance of power" system. European nations who refused to recognize Hungarian independence did not thereby imply they would acquiesce in any claims to the area other than those of Austria; nor did they mean to imply that they would intervene to help Austria. It was the pressure to renew commercial arrangements at the earliest opportunity at which stable order on some basis could be restored that usually led to the actual ceremony of recognition.

An entity claiming to be a state was held to the norms of the international community regarding state conduct whether or not it was recognized as such; for example, the exercise of belligerent rights and obligations. Withholding of recognition did not imply an outlawing of the new entity. Rather, apart from its function in protecting the prior claims of other states, the withholding of recognition put pressure on the new entity to observe the rules of the game and to accept obligations arising from succession. Non-recognition was a means of insuring that the new entity was brought within the existing system on terms consonant with the interests of the great nations.

In sum, legal doctrine and practice associated with recognition of states was primarily related to the security problem of the great nations in a "balance of power" system; that is, to maintaining a territorial status quo among the great nations in Europe through a system which insulated areas from conquest, which opened them on equal terms to all, and which collectively guaranteed their independence. Such legal doctrine could not work, as all acknowledged, in those parts of the world that were uncivilized and essential to commerce. But these parts of the world were not directly and intimately related to the European "balance of power" system until the industrial base of modern warfare became an important factor. The creation and admission of new states was fostered by common objectives of the great nations of the "balance of power" system, discounted in Afro-Asia by the common interest in maintaining European standards of economic morality and at least minimal standards of law administration.

Before the Wilsonian interlude, competing claims to territory were weighed primarily in terms of security. Secession would be forcibly resisted, and insurgents could rarely (save where it forwarded common economic objectives and the spread of European standards—for example, Greece) expect help from other states. When the inability of the former claimant to maintain control became clear, the new entity could be, and usually was, recognized as independent by others. Historical claims were formally abandoned, more quickly in the nineteenth century, when it prevented important trade in the area, than had been customary in the eighteenth century. New claims to the area could only have their basis in force, and this was not tolerated by the "balance of power" system. Where such force appeared a danger, collective settlement was the usual solution.

Before discussing the changes which result from political changes in the twentieth century, let us look at the problems associated with governmental recognition during the "balance of power" period.

RECOGNITION OF GOVERNMENTS

At the outset we should make clear that there is nothing in the legal doctrine distinguishing states from their governments, which implies that a change in the former necessarily has greater political consequences than a change in the latter, either internationally or internally. Because a change of state was accompanied by a territorial shift and a concomitant shift in popular allegiance from one sovereign to another, it always raised different and often more serious problems. Differences primarily arose from the fact that the security of third states is usually affected more by the rise, demise, consolidation, or dismemberment of states than by changes in governments. From this generality, however, one must not infer greater political consequences as a matter of course. Again the corporate analogy is useful. A change in the management of a corporation may have much more impact on stockholders and competitors alike than a merger of two corporate entities. Similarly, the French Revolution produced Napoleon and a messianic France; by comparison the vacillation of Norway from Denmark to Sweden to independence was a simple problem.

In the "balance of power" system, internal changes among ruling elites were of no concern to other states as long as the new elites accepted the norms of the international system. Meddling in internal affairs was incompatible with the basic political norm of flexibility of alignment; too much sympathy or concern with one domestic group in contrast with another affected the flexibility of alliances and might even have embarrassed equality of trade opportunities for the nationals of the "meddling" state. This does not mean that such shifts did not have some impact on international relations, for, internationally as well as domestically, personalities played a role. But all the formalities of international relations—the custom and mode of intergovernmental communications, the code of diplomatic conduct, the ceremonial rules and practices of diplomatic intercourse —were designed to protect against an undesired involvement in domestic politics. How a state treated its own nationals was of no concern to others; "human rights" that did not affect foreigners were matters for domestic law, simply because involvement would have been incompatible with the flexibility of alignment of the "balance of power" system.

Two situations are commonplace and have traditionally raised recognition problems; both are normally concomitants of violent unconstitutional changes of government, but not all unconstitutional changes raise these problems. The first is the problem of choosing between two claimants to governmental status—typically the prior government and a revolutionary group—each seeking, for domestic political reasons, the support that foreign recognition normally gives. The second situation, which often accompanies the first, at least for a period of time, is the attitude of a successful revolutionary government toward its international obligations, its willingness to abide by existing law norms and to assume the burdens of governmental succession. In the absence of another claimant with reasonable hopes of exercising effective internal authority we may ask whether or not this is really a question of accepting the revolutionary group *qua* government, or whether, more simply, it is a question of the terms on which future relations will be based. The decision concerning recognition really has nothing to do with the revolutionary change or the unconstitutionality of the process, save insofar as a genuine revolution, as opposed to a simple *coup,* has often been accompanied by excesses raising such questions.

These problems are most easily approached in terms of the consequences of recognition and non-recognition. Recognition of a new government normally results in increased prestige and stability at home; access to state funds on deposit in other states; access to private and governmental loans because of legal ability to pledge the state's credit; diplomatic and consular status for its agents in the recognizing entity; access to foreign courts and immunity from foreign process; establishment of normal trade relations; a capacity to request assistance from the recognizing government in the form of financial assistance, supplies, and even military aid; respect in other states for its laws and decrees; and benefits of existing treaty arrangements. The absence of formal recognition has the effect of suspending most or all of these rights insofar as the non-recognizing state controls them. They may be accorded to another claimant, or they may simply be suspended.

Thus refusal to recognize may be a convenient way for a state to bring to bear a number of pressures by the expedient of inaction until appropriate assurances are forthcoming. Where there is no competing claimant in any realistic sense, political inaction may (and often has) confused the local judiciary, but it avoids a formal suspension of rights, renunciation of agreements, and so forth—steps that have an air of decision and finality and that might invite retaliatory action by the unrecognized government. A simple refusal to recognize presents no problems of internal administration and responsibility, is unostentatious, and avoids commitment—all at the cost of some judicial frustration and irritation in the non-recognizing state. It has, too, a tactical advantage, for it is harder for the unrecognized government to retaliate; the recognition issue runs one way only, and inaction is always an elusive target. It does, however, make normal commercial intercourse more difficult for both states, and endangers rights of nationals within the foreign state if its unrecognized government actually takes retaliatory measures.

Revolutions toward the end of the eighteenth, and during the nineteenth centuries were often popular revolutions reflecting major social change. They were anti-monarchical (or, at least, designed to decrease the powers of the monarch) and they brought into question the social and constitutional system common to most of Europe. In the early "balance of power" period intervention to help another monarch put down revolution was not uncommon; there was a community of anti-democratic interest among ruling elites. But foreign assistance became increasingly difficult to give or receive in an age of nationalism. To meddle thus in foreign affairs was likely to cause division of opinion at home, and was, after all, dangerously close to violating all the political principles of the "balance of power" system itself. Failure to put down a foreign revolution made friendly relations with the new government considerably more difficult.

Nonetheless the lesson of the French Revolution was not quickly lost on the rest of Europe. The change of government affected a drastic change in the whole character of the French state. France became expansionistic, with virtually unlimited aims. In addition, the revolutionary appeal of France led to internal instability in the attacked states. This appeal impeded the operation of the "counterbalancing" mechanism and also interfered with flexibility of alignment. Revolutionary France was not a conforming member, and almost overthrew the system. The experience was enough to produce fears whenever a state was governed according to revolutionary principles. Dynastic legitimacy was, of course, threatened. Much more important was the potential threat to the working of the state system itself, at least until general changes in Europe occurred and states of revolutionary origin demonstrated their ability and willingness to conform internationally.

In this period there grew up a distinction, often without a difference, between recognition of a *de facto* government and recognition of a *de jure* government. It was intended to be an invidious distinction indicating distaste for revolution and expressing the opinion of the recognizing state that the government recognized was not the "lawful" government, that is, that it had not succeeded by constitutional means. It thus preserved the idea that governmental succession should be in monarchical terms and preserved such claims for an indefinite future. Should the revolutionary government fall, or should it fail to conform to the norms of the international community and require collective intervention, crowned heads envisaged a "restoration" of the *de jure* monarch. Apart from this function of preserving an historical claim, the distinction had no legal significance. Those who approved popular government, for example, the United States, avoided the distinction as a means of expressing their approval of popular revolutions.

The "balance of power" system required political alignments that were practical rather than ideological. In dealing with problems of government succession, states attempted to maintain standards that were independent of political preferences and conservative of the existing order. States had to continue to deal with an existing government until that government had lost effective control of its state machinery beyond reasonable hope of counter-revolution. Premature recognition of a new government, like premature recognition of a new state, looked like interference in domestic affairs that might be resented later on, should the recognizing state miscalculate concerning the winner. In addition, no one state wished to encourage similar conduct by other states on the opposite side of the dispute.

Recognition never was the all or nothing proposition that most theories suggest. As a revolutionary movement progressed from occasional acts of subversion to organized revolt and began carrying out governmental functions within an area, it began to be treated accordingly; that is, the rebel government began to acquire rights and duties consonant with the facts. A state of civil war was recognized, and the rebel government acquired "belligerent status," which meant that it was treated as the government for many routine purposes, although no new state was yet acknowledged to exist, nor did the rebel government succeed to rights of the old state. It was, however, not outside the international legal system—not an outlaw. Ships flying the flag of and under the control of the rebel government were not subject to seizure, and various of its public acts were respected as authoritative. The rebel government might have limited access to trade, commerce, and loans in other countries, but not on the same advantageous terms that a recognized government of a recognized state could obtain. Other states respected its territorial claims and the fact that it exercised within an area the functions of government, and held it responsible as a government for customary international obligations to foreigners within the area. However, this limited form of recognition did not give the rebel government access to formal arenas of state interaction. Until this century these arenas of interaction were not multilateral and were, therefore, under control of the several states individually. Diplomatic exchange, consular exchange, and local courts were the principal examples of such arenas.

The effort was to act "correctly." In point of fact, European sympathies were (at least among the governing elite) almost always on the side of the existing government. There was no desire for ideological reasons to encourage popular revolutions, and trade and commerce were unlikely to gain from local violence. But once a new group was clearly in control, political interests (especially if the nation were a major state) and trade interests (in any event) argued for the restoration of normal relations. Often assurances were sought and given with regard to the new government's acceptance of the obligations incurred on behalf of the state by its predecessor, its respect for existing treaty rights, and its promise of non-discriminatory commercial treatment of nationals of the other states.

Normally these were not serious problems, though there could be dispute about details. A revolutionary government did not like to be saddled with the debts that its predecessor had incurred to put down the now successful revolution, or with claims for damage to the property of foreigners. But the major nations generally insisted effectively on assumption of these obligations as a condition of recognition. At least during the height of laissez-faire capitalism, most of the economic conditions ultimately represented the common interest of all nations, for even those that had to accept immediate liabilities had a long-term interest in an international system in which these obligations were met.

We can find exceptions to these norms. Local *coups-d'etat* have sometimes been instigated by foreign governments to secure a new elite that is likely to be more favorably inclined towards a particular project; a classic example is the secession of Panama from Colombia, where a new state was quickly recognized by the United States, and the Canal Zone thus secured.

There were limits to the effectiveness of refusal to recognize a new government as a sanction to secure existing rights. Claims sometimes had to be compromised, particularly if the new government represented a major nation. But there was common acceptance of the principle of governmental succession and responsibility, and it was generally adhered to in the "balance of power" system. The pressure by the major (creditor) nations was, of course, resented by debtors who would have preferred recognition followed by settlement rather than preceded by it.

RECOGNITION IN A LOOSE BIPOLAR SYSTEM

During the "balance of power" period, recognition of both states and governments was related to enforcing international normative standards in which great nations had a common interest. Seldom did the withholding of recognition hinge on considerations of concern or political advantage to an individual state. To the extent the process of alliance was genuinely flexible, as it usually was, a new state did not represent a threat to one grouping of states and an advantage to another. And the same was true of new governments that acquiesced in the economic norms insisted upon by all the great nations—that paid their debts, respected rights of foreigners, and opened trade and commerce to all on equal terms.

Therefore, until the First World War, the doctrine and practice associated with recognition was reasonably consistent and reasonably related to its underlying functions. During the transition to the present loose bipolar system, new developments strained the process; various new criteria were offered and rejected. In the first place, the security system based on flexibility of alignment was breaking down, so that existing recognition doctrine no longer satisfied the interests of all states. Second, economic principles—the common capitalist framework—were less universal, and the role of recognition in securing continuity of obligation atrophied to an extent. In a bipolar system, with enduring alliances among bloc members, partners can scarcely be aloof and unconcerned about domestic political or economic policies of one another, or, indeed of the uncommitted nations each bloc is seeking to attract.

The creation of new states at Versailles seemed within the European practice of formal acknowledgment of status through collective agreement. But the criteria of the territorial divisions were different in important respects. The victorious European nations were set on reducing the number of great nations by the dismantling of Germany and Austria. Wilson was insisting on self-determination untested by revolutionary experience. Small states were given more than a peripheral role. The system established by the postwar treaties was, as a result, unrelated to the older security system, and had to depend for its durability on the unproved collective capacity of the League of

Nations to organize resistance to forcible territorial changes, and on the stability of national governments that had arisen without the unifying experience of violent overthrow of a foreign sovereign.

Under the League, it was extremely difficult to know just where security lay, save in a state's own capacity to resist aggression. Alliances were frowned upon, although occasionally they were made; no effective substitute mechanism existed. Nor was the task made easier by the emergence of a Communist Russia, in many respects a phenomenon comparable to 1789. Russia could not quickly turn forcibly messianic as had France. It did not, at least for the time being, represent any threat to external security. But Russia's revolutionary ideology, its network of internal subversion, and its repudiation of international economic norms greatly alarmed other important nations. The Communist government repudiated all the obligations of its predecessors. It went even further, because it repudiated the whole ideological and institutional basis of international trade and commerce and could not, through economic pressure or intervention, be made to conform. Understandably recognition was withheld. But the Communist government was able to withstand this kind of mild economic coercion far better than those who sought to invoke it. It was a moderately important trading nation and it had eliminated all domestic political pressure from private commercial interests. Other nations did not have this freedom from domestic pressure, and, as it became obvious that counterrevolution would not occur and that debts would not be honored, pressure from local trading interests and left-wing sympathizers joined to demand recognition of the new government. With some face-saving, the various states yielded to such pressures.

Analogous problems occurred in the interwar period. Italy conquered Ethiopia. Despite the clearly aggressive nature of the conquest, and its violation of the League Covenant, the territorial change thus brought about was formally recognized by a number of states. In this instance, at least, as with the recognition of the Soviet government, there seemed to be sufficient economic and political reasons to warrant formal acceptance of what could not be changed by unilateral action. In Spain, too, the norms of the "balance of power" system were violated and assistance given to insurgents by the Fascist governments. Although the Western democracies maintained a traditionally proper attitude, or even refrained from exercising their legal right to aid the lawful government, others did not, and were quick to recognize the legitimacy of the Franco regime they had helped put into power, while Russia, *per contra*, withheld formal recognition. The details are unimportant as compared with the increasingly obvious fact that common standards were disappearing and new criteria, based on ideological and political alliances, were taking over.

In the loose bipolar international system that has been emerging since the Second World War, the common interest in maintaining the independence of other states—at least with respect to flexibility of alignment—is tenuous and preferable only to having a new state align itself with the opposing bloc. Each of the bipolar blocs has an interest in keeping the uncommitted states at least neutral and independent of the other bloc. Since most uncommitted states are in areas that were colonial or dependent, common sentiments produce some cohesion in their policies, at least with respect to independence and United Nations membership. Both blocs must perforce support these demands, even though, from the standpoint of the NATO bloc in particular, serious disproportions arise in voting procedures in multilateral forums. It is difficult to take Yemen seriously as a state, and Libya has had serious problems maintaining its stability. In the "balance of power" period such territories could hardly have received the stature they receive today.

If new uncommitted states receive relatively full membership in formal arenas, new committed states are treated more harshly by the opposing bloc. Each bloc has a direct interest in making it as hard as possible for new states associated with the other bloc to acquire full rights in the society of nations. In some cases, this activity has the purpose of making the existence of the new state precarious and maintaining the possibility of its demise. Soviet policies toward South Korea, South Viet Nam, and West Germany, and American policies toward North Korea, North Viet Nam, and East Germany, have this end in view. Soviet policy toward the Taiwan regime is directed towards impugning its legitimate status as a step toward its destruction. In these cases each bloc seeks the isolation and weakening of adherents of the opposing bloc.

United States policy toward Outer Mongolia is a function, in part, of its policy toward the Taiwan regime. It neither seeks the destruction of Outer Mongolia nor the amelioration of the policy of that state. On the other hand, United States policy toward Communist China and the earlier Soviet policy toward West Germany are somewhat different in purpose. It is safe to assume that the continued existence of these regimes is not in question. Eventually some sort

of policy adjustment must be made to facts, which, although undesirable, are hard and obdurate. But these policies will not have any
relation to those of the "balance of power" period, which were designed to insure the maintenance of universal standards supporting
the common interests of the important nations.

Although United States' policy toward China is ostensibly designed
to secure China's acceptance of the principle that force should not be
used to change the status of claimed but unheld territories, it in
fact seeks in addition to enforce a particular interest, namely, an
American interest in maintaining the Taiwan regime. On strictly
legal grounds, it would be as easy to support the Communist regime's
forcible conquest of Taiwan as it now is to oppose such conquest.
Both regimes, after all, claim jurisdiction over all of China—a classic
condition for civil war. And both regimes were engaged in combat,
even though distant and ineffective, until the United States was able
to enforce limitations on the Taiwan regime. Soviet policy toward
West Germany is equally *ad hoc*. It is designed to serve specific and
particular objectives of Soviet policy rather than to implement
universal normative standards.

Clearly the standards of recognition that prevailed in the "balance
of power" system cannot prevail today despite occasional doctrinal
echoes from the past. Clearly, too, we cannot draw the inferences
from recognition or non-recognition which might have been drawn in
a "balance of power" system. Neither the conditions nor the policies
which produced consistency in the past are common today. Here, as
with as much doctrine inherited from the "balance of power" system,
rules geared to the relationships of independent states in an exclusively state-oriented system, operating according to the principle of
flexibility of alignment, cannot be transposed onto a political system in
which the important relationships are interbloc rather than interstate,
and values once common to the great nations and imposed on all are
no longer common to the two blocs.

Territorial changes of formal status are most likely to occur in
Afro-Asia. Here, movements from dependency to independent status
have been and will continue to be movements from legal ties to the
West to uncommitted status. Such movements will be supported, as
they have been supported, by the Communist bloc for the simple
reason that they weaken the hold of the West.

From the Western point of view many of these changes of status
are untimely (despite ideological sympathy with independence by
Americans) but often inevitable. Western nations seek to apply
traditional law norms that justify the forcible putting down of revolt,

as in Algeria. However, the difficulties of using force to prevent secession, coupled with the effect on other uncommitted areas of such attempts and the fear that revolutionary governments will turn for help to the other bloc, make for moderation or acquiescence. An independent status of the new state vis-a-vis the two blocs is preferable to the new state's adherence to Communism. Hence wherever the old colonial nations cannot relatively easily maintain the status quo, there is pressure to preserve lesser ties such as Commonwealth status, and a willingness to retreat to complete independence if pressed. This procedure is comparable to that of the nineteenth century, with these differences: There is little insistence that the new state have the stability required in the past, or that it be committed to laissez-faire economic policies, though in each case the West attempts to maintain these standards insofar as it is able. Bloc solidarity usually prevents recognition by members of the bloc prior to recognition by the claimant nation of the new status, but also results in considerable pressure on the colonial nation to grant recognition.

The uncommitted Afro-Asian nations themselves will be quick to recognize any claims by local political elites for "independence," but this means for them non-commitment by way of formal ties to either bloc. It is not really the flexibility of alignment principle of the "balance of power" period that they are supporting, but neutralism vis-a-vis blocs. They are often quite prepared to intervene in one another's affairs, but will denounce any forcible intervention by East or West, even if requested by the government of an independent state. United States assistance to the government of Lebanon in 1958 is a case in point and, India, for example, denounces the Portuguese enclaves in the Indian continent, but is wholly uninterested in their independence or even in the wishes of their population. These new nations are primarily interested in neutralism for the area, not in independence in the older sense.

Recognition of independent states in the uncommitted world of Afro-Asia by East and West and by other uncommitted states does not affirm the flexibility of alignment principle of the "balance of power" system. Their status is secure to some extent from either of the blocs. Vis-a-vis other uncommitted states they may have to depend on their own resistance.

Recognition of new governments raises problems where the effect of governmental change is to change the relationship of the state from uncommitted to committed status, or more dramatically from one bloc to another. Short of this contingency other states will formally apply traditional norms. Since a shift to the Communist bloc would almost certainly be the product of revolution, the United States urges the importance of constitutional changes and supports the legitimacy of intervention on behalf of an existing government to insure that changes are orderly. This is consistent with the early norms of the "balance of power" system, when there was often intervention to insure monarchical succession, but was seldom resorted to in the nineteenth century. Whether this kind of intervention can be made tolerable today to the uncommitted states is doubtful. The principle is too broadly stated, for it would require uncommitted states to support domestic governments of neighboring states of which they may disapprove on ideological grounds, when their only interest is in preventing a domestic change that would thrust one of their number into one of the blocs. Thus the legitimacy of support may be maintained, but the only intervention worth the political risk may be where the evidence of an impending change of status is sufficiently strong to gain the support of uncommitted nations. Given their fear of the restoration of Western colonialism—baseless as this fear may be—it may be almost impossible to gain such support.

A change of government by force within a bloc that does not involve a change of bloc commitment will be subject to traditional norms. A new government established by force which seeks to move the state from one bloc to the other bloc, however, is not likely to be tolerated. A new revolutionary government that seeks to become less committed may achieve recognition if its path is moderate and its relation to the bloc maintained in important respects. In addition, the genuine American belief in non-intervention makes it more difficult for the United States than for the Soviet Union to respond forcibly even to change of bloc. And this fact may introduce a dangerous asymmetry into the situation.

If one looks at recognition today in terms of the purposes of traditional doctrine, one is struck by the fact that the continuities that are important now are the continuities of bloc status. Traditionally, the purpose of the distinction between states and governments was to enforce agreed-upon norms of commercial continuity among states, to insulate these norms from governmental changes brought about by domestic politics, and to maintain the state's independence as a participating member of the "balance of power" system. But such norms today operate only when they do not affect interbloc relations. If a change of government presupposes a shift from one bloc to another, distinctions aimed at preserving other continuities of relationship may be without appeal.

This point can be illustrated by reference to the Communist revolution in Russia in 1917. The relative identity of population and territory represented by the new Soviet government with that previously represented by the old Russia provided the framework within which other states could assert a claim that the Soviet Union assume the obligations of the Russian state. The other great nations had a distinct interest in pressing this demand in view of the political and economic norms they were attempting to maintain. Clearly, however, the Soviet Union was opposed in a very basic sense to these norms; and, since the other major nations were unable to impose the norms on the Soviet government, the consequences resulting were those that traditional doctrine attached to a new state, rather than to a mere change of government; that is, continuities were not importantly preserved.

A similar situation exists today whenever there is a shift of government amounting to change in the status of a state vis-a-vis the two blocs. The important continuities on which the distinction between change of state and change of government rests, disappear, and the old state becomes in effect a new one in its relationships with members of both blocs. Continuities that were related to its prior bloc or independent status cannot survive the change; those that are unrelated to such status may still be enforceable. For instance, if Italy were to go Communist, the other members of NATO would have an obvious interest in denying Italian participation in the Organization; and any interest Italy would have in remaining in the organization would be of a subversive nature.

Hence the problem of sorting out such relationships exists, and cannot be solved by the lump-sum approach that has been associated with governmental succession and recognition in the past. Non-recognition often has little significance today, save that the details of recognition have not been worked out to the satisfaction of the non-recognizing state. Such a state hopes, by non-recognition, to salvage what it can, and to preclude from as many arenas as possible a state now committed to the opposing bloc.

Conclusions

The most difficult problems today are those which exist on the geographical frontiers of East and West: China, Germany, Korea—divisions between blocs of existing national entities with historical identity and a desire for national unity. From a functional viewpoint two states presently exist in all three cases. The territorial division is reasonably stable, assuming the present nuclear balance is stable, and probably will remain so until it can be adjusted by interbloc agreement—an agreement which would be conditioned on neutralizing the unified area effectively—or internal dissolution of one of the states. Yet leading members of the two blocs are reluctant to acknowledge the permanency of the existing arrangements, and seek to discourage any formal acts, such as recognition, that would be identified with a durable status quo, and would as a result affect future bargaining. Although the governments involved may claim to be legitimate successors to the whole area, it is clear their claims cannot be made effective. They seek, with varying success, some recognition of the legitimacy of this claim in various arenas.

Problems of admission to various arenas and succession to various rights have been differently resolved by different states. Today the doctrinal basis of recognition is more confused than ever, in part because we are faced with new problems arising from the existence of multilateral arenas. The United States has sponsored the Formosa regime as the successor to "China" in all arenas, and Russia has sponsored the Peiping regime for similar purposes and similar reasons. Russia has had more success with Peiping (as the United States has had more success with West Germany) because self-interest in economic terms for many countries has indicated the appropriate claimant. In addition West Germany clearly has popular support and economic power; similarly, the Peiping regime might be able to retaliate effectively against non-recognizing states in South East Asia. Anti-Westernism and the evidence of territorial continuity also play a political role. What is most important, however, is that American non-recognition of the Peiping regime clearly has nothing to do with supporting in any meaningful way the claims of Formosa to the mainland although the United States does forcibly support the status quo.

Succession to state rights in terms of United Nations participation ought to be a matter for that Organization to decide in accordance with criteria related to the purposes and functions of the Organization. Two claimants contest China's seat on the Security Council. Neither claimant has a clear basis in fact for claiming to represent the territory or population of the state that signed the Charter. The Nationalist regime exercises control only within Taiwan. The Peiping regime can carry out its obligations on the mainland, but has been labeled an aggressor and continues to employ some force to secure objectives in Quemoy and Matsu. Whether or not either government sufficiently corresponds with the expectations originally involved in giving "China" a permanent seat is questionable. The determination of this question lies in selecting the continuity that is important from the viewpoint of, and to forward the objectives of, the United Nations Organization. Who occupies that chair is not determinative of who occupies the embassy at Washington, Moscow, or London. The continuity of relationships important in these arenas may well be ordered by a different set of purposes.

The United States has often maintained that the decision to recognize a new state or new government is a "political decision," not subject to international law and resting in the unfettered discretion of the several states. This position is a perfectly tenable position only as long as there is no attempt to draw unwarranted inferences. A state cannot, from that premise, control legal consequences in arenas where other states participate and as to which other states have an important stake. Refusal by the United States to recognize Red China would not of its own force prevent Chinese admission to the United Nations or any other multilateral arena; it would not, save for the veto possibility, prevent Red China's succeeding to the Chinese seat on the Security Council; it would not justify use of force by the United States, or by the Taiwan government, against Red China (nor, indeed, would recognition of Red China justify the use of force against Nationalist China, for it would be equally possible to find Formosa a state for Charter purposes). A good deal of older precedent about recognition would be invoked in favor of various positions by states deciding such questions within the United Nations, as, for example, it was in the case of admission of Israel. In this sense, and for Charter purposes, recognition has become a collective subject for joint determination. Furthermore, Charter purposes are closely related to the important purposes served by recognition doctrine in the past; that is, preventing forcible change of the status quo.

From this collective "recognition" one cannot, however, infer any obligation on the part of individual states to recognize for non-Charter purposes a new state or government. The Arab states are not obliged to recognize Israel for any purposes save those encompassed by the United Nations Charter. Internal consequences of recognition—those within the unilateral control of states—have become severable from consequences in which there is a genuine international interest. With

United Nations procedures as they are, and with a process within the United Nations of determining collective international interests, it is safe to say that recognition by individual states may be a purely political act not subject to legal criteria. Who occupies China's seat in the Security Council does not have to be decided by the same normative criteria, or by the same decision-making process, as does the question of who is entitled to China's bank account at the First National City Bank. There may be excellent reasons for deciding both questions the same way. But the international interest in the former decision is far clearer than in the latter. In the "balance of power" system analogous decisions tended to get lumped into recognition doctrine. Today new decision-making processes make them more easily severable into separate problems for different decision makers invoking different criteria.

6

SOVEREIGNTY AND TERRITORIAL RIGHTS

THERE is no more confusing concept in international law than "sovereignty." It has been used indiscriminately in a number of different meanings by decision makers and scholars alike. Probably the reason for vague and inconsistent usage lies in the fact that, like "freedom" and "democracy," sovereignty is a highly emotive symbol calculated to induce a favorable response from most audiences in an age of nationalism. As a consequence, it is not very useful for purposes of either analysis or description.

Most frequently sovereignty is used in two related meanings: First, it is simply a synonym for "independent," signifying that government officials are not under the formal control or supervision of officials of another state in the exercise of governmental functions. Second, it is used to convey the idea that, within a defined geographical area, the prescription and enforcement of formal norms (law) are vested exclusively in state officials—that is, vested in persons playing formally defined roles in the governmental subsystem of the state that claims the territory involved. Usually this is referred to as "territorial sovereignty." The common thread of these ideas is the exclusion of any formal power vested in officials of other states to perform governmental functions on behalf of or in the territory of a sovereign state.

The historical relationship of this general concept to the emergence and existence of the nation-state, and to the requirements of the "balance of power" period, is clear enough. The bases of state power lay in control over activities within its territory supplemented by ties of allegiance of its population—power not formally divided

135

or shared with any transcending body politic. Sovereignty was "absolute" in the sense that it was not formally shared and that others were excluded from a state's decision-making processes. For reasons already discussed, states were jealous of these prerogatives; indeed, the political system depended upon them. Alternatives to sovereignty were either subordination of policy to another state, or an enduring relationship inconsistent with flexibility of alignment. But, in a system where there are many sovereigns, sovereignty can only be absolute with regard to a limited area and a limited number of persons, and even here formal qualifications may exist.

We can bypass much of the inconsistent and confusing usage of language by keeping in mind two points: First, we must think of sovereignty in relational terms. What is the claim being made, and against whom is it being asserted? Second, the claim to sovereignty is a claim to formal authority and not necessarily to effective control. Let us discuss these points separately.

Sovereignty over territory and population was, traditionally, a claim asserted by a state against other states to absolute and unfettered formal authority within the territory, to the exclusive exercise of governmental power within the area so far as other states were concerned. This claim was not derived from any external source and was not subject to any external controls imposed by others. It was, of course, subjected to formal limitations vis-a-vis external participants (other states) in the form of treaty provisions or customary rules of international law. Conceptually, however, these formal restrictions were not imposed by others but were voluntarily consented to; they were thought of as auto-limitations which were themselves expressions of sovereignty.

Other limitations on the authority of a state might exist in the form of constitutional limitations with regard to internal participants (individuals, associations, or political subdivisions). But these are not asserted by or against external participants, and so are not relevant to relationships with other states. Indeed, for another state to invoke such limitations on its behalf would be to question the sovereignty of the entity it was dealing with, or, equally inconsistent, to regard itself as an internal participant. As to external participants, the only formal limitations are those contained in international law.

A few illustrations may help to make this point clear. The States of the American republic, for example, remain sovereign in their relations with each other and, in areas not delegated to the federal government, with the federal government as well. Oklahoma officials may not perform governmental acts in Texas without the consent of Texas. To do so would violate the territorial sovereignty of Texas because the Oklahoma officials can point to no formal source for their authority to perform such acts. Since the United States is a federation of delegated and limited powers, the same would be true of the federal government in areas of authority not delegated to it by the Constitution. Whatever authority the federal government has is derived from that document. Yet neither Texas nor Oklahoma is sovereign in relation to other nation states; all power over foreign relations is delegated to the federal government. External participants, therefore, treat the United States federal government as though it were sovereign over the whole of the territory.

By the terms of the Constitution, States of the United States are forbidden to enter into foreign relations, as these relations are the exclusive domain of the federal government. They are not, therefore, "states" within the usual definition since they have not the requisite capacity to enter into relations with other states. For other nation-states to seek to enter into relations with any of the several states would be to interfere with the internal relations of the United States, and would be an interference with the sovereignty the United States claims in relation to external participants. As is sometimes said, so far as foreign states are concerned, "Texas does not exist."

A somewhat similar situation has often existed in the case of so-called dependent states. The typical situation was for a local ruler to delegate all control over foreign affairs to a European state while retaining formal control over internal participants. So far as other foreign states were concerned, a dependent state might be regarded as being similar to Texas. But there was one important difference. The claim of the "protecting state" in these cases was quite different from that asserted by the United States; the protecting state did not claim sovereignty over the area with relationship to either external participants or the local ruler. It merely claimed a capacity to act on behalf of the local ruler with regard to other states, an agency relationship. In the areas where such anomalous states existed, major nations would have resisted a claim by another European nation to formal sovereignty. A claim of sovereignty by a protecting state in relation to other states would have implied an enduring and absolute relationship that, in such areas as the Middle East, other major nations were simply not willing to tolerate.

Thus, the situation of a dependent state and that of a member of a federated union of states, such as the United States, were both factually and formally different. Who was sovereign in the case of a dependent state? Suppose a foreign state invaded the territory. Whose sovereignty would have been violated? Clearly, we would think, it would be the sovereignty of the local potentate, since he was the only person claiming sovereignty over the area. Yet such states were commonly called "non-sovereign."

The reason sovereignty was used in the sense of freedom from control by any external political entity during the "balance of power" period is clear. The very essence of sovereignty was thought to be this freedom from external control. States that were not free from such control were not considered sovereign. Hence, frequent statements that sovereignty is "indivisible," and the common thought that at some point a state could lose its sovereignty if it gave to another state too much control over its normal governmental functions. It was permissible for a state to limit its own formal authority by formal agreement and to acquiesce in customary norms restricting its exercise. But it was thought that for a state to allow another state to exercise governmental functions to any great extent within the former's territory, or in international affairs on the former's behalf, would mean losing, or be inconsistent with, the former state's sovereignty. How much was too much was an open question.

For the past two or more centuries of their development, nation-states have been insistent upon exclusive control over governmental processes. Joint institutions for decision making would have impeded the necessary flexibility of alliances. For a state to allow a foreign government to exercise authority within its own territory suggested foreign domination and an inferior status in the community of independent states. Accordingly, it has often been said that such arrangements are inconsistent with sovereignty. Indeed, they were inconsistent with that amount of formal authority that was required by the political system of that period for a major participant.

In the "balance of power" system, the only participants were states, and to participate, as we have seen, a state had to retain independence over its own governmental processes. This degree of independence was often associated with sovereignty. In the contemporary world, however, there is no need for the same degree of exclusive and independent authority as was required in the older system. Independence and freedom from interference in a state's internal affairs are not requirements for political security in the loose bipolar system. New political entities—both universal such as the United Nations and regional and functional such as the Common Market—have come into being as actors in the international system.

States have entered into constitutional relationships with each other and with supranational authorities. They have limited their formal authority with relation to other participants and have actually delegated typical governmental powers to new entities in a way which would have been inconceivable in the "balance of power" system.

Let us return to our example of the United States and compare it with the Common Market. The Common Market is not a federation in which the participating states give up all relations with external participants by delegating such relations to a common authority. It is as though the Constitution of the United States provided that the federal government could control the relationship of States with foreign states on some matters but not others. In the "balance of power" system, this would have made no sense; it was for reasons of security, in part, that the complete federal system was created. Today such a delegation of powers to a supranational authority is not only possible but, in Europe, has occurred. Identifying sovereignty with the independence required of the "balance of power" system would, of course, raise serious doubts as to whether the Six of Europe retained their sovereignty, and would probably mean regarding the Six as a federation. But if we think of sovereignty in relational terms, we can take such delegation of power to a supranational entity in stride. Members of the Community are no longer sovereign with regard to matters where the Community has authority to act as an entity, but the members retain sovereignty in all other respects with regard to both internal and external participants.

Is the Common Market a sovereign entity? In the sense that it exercises exclusive and ultimate authority with respect to certain important governmental functions within the territory covered by treaty, that it enters into binding relations with states and other supranational entities external to the Common Market, and that it possesses some of the immunities and rights normally considered attributes of sovereignty, it undoubtedly is a sovereign entity. If, on the other hand, one considers sovereignty to imply broad territorial jurisdiction, the Common Market would not be sovereign. Although the areas in which the Common Market exercises ultimate authority are of the greatest importance, it remains primarily a functional rather than a territorial authority. These distinctions, however, are becoming more hazy and of less importance as the organizational characteristics of the entities participating in international politics continue to change.

It has already been noted that sovereignty refers to formal authority and not necessarily to effective control. The formal authority of officials may be contrasted with actual control over relevant value processes. States may be formally independent of other states, but this does not prevent us from recognizing that, by other criteria, some "states" are "satellites." The more transactions cross national boundaries, the more interdependent peoples everywhere become. As a result there is less effective operational scope for the exercise of exclusive formal authority. Limitations on sovereignty are therefore factual as well as formal.

Whenever there is a complaint that, by a treaty or by participation in an international organization, a state is giving up a portion of its sovereignty, the complaint may well be correct in the sense that the state, by such participation, is limiting somewhat its formal authority to prescribe and enforce unilaterally certain decisions. But the state may, at the same time, be increasing its effective control—or even its formal authority—over another group of decisions affecting the same or other value changes; and it may, furthermore, be disclaiming a formal authority that it could not use for purposes of effective control.

Recent claims by Latin American states to formal authority over coastal waters extending some two hundred miles to sea represents an effort on their part to increase their effective control over whaling and fishing activities conducted off their shores by non-nationals. Rejection of these claims by the United States, along with the counterclaim that sovereignty extends only three (or six) miles seaward, represents an effort on the part of the United States to increase its effective control over a variety of activities that depend on other bases of authority and that the United States does not wish to subject to the control of others; the movement of naval vessels on the high seas is an example.

States are organized along territorial lines, and it is the capacity of government to order activity and control value changes within a prescribed area that is the source of government's political power. Therefore, it is particularly important to define territorial boundaries and to subject to rules, insofar as possible, the acquisition and loss of territory.

CLAIMS TO TERRITORIAL SOVEREIGNTY

Acquisition of territory: conflicting claims. The geographical boundaries of a state are well defined of necessity in areas where there is sufficient population to require the presence of officials exercising governmental functions, and they may be well defined elsewhere as a result of explicit agreement or that implied in consonant claims. Yet, even today in many parts of the world, Afro-Asia and Latin America in particular, inconsistent claims or boundary disputes exist. Where the area is unsettled and its resources unexploitable, as is usually the case, such disputes have low-level intensity, and there is little incentive to settle them. Claims are preserved in various ways against future contingencies. The boundaries of Israel, on the other hand, are a matter of very intense feeling in the Middle East. Elsewhere, among Arab states, the presence of large quantities of oil has led to the necessity of establishing firm boundaries. Private investors have often hesitated to invest where boundaries are unclear; an exploitation grant by the wrong state, like the purchase of property from someone other than the owner, would be a poor investment.

In the past, disputes over national boundaries have been settled in a number of ways: by force (with or without a claim of right), by claims acquiesced in over a period of time by others, by judicial decision, and by fiat or by arbitration of the great nations. Once established, whether by agreement or by unilateral claim, national boundaries are usually defended by the armed might of the claimant state against any efforts by others to exercise, within the bounded area, the functions of government without the acquiescence of the claimant state. These boundaries are also supported by an interesting strategic consideration—it is always easier to agree on the status quo than on any particular modification of the status quo. To the extent that agreement is more important than minor change, the reinforcement of the status quo is obvious.

Still another strategic factor enters—the von Neumann-Morgenstern utility assumptions. According to these assumptions, the value of any commodity depends upon the preference for gambles. Thus, it does not follow that one ought to be indifferent between not gambling and wagering $5 to gain $10 or $0 in an even gamble. If having $5 is more important for some reason than a 0.5 probability of getting $10 and a 0.5 probability of getting $0, the gamble should not be accepted. If the gambler badly needs something that costs $10, the gamble may be desirable. Since most states have adjusted to the status quo, the gamble of war to change the status quo for a minor gain is a bad gamble. If we eliminate satisfied and weak states, both of whom have an interest in maintaining rather than changing the status quo, the remaining states, although they may desire to change the status quo, are small in number. If they attempt to change the status quo, they are likely to range against themselves a preponderant coalition, particularly in a "balance of power" situation. But this serves to reinforce the norm that maintains the jurisdiction of a state within a historically given status quo.

Obviously, however, the status quo is not always maintained and sometimes it is changed by force. This new status quo, after a period of time, is reinforced by the same values which tended to maintain the old status quo. This consideration helps to explain why forcible change has been sanctioned by international law. In the absence of a central political government which can restore the old status quo at little cost because of its preponderant capabilities, or create a new one by legislative enactment, this principle minimizes costs to states in the international social system. Blood feuds, such as that of the Hatfields and the McCoys, are very costly and can be sustained only on the basis of particularistic and ascriptive qualities that characterize the clan, rather than the sort of qualities that characterize modern nation-states. However, some of the ex-colonial nations still have value systems not fully in harmony with the universalistic, achievement value orientations of the modern industrialized state and may behave in a manner that does not seem rational from such a standpoint. Whether universal organizations, such as the United Nations, can introduce a measure of peaceful change remains to be seen.

Generally, the state exercises formal authority within historically given boundaries. Peaceful occupation for a number of years, or prescription, is the most common and successful basis for a claim. In addition to the already-mentioned strategic considerations that reinforce prescription, there is the fact that most boundaries bear some relationship to "natural" factors, such as mountains, rivers, race, nationality, religion, or language, or the strategic security requirements of a particular state. Even principles of "fairness" may be asserted. Germany claimed *lebensraum;* Egypt resents its bad luck with regard to natural resources, and seeks "equitable" adjustment by various means.

These factors, however, do not always operate in the same direction. Different principles of boundary construction give rise to different boundaries. If anyone believes that boundary construction is a rationally ordered process, subject to clear decision rules that prescribe unique solutions, the belief is not likely to survive the attempt to arbitrate a serious boundary dispute. Should Cyprus have been allowed to opt for Greek rule? Cyprus is closer to Turkey than to

Greece and moreover is strategically more important to Turkey. But the majority of inhabitants are Greek. Moreover, Cyprus can be divided into two areas, one of which has a Greek majority while the other has a Turkish majority. An island does not necessarily constitute a "natural" unit, and may be divided; the Dominican Republic and Haiti occupy one small island. Shipping lanes are as common a mode of communication as roads and, depending upon natural conditions and the state of technology, two seaports may be more closely connected than two cities separated by an equal length of terrain.

One of the most important considerations is related to the expectations and beliefs of the inhabitants of the area, and the extent to which these inhabitants are prepared to resist forcibly a range of possible solutions. The fact that a large majority of the people on Cyprus wanted to join Greece, or, as a second choice, wanted independence, made the British position untenable except at a moral price that the British were not willing to pay. The fact that the Greeks have easy access to the Turkish part of the island and that the areas are not sharply separated made the division of Cyprus impracticable, though a similar arrangement had been successful in Ireland. It may be suggested, however, that had the pro-Eire minority in Ulster been substantially larger, even though still a minority, division would have been impracticable in Ireland, also. The solution eventually employed in Cyprus—independence, minority guarantees, and bases for the British—also had precedent, although guaranties to minority groups have not always been successful.

In the end, boundaries can be maintained when the maintaining force has the capability and the desire to maintain them at a price the other side is not willing or able to pay to change them. Thus in the long run, the future of Taiwan is doubtful, but that of the coastal islands off China, such as Quemoy and Matsu, is virtually certain. They will eventually revert to the mainland regime. Regardless of whether the character of the Chinese state has changed or not, islands situated immediately adjacent to the mainland of a major nation, and viewed, for historic reasons, as legitimate possessions are not likely to remain outside its control indefinitely.

Historically, national boundaries have changed whenever minorities were willing to fight to change them and were able to mobilize sufficient force to get their way. The nationality disputes in Europe ran that course and the ex-colonial nations are now experiencing the same national revival. Moreover, just as Hungary continued to repress non-Hungarian nationalities within its territories after it gained autonomy within the Austro-Hungarian Empire, the new nations will be tempted to oppress those minorities within their midst that cannot achieve nationhood for themselves. It would be a major achievement of contemporary statesmanship to establish rules and other institutional means to mitigate such oppression.

The Palestinian question is cut from the same cloth. Arabs are insistent upon Arab nationhood but seek to deny nationhood to the Israelis. The solution to date has depended upon force. But once a solution has been maintained for a period of time, this solution tends to gain support against possible alternatives, particularly when these alternatives would involve high costs in both human and material terms.

The fact that boundary disputes have often been forcibly settled and the difficulty of formulating precise and definitive doctrinal criteria does not rule out possibilities of peaceful solution. Weighing and selecting from among conflicting normative criteria is the daily task of judges and statemen, though the techniques employed are not identical. Disputes of low intensity may be (and often have been) settled, mediated or arbitrated—the arbitrator employing judicial techniques to apply those criteria which, in the particular factual situation, seem to him most persuasive. The Permanent Court of Justice decided a number of moderately important boundary questions. Where disputes run to a higher intensity they may nonetheless be settled if an independent authority can impose its judgment on the parties. This was frequently the case in the "balance of power" system where the disputes involved smaller states. The British have sought to do this in Cyprus, and the United Nations, with backing from the Western democracies, might be able to do so in the Middle East. Such an authority is likely to employ both adjudicative and mediatory techniques, and may even broaden the scope of decision (for example, dealing with minority and refugee problems) in an effort to make acceptance of the award preferable to the costs and risks of attempted forcible changes.

When a territory previously acknowledged to be under the formal authority of one state is taken by another without consent, the process is called "annexation." When the territory is formally given up to the new claimant by the old—even though this may be done under threat of force or under compulsion following war as, for example, by the Versailles Peace Treaty—the process is technically referred to as "cession." Occasionally cession is genuinely voluntary, as was the sale of Alaska to the United States by Russia, or the exchange of Heligoland for Zanzibar by Germany and Great Britain in 1890. The changing status of Alsace-Lorraine provides a number of examples of forced cessions. The legal consequences of annexation and cession, forced or voluntary, are said to be the same, but it is clear that any coerced deprivation, unless followed by a genuine attachment of a substantial proportion of the population to the new sovereign, is far less stable, and old claims may be effectively revived and reasserted at an opportune future time.

Conquest of an area does not automatically result in annexation. There must be an intent to annex before formal status is changed. Thus territory occupied in wartime remains subject to the sovereignty of the pre-existing state (that is, the state continues to exist) although its government is obviously deprived of its normal authority and officials act at the direction, or sufferance, of the occupying state. However, pre-existing domestic laws normally remain in existence unless explicitly countermanded by occupying forces, and there are rather vague limits to an occupier's legal capacity to change domestic law without announcing an intention to annex; usually, it has no interest in upsetting normal routine within the area. But this is perhaps less true today, where, as in the case of Germany, reconstruction of the pre-existing state was a war objective. In the "balance of power" system, with its flexibility of alignment and limitation of objectives, both the extent of territorial occupation and the degree of interference with domestic political norms tended to be limited. Otherwise, the national independence consonant with flexibility of alignment or, conversely, the potential availability of the present enemy as a future ally might have been damaged. Obviously these constraints became less effective as the European system became more rigid after 1870, and they are even more subject to question during the present bipolar period.

The older tradition was reinforced by two situations then common: either a common European legal system or else a native system which Europeans generally tolerated, at least for natives, or else totally abrogated through annexation. Today ideological goals are almost sure to be present (assuming a population still exists) and, as a result, more changes in the local law will likely be made. In 1945, despite the "unconditional surrender" slogan, the Allies disclaimed any intention to annex Germany, but did wish to vindicate their objectives by insistence, for example, on punishment for war crimes and on the return of, or compensation for, property confiscated from

Jews. This factor caused some confusion in the relevant doctrinal criteria, a confusion compounded by lack of harmony among all the occupying nations who could scarcely be viewed as having consistent objectives.

Contemporary doctrine regarding the permissible use of force by a state presumably makes forcible territorial acquisitions, save temporarily as a measure of "self-defence," illegal. From the Covenant to the Charter efforts to discourage forcible transfers of territory have been an avowed purpose of many nations. In 1932 Secretary Stimson announced a "non-recognition" policy where transfer was forcible, aimed initially at the Japanese in Manchuria and applicable also to the Italian conquest of Ethiopia and Russian annexation of the Baltic states. The United States has repeatedly reaffirmed this policy, as have inter-American conferences since 1933 and the Draft Declaration on the Rights and Duties of States, prepared in 1949 by the International Law Commission. The United States currently urges this principle as the reason behind its refusal to recognize Red China, where its application is a little more questionable, perhaps, than it is in the continued refusal of the United States to recognize Russia's annexation of Lithuania, Latvia, and Esthonia.

As we saw in Chapter 5, non-recognition may have consequences that give it some deterrent effect, and it helps to keep alive claims related to the *status quo ante*. But unless steps can be taken to restore the *status quo ante* before too long a passage of time, difficulties are likely to arise. Insofar as non-recognition is aimed at changes of status within the opposing bloc, there will be both little deterrent effect and little pressure to recognize the change. Non-recognition may work somewhat more effectively when applied to the actions of a member of the same bloc.

In the loose bipolar system there are fewer constraints, save in the uncommitted areas, on forcible annexation and cession than existed in the "balance of power" system. On the other hand, new techniques of effective control over bloc members are likely to make forcible annexation, such as occurred in the Baltic, less likely. In the West, techniques involving supranational groupings will be exploited to create bloc solidarity and to attract new members voluntarily by the offer of considerable economic advantage through subsidy. In the Eastern bloc, Communist Party control over puppet governments and effective (though not formal) annexation through internal subversion, perhaps assisted by "volunteers" and technicians in revolutionary tactics, are the likely mechanisms for annexation in fact. This latter technique, however, is a sham in terms of the legal norms about force that are verbally acquiesced in by all participants.

Maritime claims. Claims by coastal states to exercise sovereignty over adjacent oceans to the exclusion of others were made by major nations in the very early beginnings of the "balance of power" system, but were incompatible with it, and with the common objectives of its important members, in the developed system of the nineteenth century. "Freedom of the seas" is a nineteenth-century achievement, though the doctrinal proposals date at least from 1604, when Grotius wrote his famous *Mare Liberum* in an effort to justify Dutch commerce with the Indies in the face of Portuguese claims, with Papal support, to monopoly. The Englishman, Selden, wrote an exhaustive reply to Grotius, significantly entitled *Mare Clausum,* and ran into difficulties when he sought to reconcile special British claims to British seas with British claims to free navigation elsewhere—a casuistry that required two volumes. Therefore, five hundred years ago we find the English King calling himself "Sovereign of the Britannic Ocean" and "King of the Seas," Denmark claimed the Baltic and North Atlantic, Venice was "sovereign of the Adriatic," and so forth. The great maritime nations sought to make others acknowledge these claims, even when they were not disposed to interfere with navigation or, as was sometimes the case, exact tribute for travel upon their "territory." Until quite recently the curious custom of ships dipping their ensigns to a British Man O'War—as though doffing their hats to Her Majesty—survived. Coastal states that were not great nations made more modest offshore claims; a "league" (differently measured as between three and four miles) was the common claim along the shores of the Mediterranean (where it had some connection with the range of cannon) and of the Baltic and North Sea where it arose independently of the southern rule (from efforts to preserve neutral status).

The doctrine associated with "freedom of the seas"—the idea that the oceans were open to all and subject to the exclusive authority of none—was the result of a marriage of laissez-faire economics to British gunboats. The major maritime nations had a common interest in opening the seas to free navigation by merchant ships for purposes of commerce, by naval forces for purposes of security, and by fishermen for exploitation of natural resources. Coastal states that continued to make formal claims to excessive areas of the ocean—the Danes, for example, who claimed waters sixty miles in width around

Iceland and Greenland—could not hope to assert effectively such claims in the face of Dutch, French, and British seapower. The great maritime nations would respect only what they claimed themselves—the old league, or three to four miles—and, even within this area, insisted upon the right of ships in "innocent passage" to navigate close to shore without hindrance. In addition, insistence on closure of the seas would have interfered with the flexible alignment process of the "balance of power" system.

Freedom of the seas was part and parcel of other contemporary freedoms, and its statement has been equally dogmatic, absolute, and very nearly sloganized, as has "free enterprise," as an article of faith. Most importantly, freedom of the seas meant unfettered peacetime navigation; it has been used to justify fishing, laying cables, and other activities. The consensus that supported freedom of the seas and made it effective was that of the major maritime nations, accepted by—or imposed upon—the rest of the world. Just as Selden's *Mare Clausum* was a product of mercantilism, so the nineteenth century's *Mare Liberum* sprang from expanding capitalism— from a world without significant trade barriers, tariffs, exchange regulations, quotas, state monopolies, subsidies for defense, and similar evidences of economic provincialism.

From this historic achievement to current chaos seems a long step. The observer today is instantly struck by the increasing demands of coastal states which are not also maritime nations for exclusive authority over large parts of the world's oceans. These range from the extreme (protested but still effective) claims of Chile, Ecuador, and Peru, to a marginal belt two hundred miles in width, down to a number of twelve-, nine-, six-, four-, and three-mile claims, with the maritime nations generally supporting the three-mile claim, and a minority of other states in accord with them. Negotiations in Geneva in 1958 and 1960, based on work done by the International Law Commission, failed to get agreement on any width from two-thirds of the group, though substantial agreement on most other points of four related conventions was reached. Despite formal resistance by the United States and the United Kingdom (the latter willing to back up its demand with some show of force even against its NATO ally, Iceland), the number of nations moving toward the twelve-mile maximum increases almost every month. Current unresolved disputes involve Mexico and the United States, England and Iceland, Sweden and Russia, Japan and South Korea, and Japan and Australia, to mention only the more serious ones. Aristotle Onassis, the Greek shipowner, recently paid a fine of three million dollars for whaling in "Chilean waters" 187 miles from shore.

There are several reasons for this changed state of the law. Basic, of course, is the changed political system coupled with loss of faith in expanding capitalism as the path to economic development. The major nations no longer have a common interest in minimizing claims of coastal states, though it remains in the interest of maritime powers generally to do so. Iron-curtain countries are not major maritime nations, and are quite willing to support twelve-mile claims if for no other reason than the divisive effect such claims have on the Western bloc. Furthermore, the framework on which agreement was sought (also a reflection of contemporary politics and the danger of a representational system based on one vote per state) for the first time gave coastal states which were not also maritime powers a real voice in the decision. For reasons of national pride and economic nationalism the new small states, and those in Latin America whose voice had too long been ignored, voted for big slices of sovereignty. If the high seas were up for grabs, what had they to lose in getting their fair share?

At least three developments of a technological nature are relevant. First, most of the world's fish are found close to shore—within twelve miles but not within three. Ocean-going trawlers are a relatively new invention and have enabled fishing entrepreneurs to venture far from home waters and to catch, as compared with older methods, huge quantities of fish. This has raised some questions of conservation of the world's fish supply, particularly in historic fishing grounds shared by many. More importantly, it has injected foreign competition into areas of the coastal state's economy with depressing local effects. In countries like Iceland and South Korea, with backward technology and great numbers involved in fishing activities, the appearance of English and Japanese trawlers has been bitterly resented; the rich get richer at the expense of the poor, or so it seems to the unemployed fishermen. A twelve-mile limit and exclusion of foreigners, whether or not related to "conservation" in any meaningful economic sense, at least conserves the local fishing industry from foreign competition.

The second technological development is closely related to the first, and stems from a similar development in the shellfish, particularly oyster, industry. Some of the great oyster beds of the Pacific extend to far beyond the traditional limits, and foreign competition armed with technological advances has had a similar impact on backward economies. Here again the conservation issue is partly real and partly false.

The third development has been the discovery both of oil and the means of recovering it in relatively deep waters. Unlike fishing, though not wholly unlike cultivated oyster beds, oil recovery involves the need for geographical division of drilling rights, and, in a property system, some need for administration. It also provides a nation with a new and unclaimed source of public wealth in an area immediately adjacent to its own land.

Were it not for the seriousness of these problems and the difficulty of their solution, the events of the last few years would read like a comic opera script. The United States, with more interest than any other nation in preserving norms of free enterprise and free navigation, upset the applecart in 1945 when President Truman made two famous declarations. The first claimed "exclusive jurisdiction" over the resources of the Continental Shelf, with the important qualification that this did not affect the status of the superjacent waters as "high seas." The second, issued simultaneously, qualified the qualification by asserting our "jurisdiction and control" over fishing in these waters, exclusively where the waters had been fished only by our nationals, and jointly with others whose nationals had historical fishing claims. Both proclamations made vague, though probably sincere, invocation of the need to conserve natural resources.

Thus was Pandora's box unlocked. Proclamations by others were printed with the abandon of Confederate currency. The oil sheiks followed suit, as the United States had expected and probably hoped (in view of American Middle East oil interests) they would. Australia, long concerned about protecting her oyster beds from the Japanese, found our precedent the answer to a vexing problem; so enamoured was she that she applied it to the continental shelves surrounding her island Trusteeships as well. Oysters, said Australia, were really more like oil than fish, so there was no need to pay attention to historic claims, which were not so terribly historic anyhow. The niceties of American qualifications were lost on America's neighbors to the south. Jurisdiction without sovereignty, according to the Latin American countries, was a "juridical impossibility"; hence the United States must really have been claiming sovereignty; and sovereignty implied jurisdiction over all activities since (in their view) it was theoretically indivisible. Latin Americans claimed sovereignty over their shelves, to the resources of those shelves, to the waters above, to the fish therein—reserving any rights they might have to anything they had not thought of. Argentina's shelf extends in places for more than a thousand miles—a sizeable acquisition of real estate for the price of printer's ink. Her neighbors to the West, without a shelf, saw no justice in this foible of Nature's so they claimed a modest two hundred miles to make up for such discrimination and lack of equality. Iceland and Korea claimed their right to exclusive fishing above their shelves, thus endeavoring to export unemployment in the fishing industry back to the United Kingdom and Japan. The Arabs, anxious to close the gulf of Aquaba to Israeli shipping, opted for at least twelve miles. It was against this background of short-run policies and domestic politics that the Geneva meetings sought—unsuccessfully—to resolve conflicting claims.

Claims to full and exclusive authority over maritime areas are not difficult to distinguish in important respects from similar claims over settled land areas. Some exercise of authority by coastal states is relevant to enforcement of local laws, particularly those regarding customs controls, sanitation (protecting recreational areas from spoilation), and communications cables in shallow water. Other claims may be related historically to security, but under modern conditions—both technological and political—such claims can scarcely serve security purposes adequately. Additional claims may be justified on the basis of the need for some law administration to protect capital investment related to the exploitation of maritime resources and perhaps to conserve them from economically wasteful exploitation. Oil, which requires fixed installations and exploitation of fields as a unit (unitization), would seem to need some legal regime, and perhaps the coastal state provides the most convenient source of administration to protect both the resource and the investment and prevent injury done by drilling to existing cables, navigation, and fishing; similarly, oyster beds that have been artificially seeded require some protection from exploitation by non-investors in their productivity. These activities may be contrasted with fishing, where the only investment is in movable equipment and can be most easily administered through the protection of the flag state rather than regimes shifting with location. There may, of course, be a need for preserving fishing resources from uneconomic exploitation—salmon and seals present examples—but conservation schemes have not in most cases as yet been backed with persuasive evidence of any objective need, and more often than not appear to be "conservation" for the coastal state—a monopoly arrangement—rather than a genuine program to protect a shared resource.

Obviously, not all these conflicting demands will everywhere be satisfied by a given territorial margin. A claim to sovereignty over a broad marginal sea irrationally affects uses by others for purposes such as navigation, thus subjecting matters previously thought to be beyond coastal control to a legal status phrased in terms of the most exclusive language of formal national authority. Coastal states outnumber maritime states, and are presently disposed to think in terms of short-run national economic interests. Rational argument has not yet persuaded many to give up their narrow views for the view based, essentially, on bloc integration economically and militarily (though phrased in terms of universality, not blocs) any more than national statesman have been able to persuade farmers and labor unions that smaller shares of larger pies are preferable to larger and larger shares of smaller and smaller pies. In the short run, claims to sovereignty for purposes of excluding foreign economic development and exploitation—the major reason behind these claims —is good local politics.

Claims to the continental shelf and its natural resources, but excluding superjacent waters, by coastal states are generally acknowledged, but there is not now a generally agreed width to the territorial sea; only a few Latin American countries, however, claim more than twelve miles. It seems probable, despite strong opposition from the maritime powers, particularly the United States and United Kingdom, that claims in excess of three miles and perhaps up to twelve will be generally conceded, subject only to a right (not satisfactorily defined) of "innocent passage" within such waters. The United States presently takes the position that it need not recognize a width greater than three miles since that is all it claims and no greater width has generally been agreed by the international community. This is a tenable, though hardly persuasive, position on strictly doctrinal terms. It is untenable practicably over any extensive period and may be assumed to represent nothing more than a bargaining position. Perhaps by separating the problems in the manner suggested above, by subsidizing those states suffering from the technological impact of new fishing boats, and by lining up support through bilateral arrangements of this general nature, the United States can persuade a number of bloc members to modify existing claims. For most smaller, underdeveloped coastal states the real problem is fishing, and the solution of this problem by means of subsidy would do much to reduce intrabloc disputes.

From the viewpoint of the United States, claims to sovereignty, whatever the context, are almost certain to be unfortunate. The general objective of the United States is to create bloc solidarity, to accommodate as many bloc members as possible, and to knit economically and politically as many members as it can into a viable system through common institutions. Exclusive and broad claims are usually divisive, and make bloc objectives more difficult and more expensive. Hence, despite occasional noises from the Senate, the United States keeps attempting to push a view that will lead to reasonable accommodation of bloc interests (usually phrased in terms of universality) rather than concentrating upon the "right" of one state to exclude, or prescribe the terms for admission of, foreign nationals.

If, instead of talking about the whole bundle of exclusionary rights that usually accompany the idea of sovereignty, we can encourage states to concentrate on particular problems of fishing, oil and other shelf resources, security measures, and so forth, there is greater chance for terms and conditions that integrate rather than divide bloc members. The position is sound both doctrinally and historically, for it is clear that customary law actually developed in this way, and that one uniform width of territorial sea will not solve all problems to every state's satisfaction. What may be reasonable for customs enforcement is not necessarily equally suitable for conservation.

The bulk of present claims are based on some presumed economic advantage founded upon short-run policies of economic nationalism, increasing immediate capital resources for nationals at the expense of long-run efficient production and exploitation. But the form in which these claims are stated—as increments to "territorial sovereignty"—has far broader implications that would be difficult to justify in any particulars. We need only look at the broad and open-ended bundle of rights included within the ordinary concept of sovereignty, to realize how much is being claimed. For example, the entrance to the Panama Canal, always considered to be through "high seas," would, with a twelve-mile limit, be within the "territory" of Panama, and that undefined term, "innocent passage," would then be a crucial one for the variety of purposes, economic and military, that the Canal serves.

For reasons similar to those discussed above, there has been a tendency to close off bays previously regarded as open to all as parts of the high seas, and to seek to expand territorial waters by new "straight-line" measuring devices. The method of straight lines projected "in the general direction of the coast" from promontories was introduced by Norway to protect her fishermen and had the result of greatly enlarging what had previously been regarded as Norwegian territorial waters, while at the same time allowing her to maintain a verbal consistency in terms of mileage. This method of measurement was approved by the World Court in 1951 over the protests of the United Kingdom. Obviously there is a tactical advantage to states such as Norway, with maritime interests the world over and fishing problems at home, in taking advantage of an unusual coastline to project her historical claims further in fact from her coast while maintaining support for only a four-mile limit. Indonesia has been less subtle, simply closing off huge bay areas unilaterally.

Airspace and beyond. When man first began seriously to succeed in flight it was urged on the one hand that the air, like the sea, should be *res extra commercium,* free to all users, and on the other that the underlying states had sovereignty over airspace. Governments were not really concerned over the possibilities of flight until the years immediately before the First World War, when the French, alarmed by increasing numbers of German balloons, manned by military personnel, over France called an International Air Conference in Paris in 1910. This Conference did not complete any Convention, but it was already obvious that the advocates of sovereignty for underlying states were going to prevail. In 1919, with the experience of the war behind them and with air travel being on the threshhold of commercial use, states formally took this view in the Paris Convention of that year. Those states that were not parties to the Convention, subsequently enacted similar national legislation. The position was further consolidated at Chicago in 1944 in the Convention setting up the International Civil Aviation Organization, Article 1 of which reaffirmed that "every State has complete and exclusive sovereignty of the airspace above its territory." No definition of "airspace" is included in these Conventions.

This development is what might have been expected. Indeed, in retrospect, what is surprising is the vigorous nature of the arguments made by some that the air should be "free" to all users. From the outset, the military significance, at least for observational purposes, of air activities was apparent, and as a consequence states were concerned to regulate and control foreign flight instrumentalities over their territory. In addition, flight was regarded as dangerous, not merely for those who participated but also for those on the ground, and it was generally thought that, for this reason also, overflight must be regulated by the underlying state.

An administration analogous to that of the high seas was unobjectionable over unclaimed areas, principally polar areas and the high seas, but it was generally agreed that, over populated territory, flight should be controlled by the underlying states. By 1944, when air traffic had proved itself commercially, these reasons were reinforced by the desire of many states to participate in commercial aviation across international boundaries. In view of the pre-existing law, the United States, with large commercial interests, felt it must concede sovereignty but sought to get agreement on the so-called Five Freedoms; overflight, landing, and discharging, loading, and carrying international traffic.

As the most powerful operator state, the United States was interested in establishing, for commercial purposes, a regime similar to that supported by maritime states on the oceans. Virtually all other countries with commercial aspirations resisted, using their claim to sovereignty to bargain for their "share" of traffic and to prevent competition; most airlines were government owned or subsidized. States were willing to accept generally rights of overflight and landing for non-traffic purposes in peacetime for "non-governmental" aircraft (that is, for commercial and private aircraft) but would not go further. They were generally disinterested in competition for commercial traffic, and insisted on a number of qualifications, related to security and to safety considerations, for even the first two of the Five Freedoms.

Airspace over the high seas was acknowledged to be open to all, but it was successfully contended that no right of innocent passage for aircraft over territorial waters existed (a consideration that, as one can see from a map, makes the impact of expanding territorial waters quite significant to air traffic in some parts of the world). This divergence may have been related to security and also to the fact that, unlike small ships, passage of aircraft close to the coast cannot be justified so easily in terms of navigation or safety. Actually, even the width of the territorial sea is quite inadequate for security purposes, and states with extensive coastlines such as the United States have established Air Defense Zones far over the high seas, within which aircraft must identify themselves. Failure to do so is not, however, automatically accompanied by forcible sanctions, though it may result in a commercial line losing any privileges it presently has within the United States if the aircraft actually proceeds to enter United States territory.

With the impending conquest of "outer space" claims to sovereignty over airspace have taken on a new significance. Neither the United States nor Russia has sought the permission of other states for their space activities to date, and it is highly unlikely that either will do so. To date, no state has objected formally that its sovereignty was being violated. From this it might be possible to infer that present claims to sovereignty stop somewhere short of the perigee of satellites so far launched, and that whatever law applies beyond this "boundary" it is not unilaterally to be determined by the "underlying" state. Many scholars, in their anxiety to find a clear-cut legal answer, have suggested that, above the boundary, space, like the high seas, is free, and have agitated for a clear boundary between the two legal regimes. Conceding that states are sovereign over their airspace, they seek a linear measurement of how far "up" this sovereignty extends.

To endeavor to find a solution to this question by interpretation of terms like "airspace" or "aircraft," as used in the Paris and Chicago Conventions, is to pursue a mirage. Some of the terms are not defined; others have important ambiguities. Extra-documentary definitions, both in past and present usage, vary with context and purpose, as well as with changes in scientific understanding and technological progress.

Numerous suggestions have been put forward by those who believed that outer space was or ought to be distinguished from airspace to locate the boundary they feel is legally relevant. Some have been based upon supposed geophysical or astronomical constants; some on beliefs (usually scientifically wrong) as to the maximum heights attainable by aircraft; some on arbitrary altitudes varying inversely with the "internationalism" of their proponents. The same writers, in efforts to keep up with rapidly developing technology, have been forced to revise more than once their various proposals.

The difficulties of fixing a meaningful boundary may well be insuperable. Neither the physical characteristics of flight-craft, nor any other relevant factor, can be reasonably expressed with regard to a fixed and stationary line. If in order to avoid these difficulties an arbitrary line is fixed so low, or so high, as to include all foreseeable space activity within a desired category, the result would be either to fetter space activities by inapposite rules that would require multiple consent for any project, or to interfere pointlessly with the existing international aviation regime. In this respect, the problem resembles that of claims to territorial waters.

More important, the achievement itself would be totally without meaning. For example, artificial satellites launched in geocentric orbits have come closer to the ground at some points than at others, in some cases the perigee falling below the line previously proposed by some of the well-informed experts. Yet it would make little sense to impose one legal regime or status at one end of the orbit and a wholly different one at apogee.

The very notion of horizontal boundaries assumes that up to some altitude the space "above" national territory bears in some respect a special relationship to the underlying area, whether for reasons of safety, of defence, or of commerce, or for other reasons. In other words, the concept of horizontal boundaries presupposes the validity of vertical boundaries. Yet, beyond some varying limit, the fact that an object is located or an activity is taking place "above" a certain spot on the earth's surface has no necessarily relevant connection with that spot. Some activities in space require line-of-sight connection with a given area on the earth but do not require that the particular line-of-sight remain within projected vertical boundaries enclosing the state in question. An object projected from outer space toward the earth's surface would not be projected from a point "above" its target. Nor could a state afford to delay defensive counter-measures until projectiles came within its vertical boundaries.

It is always tempting to try to make fast a line from the known to the unknown, particularly, perhaps, for lawyers, whose job, after all, is order. Thus writers have sought to transpose wholesale the law of the sea to outer space. But, although this is tempting and undoubtedly relevant in part, there are innumerable differences that argue against any such wholesale transfer of doctrine, developed over centuries, from one area to another. As compared with activities on the high seas, for instance, the present use of outer space presents fewer commercial and economic aspects; its military potentiality represents a relatively higher fraction of its present total importance; the users for some time to come will be relatively few and will probably be, for the most part, governmental entities or possibly international agencies. As compared with conventional airspace, the distances, speeds and times involved in usage are dramatically different, as are the methods of launching and landing; the military threat is of a different character and, at least for the time being, of a different order of magnitude; the commercial and economic possibilities are less well known, but potentially far more extensive.

The futility of mechanical adoption of the law of the high seas does not mean that past experience is irrelevant. Indeed, reflection on that experience (and particularly on current problems discussed above on maritime boundaries) may help to anticipate problems and their solution. The law of the sea may afford hints as to the accommodation of activities such as navigation (space-flight), fishing (exploitation of mineral or energy resources), and cable laying (communications) to activities or security needs like naval maneuvers, customs protection, and so forth. Decisions on the registration of space vehicles may draw upon experience with regard to both maritime and air vessels and may analyze both the successes and failures apparent in that history.

These problems, in no event easy of solution, are complicated somewhat by the high degree of interdependence between a variety of uses and objectives in space. In this respect space presents problems analogous to those of the atom. Scientific knowledge about cosmic radiation may be used for radiological warfare; television and radio relay stations may be used to hinder as well as promote communications; geodetic and meteorological observations have the same duality of function; most important, of course, the technology relevant to the exploration of space is equally relevant to the launching of intercontinental ballistic missiles.

It is not difficult to make a catalogue of foreseeable problems presently raised by the conquest of space. A partial list might run as follows: problems of radio spectrum management and of the allocation of radio frequencies; conservation of space to prevent a state from propelling into orbit large quantities of radio-active "junk"; radio and television relay satellites; weather forecasting and control; damage to subjacent states, aircraft and vessels; nuclear explosions in space; repossession of space projectiles and repatriation of personnel; coordination of space programs, registration of projectiles, and sharing of scientific information; and so forth. The only thing these problems have in common is that none will be solved satisfactorily by any claim as to "sovereignty" up to any particular altitude.

The security problems raised by space technology are similar to those raised by atomic energy, and will probably remain unresolved in the immediate future for the same reasons. An *ad hoc* United Nations Committee tentatively explored in 1959 problems of space activities for "peaceful purposes"; it considered methods of disseminating scientific information, and catalogued some of the legal problems raised. This was a useful first step to ordering problems and solutions. It is unlikely, however, that space activities will be put under control of an international agency until problems of missile inspection and bases are solved, but it is entirely possible that an organization similar to the International Atomic Energy Agency will be created to promote dissemination of information and to make suggestions and recommendations to states engaged in space activities.

Smaller states are unlikely now to push their claims to sovereignty very high, and everyone may be most easily satisfied if the "boundary" problem is left unresolved. Neither the United States nor Russia is prepared to subject activities with a high security element to unilateral decision by any number of smaller states who would then have to consent to various activities "over" their territory. Nor do decision makers in these states themselves really wish for this kind of decisional mechanism. In all probability, concentration will be on the particular problems listed above, and only if there is wide division of opinion on these will states resort to pushing their contentions about sovereignty in outer space as a bargaining device. In effect, national programs will continue unfettered by substantial formal legal requirements as long as the military connection predominates, though the United States will be desirous to demonstrate its internationalism by utilizing the United Nations Space Agency (if one is created) as an arena for the airing of opinion. For the general reasons that support American use of the United Nations as an arena to mobilize international opinion in its support, it will desire to give as many smaller nations as possible a sense of participation in the conquest of space while not subjecting any activities to formal controls inconsistent with unilaterally determined security objectives. The U.S.S.R., with smaller voting strength and less need for the UN as a supranational mechanism to tie together its supporters, will be more cautious, but may well be forced into limited participation. The Soviet Union is presently following the familiar pattern of dilatory boycott of UN activity on procedural grounds, and may continue to do so as long as possible. But it is more questionable whether Russia is prepared to stay outside an agency, which will have little formal power, at the cost of some loss of support in non-Communist countries.

Missiles raise problems that satellites do not. Although satellites might be used for some military purposes, assuming improvements in technology, missiles are thought of as primarily military instruments.

The flight of a missile over the national territory of a state therefore might lead to complications that the flight of a satellite does not. Moreover, the peacetime flight of a missile might serve as a precedent for time of war; if argumentation was in traditional terms of "sovereignty," it would be neither use nor violation of territory, provided the overflight were at a very high altitude. For this reason the peacetime flight of a missile over the territory of a non-cooperating state is sure to be protested vigorously and probably successfully, regardless of the height at which the missile passes over national territory.

Polar regions: space bodies. Every schoolboy is familiar with the great explorers of yesteryear whose general practice, upon discovery of territory, seems to have been the planting of flags and the claiming of the new lands, generously described, for their sponsoring monarchs. As we have said, over most of the inhabitable world these claims have been variously settled—leaving a few boundary problems of minor importance. Antarctica remains, so to speak, the last outpost in an otherwise claimed world. Here a number of states have put forward conflicting claims to parts of the icy wastelands. Although these wastelands are not and may never be permanently settled, they do have some potential for scientific experimentation, a possible economic utility in terms of mineral resources, and only rather marginal military significance—as made evident by the recent agreement by twelve nations not to use Antarctica for military purposes. But the possibility of new worlds to conquer in space—planets and particularly the Moon—has stirred new interest in Antarctic claims on the theory that a solution here may be precedent for a solution in space. Again, however, as in the analogies between the high seas, airspace and outer space, there are relevant differences as well as similarities, and even were conflicting claims to Antarctica resolved—which does not seem likely—the parallel is not wholly convincing.

We have already stated that the modes for acquiring sovereignty over land areas, and the land included within a claim, have historically varied with context and have depended on a number of considerations. Where land has been inhabited, sovereignty has depended in recent times to an important degree, though not exclusively, on the views of the inhabitants, particularly where these views have been so strongly held and vigorously pressed as to make them relevant to the maintenance of order. Uninhabited areas—or areas that, in the recent past, were inhabited by non-Europeans—

have raised boundary problems that have been settled by weighing "natural" factors against historical claims to title. The difficulties of making any single criterion determinative have already been discussed. Claims in Africa, for example, were settled by multilateral agreements reflecting no one standard and involving a good deal of political trading. Force and the threat of force have very often played the determinative roles, although, with rare exceptions, the use of force has been justified by reference to legal doctrine in substantiation of the claim asserted.

The highest credentials to a claim of sovereignty are found in effective occupation of an area for a substantial period of time; that is, settlement coupled with the actual exercise of normal governmental functions within the area. The exclusive nature of a claim to sovereignty requires that any other claimant object, forcibly if need be, to the exercise of authority by the first state. Nor is there any problem where an area is unpopulated but completely enclosed by borders that are effectively occupied. The problems come when there is an effort to extend sovereignty over areas not enclosed within acknowledged borders and not populated. Here, too, there are claims to sovereignty by virtue of occupation, but there being no need to exercise normal functions of government "occupation" becomes an equivocal term. It is bolstered by claims based on discovery, continuity, or contiguity.

Discovery is a self-explanatory concept, although who discovered what and when may raise difficult factual questions in determining historical priority. In addition, it is not easy to determine from a coastal landing the extent of the area discovered; for example, did Columbus discover the whole of North, Central, and South America? Hence discovery ordinarily supports at most a prior claim to something that will be determined later by acts of occupation. Discovery gives, so to speak, a first opportunity to settle and occupy some area. The claim may be bolstered by such acts as mapping and exploration, somewhat like the staking out of a mining claim. If, despite prior discovery, the area is in fact settled by others, the claim based on discovery will, at least after a period of time, give way to that based on effective occupation, either because occupation is a superior basis or simply by virtue of prescription.

Continuity is based on the idea that a continuous land mass forms the normal territorial basis for a state. Often "natural" factors set limits, particularly when they are obvious and carry a security connotation with regard to the area actually settled. Claims to the continental shelf, for example, were based on the idea of a continuous land mass projecting to the point of steep declination or, in some formulations, to the point where occupation (exploitation of the shelf itself) was no longer possible. Claims based on continuity may prevail so long as there are no other claimants to the area at the time. Most such problems simply become border problems where the oceans are not the delimiting line.

The third basis—contiguity—is similar to continuity, but is applicable to claims that the former will not support, usually coastal islands. The theory is that these are related to the larger land mass, even though outside territorial waters, either for reasons of security or simply because of nearness. As with continuity claims, which can and do run into similar claims of others, so, too, can islands be regarded as contiguous to more than one land mass. How close an island has to be to be regarded as contiguous is open to question; a claim based on contiguity will be subject to objection if too much of the high seas lies between the area being claimed and the area to which it is claimed to be contiguous. Both continuity and contiguity require the projection of certain boundaries into the area claimed, and it is clear that the lines of projection of more than one state may result in overlaps. Thus particular principles governing claims to territory, when applied, may give rise to inconsistent claims. This has in fact happened in the polar regions of Antarctica.

It should not require much reflection to see that geographical claims of this sort must depend to a large extent on the particular context. Claims based on security considerations must be viewed differently in the contemporary world from the way they were viewed in the "balance of power" period. Claims based on the possibility of economic exploitation might have been seen primarily as administrative problems until the more recent trends toward state monopoly added the new ingredient of direct state involvement. In the absence of settlement, nearness plays a seemingly relevant role for one in search of objectivity; so too, perhaps, does the age of the claim, the extent to which it has been consistently put forward, and so forth. But ideas of discovery, continuity, and contiguity cannot provide a consistent hierarchy of claims in all situations, and resolution will depend on a balancing of these claims with other criteria based on more specific contextual considerations.

There are, for example, quite relevant differences between claims to arctic as opposed to antarctic areas, though in both instances the claims are based largely on theories of continuity and contiguity (encompassing large areas of frozen ice and high seas) drawn in accordance with vector lines. In the Arctic, lines drawn in this fashion form reasonably clear boundaries because of the accident of land masses. Far more important is the fact that the Arctic is a bloc boundary between the Soviet Union and Canada (in particular) and thus the line takes on security connotations of first-rank importance. Any principle of division that is mutually satisfactory is likely to be durable, and serves the immediate purpose of avoiding potential incidents attributable to the flight of military aircraft in the Arctic.

The Antarctic does not carry such a security connotation, nor do vector claims seem to provide quite as handy a division. Here, a number of claimants assert sovereignty over parts of the Antarctic on theories of discovery, continuity, contiguity, and various acts of occupation (mapping, scientific exploration, and so forth). Present uses of the area are confined to scientific exploration, and these uses would not exclude other nations from exercising similar uses. Potentially there is some possibility of economic exploitation, but this, like permanent settlement, does not seem feasible in the foreseeable future. Under these circumstances there is little incentive to nonclaimants to acquiesce in any claims to sovereignty over parts of the area, for there is little need for any exercise of exclusive governmental authority.

The United States has, for some years, neither recognized claims of others nor put forward claims of its own, although it has reserved the right to do so. The Soviet Union has taken much the same position, insisting that it will recognize no settlement in which it does not play a role. Both countries somewhat tentatively and unofficially had suggested an international administration, directly or through UN Trusteeship arrangements, but this had been strongly opposed by Latin American claimants. The intensity of feeling that countries such as Argentina and Chile have regarding their claims to what, at the moment, are essentially wastelands cannot be explained on rational grounds; it is, perhaps, analogous to the pride of Texans in having had (until recently) the biggest state in the Union.

The United States is reluctant to acknowledge even the claims of its bloc partners, though these would be preferable to Soviet claims, partly because of the possibility that such nations might impose restraints on scientific experimentation within the areas. Nor does the U.S. wish to be a Solomon among its friends. Furthermore, the attitude of Latin Americans toward "conservation" of resources of the high seas has not encouraged confidence in the wisdom they would exercise in exploiting mineral resources of Antarctica. A dilution of unilateral control through some form of internationalization would be preferable, even though this would involve some Soviet participation in decisions.

The Soviet Union, for security reasons, can scarcely expect its potential claims to be acknowledged by other claimants. Nor is the Antarctic presently of major importance to the U.S.S.R. The Russians, because the area may raise some strategic questions, probably prefer a form of organization and administration that gives them a permanent voice in the control of the area to one that does not, and, hence, the Russians might be expected to accept international control. The recent twelve-nation treaty on the Antarctic, a treaty not yet ratified by the United States, provides for the non-militarization of the Antarctic by the signatory nations. The Soviet Union and the relevant Latin American states are parties to the agreement, which also provides that the signator nations will use the Antarctic only for peaceful scientific purposes. The treaty, which remains in force for thirty years, after which a signator may raise the question of modification of the treaty provisions, also provides that the signators will not make new or enlarge old territorial claims during the life of the treaty. The agreement, however, does not prejudice existing claims.

Space bodies raise rather different problems because of the possible higher military potential. Conceivably, if either the United States or the Soviet Union gets a long-term head start on inter-planetary flight, it may be in a position to dominate moon settlement and to establish bases which at some future time might permit earth hegemony. Although present technology does not lend credence to—and indeed tends to discredit—such a fear, rapid technological innovation is a feature of our time. Fear of the potential consequences of the attempt to establish military bases on the moon might itself be sufficient to generate considerable unrest on earth. The risks and uncertainties involved might well persuade the United States and the Soviet Union to agree to international colonization of the moon without military advantage. The problem of mineral rights is hardly likely to be a serious one, because of the costs of transportation. The moon is not likely to prove important as a base for interplanetary flights for quite some time, but, if and when this problem does become relevant, international bases could probably service the space fleets of all nations in a satisfactory fashion.

In other areas (such as Greenland) the lack of the exercise of significant effective authority has been mitigated by the fact that little human settlement occurred within the areas under question. Therefore, claims have been acknowledged despite very limited occupation. In addition, it has often been recognized that the security of the area may depend upon the control of adjacent territory. Some leeway therefore has usually been given in determining the geographic extent of claims. On the moon, however, it is unlikely that even consistent stationing of men over a large uninhabited area will be sufficient to establish a claim to the whole area, if the moon is of great strategic importance to both sides. Undoubtedly, the attempts to establish counter-claims will be based upon some putative legal principle, for instance, establishment of some bases in the same area. But, in the final analysis, the matter will rest on the fact that no principle that fails to provide for the security of the major blocs can gain sufficient support to be accepted. The easiest method of overriding dangerous national claims will rest on the assertion of an international interest or, what is much the same thing, the assertion that the moon is the common possession of all. A similar solution for Antarctica in this respect might be useful precedent.

Legal doctrine based upon discovery, occupation, contiguity, and continuity is not irrelevant to the solution of claims to polar areas or space bodies, even though clearly less relevant than in the past; indeed, some form of occupation may be decisive. These principles will form the bases for various national claims, as they have in the past, and hence are important to those who wish to justify claims, or, as in the case of both the United States and Russia in Antarctica, as a tactic for refuting claims by others. The almost impossibly difficult job of agreeing to any national division, or the absence of any real need for the exercise of national control in the areas, join with the potentially high costs of disagreement, to argue for non-militarization and for a form of international administration. This solution, of course, is a direct and obvious reflection of the changed political structure of the world. In the nineteenth century there was, in reality, no alternative to division of areas among existing nations— for example, the African settlement—for the division of an area into spheres of influence helped to stabilize the "balance of power," while, in the present age, national exploitation might unstabilize the currently tenuous bipolarity.

Colonial administration. Claims to exercise sovereignty over territory have not always been claims to contiguous areas to be incorporated within the territory of the claimant state. States have also claimed full sovereignty over areas widely separated geographically. Natives of colonial areas were not usually given full rights of citizenship, and (with rare exceptions) such areas have not been formally incorporated within the territory of the claimant state. The claimant state has generally established a special system of law administration, sometimes permitting a considerable latitude to native leaders to administer native law, but exercising a general control and supervision over the processes of internal government as well as, of course, over foreign affairs.

Since the claims to formal authority over colonial areas were usually claims to sovereignty, there is no reason to distinguish this situation legally from other territorial claims. Sometimes the word "sovereignty" was avoided and broad claims to "jurisdiction and control" (or similar language) substituted. Whichever verbal formula was used, it was true that whatever local autonomy existed was granted by the colonial power and the residue of formal authority remained with it. The authority of native princes or tribal leaders was, therefore, limited to what was authorized by the colonial power.

Typically, within the "balance of power" period, a state did not permit another state to exercise any governmental functions within its territory, but insisted on a monopoly of local law administration. At the other end of the spectrum was the wholly dependent area, in which all the functions of government were exercised by a foreign state. In this case, local authorities possessed limited jurisdiction, the colonial power sovereignty. But the broader the area of formal authority that was granted or acquiesced in by the colonial power claiming sovereignty, the closer the dependent area came to a functional independence. We could as easily begin by reversing the granting concept. We would arrive functionally at the same result, if we imagined that the sovereign were to grant a foreign state extremely broad authority to perform governmental functions within the area or to represent the area with regard to external participants. Just as the dependent area could approach actual independence, so could the formally sovereign state approach a factually dependent status.

The treaty between Panama and the United States with regard to the Panama Canal Zone, for instance, provides that Panama grants to the United States in perpetuity the right to maintain and operate the Canal, and, within the specified area, grants the United States all the rights it would have if sovereign. The language implies that

Panama remains sovereign, but that the United States enjoys, in perpetuity, all the rights of sovereignty.

NON-SOVEREIGN TERRITORIAL JURISDICTION

Mandates and trusteeships. During the First World War, a number of proposals looked toward some form of international administration of colonial areas not yet ready for self-government. Anti-colonial forces among the Allies pressed for internationalization of areas previously subject to German hegemony, and Wilson added his powerful voice to such efforts. Direct international administration did not, however, appear plausible, and it was thought preferable to concentrate administrative responsibility in one state while providing some form of international supervision under the auspices of the League of Nations. Arguments to this effect were reinforced by studies of older attempts at joint administration, particularly the Condominium, where two or three states had attempted, as in the Sudan, Samoa, and the Hebrides, to share administrative responsibility. Such experiments, as might have been expected in the "balance of power" system, were notoriously unsuccessful. Their principal advantage was that they scrupulously avoided locating sovereignty anywhere, thus, according to Lord Cromer, creating a "hybrid State eminently calculated to shock the susceptibilities of international jurists." Rivalries among the administrating states, different currencies, taxes, schools, budgets, languages, laws, and so forth, increased discord among the administering officials while scarcely serving the interests of natives. Such areas were usually those in which there had existed historical rivalries, and the Condominium simply, *faute de mieux*, formalized and perpetuated them as an attempt to preserve the status quo.

For these reasons there was considerable scepticism about any form of joint international administration over former German colonies in 1919, and it was felt that the older form of a Protectorate with international authorization and supervision had more prospects of success; in 1919, supranational authority did not exist, and the fiasco of "international administration" (meaning administration by two or three states) was to be avoided. Hence former German colonies were divided up among the Allies; an "advanced" nation, the Mandatory, was to provide the necessary "tutelage" in areas not yet ready for self-government. In the case of the old Turkish Empire, the territories were considered as having reached the stage at which they could be regarded as potential independent nations subject merely to administrative advice and assistance until they could stand alone. Other peoples, especially those of Central Africa, were considered to be at such a stage that the Mandatory would have to perform the functions of government, with the proviso that the natives were not to be armed except for internal police purposes, and that all members of the League were to have equal opportunities for trade and commerce within the area. Finally, some territories in Southwest Africa and some South Pacific islands were so sparsely inhabited that they could be best managed as part of the integral territory of the mandatory state.

Thus, conditions of mandates were laid down in various terms, and the League created a permanent Commission to receive reports from the Mandatories and make recommendations to the League Council. But the Commission lacked ability to compel the Mandatories to do anything, and could not even investigate conditions, if the Mandatory objected to such investigation. There were no substantial differences in fact between League obligations under a mandate and the way in which England and, to some extent, France handled their colonial empires; legally, the Mandatory had an international responsibility not acknowledged in a colonial system. Sovereignty was not in the Mandatory, who exercised governmental authority under the Covenant, but that made little practical difference except, perhaps, that it prevented a relapse into a formal colonialism and thus kept alive the idea and hope of eventual self-government as a matter of legal right.

Roosevelt shared with Wilson a conviction against colonial administration, and was with some difficulty convinced not to press formally for dissolution of the British, French, Belgian, and Dutch empires. The Draft Charter prepared at Dumbarton Oaks was silent on this subject; at San Francisco, anti-colonial feelings were expressed in the trusteeship proposals of the Declaration Regarding Non-Self-Governing Territories. Under the United Nations system, the General Assembly exercises supervision over the governance of trust territories except when they are designated as "strategic," in which case the Security Council exercises supervision subject to the veto. Some Pacific islands seized from Japan by the United States during the Second World War have been placed in this category, thus avoiding annexation, which is particularly distasteful to the American public. The General Assembly and the Security Council have the assistance of a Trusteeship Council which replaces the Mandates Commission of the League of Nations. The Council has powers to investigate and hear complaints without consent of the Trustee state.

The trust territories of the United Nations include the mandates of the League, territories removed from the jurisdiction of the defeated Axis nations, and territories voluntarily placed under the trusteeship system. The last category is still unused, perhaps because former colonial areas have passed directly, and quickly, into independence. On the other hand, all League Mandates, except Southwest Africa, have been placed within the Trusteeship system. As of late 1960, only three African Mandates have not become independent states.

The system remains essentially a voluntary one under the United Nations as it was under the League but, as already mentioned, the UN system places certain powers in the hands of the Council which insure that international attention can be focussed on problems in Trust Territories. The Council can investigate, and on many occasions natives have been brought to New York to testify about conditions. Publicity and moral suasion have been quite successful because of the practical influence of the ex-colonial nations (and the desire, for instance, of Great Britain to satisfy ex-colonial members of the British Commonwealth such as India), and because of the self-restraint of the administering Authorities who, on the whole, subscribe to the belief in self-rule and feel constrained to create conditions that make self-rule possible.

Leased areas. Competition among the European nations for control of colonies became more acute as the industrial base of modern society became clearer, and as new areas of the world were opened up to extensive trade and commerce. Efforts to arrive at agreement with regard to potentially important areas not easily subject to conquest sometimes took the form of "spheres of influence," as in China. These were agreements among the European states to which China itself was not a party. They were accompanied and consolidated, however, by a number of "leases" between European states and China, whereby the European states coerced acquiescence in a number of commercial, judicial, and, more exceptionally, "territorial" rights to such cities as Kiaochow (Germany), Port Arthur (Russia), and Kuang-chow Wan (France). In these cities, the "lessee" had virtually unlimited authority, administering the city with the same powers it would have within its own territory, but acknowledging nominal ownership, or sovereignty, in the lessor. Kiaochow and

Kuang-chow Wan were restored to China in 1922, and Port Arthur to Communist China in 1952.

Similar arrangements in Panama were made in connection with the Canal Zone, and earlier forced arrangements of a similar nature were imposed by the great European nations upon Turkey in the nineteenth century. For example, the Berlin Congress of 1878 gave Austro-Hungary complete jurisdiction over Bosnia and Herzegovina, but left sovereignty in Turkey. Except for the Canal Zone, however, such broad grants of jurisdiction to a foreign states are things of the past, and, in the future, any analogous arrangements are more likely to have a supranational character.

In contrast to these earlier leases are the military bases leased to the United States by the United Kingdom in 1941 for a period of ninety-nine years. In the area of these bases, and others negotiated for lesser periods in Africa and Europe since the Second World War, the United States has exercised a more modest and limited jurisdiction tailored to the problems of security and discipline involved in military operations, but including little authority over nationals of the leasing state. Sovereignty over the area is explicitly stated to remain in the leasing state, though the extent to which officials of that state can exercise authority within the base area is limited, and arrangements for the lessee's turning over persons who have committed offenses against the laws of the lessor is provided in the applicable treaties.

"Extra-territorial" rights. The final method of exercising jurisdiction in the territory of another, unaccompanied by any claim of sovereignty, was that of the consular courts until their general abolition, and today (though usually in connection with bases) of military authorities with regard to military personnel. As in the case of leased areas, the consular courts were imposed upon foreign states whose law was thought to be uncivilized and unsuitable for dealing with commercial matters or with the criminal prosecution of Europeans. China, Japan, and Morocco are examples. A controversy to which a European was a party was tried by consular and not by local authorities. With regard to limited categories of offenses military authorities today have a similar, though more restricted, competence. In both instances it involves a limitation upon the jurisdiction of the "host" state and the exercise of a limited governmental authority by a foreign state within territory claimed by another.

Conclusion. Major rights of a foreign nation in territory are bound to collapse if a strong state emerges within the territory. In the "balance of power" period, extra-territorial rights in Japan were given up when Japan was ready to play a full role in the system. It was desirable from the standpoint of all states to permit this, for it gave greater stability to the system. For Great Britain in particular, it meant that Japan could emerge as a counter-weight to Russian expansion into China. China, as distinguished from Japan, was a weak nation incapable of participating effectively in international politics or of helping to stabilize the "balance of power" system. Extra-territoriality was not sufficient to protect Western interests. The danger that a particular nation might establish hegemony over China was present. The leases established rights that protected against such individual hegemony, and had the additional function of preventing native interference with international commerce.

In the loose bipolar system, flexibility of alignment is out of the question. The United States and the Soviet Union are in opposed blocs. The minimum degree of agreement required for a division of the spoils is lacking; moreover, the Soviet Union has a direct interest in instability. Since, for the most part, colonies are held by Western European nations allied with the United States, the Soviet Union has a direct interest in supporting claims to independence. The United States finds it difficult to support or to oppose these claims, although, in the end, it will probably have to support them. The net result, therefore, must be the elimination of the colonial system. As of the date of editing (early November 1960) it appears that a resolution advocating independence for all colonies will be adopted by the UN General Assembly.

The same is true, in all probability, of lease arrangements, except perhaps with a bloc member whose goals are the same and where the jurisdiction exercised is narrowly limited to what is reasonably necessary. In the emerging new nations, such leases, because of their military nature and because of resentment against foreign interference generally, are unlikely to stand up for long periods. The United States is already vacating its costly Moroccan air and naval complex; and it seems quite probable that the conditions under which the United States holds the Panama Canal Zone will have to be considerably modified in the near future.

There are other reasons why territorial rights in foreign states are unlikely to be important in the future. Law administration can be organized along either territorial or functional lines. As problems of interdependence arising out of contemporary technology make geographic boundaries and the geographical organization of authority more and more clumsy, it seems probable that internationally, as domestically, we will turn more and more to a system of law administration that emphasizes function and purpose; that is, to the creation of functional agencies with limited power to prescribe and enforce rules related to defined objectives.   In the United States this is apparent with regard to federal agencies, regional school authorities, sewage commissions, or fire departments.   Internationally, we see the same development in the Specialized Agencies of the United Nations, of the European Community, and of Customs Unions.   The problem of territorial sovereignty may be transcended by slicing international problems functionally, and assigning roles to supranational and intergovernmental agencies whose formal authority is derived not from any control over territory but from their capacity to deal with particular problems.

7

JURISDICTION

The terms "sovereignty" and "jurisdiction" are related, often interchangeable, but not identical. Jurisdiction refers to the competence of various officials to prescribe and enforce rules with regard to particular persons and events. Such jurisdiction may be a claim to exclusive authority, or it may be concurrent with, or even subordinate to, the authority of other decision-makers. Jurisdiction may be derived from sovereignty. But a state official may exercise authority of a more limited nature without making a claim to sovereignty over the area involved. For example, no state has sovereignty over the high seas, but a state may exercise a limited authority over persons within the area, or with regard to events taking place there.

"Territorial jurisdiction" exists with regard to all persons, property, and events within the state. Exceptionally, such authority[1] may be extended beyond territorial boundaries of the specified state, by agreement with other states, by being implied from custom, or by being made explicit through treaty, and, similarly, such authority may be curtailed within territory by the same process. In addition, a state has jurisdiction over its nationals, and may prescribe policy with regard to such persons, wherever they may be. Since nationals of one state may be within the territory of another, "personal" jurisdiction is concurrent with, or (in the view of other authorities) subordinate to, "territorial" jurisdiction.

A little reflection will indicate that it is not easy to relate formal authority to territory in any comprehensive way. Within the world community methods of policy prescription are territorially organized within a framework of separate sovereignties. But the values that states seek to achieve jointly and severally, as well as the means of

---

[1] This should not be regarded as a contradiction of Hohfeld's contention that jurisdiction over property is really jurisdiction over persons with respect to the use of property.

achievement, are not so easily related to geography. People and wealth move across state lines with relative ease. It is this latter fact that is one source of difficulty. Another is that persons may commit acts outside a particular territory, but such acts may still have important effects on the distribution of values among persons within the territory.

In what respect is the authority of officials related to territory? Are legislators empowered to prescribe only with regard to acts or events that, in some sense, take place within the state's territory? If so, there is considerable difficulty in determining when a complex event occurs "within" geographical limits. Assume, for example, that there is a world-wide cartel to restrict production, pool patents, and control prices of radios; what states have jurisdiction to punish what participants for what acts taking place where? But, even if we ignore this difficulty, how can we determine whether a prescription can be enforced against persons who have, since the relevant acts, left the state for another; what officials, applying what rules are responsible for such enforcement? Is, for example, the competence of judges to adjudicate a controversy related to the fact that the relevant events took place within the territory? Or is the competence of judges related to the fact that the court has control, either over a defendant or over sufficient property belonging to him, to make its judgment effective—in this case, because he or his property is within the state's territory? Or may the court render a judgment even though the defendant is not himself within the territory and has not any property within the territory, in the hope of later vindication should the defendant come within territorial limits? Does competence based upon territorial sovereignty refer to the time of the relevant acts, to the time of adjudication, or to the time of enforcement? If it is the former, how is it made effective? If it is the latter, what standards are used? And, finally, we must remember that a decision made effective through control exercised over persons and property within territorial limits can remain effective only if undisturbed by other states with comparable power at the time or at some future time.

In point of fact all these considerations have some relevance. In terms of law enforcement, it is quite accurate to measure official authority with regard to geography. With minor exceptions, a state official cannot seize persons or property not physically present within state territory. In this respect, legal process is "territorial," and it is possible to say with Justice Holmes that the "foundation of jurisdiction is physical power." It is also true that courts are reluctant to render judgment in the absence of the defendant, or at least his property, for the reason that it will not be effective unless a foreign state enforces it; and, in the absence of treaty, the foreign state is unlikely to do this. In addition, there are considerations of fairness as to the place of trial (venue) that are difficult to resolve in the absence of one of the parties. Therefore, Anglo-American courts have tended to conceive judicial jurisdiction in terms of their capacity to enforce a judgment against the defendant. Finally, it is also true that states are primarily interested in conduct that directly affects persons and property within their borders, and that, as a result, most laws envision events taking place within the territory rather than abroad. This idea—sometimes called "legislative jurisdiction"—also has a territorial connection, although, as we shall see, the connection is often difficult to specify.

To relate law to physical power over persons and property within territorial limits is, however, to employ a misleading point of departure. This relationship of law to physical power rests, in part, upon the truism that the effectiveness of any prescription ultimately depends upon power to coerce compliance, and, in part, upon the importance of preserving self-determination in the exercise of local rule. The relationship cannot, therefore, be ignored. But to the particular decision maker, possession of physical power does not determine appropriate policy, the wisdom of its exercise, or the substantive rules to be applied (domestic or foreign) as the guide to decision. The policy so formulated is, of course, one related to problems of the larger community—such problems as: the fact that there exist (generally) only national courts to decide disputes involving interstate facts and policies, the fact that policy prescription and administration are geographically organized, the fact that various types of political power are shared.

These are problems of both private and public international law. The distinction between the two categories is not altogether clear, and there is considerable overlap. Officials of a foreign state cannot sue in local courts to enforce their laws with regard to events over which they claim legislative jurisdiction, and local officials will not do so for them unless authorized by local legislation; such authorization, generally speaking, would arise only as a result of treaty arrangements granting reciprocal rights and duties. At the same time, foreigners have long been entitled to access to national courts and to impartial justice in the prosecution of their cause. As defendants, too, they are entitled to all the protection that would be accorded nationals. Indeed, trade and commerce would be virtually impossible otherwise. But in transnational situations the unfairness and impracticality of courts adjudicating disputes in terms of local standards and rules of law is obvious. In adjudicating such matters, the judiciaries of all countries adopted the practice of selecting applicable rules from foreign legal systems as well as from their own. Such a practice came quite easily in early times as being merely an application of a common law of nations.

Use of foreign law by local judges raises no great problems if the substantive rules are viewed in universal terms, are widely shared, and are derived from custom and from voluntary acts. Neither courts of admiralty, administering a common law of the sea, nor the courts administering the law merchant, were consciously concerned with more than variations of custom; the same was true of civil courts administering a common law derived from Rome. But as we move away from substantive universals and obligations voluntarily assumed or conceded to those imposed by community fiat for the realization of group values, the "due process" problem takes on added dimension and difficulty. Positive law as the conceptual source of rights poses immediately the question of whose positive law is to be used, and leads to a jurisdictional approach; that is, to an allocation of competence to prescribe. Then, too, as rules are conceived as expressions of sovereign policies rather than individual rights derived from nature or reason, a political element enters the conscious appraisal of doctrine. It is one thing to argue that a court should adopt a foreign rule of decision as its own because fairness or justice demands such adoption; it is quite another to do so simply because another state has prescribed a particular result. The requirements of justice and foreign prescriptions may often equate, but not necessarily. Problems as to the scope of judicial discretion arise.

As soon as a foreign prescription involves a departure from customary and widely shared standards, it begins to present a problem of foreign policy—a "political question"—for local courts, and such courts have traditionally sought techniques and doctrine for reducing the possibilities of political involvement. Common-law courts have, therefore, refused to enforce claims based on foreign penal, political, or revenue laws; civil-law courts have reached approximately the same result by refusing to give effect to foreign *ordre public*. As to such laws, courts in all countries have sought political guidance from other branches of the local government.

PRIVATE INTERNATIONAL LAW

In the field of private international law, or the conflict of laws, what were once conceived as universal rights, based on the law of nations, became nationalized towards the middle of the nineteenth century. As already indicated, this resulted from increased amounts of national legislation replacing customary law, from positivist theory, and from the general aura of nationalism which pervaded thought. In addition, it became increasingly obvious that, despite a good deal of universal doctrine, there were marginal variations in the way controversies were decided—that the same choice of applicable law was not always made by judges sitting in different countries.

Efforts to maintain a maximum amount of uniformity in the rules applied usually took the form of determining which state had "legislative jurisdiction" over the relevant events, and often this involved references to the "territoriality of legislation." At the same time, national courts wished to preserve the integrity of their views as to the proper foreign law to apply, and, therefore, they said that rules as to choice of law were, like all the rules they as national officials applied, of national origin. This has caused considerable semantic confusion.

Concepts of territorial sovereignty breed theories of territorial law —jejune notions of an omnipresence that cannot brood more than three miles from home. The territoriality of law can be used to explain why the forum always applies its own law, and, equally well, to explain why it applies foreign law. It is simply a question of where we get on the merry-go-round and where we get off; which sovereign we are talking about, and what we do mean by "law." European thinking has traditionally been oriented from the viewpoint of the sovereign whose legislative rules ought (in someone's opinion) to apply; it claims, therefore, for this law an extra-territorial effect—extra-territorial in the sense that it will be applied by states other than the one that enacts it. Anglo-American practice, on the other hand, has always started at the other end of the spectrum —in terms of the decision maker adjudicating a dispute. Foreign law can have no effect within his territory because law is territorial— national judges apply only national law. The practical results, of course, may well be the same under either approach.

A rational approach to such problems would be premised on the thought that each state should use the means available to it to make its policy effective in and with regard to the international community.

Doing so requires invoking principles that are at least potentially persuasive as international precedent for other decision makers, and that, therefore, take cognizance of the policies of other states. If they are to fulfill their function as stabilizing forces in the world community, decisions involving international facts should urge and imply reciprocity on like terms. The objective of each state should be to make effective the compatible policies of all. To a considerable extent this objective is at least pursued within the area of "private law" by using foreign law as a guide to local decision. Thus an American court may well decide that rules enacted by a foreign state having "jurisdiction" over the events should be applied by the court in arriving at a judgment. Often, however, the foreign law applied is selected through a mechanical application of choice of law rules rather than through a discriminating clarification of underlying goals and the correlation of facts with the policies of the various states involved. Presumably a local decision maker should think directly in terms of foreign claims to regulate the consequences of particular events, and should refuse recognition only if the claims run counter to the forum's conception of due process (fundamental fairness) or to its public policy, or to the co-equal claims of another state to regulate the same events.

It would be pointless to ignore local power or the valid policy of self-determination it encompasses; Holmes' aphorism is scarcely as "factually unsupported and functionally unsupportable" as some would have it. To ignore it would be to ignore the final determinant of whose policy, and therefore what policy, prevails. To that extent, Holmes, in company with Story, was on solid, if self-evident, ground. But equating jurisdiction and power in this sense neither refutes nor even takes issue with those who insist that law is cast in more purposeful terms. Of course it is, and rightly so; each sovereign uses its capability to make effective what it conceives to be appropriate policy, and over a wide area there is agreement or, at least, tolerance. So long as formal authority is organized and administered territorially, there is a mutual and reciprocal interest—in the words of Justice Story: a "sense of the inconveniences which would otherwise result"—in extending areas of tolerance. The strongest case, of course, is presented by the executed judgment or decree—the exercise of territorial power-in-fact by a foreign official. Whether courts concede the "jurisdiction" of the foreign sovereign or refer directly to the Act of State doctrine (which provides that, without political guidance, courts will not redress wrongs based on the acts of foreign officials), plaintiffs are normally relegated to diplomatic channels for redress. Thus where a sovereign possesses and exercises physical power over persons, his competency to do so will rarely be questioned in courts abroad.

Judicial equation of jurisdiction with power to enforce a prescription within territorial limits is, then, less an endorsement of principle than an acceptance of fact. It merely recognizes the realities; the deficiencies of a legal system involving multiple decision makers, limited power and differing doctrine; and the circumspect role of judges in resolving political problems. It need not be sanctified as principle and, in fact, a different result may well obtain for prescriptions unreduced to *faits accomplis*. There may be much policy cross-reference—*res judicata*, deference to the views of other sovereigns, and awareness of possible political complications. But these considerations are less strongly felt where the complication of territorial sovereignty is removed. Legislative or judicial acts designed to regulate events or persons not within local territory stand on a lesser footing in the international community.

It scarcely requires argument that physical power over the defendant, or his property, is indefensible as the exclusive criterion of either legislative or judicial jurisdiction. No one seriously asserts otherwise. Venue in all countries is linked with fairness and convenience, most often measured by domicile or residence, the place of relevant acts or events or property, or prior agreement. The application of legislation to persons or events is, like all rules, a function of its purpose, limited only by the due process principle that the defendant should have had fair opportunity to apprise himself of its potential application, and the legislative claims of other sovereigns to regulate differently the same events. Ultimately, of course, enforcement depends upon the views of a sovereign with the capability of enforcing his decisions. But there is no reason to invert a political limitation into a legal principle.

There is general agreement that a state is primarily interested in events that affect its own safety, public order, and the integrity of its social system; that is, the distribution of values among those who, by virtue of citizenship or residence, identify themselves with a particular community and seek the protection of its laws. As the impact upon values of this national community becomes more remote, the public interest is less and the area of tolerance for divergent rules correspondingly increases.

A claim for the application of personal or territorial law involves matters of sovereign concern. Relationships among its own nationals or residents, particularly continuing relationships, such as marriage and employment, may be of importance to the sovereign irrespective of where the relevant events occur. Similarly, if the conduct of others affects local values, the state may seek to subject such conduct to its standards. A state may or may not be concerned with acts of its citizens abroad. In terms of its impact upon local values, the place of occurrence of relevant events may or may not have significance. In the absence of a specific prescription embodying a definable policy it is not possible to determine abstractly the scope of statutory or customary law with regard to either persons or events.

The claims of a sovereign to control the conduct of its citizens are, in due process terms, somewhat broader than the claims it can fairly make with regard to others. There are obligations imposed upon nationals and residents that can only be imposed on foreigners in more limited fact circumstances. An obligation to pay taxes, for example, cannot fairly be found against non-residents except with regard to local transactions. The same is true of an obligation to defend in local courts. And a general familiarity with legal standards of a state's national law may permit that sovereign to extend the prescriptions of its national law to foreign acts by nationals, when its policy is served by doing so, more freely than would be reasonably possible in the case of those whose contact with the standards involved is insubstantial.

Where a sovereign possesses the means to enforce its judgments, its jurisdiction is unlikely to be questioned elsewhere. But the fact of physical power does not legitimize the exercise of such power, particularly if the claim is based on foreign rules and if the venue is an inconvenient one. If the forum refuses effect to foreign judgments unless executed abroad, there is a pressure to sue only where power in fact is present. This practice may protect citizens against foreign law and foreign judicial procedures, but, since other states are likely to reciprocate, it does so at the price of sacrificing local claims against foreigners. Furthermore, as the movement of people, the conduct of business and the dispersal of wealth become increasingly interstate, power over these elements is more widely shared. It is therefore to the interest of all states to formulate reasonable criteria of proper place of trial without regard to the existence of physical power to enforce.

If we could hypothesize uniform principles and standards of judicial administration, the policy issues with regard to both claims and concessions to render effective judgments would be drawn exclusively in terms of fair notice and reasonable venue. Indeed, even with the possibility of different rules and methods of fact finding and trial, procedural uniformity would seem more important than achieving substantive uniformity. When called upon to enforce a foreign judgment, a state can always cast out decisions that offend its sense of justice. The standards of what constitutes fair notice are relatively easy to formulate and are, in fact, widely shared. Venue is more difficult, unless states were to agree that defendant has an obligation to appear wherever venue is *prima facie* reasonable—for example, any state where connection with the events is sufficiently evident to make possible the application of its law. Such a principle, spurred by the ease of modern travel, has been slowly evolving, but it requires a counter-principle or practice that will cause dismissal if venue is in fact unfair. Although this result has been virtually arrived at in the United States, the counter-principle has not expressly appeared in other countries.

The "Territoriality" of Public Law

It was noted earlier that courts will not, without legislative guidance, give effect to foreign prescriptions that involve public order, fiscal or revenue policy, or other "political" matters. The line between "private" and "public" law, however difficult to draw in practice, has these considerations in mind. Appropriate arrangements can be arrived at by a process of diplomatic negotiation and results may be embodied in formal treaties. But courts will not on their own initiative create reciprocal rules within this area, and foreign officials may not prosecute governmental policy in local courts.

The classic examples of public law are rules concerned with the prosecution and punishment of acts regarded as criminal. Since no "extra-territorial" effect is given to criminal statutes in the sense that local courts will not apply foreign rules, each state punishes only acts that are criminal under its own legislation. There is no choice-of-law problem as such, though it is entirely possible for the same acts to constitute a crime by the law of more than one state. Territoriality in its other meaning also comes into the doctrine, primarily because statutes have generally been drafted, or interpreted by courts, to be applicable only to offenses occurring within the territory of the state involved—that is, where at least some of the acts constituting the crime, or closely related to it, took place within the geographical boundaries of the sovereign. According to common law venue was laid at the "place" of the crime, and as in private law matters, venue merged into jurisdiction and joined forces with sovereignty. In civil law, laws relating to the *ordre public* were from the outset classified as "territorial," and thus were not entitled to extraterritorial enforcement by other states.

Since crimes in both law-systems were considered offenses against the sovereign, there was a conceptual barrier to considering, for example, a murder taking place in State *A*, as an offense against State *B*. This idea was inverted and given positive expression by saying that, because each state was sovereign within its territory, no other state could punish conduct occurring there without derogating from, and thereby offending, the sovereignty of the territorial state. The time-honored exception, and transparent theoretical inconsistency, is the competency of a state to punish its own nationals for acts committed abroad. This latter "jurisdiction" is widely regarded as subsidiary to that of the *lex loci,* though some consider it concurrent, and a few, if we may judge from their refusal to extradite nationals without any obligation to prosecute locally (though claiming nonetheless the right to try foreigners for crimes committed in their territory), still pursue a policy of catch-as-catch-can.

Obviously, as in the case of conflicts doctrine, the key to territoriality lies in defining the connecting link. Since the purpose of criminal prosecution is principally protective, and, since states have been almost unbelievably provincial and backward with regard to international assistance in criminal prosecution, there has been a good deal of cheating around the edges in terms of a state's extending its competency in order to meet the problems of rapid communication, transportation and resultant interdependency. The fetish for a territorial link, coupled with common law and constitutional venue and jury requirements, has led to attempts to maintain the fiction that each state punishes only crimes committed locally.

Statutes have, however, provided for local punishment, if any of the acts or omissions connected with a crime, although not in themselves doctrinally significant, have been committed locally. This has been bolstered by other statutes redefining "crimes" and creating new ones to provide a geographical point of reference, however slight, within the boundaries. Conspiracy and attempt doctrine and principal-accessory concepts have also been used to reach far abroad. Only occasionally has ingenuity failed when there was pressure to find a territorial act, and in these cases, such as counterfeiting and in offenses against state security, the protective principle has been frankly espoused, and the need for a territorial connection abandoned.

Some maintain that a state has competency to try anyone for an offense against its nationals (or their property) under its own law, even though they were located outside the state at the time of the crime. This view, however, has been severely criticized as too extreme. The criticism usually is based on the assumption that the acts were not criminal where committed. It could also be argued that trial may put too heavy a burden on the defendant in terms of producing witnesses.

The result of these expansions of jurisdiction through redefinition of both crime and its locus has been to make more than one law applicable to many offenses, a situation clearly in conflict with the theories of exclusive territorial sovereignty and equally at odds with the belief that one law must govern all legal relationships. Criminal statutes have not attempted to disguise the tenuous connection with territoriality. Virtually any act or omission within a state is sufficient if there is an intent to commit a crime somewhere; the converse of this "subjective territoriality" is "objective territoriality," which admits the competence of a state to punish a person who, though all his acts are outside the territorial limits, "willfully puts in motion a force to take effect in it." The latter is distinguishable from an unqualified protective approach and also from the so-called passive personality theory, which would by local criteria of crime and local trial try foreigners for criminal acts against nationals even though such acts may be committed abroad, but it is nonetheless a formula capable of considerable expansion. Lack of clarity is inevitable so long as the theory is phrased in terms that, though strained, seek to give it a territorial flavor by using fictions that confuse physical acts within the state with the consequences of the proscribed conduct, and that indiscriminately merge considerations of venue, notice, and legislative policy.

We may concede without argument that the limits of power are territorial, with only narrow exceptions, at the level of administration. Effective prevention of and punishment for crime depends upon being able to lay hands on the alleged culprit. There is, too, general agreement that a state is primarily interested in the punishment of acts or omissions which directly affect its own security, that of persons and property within its boundaries, or that of its citizens, domiciliaries or residents. We could, however, reasonably maintain that there is a common interest in punishing "crime" irrespective of where it takes place, at least to the extent that there is agreement on what acts are "criminal," what is reasonable punishment, and what constitutes fair procedure. The policy that crimes committed in one state are of no concern to others is a short-sighted and self-defeating one that, in the absence of treaty arrangements, results only in harboring and protecting criminals. Fortunately the pressure of mutual interest led to a rash of extradition treaties after 1850. Some provincialism remains with regard to extradition of nationals, but by and large states are now willing, on a reciprocal basis, to aid a foreign state to secure the person of the accused when the acts would be regarded as criminal by substantive domestic standards.

A "universalist" view with regard to acts or omissions generally regarded as criminal would permit prosecution wherever the offender could be brought into custody. The failure to take this position can be explained rationally and supported by the difficulties of procuring and presenting evidence at a distance from the place of the alleged acts, and by the consequent unfairness to the defendant. The refusal to extradite, in the absence of reciprocal treaty obligations, is more difficult to justify, but can be explained partly by the protection customarily thrown around the use of public power in criminal cases and the judicial requirement for explicit authority to deprive an individual of freedom. The almost entirely accepted practice of not extraditing for acts not locally considered crimes is similarly explicable. In addition, it is probably desirable to reserve judgment with regard to alleged crimes, the definitions of which might conceivably offend the extraditing state's sense of justice.

Insofar as extradition treaties and practices exhibit a general willingness to use local power in aid of prosecuting common crimes, we could say with some accuracy that, given substantive limits, the problem is simply one of venue. The common interest in criminal prosecution has to this extent superseded jealousies founded on sovereignty and the irrational position that crimes committed in one state are of no concern to others. Viewed in this light, criminal prosecution shows similarity to conflicts doctrine with the difference that selecting a fair and convenient forum is particularly important. The failure to extend extradition to the full length of a foreign state's claims is not unlike the occasional refusal to apply foreign law in private controversies, and similarly is based on the public policy of the forum. In criminal matters, however, the public policy is placed beyond the power of the judiciary to determine, and extradition treaties, consistently with customary principles of specificity in criminal cases, set quite narrow limits upon judicial discretion.

The continual reaching out, or "self-help," in criminal jurisdiction results partly from the failure to devise efficient methods of administrative assistance across international boundaries in terms of both prosecution and investigation, partly from the desire to extend the state's policy as far as possible. To the extent that the conduct itself is commonly considered criminal, jurisdiction amounts to no more than broadened venue and is objectionable only insofar as it might, on particular facts, put an unfair burden on the defendant in terms of securing evidence, or possibly, be a less efficient place to prosecute for the same reason. By thus allocating responsibility on a multi-state basis when the criminal conduct has more than local relevance, the general level of law enforcement is raised and, we might hope, the groundwork is laid for future administrative cooperation.

Since each state has, by its own law, an interest in prosecution, exchange of evidence and cooperative investigation is encouraged. The criminal, wherever prosecuted, is protected by the almost universal acceptance of double-jeopardy, or *non bis in idem*, doctrine. It is worth noting that there is no insistence that one law govern criminal conduct, and, for extradiction purposes, variations in details of punishment prescribed, or of conduct considered criminal, are unimportant if substantial equivalency exists.

Where the conduct is not universally proscribed, different policies are present. One policy involves the fairness of subjecting defendant to punishment in accordance with prescriptions not within his reasonable foresight at the time of acting. Although *mens rea* is not a necessary ingredient of crime, there is a widely shared belief that in its absence there ought to be quite clear notice that the activity in question is prohibited—the clarity of the notice varying directly with accepted ideas of individual morality and with the harshness of the punishment. Here, territoriality may serve a real and useful function, since physical contact with a foreign state constitutes at least some notice of its laws and customs.

An individual traveling abroad is conscious of an obligation to obey local laws, and he generally knows that they may differ somewhat from those to which he is accustomed. A business enterprise is perhaps even more aware of potential prescriptions with regard to "business done" in a foreign country, at least where such business is more than incidental. Particularly is this true where the conduct is proscribed by many states, although perhaps not all, thereby increasing general awareness of areas of potentially prohibited acts. It is, for example, common knowledge that the sale of securities or insurance, the practice of certain professions, compliance with pure food and drug laws, and the number of wives one may have at the same time, are often subject to criminal sanctions.

How much territorial contact is necessary to put one on notice depends on the nature of the act and the notoriety of the proscription. Where the impact within a foreign state is reasonably foreseeable, and where the matter is one that is often subject to criminal sanction even though not so regulated at the place of commission of the act, it may be sufficient to subject the actor to the legal process of the place of impact if he can be taken into custody there without objection by other states. The case is, of course, even stronger where the particular actor intends to violate the law in question, for here the general interest in order and respect for law is put in issue. The physical act within the territory has no magic in itself. The real issue is due process—the fairness of subjecting the offender to rules that were unfamiliar to him, and the fairness, perhaps, of designating the foreign state as the place of trial.

The second major policy consideration where the conduct is not commonly recognized as criminal concerns the quality of the prohibition and punishment. Criminal behavior goes to the very roots of social organization, and, because individual freedom is often in issue, the limits of tolerance are narrower than in other fields of law. In many countries certain activities are highly favored and any public encroachment by way of limitation is viewed with jaundiced eye. Take, for example, freedom of speech and press. A foreign law with regard to criminal libel that attempts to touch newspapers and radio broadcasts that were published or that originated elsewhere is likely to be claimed a violation of territorial sovereignty.

In these and in similar cases where conflicts of policy exist, there is much more at stake than mere venue. Some effort to assign competence on a territorial basis may be useful, but only if it helps to prevent sharp conflicts. Resolution at a substantive level is preferable. It is, for the same basic reason, usually urged that one state should not punish for acts committed outside its territorial limits when the acts are, in some positive sense, required or, more doubtfully, privileged. Conversely, courts have been reluctant to order a defendant in a civil case to commit abroad an act that is or may be in contravention of the law of the sovereign in whose territory he must perform. In part this self-denial relates again to ideas of fairness (damned if you do and damned if you don't), but it also reflects a conscious self-restraint by the judiciary where other states have different views strongly held and potential power to enforce.

As the foreign norm becomes increasingly offensive, any ideas of territoriality are cast aside, and political protest goes directly to the nature of the norm rather than to the place of the act. This is so particularly if a state's own nationals are involved, but today, even with regard to foreign nationals, alleged denials of justice are likely to be subject to diplomatic protest. There is a gradation of policy differences, and territorial competence serves as a sort of intermediate position. In a sharp conflict that does not go into basic issues of human rights, territoriality is employed as a rationale for claiming and recognizing dominant interests on the part of one state. Differences are tolerated, and resolution in fact depends upon the ability of the prosecuting state to enforce its prescriptions. Admittedly, there is nothing very satisfying in thus leaving matters to chance, but surely we can accept the imperfections of political institutions in the world community without perpetuating confusion between the territorial organization of law enforcement and the policy aims of legal doctrine.

Where the territorial interpretation of legislation goes beyond fairness in terms of notice and venue to an attempted allocation of sovereign competency to determine substantive policy, we move from judicial to predominantly political norms, with all the limitations on the judicial function that necessarily follow. Particularly perplexing are extensions of police power resulting in economic regulation of business and trade or the seizure of property. Domestically, policies dictating such action are arrived at through legislation, and courts have retreated to a test of factual reasonableness that rarely leads to constitutional veto. If it can be shown that the regulation bears a factual relationship to health or welfare and is equitably administered, it is likely to run judicial fire successfully.

Presumably the same constitutional tests and the same interpretative criteria govern business done internationally or owned or conducted by foreigners. But the national interest is here more obscure, for what benefits the citizens of one state, may do so at the expense of others. Extra-territorial application of our anti-trust laws, the administration of exchange controls and nationalization of industries are among the more important current problems. Where what is sauce for the goose is something else for the gander, power to enforce locally through unilateral determination of appropriate policy is unlikely to give a mutually satisfactory solution.

The high seas.   Territorial sovereignty extends to the outer limits of territorial waters, which, increasingly, looks to be at least six and perhaps twelve miles despite United States' claims for no greater than three.   Beyond this lies the high seas, an area in which no state claims exclusive authority.   The high seas can usefully be thought of as an area open to all and belonging to none, a sharable resource of the world community.   "Freedom of the seas" has meant primarily the rights of ships of all nations to navigate without interference from other states and to fish in waters not subject to the sovereignty of the coastal state, plus the right to lay submarine cables, and the freedom of overflight for aircraft.

These rights are, however, subject to some qualifications.   They must, of course, be exercised with due regard to the rights of others to share the common resource; for example, rules of navigation must be complied with when they are sufficiently common and well-understood to make a failure to comply hazardous to other users, and all states possess a competence to hear causes between private parties for failure to comply with various rules of admiralty common to many nations.   Submarine cables should not be laid in areas where there is frequent anchorage, and, reciprocally, ships should be careful not to interfere with cables already laid; for example, a vessel trawling in deep waters should be careful not to break a cable.   Conventions on this subject exist among important maritime countries giving each a right to investigate and report negligence by ships flying flags of the other, and involving a duty on the part of the flag state to make the guilty party answer in damages.   Similar conventions exist with regard to the conservation of fisheries shared by various states.   Since these conventions only bind the signatory nations and ships flying their flags, they may not be enforceable against others.   If such resources are rationed among current users, the temptation to others, who can evade the regulations, is correspondingly increased.   This problem was the subject of a proposed Convention on Conservation of Fishing and Conservation of the Living Resources of the High Seas, adopted at the Geneva Convention of 1958, but not yet ratified by a significant number of states.

There are other qualifications.   In time of war, freedom of navigation is circumscribed by the acknowledged right of belligerents to "visit and search" ships of all flags, and to confiscate any "contraband" they may discover. Rights of blockade, greatly expanded during the last two wars, also exist, permitting belligerents to close off large portions of the high seas to all flags. Even in peacetime, states sometimes claim similar rights, closing off large areas during naval maneuvers and, more recently, atomic testing and missile recovery. In the cold war context, dramatized by new technology, other qualifications on freedom of the seas have been unilaterally claimed and generally acknowledged. One example is the extension of Air Defense Identification Zones far out over the seas, with rules requiring all aircraft within the Zone to report and identify themselves. In addition to such security demands, coastal states have also occasionally extended their jurisdiction for certain limited purposes into areas beyond their territorial waters; actions undertaken to prevent pollution and smuggling, are examples. And problems of disposal of atomic waste raise other questions of how far a coastal state may extend a claim of competence to forbid such acts of disposal, or regulate them, if it believes itself endangered.

To put it simply, "freedom of the seas" is more slogan than doctrine. The high seas, although subject to no state's exclusive control or sovereignty, are not free from unilateral regulation by affected coastal states for specified purposes, or from the whole community of nations to preserve their character as a shared resource.

The usual method of regulating activities on the high seas is by the flag state to control all ships flying its flag, but to protest, in most cases, any attempt by public vessels of other states to do so. A ship must be registered and may fly only one flag. The flagship is usually regarded as analogous to a piece of territory of the flag country, at least in the sense that its laws apply to all that goes on aboard; but, unlike other forms of territorial jurisdiction, this "territory" may pass into the "territory" of another state, in which case the jurisdiction is regarded as concurrent. In addition, of course, a state may legitimately claim to regulate the conduct of its nationals on board such ships, but not, presumably, in a way which interferes with the control of the flag state.

Recently a number of difficulties have occurred with regard to the notion that the flag state predominantly regulates all conduct on board a ship, and the ship itself. These difficulties stem from the fact that, in many states, foreigners may register their ships and become entitled to fly that flag. National regulation of flagships in the form of safety requirements, minimum wages for crews, and other forms of social legislation have greatly increased the cost of operations under United States, United Kingdom, and some other flags. This has resulted in American owners registering their ships under so-called flags of convenience, such as the Liberian and Panamanian, as a method of evading United States regulation. Unions have been understandably much agitated, but, as yet, the United States has taken no steps to regulate Americans who do so; indeed, the Maritime Commission has supported the practice, as has the Navy. The reason is that they believe, without "flags of convenience," Americans would simply go out of the shipping industry, and a potential military resource under effective United States control would thus be lost.

At the Geneva Conference on the High Seas this problem was much discussed under pressure from some of the maritime states and the maritime unions. A provision vaguely requiring a "genuine link" between the flag and the ownership was included, but does not promise to be effective.

IMMUNITIES FROM JURISDICTION

By treaty, customary international law, and municipal regulation, certain immunities from territorial jurisdiction are recognized. These include foreign states, international institutions, diplomatic representatives of foreign states and international institutions, public ships and armed forces, and, to a lesser degree, private foreign ships within territorial waters. Although there is a wide area of consonant practice among states in these respects, variations of doctrine as to the extent and nature of the immunity do exist. In addition, it is by no means clear in many cases whether the rule is one of international or national law, and as a result, to what extent it might be unilaterally modified or abrogated. In general, reciprocal advantages support the practice and general principles involved, even though differences of interpretation and application of rules occur.

Sovereign immunity. The general rule of international law is that foreign states (and heads of foreign states) are immune from all foreign process. The rule had its origin in the personal immunity of a foreign Sovereign, and was later extended to the state as a juristic personality when republican forms of government became more common. Sovereigns were thought of as being above worldly law in their own realms; to subject them to foreign laws would have been even more offensive. Sovereigns were formally equal; one could not subject another to its laws or legal processes. Jurisdiction over sovereigns would also have been inconsistent with the independence necessary to the desirable functioning of the "balance of power" system.

The immunity granted foreign states has, until recently, been extremely broad. In the absence of its consent, a foreign state was not subject to local legislation, and could not be sued in local courts. In addition, property belonging to the foreign state, or subject to its possession and control, was not subject to seizure, detention or other legal process—unless, of course, as an act of reprisal or a wartime measure. Property problems have, particularly in recent years, caused certain technical difficulties, and in minor respects the immunity is qualified. For example, suits relating to title of land may be heard even if a foreign state is in possession, unless the property is being used as a legation. Similarly, property may be condemned as part of a public works project; and a trust fund or corporate shares in which a sovereign is interested may nonetheless be administered by local authorities under local law. But these are minor inroads. A far more important issue arises as to whether or not the customary immunity should not be drastically cut down, and several states, including the United States, have already acted to reduce the scope of this immunity.

In recent years, two related developments have taken place. First, in many states the immunity of the local sovereign under local law from suit by private persons has been almost abolished. Suits may customarily be brought today on government contracts and for negligent acts of public officials; for example, the state is responsible for the acts of the careless postal delivery driver who injures a pedestrian. This suggests that states regard sovereign immunity as less important than in prior years, but does not necessarily mean that they are willing to have these issues litigated in foreign courts.

Secondly, as an incident of socialism, states are engaging in many activities previously regarded as "private." States are widely active, in one form or another, in business and commercial activities, often in competition with private enterprises performing similar services. Should these enterprises be immune from local taxation, regulation, and judicial process enforcing claims by individuals simply because they are owned by foreign states? Today there is no uniform rule or practice. The Soviet Union maintains that immunity should be preserved even for these activities. The United Kingdom has a similar rule. Italy, Belgium, and the United States will not grant any plea as to immunity for activities that they regard as commercial, but (despite the fact that they allow suit locally against themselves) will continue to grant it for other activities of a "governmental nature." The United States' position is not entirely clear, though announced by the State Department in 1952 as government policy, for the reason that courts could, in the absence of legislation, constitutionally refuse to follow the policy, and no cases have been litigated where the principle has been judicially stated.

The legal capacity of a state to cut down unilaterally on the amount of sovereign immunity by designating areas of activity with regard to which it will subject a sovereign to local jurisdiction, illustrates some of the equivocal features of customary international law. It could be based, as the State Department's memorandum seemed to be, on the theory that custom and practices had changed elsewhere, and that commercial activities did not seem to be within the purpose of the rule as originally expounded. Or, alternatively, it could be based on the theory that the "customary" rule is merely one that is implied whenever, without a contrary condition being imposed, a foreign sovereign is permitted to conduct activities within another's territory. According to this latter view, a state could impose whatever conditions it wished on a foreign sovereign provided only that it specified the conditions in advance.

Public vessels. The immunity of a foreign man-of-war or naval vessel in territorial waters is similar to the immunity of the state itself, and could be regarded simply as an incident of sovereign immunity. A ship belonging to a foreign sovereign, or in its possession, would be immune from any local process simply under the general rule. A ship, however, unlike most property, is a place where various persons live and where acts may take place. Therefore the issue is not merely the seizure of the ship itself, but the extent to which local authorities can regulate activities on board, or remove persons on board who have committed offenses ashore.

Some authorities regard the ship as a "floating island," as part of the "territory" of the state whose flag she flies. Under this theory, acts on board would be exclusively governed by the law of the flag, and local officials could not board the ship, without the consent of its commander, for any purposes whatsoever. It could even be extended to the point of denying any duty on the part of the captain to turn over a fugitive from justice, and a right on his part to grant asylum, on behalf of his sovereign.

A preferable position would be simply to recognize the policy considerations involved by granting a considerable immunity to a foreign man-of-war visiting a local port. The conditions of the visit would be those implied from the duties of the vessel and what would seem to be a reasonable arrangement in view of the legitimate interests of both states. We can arrive at this position theoretically by the complementary devices of saying that the matter is governed by local law which concedes certain "customary" and reasonable immunities, or that, by allowing it's ship to enter a foreign port, the sovereign waived by implication immunities not strictly necessary to the performance of its duties. Under these arrangements it would be a duty of the ship's captain to insure that the vessel observed local quarantine, sanitary, and health regulations, that the crew did not assist in breaches of revenue laws, that any fugitives were turned over to local authorities, and that any members of the crew were punished for infractions of local law. Authorities of the port state would have no rights to board the vessel for any purpose without the consent of the captain, but the failure of the latter to abide by the conditions detailed above would be grounds for state liability enforced through diplomatic channels.

It seems reasonably clear why a foreign government will not permit local authorities any control over activities on board a man-of-war nor grant any right to search the ship. Before public vessels were used extensively for commercial purposes, there was no distinction with respect to immunities between one type of public vessel and another. But the considerations that support these immunities do not apply equally to public vessels engaged in commercial activities. One of the commercial activities referred to in the section on sovereign immunity is shipping. As more and more public vessels are used in commercial pursuits, we can predict that they will increasingly be treated in the same way, and for the same reasons, as private vessels similarly engaged.

Foreign armed forces.   Armed forces admitted to the territory of a state enjoy a limited immunity. In earlier times this rarely occurred except during wartime, where an ally might be granted permission to bring his forces upon the territory, or where troops were in passage from one state to another through the territory of a third. It was suggested under these circumstances that a force was entitled to extensive immunity, because to hold otherwise "would be inconsistent with its continuing to exist as an efficient force available for the service of its sovereign." Under this view, and especially in wartime, the commander of the forces would have exclusive authority to punish and discipline members of the force; the members themselves would not, however, be immune from local laws, and the commander could waive, on behalf of the state, any immunity from local process. Where he did not, he would be under a duty to punish them for offenses committed against local law.

The extensive stationing of troops on foreign soil in peacetime as an incident of bloc activity has led to a narrowing of the immunity granted by the host state. The NATO Status of Forces Agreement, which is perhaps the leading model and therefore could be said to represent "customary" law as well as being a treaty binding its signatories, provides for concurrent jurisdiction by the sending and host states over all offenses, with a primary right in the sending state to try offenses in line of duty or involving personnel or property of the armed forces exclusively, and a primary right on the part of the host state to try all other offenses. Foreign forces are also given certain rights that would be implied from their status; for example, the right to bear weapons, use motor transport without local licenses, etc. Additional provisions cover problems of law enforcement and security within the area of military bases, with primary jurisdiction in the sending state.

Private ships: peace of the port and entry in distress. In general, private ships, and personnel on board, are subject to the law of the flag whether on the high seas or in foreign territorial waters and ports. When in foreign territorial waters they are, however, subject to the concurrent jurisdiction of the territorial state. This jurisdiction is, however, qualified by certain "customary" immunities.

The authorities of the territorial state are not normally interested in maintaining discipline among the crew, or punishing minor infractions. They have, however, asserted an interest in all crimes on board ship within their waters that "disturb the peace of the port." This has usually been interpreted not in a literal sense, but in a sense that merely includes any crimes of a serious nature. In addition, private ships must comply with all local fiscal, port, and health regulations. They are subject to inspection by local authorities, arrest of persons on board, and punishment of such persons for any infractions of local law. They may be attached and sold for the satisfaction of any judgments against the owner or claims of the crew for wages due.

There are two exceptions to the exercise of this extensive jurisdiction by the territorial state. First, a vessel not proceeding to a local port, but in innocent passage through territorial waters, may not be seized nor may personnel be removed from her, unless the "peace of the port" is disturbed, or the passage is not "innocent"; for example, the ship may be violating local navigational, security, or sanitation measures. Second, a ship that enters an unintended port under distress, due to weather or breakdowns of equipment that would endanger the lives of the members of her crew if she continued on course, is immune from local process for whatever is considered a reasonable period of time in which to make repairs.

These immunities are of quite ancient vintage. We may doubt that they stand on very secure footing today, since the trend has been for the territorial state to assert ever increasing authority over ships within its waters. Maritime nations will support innocent passage doctrine strongly, but even the British have taken the view that local authorities have complete jurisdiction over private vessels in port, though they customarily do not exercise it to its fullest extent. And when the question of immunity from local jurisdiction of aircraft entering in distress arose—a rule granting immunity would be equally as supportable or unsupportable as the older rule about ships—immunity was universally agreed not to exist.

Diplomatic and consular personnel. Diplomatic officials have complete immunity from local process but not from local laws; that is, in theory they have a duty to obey all laws of the territorial state, but they may not be prosecuted in local courts or arrested by local officials for such offenses unless the state that they represent waives their immunity. The immunity, therefore, is that of the state in the person of the diplomat, and is not a personal privilege belonging to the diplomat. The exemption of the plenipotentiary from jurisdiction was first given specific formulation in Gentili's advisory brief for the British Crown at the end of the sixteenth century, in the case of a Spanish Ambassador who had engaged in a plot against the British Crown. There seems to be greater advantage for all states in treating plenipotentiaries as inviolable, and in handling grievances against them as grievances against the states they represent, than in attempting to punish them for their acts.

Although modern communications are now reducing the importance of the representative function, there was a time when the ambassador actually did represent his state in the sense that he had to make on-the-spot decisions of the most grave importance without having the opportunity of consulting his government at home. Any action against the plenipotentiary would have broken the slender thread of diplomatic intercourse at an exceptionally delicate link. Such action would have compounded rather than reduced the consequences of an ambassador's misbehavior. In addition, of course, seizure of an ambassador or invasion of an embassy, particularly in these democratic times, but also in the past, would only inflame the public and add imponderable difficulties to the burden of harassed negotiators who, in the effort to smoothe international relations, already carry an almost impossibly large burden.

Similar reasons explain the extention of immunity to the minister, the lower ranking members of diplomatic staffs, their families, their residences, and, for some purposes, their servants. Most states require that an individual be entered on a diplomatic list before the immunity becomes effective and argument might be made that the list is too large and has been extended to cases where it serves no national or international interest.

Immunity from process is not to be construed as immunity from liability. British courts, for instance, force the insurance agent of a diplomat to pay damages even though process cannot be served against the diplomat. And, in many cases, it is expected either that waiver of immunity will be made or that, if he is allowed to return to his state after the commission of a delict, the diplomat will be punished by his state for the delict. The salary of the diplomat is exempt from taxation by the state in which he is located, but he is not necessarily exempt from taxes at the source.

The embassy and other diplomatic residences are also inviolable. But there is a corresponding obligation for those within not to use embassies for purposes contrary to the law of the host state. They are not to be used for offering asylum to fugitives from the ordinary criminal law, nor are they to be used as places of detention. The case of Dr. Sun Yat-sen, leader of the Chinese Revolution, is in point. In 1896, Dr. Sun was enticed into the Chinese Embassy in London and held for deportation to China, then under the rule of the Manchu Dynasty. Great Britain immediately demanded his release and was successful in this demand. We may wonder what would happen if a similar case were to occur in 1961 in the Soviet Embassy in London, and the Soviet authorities were to refuse to surrender the individual.

Whether an embassy can be used to house political fugitives often raises delicate questions. It is common practice in Latin America to allow political refugees to seek asylum in foreign embassies. Determining when a refugee is a political refugee and not a common criminal is often difficult. After the revolution in Guatemala, in 1954, the new Castillo Armas government demanded the return of political refugees accused of murder, torture, or of other crimes not political in nature. This demand was rejected and the refugees eventually were permitted to leave the country under foreign protection. On the other hand, the Hungarian government, which claims that Cardinal Mindzenty had been convicted of ordinary rather than political crimes, refuses to permit the Cardinal to leave the United States Embassy in Budapest under safe conduct, but will not invade the Embassy to seize the Cardinal. Although the Hungarian government has demanded the person of the Cardinal, and has accused him of engaging in activities detrimental to the state while he was in the Embassy (certainly a violation of the privilege of asylum if true), it has not done anything effective to enforce its demand. The United States rejects the contentions of the Hungarian government with respect to the crimes of the Cardinal, but has not been able to secure his removal from the Embassy under safe conduct.

Whether the Latin American rule may be made to hold within Communist territory is subject to some doubt. On the other hand, the Communist states are not prepared to invade embassies. On the surface at least, the rule is saved by the contention that the Cardinal is not a political refugee. Indeed, he probably did break the criminal law of the state, but these are laws a political opponent of the state would almost necessarily break since Communist states so circumscribe opposition that criminal laws are almost necessarily broken as a by-product of political opposition. As long as Communist states feel the need to capture and to punish their enemies, wherever they are, it will be most difficult to enforce universally the rule of political asylum that characterizes most practice outside the Communist bloc.

Consuls are in a different class from ambassadors and ministers— a much less sensitive class. They may not even be nationals of the state they represent. They have variant exemptions from process; they are not usually taxed or required to serve on juries. But they are not wholly exempt from civil or criminal proceedings, except that efforts are usually made to prevent such proceedings from interfering with their conduct of consular business. Their consular records are inviolate. In the past, consuls from European nations have sometimes exercised criminal and civil proceedings over their countrymen in some non-Christian states or territories—a procedure that often implied distrust of local law or process.

8

RESORT TO FORCE: WAR AND NEUTRALITY

VIOLENCE and the threat of violence have always played roles in politics. All systems of law-government have means of legitimizing resort to physical force in order to enforce policy under some circumstances, and they do so on both moral and practical grounds. The central problem of law-government in all communities is to develop principles and procedures which can effectively control and minimize resort to violence. Modern technology has made this problem particularly urgent in the international community; it is common knowledge that its resolution may be closely related to human survival.

Controlling and minimizing resort to violence are distinct, though often related, concepts. We attempt to subject physical force to processes of law-government—to constitutional norms and procedures —to insure that it will be used only to enforce "law and order." In a developed system of law-government this means that only government officials may employ physical coercion (with very narrow exceptions such as self-defense, or civilian arrest), and these officials may employ it only in accordance with norms formally established as law through the governmental system. Force is not thereby eliminated from politics; it is simply subjected to formal controls, to the governmental process. It is scarcely necessary to point out that the process itself —the method of formulating community policy—varies widely from polity to polity, and may be quite unsatisfactory to some participants or to members of the community denied any formal right to participate in political processes. It is also clear that government officials may themselves violate the norms and processes which are formally binding and resort to force to cut off protest.

The point to be emphasized here is that even within developed legal systems resort to physical violence continues to play a role. Since no system of law-government can be neutral in the distribution of values, a process determined by community policy, acceptance of the legitimacy and necessity of force in support of law and order does not mean that all processes of decision making, or even all decisions, are regarded as equally legitimate by all members of the community. Thus whether the use of force in support of community policies is regarded as legitimate depends upon the extent to which paticipants regard the decision-making processes themselves as acceptable or tolerable, and upon the paths that are open for non-violent modification of the system and of the actual decisions adopted. Differences in attitudes towards force in support of law and order and force in opposition to the rules enforced depend in part on evaluations of the process itself; that is, upon conceptions of the legitimate form of government (favoring representative government over dictatorship for instance) or doctrinal argumentation (the existing government has violated the Constitution, or human rights, or natural law). The duty to obey and the right of revolution have walked hand in hand through history.

Domestic experience indicates, then, that maintaining order has always involved some coercion and resort to force, or the threat of force, as the ultimate sanction for community policy, however such policy has been determined; a government must be prepared, if necessary, to use violence to enforce the law. This obviously does not mean that all law is found at the end of a policeman's nightstick, but merely that the nightstick is present in any system of law-government. So, too, is the possibility of forcible opposition to government. The extent to which a government relies upon physical coercion—including extremes such as massive or isolated acts of terrorism—has varied greatly from one polity to another. A number of factors, both environmental and predispositional, are clearly relevant. Not all domestic political systems have been able to create durable systems of order, and not all that have succeeded in achieving internal stability have done so in accordance with principles and processes that would be acceptable in other national communities. In many countries governments have relied heavily on specialists in violence—armies and secret police—to prevent opposition to governmental decisions, and maintain order on a basis preferred by the dominant group. The threat of foreign domination is one important factor in promoting national solidarity and legitimizing domestic government; maintaining internal order is a factor in maintaining external security, and professional armies needed for the latter function could be used to promote internal stability as well.

Minimizing resort to violence is also a common feature of most systems of law-government. This may be true in part because most social systems value agreement, persuasion and compromise, moderation and toleration of the expression of a variety of different opinions as to community policy. War, revolution, riot and other forms of disorder always involve deprivation of other values to members of the community. Furthermore, widespread resort to violence involves risks to all participants; strong action may—and, very likely, will—involve the risk of strong counteraction, except where force is overwhelming and certain. Thus, both governmental elites and opposition leaders must measure the value of political objectives against estimates of political costs. There is constant pressure to economize on force, and to scale down political objectives if the price appears disproportionate. Ends and means of political action constantly interact.

Controlling and minimizing resort to violence come together insofar as order itself is a value pursued by all participants. One aspect of government is to determine community policy; a second aspect is to enforce it; the two interact insofar as it is important to decision makers to determine what policies are enforceable, under what conditions, and at what cost.

In general terms, many of these same considerations operate in the international community, in interactions of nation-states. We emphasized this point in Chapter 2 when it was pointed out that, in the "balance of power" political system, the objectives of war were characteristically limited objectives, and that extinction or complete conquest of the defeated state, even if technologically possible, was not in the interest of the victorious state.

Environmental conditions in the international community are obviously different in major respects from those in the nation-state. Most important is the absence of any real sense of "community" or "mankind." The absence of common identification—the elevation of national objectives over international ones—has made it extremely difficult to find ways of formulating a community policy in sufficiently inclusive terms. As we have seen, international law-doctrine tends to be formulated in terms of what states may and may not do, emphasizing bargaining and reciprocity rather than the commonality of values and objectives. For reasons already discussed, arriving at common institutions for prescribing an inclusive community policy is made more difficult by the demands of security and survival, by the fact that the ultimate arena of interaction has always been the military one, and the perspectives of participants have been heavily influenced by expectations of violence and fear of catastrophe. This continues to be true in interbloc affairs. If thermonuclear stalemate is achieved—if the United States and NATO, on the one hand, and the Soviet Union and its bloc, on the other, develop extensive protected second-strike forces[1]—the damper on the resort to large-scale violence will be reinforced most strongly. So long as the possibility of mutual destruction, of two Carthages rather than one Rome, is present, there would seem to be an effective sanction of self-interest in limiting too extensive a resort to war.

RESORT TO WAR: FROM THE JUST WAR TO THE CHARTER

Efforts to control and minimize force in international relations have occupied more attention from scholars and statesmen alike than any other aspect of international law. These efforts can be seen in three broad and related categories: First, efforts to control the use of force in international relations by doctrinal statement of the conditions under which states legitimately might use military measures to secure objectives; second, the law of war, composed of rules and practices governing hostilities among participating nations; thirdly, the law of neutrality, setting out rights and duties of belligerents and neutrals vis-a-vis each other.

Efforts to prevent the resort to war have always, as have their domestic counterparts, taken the form of doctrinal limitations on the use of force, confining it to support of law rather than to use as an instrument of political gain for particular participants. Hence the doctrine of the *bellum iustum*, seized upon by Roman historians and philosophers, to bring force to the support of a legal system. Although violence itself was conceived as simply a part of the natural order of mankind, recourse to arms in a particular case could be had only for an injury suffered and after the refusal of the guilty party to make atonement. To make sure a just cause existed (and

---

[1] A second-strike nuclear force is a nuclear force that will be available for purposes of retaliation even after an enemy has attacked first.

to make sure of Divine assistance) the doctrine was, in a fashion similar to our own Constitution, internally subjected to checks by reference of the justice of the cause to a collegium of priests to insure the war was both legally justified and religiously favored.

This idea of the "just war" had a great impact upon Europe from the time of Augustine until the developed positivism of the "balance of power" period. With Augustine it served both a controlling and a limiting function, for Augustine saw the just war and the just peace as being interrelated. Writing in the conceptually unitary system of the Roman Empire, he saw the purpose of war not as victory but as the restoration of an ordered and lawful society. War had to have a just cause; it had to be preceded by an unredressed injury, and its purpose had to be simply to right the wrong. Force had to be proportional to the injury suffered, in terms of punishment and redress. To seek more was to convert a just cause into an unjust one. Although he did not use the word "reprisal," Augustine essentially saw "war" and "reprisal" as equivalents, as did some of his successors in the later Empire period.

To attempt to pursue in any detail the interesting evolution of the concept of the just war would go beyond the scope of this study. But a few brief notes may make doctrine more understandable. The great moralist of the Middle Ages, Aquinas, added to the need for a just cause the fact that the belligerents must be animated by the right intentions, thus introducing a subjective test. His followers contributed a number of detailed distinctions and categorizations of when a war could be considered just and when it could not. But all these writers remained true to the tradition. The purpose of war was to right a wrong and to restore the status of peace; wars of aggression were unjust. The objective of war was the maintenance of justice in the common good; that is, to punish lawbreakers.

With the breakup of the authority of the Church, with the coming of the Reformation, and with the emergence of nation-states, the doctrine began, within the same verbal framework, to undergo subtle changes. The doctrine remained, with Vittoria in 1532, largely in the Augustinian heritage, except for the novel suggestion that war was an essential element of sovereignty—but still its use was to right a wrong received. To Ayala, writing fifty years later, the justice of the cause, although still important, was a matter of "politics and equity," no longer of "law." Each was trying in his own way to answer the question posed by the breakup of the Christian Community: could a war be just on both sides at the same time? Vittoria combined subjective ignorance with objective truth to find it possible. Ayala went somewhat further. Both saw "objective" justice on one side only. Vittoria said it might exist "subjectively" on both sides, if one side were ignorant or in error. Ayala followed a similar line but said, for this reason, the justice had nothing to do with its "legality," but merely with politics and equity. Wars prosecuted in a belief as to justice were legal on both sides. To this, Gentili, writing in England a decade later, added that justice might be objectively on both sides, even though one side might be more just than the other. "Legal justice" was carefully separated from theology and ethics. War was formally lawful if the Prince said so, and, although he was obligated to search his conscience, he was considered above second-guessing. Formalism took over. And when we look to the catastrophic wars of religion that followed in the wake of the Empire, it is easy to guess why.

Grotius thought to save the demise of the concept of the just war as a method of both controlling recourse to force and limiting objectives—objectives that had been lost sight of in the religious fervor that swept the period—by seeking to throw out theological causes, which were getting people into war, and re-emphasizing the non-ideological basis of the older concept. Just causes were seen as self-defense, the protection of property, and punishment for wrongs inflicted on one's citizens; unjust causes were territorial expansion, subjugating other peoples against their will on the pretext that it was to their own good, and (conversely) the desire of a state to attain political independence of another. Again the legalistic conception of righting a wrong was emphasized. But Grotius added, or sought to add, the necessity of sanction by neutral states, or states not party to the controversy. These states should refrain from lending assistance to the state whose cause was unjust and from putting obstacles in the path of the state whose cause was just.

Grotius' theory was that judgment by states not party to the controversy would tend to support the just cause and deter unjust wars. However, in many circumstances it is very difficult to determine which cause is just. Moreover machiavellian considerations may enter into the calculations of states not originally participating in the war. Thus the formula offered by Grotius tended to spread war to the states that took sides regarding the justice of the controversy rather than to deter violence. As a result, it was ineffective to control the outbreak of war, and, once it had broken out, the principle tended to increase the extent and consequences of the war, rather than to minimize the destruction of values that accompany violence.

But the idea of using neutrals to keep the outbreak of violence within limits was an ingenious one, and the successors of Grotius, most importantly Pufendorf and Bynkershoek, seized upon it. They used the idea, however, not to control or deter the outbreak of war, but to confine it and minimize its consequences. Both insisted on the necessity of a just cause; but both cautioned neutrals to remain neutral, and not to do anything that would make them a party to the quarrel. The justice or injustice of the cause, according to them, did not concern the neutral, who, by the middle of the eighteenth century, was not to inquire into it and thus was not to "sit in judgment between his friends." The notion that all states should assist in the punishment of international wrongs was rejected. Between belligerents, however, the Grotian idea of war as punitive was maintained. The lines of doctrinal evolution into the developed positivism of the nineteenth century are clearly foreshadowed in these writings. The justice of the cause was still important for belligerents, but not for neutrals. Mid-eighteenth-century writers, such as Christian Wolff, maintained this much of the doctrine, rejecting the competing doctrine advanced by Machiavelli that war was just if dictated by reasons of state, or if it was politically necessary. But even this principle, with Wolff's disciple, Vattel, was put into practical effect by being relegated to the realm of ethics and morality: a sovereign ought not to use force against other states without a just cause, according to the doctrine, but the presence or absence of the cause did not affect the legality of the war.

Before 1800, the concept of the just war was relegated to history, and it remained there until after the First World War. Most writers in the nineteenth century explicitly rejected it, considering war as a necessary incident of sovereignty. This followed, in the usual rationalization, from the simple fact that states were "equal" and that as a necessary incident of this sovereign equality, none could sit in judgment upon another. States were obligated to keep agreements, to refrain from territorial conquest, to keep out of the internal affairs of another, and, when disputes arose, to seek peaceful means of settlement—negotiation, mediation, arbitration; but whatever they did or did not do, others could not sit in judgment on their acts. War became a "factual question"; when it existed, the laws of war and the laws of neutrality came into operation. However the war had arisen, and whatever the merits, the legal consequences as among belligerents or between belligerents and neutrals were the same. The only issue was: Did a state of war exist or not? There is no "right" to resort to war; it simply ceased to be a question of legal concern to members of the international community.

The rise and demise of the concept of the just war reflects the rise and demise of Christendom and the emergence of a fully developed "balance of power" system with nation-states playing the predominant political role in a divided, rather than a unitary, system. Within the crudely unitary system of the Empire, the requirement that a state could fight a war only for just cause, that is, to punish for specific offenses or to recover what was rightfully that state's possession, was a factor in controlling and limiting resort to violence by minor princes. Other states could pass upon the justice of the cause and the justice of the peace; the system was one of law enforcement, making no distinction between war and reprisal as means for this end. The doctrine served, too, to preserve a status quo within a common ideological framework. The Church could and did play a role in keeping force within the bounds of justice, and doctrine was aimed to assist this function.

Religious wars and the growth of nation-states led to the abandonment of the just war concept. The absolutism of competing religious ideologies made it extremely difficult to limit objectives, to keep a just peace tied to a just war or make the punishment fit the crime. The Church itself, not minor principalities, was increasingly a participant. With the Spanish school of the sixteenth century, we see war removed from "legal" restraints. Grotius, trying to restore a limiting concept, returned to justice as a legal requirement, adding neutrals to police it. But neutrals could not act in this way without the danger of violence spreading and endangering their own national existence. In addition the idea of just war became more and more incompatible with the flexibility of alignment necessary to national security in a "balance of power" system. As we have seen, there was not and could not be room in the dominant national political system for judgments based on the use of force except in the national interest—an interest identified with protecting the nation from foreign interference or conquest. Attempts to impede flexibility of alignment by legal doctrine were simply incompatible with the strange alignments that were good politics.

Abandoning any concept of the legality or illegality of war did not mean that a concern with controlling violence had also been abandoned. In a "balance of power" international system, flexibility of alignment is an essential means for limiting the objectives of the major states of the system and thus also for controlling and limiting violence and for promoting the security of nation states. The abandoning of a prior test of legality allowed the introduction of more order into rules that constrained the use of violence, minimized its destructive impact, and promoted rapid restoration of a peaceful status quo. Rules of warfare and rules of neutrality were not conditioned upon any prior test of the legality of the hostilities, but came into effect automatically when the factual state of war existed. However "unlawful" the cause of war, however aggressive the war was in intent—actual or expressed—the rules as to its conduct applied to all participants. Other states could honor their alliance agreements and participate; or else they could remain neutral favoring neither one side nor the other. They had no general obligation to uphold the justice of any cause. Finally, peace settlements were separated from the reasons for warfare, and operated independently. Thus there was no question of the "legality" of the new status quo that in any way related it back to the legality of the war itself. The dangers of ideological conflict had been demonstrated grimly by the devastation of the wars of religion. States in the late eighteenth and nineteenth centuries were far more interested in stability, in minimizing violence, and in preserving themselves from foreign conquest than they were in the justice of war. In short, by abandoning the concept of the legality of war, states found it easier to accomplish the objectives of controlling and minimizing violence.

The doctrinal device for jettisoning the older law was that of the claimed inconsistency of judgment by third parties; since no state could sit in judgment on the acts of other sovereigns, there was no way of determining whether the war was just or not. This action did not preclude states from continuing to invoke the older doctrine and plead the justice of their cause. States continued to do so, in part to build up domestic support for military intervention, in part, perhaps, to reassure other states as to their limited intentions. But it was clearly understood during the nineteenth century, by governments and scholars alike, that there was no necessary or legal relation between statements of the grounds for war and the peace that might lawfully be exacted. In practice, but not consistently, a relation continued to exist.

For roughly a century and half, the just-war concept was submerged, making only occasional reappearances in legal doctrine. War was not a question of law but of fact; the issue of its justice, or legality, was non-justiciable in the broadest sense. But this dichotomy between war and peace was sometimes inadequate politically, for there were situations in which the use of violence was, in the older fashion, limited strictly to the righting of a felt wrong. Those who sought to use small amounts of force to cure minor malpractices were frustrated by the thought that there was no remedy short of full-scale war. The world of the lawyers was divided into war and peace; the world of the statesmen saw intermediary stages in the political process. War should be reserved for major disorders; hence distinctions aimed at minimizing violence arose in practice even though difficult to fit into theory. Lesser forms of sanction were often called "reprisals"; if a few more soldiers and sailors were added, they were called "hostile measures short of war."

In each case the thought was to relate the degree of force to the offense committed, a thought that had characterized the older just war–just peace relationship, but was abandoned when war became, if not legal, at least not illegal. Older writers had found no need to distinguish between reprisals and war, because, in each case, the amount of force permissible was related to the offense alleged. But if there were no legal controls on war save those self-imposed by participants, to declare war to protect minor rights looked a bit like calling out the national guard to enforce a parking ticket. The desire to enforce accepted rules without going to such extremes was persuasive as a political matter, because it demonstrated the absence of any desire on the part of the enforcing state to increase its territory or to subjugate another population. But the scholars never liked the idea of reprisals short of war because, having decided that the existence of war was a factual question, they wished their facts clear. Did laws of war apply or not? Did laws of neutrality apply or not? If war did not exist, then the world must be at peace; if the world were not, then a state of war must exist. The law did not permit any intermediate position.

There were a number of incidents, of hostilities, or the use of some force, without declarations of war in any formal sense, or without facts that accorded with any popular conception of war. Between 1811 and 1911 there were at least forty-eight occasions, according to the Department of State, on which governments took forcible military action in support of rights of citizens claimed to have been unlawfully denied by a foreign government. For example, on July 13, 1854, a Commander Hollis of the U.S.S. *Cyane* shelled the port of Greytown, Nicaragua, and totally destroyed the city. His action, taken on Presidential orders, came after repeated acts by local authorities against Americans and repeated refusals to apologize for such allegedly unlawful acts. War was not declared. Similarly, in 1914, American marines landed in Vera Cruz when General Huerta refused to apologize for the arrest of some American sailors. The action was taken after a joint resolution of Congress approving use of military force. The Mexicans stated that the landing of marines "must be understood as the initiation of war against Mexico," to which the State Department replied that "a state of war does not exist," and that the United States was simply occupying Vera Cruz temporarily to redress various indignities.

Other well-known instances that, to quote the mid-nineteenth-century scholar, Kinglake, tended "to throw down the great landmark between peace and war," were: the "war" between Venezuela, on the one hand, and Great Britain, Germany, and Italy, on the other, commenced by the latter to collect public debts on which Venezuela had defaulted; and the shelling of Corfu by the Italians in 1923. The allies had delivered to Venezuela a series of ultimata followed by minor acts of force and, eventually, by a naval blockade. Acts were characterized as "coercive measures," "reprisals," and "semi-hostile acts"; other nations did not declare their neutrality, though, at least after the blockade in which the Allies were claiming the usual rights of a blockading force to stop neutral shipping, the United States protested on the grounds that no war had been declared. In response to this pressure, a state of war was declared to exist, but the measures taken continued to be moderate and phrased in terms of the limited objective that was causing these measures— payment of debts. Corfu, on the other hand, was a "hostile measure short of war," a "reprisal" for indignities that the Italians claimed to have suffered. That the "punishment" in this case was grotesquely out of proportion to the wrong alleged was clear.

It is hard to read this history without experiencing a touch of both scepticism and cynicism. The concept of force to support law was never really successful, even in Middle Ages, because, despite the myth of Christendom, the necessary unity was not present. The Empire was too loose and too divided. At the same time, the later division of the whole continuous process of coercion into peace and war was equally unrealistic. It made good sense to free neutrals of any formal obligation to pass on the justice of war or peace demands, and to insist that the standards of warfare and the rights and duties of neutrals should not vary with the justice of the war itself. Without an effective institutional process for determining community policy and for making it independent of the security of national participants, it was futile to expect spontaneous and overwhelming agreement as to what was "right" and what should be done to enforce the law. If the objective is to control force in support of a community policy, there must be some means of determining the policy and some means of controlling those who enforce it as well.

Yet it was equally futile to expect that statesmen could live with such a crude division of reality. There are both deep-rooted psychological reasons and persuasive political reasons for a state to identify its cause with righteousness and to limit its objectives to professed needs. If, as we have hypothesized, it is good political sense to use force for limited objectives, then we would expect statesmen to act accordingly. If, as in the case of Venezuela, other states wish public debts to be honored, these states would be foolish to expend more force than was necessary to accomplish this purpose. In the "balance of power" system we could expect third states to be neutral only if they were indifferent to the outcome in terms of their own security. The United States was sympathetic enough with the collection of debts from Venezuela, but it was extremely chary of European intervention in Latin America. European statesmen might not approve of Italian occupation of Corfu, but they could tolerate it if sufficiently reassured as to lack of any serious intent to change the map of Europe through the use of force. In short, if war were no longer formally subject to the test of legality, the older ideas nonetheless survived. The "anomalous" (from the lawyer's viewpoint) practices of "hostile measures short of war" were always aimed at enforcement of claimed legal rights or punishment for prior wrongs. Even larger engagements often continued to be justified in the old way. Russia's professed aim in the war with Turkey in 1828 was to guarantee respect for treaties. The United States, in its declaration of war on Mexico, justified the act as a method of righting prior wrongs and preserving order. And the U.S. entered the First World War ostensibly because Germany violated its neutral rights. Most importantly, the issue of war guilt was raised at Versailles after the First World War.

The Versailles Treaty represents a return to the concept of war as an instrument for law enforcement—for punishing the guilty state— and thus represents a reversion to earlier concepts. Germany had to give up parts of its territory in retribution for its wrongs, and to answer with monetary damages for civil claims. The League of

Nations was envisioned prospectively as the instrumentality whereby force could be brought within a legal framework by collective sanctions to insure the punishment of violators, a method of enforcing community policy laid down by the Treaty and by the League as a body to implement its principles. That, hereafter, force was to be confined to law enforcement in support of League decisions was reconfirmed by the Kellogg-Briand Pact of 1928 renouncing war "as an instrument of national policy" and pledging to settle disputes exclusively by "pacific means." The Treaty was ratified or acceded to by some sixty-three states. The only exception to this sweeping renunciation of war was the understanding, clarified in the course of the Treaty's negotiation, that the "inherent right of self-defense" was not restricted or impaired, and, to quote the Secretary of State, "every nation is free at all times to defend its territory from attack or invasion and it alone is competent to decide whether circumstances require recourse to war in self-defense."

Apart from the fact that saying so did not make it so, there was room for technical argument about what the Covenant and the Kellogg-Briand Pact said. In the first place, both instruments talked of war, leaving room for doctrinal niceties of the kind which had occurred in the previous century. Was "war" to be understood as excluding other uses of violence such as "reprisals" and "hostile measures short of war"? Certainly the Kellogg Pact, by renouncing only "war as an instrument of national policy" was open to the interpretation that it did not prohibit the use of force by states as a sanction, to enforce "rights"—the classic *bellum iustum,* which, as we have seen, was always conceived as a sanction for community policy—but only wars of "aggression." This interpretation was to some extent reinforced by the fact that the Covenant itself did not prohibit war altogether, but simply prohibited resort to war where the Covenant provided (in theory) effective substitutes in the way of substitute procedures. Sanctions were provided against those states who "resort to war in disregard of their covenants under Articles XII, XIII or XV." In the event of failure of these peaceful settlement methods, or on matters not covered by them (if any), a good argument for "self-help" as lawful could be made—that is, argument in favor of the just war or lesser forms of sanction.

Efforts to remedy these technical defects, as well as the gaping exception of self-determined "self-defense," were made at San Francisco following the Second World War. The ambiguous term "war" is replaced, in the key section (Article 2, paragraph 4) of the United

Nations Charter by prohibiting Members "from the threat or use of force against the territorial integrity or political independence of any state." The only important exception to this seemingly sweeping prohibition of violence is Article 51, which permits a state—or states, collectively—to use armed force against an armed attack "until the Security Council takes the necessary measures to restore international peace and security." Conceived as an interim measure of short duration, Article 51, along with NATO, SEATO and other alliances of less importance, became a cornerstone of the Western security system.

The use of force as a sanction for law enforcement is a monopoly of the Security Council, which may use forces earmarked for its command (anticipated in the Charter but stalemated by the East-West controversy) or may call upon Members to enforce its decisions. But even the Security Council has limited authority, for it may only use the force necessary to restore peace and security. The General Assembly is even more limited in its constitutional authority, for, although it may investigate, pass judgment, and "recommend," it has no explicit power to compel compliance with its recommendations. The "Uniting for Peace" Resolution of 1950 represents an attempt to transfer some sanctioning competence to the Assembly when, because of the veto, the Security Council cannot act. Its constitutionality has been extensively debated, and few of even its strongest supporters have dared to claim that it really permits full substitution of the Assembly for the Council. To so substitute would fly in the face of language in the Charter, which is, in this respect at least, capable of only minor stretching.

Two important points emerge from a consideration of the Charter. First, it by no means provides, even in theory, an extensive enforcement of any community policy other than in the case of the misuse of force by Members. A state cannot use force to violate law. Equally, a state cannot use force to enforce the law, as a sanction; nor can the Security Council, with the narrow exception of enforcing judgments of the Court—assuming the dispute to be judicially settled by voluntary submission—and maintaining order. Second, even within the narrow area of permissible use of force, the Council can be stymied by the veto.

This latter defect is, despite its publicity, the less serious. Article 51 permits self-help and the help of allies, bolstered, if circumstances warrant, by the blessing of the Assembly under the "Uniting for Peace" Resolution, should that course be elected by participants. The only serious defect of Article 51 is the limitation to "an armed attack," a limitation that may be both naive and futile in an atomic age, or, for small states, in an age of jet planes and fast tanks.

Must a state wait until it is too late before it may defend itself? Must it permit another the advantages of military build-up, surprise attack, and total offense, against which there may be *no* defense? It would be unreasonable to expect any state to permit this—particularly when given the possibility that a surprise nuclear blow might bring about total destruction, or at least total subjugation, unless the attack were forestalled. Neither the United States nor the Soviet Union is likely to do so unless one or the other is immobilized by large segments of domestic or allied opinion. The situation has special immediacy for the United States and the Soviet Union, for, unlike the situation in the "balance of power" period, no combination of other nations can protect either one if it misplays its hand.

If the situation is especially poignant for the United States and the Soviet Union, at least these two have the means to protect themselves. Small states may face similar, if not identical, perils,[2] and yet may find themselves prevented from acting by the combined opposition of the United States and the Soviet Union within the United Nations.

Even though Article 51 permits collective self-defense and even though Article 52 has been interpreted to permit supranational defensive blocs such as NATO, the Charter restriction of self-defense to cases of armed attack[3] undoubtedly is not fully adequate to the

---

[2] According to reliably informed sources, official Israeli military doctrine shifted in 1954 from one based upon defensive counter-attack, to one based upon a forestalling attack under certain conditions. Considering that Israel could be cut in two by a drive of less than twenty-five miles launched from the Gaza Strip, Israeli doctrine called for a forestalling blow if an attempt were made to deploy militarily superior armored and jet forces in that area. The rationale was reinforced by the knowledge that the Gaza Strip constituted a bad defensive, but excellent offensive, position for Egypt, and that failure to forestall an attack by superior forces was likely to result in military defeat for Israel before help could possibly arrive, even supposing that any nation desired to come to Israel's aid.

[3] Article 51 reads "Nothing in the present Charter shall impair the inherent right of individual or collective self-defense if an armed attack occurs against a Member of the United Nations, until the Security Council has taken the measures necessary to maintain international peace and security. . . . " The wording therefore does not clearly forbid self-defense prior to armed attack but only sanctions self-defense as permissible in case of armed attack. However, the restrictive term "armed attack" was included deliberately and most commentators would read the Article to forbid self-defense except in case of armed attack. On the other hand, some commentators have pointed out that Article 2, paragraph 4, which forbids the use of force, forbids only that use of force designed to impair the "territorial integrity and political independence" of states. This problem of interpretation will be discussed below.

defense problems of the present age. On the other hand, the concept "self-determined self-defense" that qualified the Pact of Paris constitutes a bottomless legal pit, and, in the thermonuclear age, may open prospects frightening to all. For purposes of a Charter provision, designed to influence and to restrain the behavior of nations, a narrow definition was preferred to one that might not be restrictive at all in application. Moreover, a state need not wait until it undergoes armed attack before complaining to the Security Council or to the General Assembly about "situations" likely to "endanger international peace and security." And a state may dramatize the danger by a little sabre rattling of its own. If hostilities are not averted, they may nonetheless be contained and terminated, unless they succeed in their objectives before action can be taken or unless the Soviet Union, the United States, or a large number of Asian and African states obstructs action. Typically each side will accuse the other of "aggression" and then claim that it acted in "self-defense." These are questions which need not be resolved unless to label one side the "aggressor" would, in particular circumstances, serve as a deterrent to like action in the future. The Charter does not require the Council or the Assembly to act unreasonably, ineffectively, or foolishly.

There are many scholars, and some statesmen, who believe that the intentionally vague language of the Charter should be made precise by more detailed definitions of "aggression" and "self-defense." But, although such definitions might contribute to clarifying doctrine for the benefit of commentators, it is doubtful if they would contribute to a more orderly world; the effect might be the contrary, for they might encourage decision makers to pronounce authoritative decisions beyond their capacity to enforce them, thus putting their own authority in issue. On the other hand, any definitions adopted would be subject to the processes of political compromise—even if adequate definition were theoretically possible—and the attempt at definition might produce ambiguities useful in the justification of more self-help than anyone presently desires. This might happen under circumstances not contemplated at the time of adoption of the definition, including circumstances that might entail the risk of nuclear war.

The seemingly more important defect in the Charter, however, is that it seems to provide no system of sanctions to enforce community policies, no forcible military sanctions for any rule other than that which forbids the use of force. To draw an analogy from domestic law, the Charter system seems to be so underdeveloped that only murder is prohibited and sanctioned by central authority, and only for murder may a state resort to self-help if the Council fails to act. Military force cannot be used to change the law; neither can it be used to support it. The only just war would seem to be that of self-defense—the official view of the Catholic Church as expounded by Pius XII.

To this interpretation of the Charter—an interpretation that restricts both the United Nations and individual Members in the use of military force as a sanction—several writers have reacted with vigor. In particular, these writers defend the position taken by the British and French at the time of Suez. The argument, most brilliantly advanced by Julius Stone, begins with the proposition that this interpretation would permit states to violate international law in any number of ways, but does not provide an adequate remedy for the injured state. Treaties could be violated, property confiscated, and all manner of customary practices breached at will. Any violation of international law, in short, that is not itself an "armed attack," cannot be sanctioned by military means. This leaves law-abiding states helpless, an intolerable and absurd situation, according to Stone. Therefore, he says sanctions are necessary, if law, and not merely order, is to be established in the world community.

From this starting point it is urged that sanctions are not forbidden to states, and that they may use force or the threat of force to enforce general principles of international law without violation of the Charter. Article 2, paragraph 4, refers to force against the "territorial integrity and political independence" of states—that is, wars of aggression, not reprisals or hostile measures short of war, which do not have territorial conquest or political subjugation as an objective, but which are merely vindications of legal rights. For the latter purposes, force may be used; a just war is still a legal one, and forcible sanctions to guarantee rights are not aggression, clearly, and are not even, in most cases, threats to the peace—provided the force employed is moderate and limited to the vindication of legal rights.

The argument is appealing and doctrinally tenable as an interpretation of the Charter. It has, however, been rejected by the majority of scholars and statesmen alike. It has some support in Western Europe, and the bitterness of the British and French, after Suez, at the rejection of this argument by the United States and by the United Nations Secretary General is well known. We could not expect it to be supported by Latin America or by the growing number of new nations of Afro-Asia. The Latin Americans have long favored a rule opposing forcible sanctions, and this rule is clearly one that usually favors the smaller nations against the larger ones, for the reason that reprisals and hostile measures short of war have never been taken by a militarily weak nation against a powerful one. Moreover, weak nations are often poorer and more revolutionary, and, thus, they more often violate existing rules of law.

One final point should be made in clarification of Charter provisions. The Security Council has authority to "determine the existence of any threat to the peace, breach of the peace, or act of aggression" and to decide what forcible measures shall be taken to "maintain or restore international peace and security." Given a different political situation than now exists, this language is expansible. A Council decision not subjected to veto could envision military measures to coerce compliance with a rule of general international law on the ground that such compliance was in fact necessary to restore international peace and security. We do not have to read the Charter in exclusively cease-fire terms. If the UN has little legislative power at the moment, we should not cast out the possibility of eventual development.

Let us shift perspective and inquire as to the realism of the Charter. To what extent, and under what conditions, has resort to force been effectively removed from the decision of individual states, or of the blocs, and put into a workable constitutional framework? How seriously should we take the Charter? How effective are the formally prescribed procedures? To what extent has force been outlawed, for any purpose—including law enforcement?

Clearly, the answers to these questions will not be found in the Charter, but outside it, in the conditions that in fact exist. Like all constitutions, the Charter will be effective to the extent to which it is in accordance with the realities of politics or to which it is adaptable to them. Like all constitutions, the Charter also influences those realities to the extent that it represents to participants an alternative preferable to other possibilities. The Charter's predecessor, the League Covenant, could not meet this test, but undoubtedly a deep change with respect to the use of force has occurred with the emergence of bipolarity and atomic weapons. This change may give real effect to the words of the Charter and to the United Nations. The United Nations may not play the role contemplated by its founders, and the reasons for its effectiveness may not have been foreseen. But that is immaterial and largely irrelevant, if, in fact, the UN can be made to work.

No one doubts that security today is largely a function of thermonuclear stalemate and its worldwide ramifications. Whatever the United Nations, as a collectivity, does or does not do must be related to interbloc politics and must, of necessity, take into account the distribution of military power in the loose bipolar system. World-community intervention will be ineffective unless supported by either the United States or the Soviet Union and preferably by both. Opposition by one of these nations, particularly with respect to cases occurring within its zone of influence, may be sufficient to compromise the effectiveness of UN intervention although supported by the other leading bloc nation. It is possible that the Korean War might have been won despite the degree of support given the North Koreans and Chinese by the Soviet Union. However, this occurred at a time when the Soviet Union was in a position of nuclear inferiority. Even in the case of the Korean War, global considerations led to a negotiated armistice. Thus, the limits of UN effectiveness in opposing the use of force are set within the framework of nuclear weapons developments and of bipolar politics.

The Charter prohibitions on the use of military force have not been wholly effective and this state of affairs may well continue. Yet the prohibitions reflect much more than wishful thinking, and few states would seriously try to modify them in the interest of accuracy. In fact many see in these prohibitions an overriding community policy for preventing total disaster, and many assert a common interest within the society of nations in opposing minor breaches of the peace (however righteous their causes) where the risk of more general atomic conflict is substantial. The opposing blocs may well support jointly, or, at least, may not oppose, United Nations action that douses minor fires without sacrificing important bloc-security interests. And many smaller nations may support such action in a world where the United Nations is their best guarantee against major nation intervention and their most effective lever in influencing interbloc politics to their own economic and political advantage.

Those who want the rule of law enforced on a world-wide basis (provided it is their rule of law which is in fact enforced) may deplore the difficulty under the Charter of collective or individual action to enforce generally accepted community norms. But conscious abstention from the just war approach has the same hard realism. To leave loopholes permitting the use of military force in support of general expectations of righteousness, however justifiable in the abstract, would be extremely difficult to keep under control in the present concrete environmental context. Although the risk of general war in some cases may be so slight that participants can risk forcible intervention to secure particular objectives, there is virtually no way to state those conditions in doctrinal terms so long as the community remains decentralized and only partly organized.

Should a series of limited wars, reprisals, or limited retaliations be politically feasible, then Charter prohibitions will either fade into obscurity or undergo doctrinal surgery. More likely, they will remain partly, though not totally, effective. What the United Nations, with the support of at least one bloc, cannot prevent, it may nonetheless moderate through the influence of the uncommitted and because neither bloc presently wants to scuttle the UN. Clearly no combination of participants within the UN framework can control either bloc under circumstances where the bloc finds its security interests vitally affected. But the United Nations may, through its "public diplomacy" and private mediation facilities, greatly moderate occasional and, one hopes, sporadic outbreaks of violence by increasing the political costs of more than modest objectives.

If so, the UN may continue to play, with increasing effectiveness, a role that approximates Charter provisions against force and, where bloc interests are not—despite sound and fury—really jeopardized, may even actually enforce modest standards of behavior in other ways. If law enforcement involves, of necessity, consideration as to what law can be enforced, then the United Nations will refrain from over-extending its efforts and will concentrate on what it can legally accomplish rather than on abstract justice.

Yet the UN must also recognize that political change is also an important element of international political life—that the international political process must be sufficiently tempered with justice to merit the support of nations and to forestall the resort to force in desperation. If our hopes must be modest, if the nuclear age places a premium upon controlling the resort to force, it is also important that we do not abdicate political responsibility. The United Nations must not do so little that justified dissatisfaction itself becomes a threat to the peace in circumstances where the organization has the capacity, given wisdom and imagination, to do more.

Neutral rights and duties. In discussing the rise and fall of the just war concept, we noted that it was related to ideas of neutrality, and to the extent to which non-participation in war is permissible.

Efforts to control military force in support of community prescriptions require states not immediately involved in a dispute to support the participant whose cause is just. This was the view of Grotius, and it presupposes a common interest in, and responsibility for, the preservation of international law. This view is, therefore, the precursor of collective security. There can be no such status as strict neutrality, because all have a common duty to support community policy and to see that lawbreakers are punished in proportion to their guilt. The relationship of non-participants in a dispute to belligerents is a function of the neutral's appraisal of the merits of the controversy, the justice of the cause. The purpose of this arrangement, analogous to domestic law enforcement, is to deter and punish violence in opposition to legal standards and to assist the prosecution of law enforcement.

The decentralization of the international decision-making process, the fact that states put their own security and self-interest ahead of the preservation of less-important community norms, and the difficulty of appraising facts and circumstances made the system ineffective. It tended to spread rather than limit hostilities, and thus was inconsistent with the equally important community objective of confining and minimizing violence. Hence, the gradual evolution of doctrine encouraged states to remain aloof from conflict by denying them the function of judging its merits. A political system that assumes that states are not required to judge the merits of a war or to enter it as belligerents requires a doctrinal framework for relations between neutrals and belligerents. Although ideas of neutrality had existed even in the earliest times, it was only during the late eighteenth and nineteenth centuries that states expounded the law of neutrality in a number of detailed and technical rules.

The law of neutrality of the nineteenth century reflects the "balance of power" system and the basic premise of flexibility of alignment. It assumes the interaction of a minimum number of great states that have relatively equal strength and are able to assert and defend their neutral rights by the threat of participation. This system permitted and encouraged non-participation as a function of "balancing." It will be recalled that, during this period, war was not illegal but was simply a matter of sovereign discretion. The rules governing neutral relations came into operation when the legal state of peace was transmuted into that of war. Wars were usually, though not always, formally declared, especially if more than quite localized and speedy "reprisal" or "hostile measures" were contemplated. One reason for this was that it gave belligerents certain rights with regard to neutrals (for example, blockade) and it brought into effect certain duties of neutrals with regard to belligerents (for example, abstaining from giving assistance to belligerents). It was also customary for non-participants to declare their neutrality for reasons largely related to avoiding participation and to gain for themselves the economic benefits of neutral status. But most importantly, and fundamental to the political system that predominated, the existence of powerful neutrals able to redress the "balance" served to limit the objectives of the belligerents.

There is no need here to review in any detail some of the highly technical rules that developed. But it is important to recognize their general purposes and to assess their future in the light of two important changes. First, the breakdown of the political system that supported neutrality; second, the changed environmental conditions that have affected the techniques of warfare.

The rules of the nineteenth century—the doctrine we inherit today —-were in general terms an effort to accommodate reasonable military needs of the belligerents to the least possible disruption of business as usual for neutrals. The neutral state could give no assistance to either side—it could not furnish troops, make governmental loans, or provide shelter for belligerent troops (with minor maritime exceptions). The commission of such actions would have permitted a belligerent to regard the act as a hostile one justifying forcible reprisals or war. Correlatively, belligerents had to respect the territory of neutrals, refrain from attempting to use the neutral territory as a base of operations, and permit normal private intercourse between citizens of neutral countries and enemy nationals. Violation of any of these rules made the violator answerable in damages to the offended state. A famous example of damages actually assessed arose in 1872, when the *Alabama Claims Arbitration* awarded the United States $15,500,000 for British violations of neutrality in permitting the outfitting of a Confederate commerce destroyer in a British port.

The most difficult and detailed area of neutrality law has been that of the relative balancing of neutral and belligerent rights with regard to commerce on the high seas. Even prior to the First World War, and the growing importance of economic warfare, military considerations required some isolation of an enemy from sources of supply of war material. To do this effectively meant stopping and searching ships on the high seas whether they were flying enemy flags or neutral ones, and confiscating contraband cargoes. As a result, the concept of freedom of the high seas, and rules with respect to its implementation, underwent major qualification in time of war.

Once war existed, a belligerent could assert against a neutral ship the right of "visit and search," to be carried on in the most reasonable way with the least inconvenience to neutral flags. If the neutral were carrying "contraband" cargo belonging to the enemy and headed for an enemy port, the ship could be taken with its cargo to the nearest belligerent port. At this point a "prize court" of the belligerent would adjudicate the confiscation of the enemy cargo and, if the neutral ship had knowingly carried the cargo, the ship as well. If, on the other hand, the cargo was not contraband, the ship must be permitted to continue to its destination, even if the destination were the enemy country.

The Declaration of Paris of 1856 laid down rules governing search and seizure with some precision. Belligerents were permitted to seize enemy contraband goods being carried to an enemy destination on neutral ships, and neutral contraband goods to an enemy destination on enemy ships. Reasonable cause to believe this might be the situation was sufficient to justify taking the ship and cargo to port for ultimate adjudication by a Prize Court. It scarcely requires prevision to guess that difficulties arose as to what was "contraband" and evidence of ownership.

In addition to the rights of seizing contraband, a belligerent had the right of blockade. If it declared a blockade of an enemy port, and had enough ships performing blockade duty to make it "effective" and not a mere "paper blockade," the belligerent could seize and confiscate as a prize the cargo of any ship, enemy or neutral, that knowingly sought to run the blockade. In other words, once a blockade existed and neutrals notified of the fact, all cargoes were treated as contraband if bound for the port in question or seeking to leave it.

From a technical viewpoint these rules always ran into some difficulty because of disagreement between belligerents and neutrals as to what was "contraband," when a blockade was "effective," and whether rights of "visit and search" were reasonably exercised. The rules broke down almost completely in the two world wars. There were several reasons for this: technological developments, particularly submarines, expanding concepts of economic warfare, and the absence of a number of strong neutrals capable of asserting their rights effectively. During each of the two wars, there was a period when the United States was the only important neutral. Once the U.S. became involved, there was no state capable of asserting neutral rights effectively save as the belligerents (from mutual advantage) might acquiesce.

Both Allies and Axis, in both wars, wished to cut off the maximum amount of neutral trade possible with the opposing belligerent. The Germans could do so only by resort to extensive submarine warfare, and submarine warfare did not permit the niceties of reasonable visit and search with escort to port of vessels suspected of carrying contraband. The British, not faced with the same difficulty, employed three doctrinal techniques to accomplish isolation of the enemy. They greatly expanded notions of what was "contraband"; they declared a long-range "blockade" of all German ports; and they justified these, and other extensions of belligerent rights as "reprisals" against the German policy of unrestricted submarine warfare on the explicit grounds that "reprisals" against enemy action were legitimate even if they had an impact on neutrals as well. In 1916, and again in the Second World War, the British adopted an ingenious administrative procedure of issuing, through British consuls in neutral ports, "navicerts" to all neutral shipping. A ship not producing a navicert was presumed to be carrying contraband cargo to an enemy destination. British Prize Courts in both world wars used a set of presumptions to relate this wholly changed practice to inherited doctrine. Virtually every product was contraband; and even foreign credits in the control of a belligerent were considered a war asset.

Because belligerents in both world wars justified much of what they did in contravention of pre-1914 custom and convention not with relation to a changed technology but by the doctrine of "reprisal," it is possible to argue that the technical rules of neutrality have come through unscathed. Nobody really believes this as a practical matter. But it would be going too far to say that some older rules and practices may not be invoked effectively by decision makers in the future. They may not have much meaning in major wars yet continue to have operative scope in minor hostilities. Indeed, Egypt is relying on traditional doctrine in her attempted embargo of the Suez canal to Israeli shipping and to contraband cargoes destined for Israel on neutral flags.

The more interesting and difficult question is to what extent the concept of neutrality has itself survived. The provisions of the

United Nations Charter outlawing war, except in individual or collective self-defense against armed attack, embody a community policy formally subscribed to by all Members. It would seem, too, to envision a common responsibility. How long can Charter prohibitions survive claims of impartiality between belligerents irrespective of Charter rules and practices? If, in accordance with Charter provisions, the Security Council labels one belligerent an "aggressor" and calls upon all Members to assist it in restoring peace and international security to the area, can Members claim neutral status without doing violence to their Charter obligations? The answer would seem clear that rules of neutrality are not supposed to operate in situations where the Security Council, and perhaps even the General Assembly under the "Uniting for Peace" Resolution, has authoritatively characterized the violence as unlawful and called upon Members for assistance. The degree of participation may vary with capacities and location of Members; but nonparticipation would seem to run unequivocally contrary to Charter obligations.

But to say this is not to give a whole and complete answer. We should not bury neutrality prematurely on the one hand, nor assume, on the other, that it exists in all situations where authoritative United Nations action has not been taken. There are loopholes in the Charter. Most important is the operation of the veto, which may prevent the Security Council from making a decision. Also, recommendations of the Assembly may not be regarded, despite the "Uniting for Peace" Resolution, as "binding" on Members. In these circumstances states may perhaps assert neutrality without violation of Charter obligations. The same is true for non-Members in all cases. And, finally, states such as Austria which are "permanently neutral" may, with some reason, regard acceptance into the United Nations as acceptance by other Members of this neutrality.

The other side of the coin is equally important. If some states do not regard neutrality, in the absence of authoritative Security Council decision, as inconsistent with their Charter obligation, equally others may regard participation in such circumstances as permissible. A resolution of the Assembly, or even the failure of the Assembly to pass a resolution by the required two-thirds majority, may be construed by some states as authorizing them to determine unilaterally the lawfulness of belligerents' claims, and act toward them in a discriminating fashion.

We have already indicated the possibility that force may be more frequently resorted to in the loose bipolar period than would seem to be permissible under the strict terms of the Charter. If this occurs, we would expect the possibility of blocs taking appropriate counter-measures wherever limited war appeared feasible. On the other hand, groupings of "uncommitted" states may well strive to remain aloof from interbloc conflicts except where the United Nations has been able to take a strong stand in the Assembly—a vote that would reflect their willingness to be involved. In addition, in conflicts affecting the two blocs but not directly involving uncommitted states, such states are unlikely to participate, irrespective of United Nations action, in significant degree. It is difficult to avoid concluding, despite the Charter, that neutralism requires something approaching neutrality in all cases involving interbloc conflict.

The rules of neutrality of the "balance of power" period rested upon the premise that the neutral states had no real stake in the outcome; that is, they rested upon the assumptions that the war would not produce a predominant coalition and that fixed alignments would not persist as conditions changed. These assumptions ceased to hold shortly after the Franco-Prussian War. But it took some time for national practice to catch up with changed conditions. Actions by the United States during the Second World War, before the U.S. was forced into the war, hardly conformed with accepted usage. Lend-lease, bases for destroyers, and patrolling operations were certainly not neutral actions and did not stop far short of belligerency. But the rule of neutrality can hardly persist in the absence of the interests that produced and supported that rule.

In the present-day world, many factors tend to reinforce this absence of interest in neutrality. Indeed, matters have gone farther than a mere absence of neutrality in war between two states. There is intervention on behalf of rebellious colonies. The ex-colonial nations feel a strong interest in all struggles for independence. Many of the governments in these ex-colonial areas would topple if they acted otherwise. How long could Bourguiba remain in office if he did not aid the Algerian rebels? Of course, this is not completely without precedent. Witness the enthusiasm in England for the Greek rebels during the nineteenth century. Periods of radical social and ideological change may force cleavages within and between nations inconsistent with flexibility of alignment even during a "balance of power" system. In the nineteenth century most statesmen regarded such inclinations as aberrations based on sentiment rather than interest. This seems extreme even for that time. It assumes that the only interests of the state in international society concern relations between states rather than also within them. But in a period when nationalism is succumbing to regionalism and supranationalism, concern with internal developments may constitute an effective lever for national action, as Nasser has discovered.

Where strong interests support non-neutral activities, it seems hardly likely that the old rules of neutrality can be maintained, unless the state that wishes to enforce these rules is willing to drive the non-conforming states into war. But, in the Second World War, Germany preferred American non-neutrality to American belligerence, and it hardly seems likely now that France would gain by declaring war on Tunisia, when it already has so much trouble in Algeria.

Neutrality is suspended not only because war is outlawed, thus involving collective action against the aggressor, but because neutrality no longer corresponds to the interests of the uncommitted states. They are quite likely to supply one side with weapons, leaders, training facilities, and protected areas for regrouping. If the uncommitted states are no longer under the obligations of neutrality, they do not necessarily retain the rights of neutrals. There can be no objection in principle to reprisals against them. The question is rather one of prudence, that is, whether it pays to engage in reprisals.

And what is true of the uncommitted nations is also true of the blocs. Neutrality serves no genuine interest when their allies or supporters are in conflict. The Communist bloc supports North Korea and the Viet Minh, for instance, while the United States supports the Republic of Korea and Viet Nam. During the conflict in Indo-China, both sides supplied their respective allies with the sinews of war. Many warlike situations in the loose bipolar period are likely to align the blocs on opposite sides. Unlike the neutrals of the nineteenth century, the blocs are not trying to protect their neutral rights. And they cannot be compelled to accept the duties of neutrals, although they may permit others to play this role. However, we do not assert that nations will not be able to assert successfully the rights of neutrals in some—not necessarily in all—cases.

These ambiguities throw into doubt the law with respect to the rights and obligations of neutrals and belligerents. The law applied to a period in which wars were limited to security objectives (this may have included national consolidation, as in the case of Italy and Germany) and thus did not affect the interests of other states except insofar as they decided to enter the war themselves. Foreign policy was not subject, in large measure at least, to internal political considerations or to supranational political programs. We would expect the law to be in transition when the international system is in transition. But it seems doubtful whether the loose bipolar system can sustain a definite body of international law governing the rights and obligations of neutrals that applies to all armed conflicts, regardless of how they originate or regardless of who participates in them.

The laws of warfare. In an area of H-bombs and other weapons of total destruction, it may seem unrealistic to talk about laws of warfare, the more so, perhaps, when we remember the brutalities of the Second World War. And so it would be, if we could assume that the only possible wars are atomic ones with virtually unlimited objectives. But so long as there is the possibility of limited wars for limited objectives, it continues to make sense to clarify and restate community policies with regard to the conduct of hostilities.

Two major policies reflected in these rules are, first, the reduction to a minimum of unnecessary and wanton destruction of values; second, maintaining, insofar as possible, conditions that facilitate the rapid restoration of a nonviolent relationship. Past customary practices have been codified in multilateral treaties, particularly the Hague Conventions of 1907 and the Geneva Prisoner of War Convention of 1949 (replacing an earlier convention). Some of these rules have to do with the actual conduct of hostilities, treatment of captured and wounded personnel, occupation of enemy territory, and treatment of local populace and property; others deal with treatment of enemy aliens and alien property located in the foreign state. The 1907 Convention is clearly outmoded by new technological conditions in several respects, but the 1949 Convention is, presumably, an authoritative statement of contemporary policy.

The central core of difficulty in the laws of war is that of balancing "military necessity" against humanitarian standards of conduct. Military necessity is almost infinitely expansible, especially if measured against belligerents' objectives. These are often stated in sweeping terms such as "victory," "unconditional surrender," or the like. What is "necessary" can only be measured in particular factual contexts and in relation to purpose or objective. It may be possible in some circumstances to separate a specific military objective (for example, the capture of a city) from broader political purposes. But it would be a mistake to think that the former are constants while the latter vary. At least in general outline, military purposes are related to and determined by political purposes. There might, in most circumstances, be a consensus that the military occupation of a city does not require wholesale slaughter of its civilian population. But what of so-called strategic bombing of cities, or the decision to use the atomic bomb against Hiroshima and Nagasaki? And consider the Korean "war" with the continuing tension between the objective of "restoring international peace and security" and what was called the "military necessity" of crossing the thirty-eighth parallel. Here, it would seem, there was an effort to resolve a difference of opinion as to the permissible political objectives by talking in terms of necessary military ones.

The more limited the political objectives of violence, the less the amount of military coercion that may be needed to achieve them, and the greater the possibilities of controlling the methods employed by belligerents. It would be dangerous to assume, despite the United Nations Charter, that there is widespread agreement on what political objectives will be considered lawful. But there is reason to believe that limited objectives may nonetheless be espoused and that, as a consequence, much of the laws of war may survive in such contexts. We might consider in this connection the efforts of the British and French in Suez to avoid unnecessary destruction of civilian property or lives, the treatment of prisoners in the Korean War, and the degrees of compliance and non-compliance with customary rules in Indo-China.

It is, of course, a mistake to relate community prescriptions about the lawful resort to force to community prescriptions regarding the conduct of hostilities. Whether the resort to force is, in terms of objectives (aggression or self-defense), lawful is a different question from whether the laws of war have been violated by belligerents. The community may fail in its attempt to control violence at the outset but still be successful in minimizing its consequences. To characterize all acts as unlawful because tainted from the outset by the illegality of the war itself would be to defeat the humanitarian purposes of the rules. There is general agreement that the laws of war apply to all situations of military hostilities, lawful or unlawful, and should not, despite occasional limiting language in treaties, be defeated by technical arguments irrelevant to their general purpose.

To many the idea that there can be law of war is very nearly a contradiction in terms, for they see war as the antithesis of law, a lawless situation in which sanctions will be largely ineffective and particularly against a ruthless enemy whose convictions about human dignity may be wholly different from one's own. They support this argument by pointing to the numerous violations of the laws of war in the last two wars, and in the Korean action. They predict that the Soviets and Chinese, on past performance, would pay little attention to the niceties of Prisoner of War Conventions and have little respect for civilian lives or property.

This argument is usually overstated, for by concentrating on the degree to which past customs have been violated in specific instances it understates the extent to which the existence of rules of war have influenced and moderated belligerent action. The realistic question is not the prediction, as to the degree of compliance or non-compliance, but whether humanitarian policies are better served by clarifying to the extent possible the limits of permissible conduct or by abandoning such attempts. No one who has examined the war crimes trials of Germans or Japanese would conclude that customary rules of war did not have genuine operative scope, even if practice was not always in explicit compliance with the rules and often fell below prescribed levels. It would be rash to predict that this past experience is irrelevant to future situations.

The argument usually embodies a second fallacy in its unspoken premise of reciprocity. The sanction supporting the laws of war is self-interest. Sometimes this may be measured in terms of reciprocal treatment, but by no means always. The fact that one side violates the rules of war may technically justify the other in taking appropriate action in reprisal. Reprisal has as its purpose forcing the other belligerent to comply. But the laws of war rest on a more solid basis of self-interest than simply reciprocal treatment. Unnecessary destruction of values is both pointless and harmful. If it stimulates hatred and fear in the enemy, it will correspondingly increase his will to resist and thus increase the military cost of obtaining the belligerent state's objectives. Soldiers who expect to die if captured will fight harder. Civilians who expect to see their homes burned and wives raped will take to arms. Nazi policies in occupied parts of the Soviet Union offer an excellent lesson in the wisdom of economizing on unnecessary and savage use of force. And, finally, to permit oneself to engage in uncivilized brutality without reason is to destroy one's own values in the process.

In future wars, there will be violations of the laws of war as there have been in the past. New technology will continue to make it hard to adjust old doctrine to new and fluid situations and to new formulations of "military necessity." The Hague Conventions are sorely in need of restatement for contemporary warfare. But so long as a Carthaginian peace is not sought, the laws of war will continue to have operative scope. This scope will be reduced, however, for in the bloc system, as opposed to the "balance of power" system, with its principle of flexibility of alignment, there is not the additional incentive that the enemy of today may well be the ally of tomorrow.

part  III

THE ORGANIZATIONAL FRAMEWORK

9

"SOURCES" OF INTERNATIONAL LAW

I<small>T</small> is a commonplace that law is a process, not a body of self-executing rules, and that the institutional framework in which doctrine is created, invoked, and applied is of decisive importance in understanding the decision-making process. It is our purpose in this chapter, and in the next, to examine this framework.

The "sources" of international law have become stereotyped; they are treaties, custom, general principles of law, judicial precedents, textbook writers, and reason. What is not made clear by the writers who describe these "sources" is that the concern here is with method and technique. How does a decision maker support or refute a claim that a given act is or is not consistent with international law? Where does he look for argumentation, support, and reasoning?

It is a common error to treat all officials who invoke international law as though their roles were identical and as though, in each case, their major motivations were to act as impartial international judges. Such an approach distorts the actual process and attempts to transfer to the international arena the judicial philosophy that, as we previously stated, was identified with Austin and the growth of a legislative body. Such an approach insists that we can and should appraise decisions only from the point of view of their compatibility with a set of legal norms that dictate a single resolution. The technique is thus wholly confused with the larger process. At most it is one part of the process, and is itself dependent on the existence of other methods of making decisions. A judicial system, as we know from our own history, operates quite differently where a developed legislative alternative exists from where it does not.

The preponderant position of the nation-state, at least as exampled by the great nations, has, of course been an obstacle to the most effective organization of the international law process, for it has meant, with *ad hoc* exceptions of international arbitrations or cases before international courts, that international law has been the exclusive domain of state officials. Primarily, it has been employed by national judges on the theory of its incorporation into domestic law, and by foreign office officials in justification or protest of national acts. In each instance, it has unavoidably been circumscribed by national objectives and national policies, since the decision-making officials are cast in national roles.

This national identification is not a fatal defect to the existence of a legal order, but it is a block to its development beyond a relatively undeveloped stage. A central authority to resolve disputes and to prescribe and enforce norms of the larger community is not a necessary ingredient of law, for other constraints exist that can make for generally lawful behavior. The essence of the legal process lies in the fact that the authority of public officials is limited by formal norms and processes, and is thus imbued with a degree of objectivity.

Formal norms may be changed and modified in various ways. In a developed legal system, the legislative process, itself subject to both procedural and (often) substantive limitations, is explicitly designed to perform the function of transforming political objectives into formally binding law-rules. In addition, however, formal rules constantly interact with informal restraints through a process of interpretation and reinterpretation, by the growth of "custom" (the process of abstracting rules from past conduct), by Reason, and by analogy. The preservation of order, as well as the sense of justice and fair play, is closely related to expectations; a consistent pattern of activity in the past creates an expectation of similar conduct in the future.

We can consider the legal process from at least two perspectives. The first is that of method or technique—the means by which an official seeks to justify a decision as one which is "lawful." As we have said, any decision with normative content may be analyzed and discussed from the perspective of its consistency or inconsistency with pre-existing formal prescriptions. Any invocation of law requires a minimum of consistency with pre-existing norms, even where these norms are sufficiently general and sufficiently obscure to permit a quite broad discretion in the particular decision maker. In other words, a decision maker is limited in his alternatives, both substantively and procedurally, by the existence of pre-existing norms.

Secondly, we can view the process from the point of view of who the decision maker is, and the role he plays in the total process. The same question may be presented to the International Court of Justice, to a national court, and to a foreign office. Each may purport to resolve the problem by reference to the same body of materials and employ similar techniques to justify its resolution. Yet the difference of role may lead to variant conclusions and variant justifications.

We will examine this problem in more detail in the next Chapter. It should, however, be noted that the great bulk of officials, national or supranational, are not charged with important roles in formulating policy in the international community. Each year thousands of questions involving international law are presented to such officials in the course of their routine duties without raising dramatic questions of national policy. Routine interpretations of treaties or other "sources" are handled routinely, and with considerable circumspection, because minor officials do not wish to become the cause of international controversy. This adds both objectivity and stability to the process, for there is general hesitation to approach the limits of discretion and an inclination to stay well within the bounds of prior practice. Problems of international law are treated just as problems of national law would be by most bureaucrats. Innovation comes only at a relatively high level of national decision making. Most officials feel a national as well as an international pressure to act with moderation and a sense of fairness, that is, within the constraints of general expectation.

For all decision makers, the recorded experience of mankind is a valuable, indeed indispensable, guide to the present and future. But they may employ history differently. Deriving principles from the past is a method of identifying and resolving problems to be encountered, the likelihood of success or failure, the acquiescence, support or opposition of others. The extent to which one can persuasively relate a decision to past decisions of others is a technique for disarming opposition and gaining acceptance on grounds of reasonableness and moderation. Consistency is a political as well as a legal virtue, for the expectations of others are conditioned by past experience and by past statements and acts. For the judge, cast in an impartial role, consistency helps to establish his lack of bias or favoritism among litigants as well as assisting future claimants to predict future judicial responses to various facts and argument. For the political decision maker, impartiality is not a formal requirement of the role, but consistency is no less important if conflict and collision are to be held to a minimum. Others must design their policies on the assumption that abrupt changes in position will be the exception, and that there is general appreciation of the virtues of principled action, even where there is disagreement as to the proper principles.

Invoking precedents found in the accepted "sources" of law serves these purposes. But the process is not, as we have emphasized, one exclusively of impartial application of pre-existing norms, discovered in the "sources," to contemporary facts. It may often involve little more in routine matters. But the process clearly involves using the same techniques to formulate new rules, to amend old ones, to terminate still others—functions we associate with the legislative process and political institutions. In the international process, the formal equivalent of a legislative process is explicit agreement, and this often proves cumbersome and difficult. Hence, to a considerable extent it may be bypassed, and new wine poured into old bottles by a purposeful rereading of history.

In a relatively static and stable society it is possible to deal with legislative problems by a process of gradual adjustment, relying heavily on interpretation of old rules and customs to adapt to new situations. It is characteristic of traditional, non-bureaucratic government that functions are structurally intermingled. The methodology of the common law was essentially the methodology of the ethical jurisprudence that marked the law-of-nature system, and that can be found today in the less-developed legal systems of Afro-Asia, despite European influence. Indeed, one of the major problems of this area is adapting Muslim law, or native tribal law, to a society that seeks salvation in economic development; discussions among Arab lawyers as to the best way of accomplishing this change are not unlike those of the Western world at a comparable time of development.

As Western society became more socially mobile and interdependent, and as technology created serious problems of social and ethical adjustment, the need for more explicit norms to deal with change led to increasing dependence upon legislation. In part this was required to coordinate the activities of governmental officials as bureaucracy grew; in part it was necessary to clarify, and thus stabilize, the new relations that an expanded commerce and industry brought into being. As we have seen, positivism replaced natural law as the dominant jurisprudence, and the basic "source" of law became the edicts of government rather than the ethical consensus of the people as expressed through custom. Change was too rapid to permit customs to evolve, and the need for certainty was too great (in economic matters, for example) to permit adjustment after the fact. In no country did this mean that past customs were discarded or that ethical ideas were found to be irrelevant. They heavily influenced the content of legislation and continued to supplement both the words of statutes and the decisions of officials charged with their interpretation and application. Legislation was superimposed on the existing system and became the primary source of authority. In civil-law systems, officials were formally confined to the written codes, but were permitted to use custom, general conceptions of righteousness, the views of scholars, and so forth, as an aid to the interpretation of rules formally enacted. In the common-law system, customary law (the judge-made rules), and legislation proceeded hand-in-hand as supplements and complements, with legislation getting the superior formal status in the event of conflict.

In the international system, legislative supplements to, or substitutes for, the tradition-oriented legal system have been more difficult to evolve for reasons already discussed at length. Theories of state sovereignty and the concomitant jettisoning of the law-of-nations approach met some of the real needs by freeing states from a number of procedural restrictions on their freedom to adjust to new international situations. States were free to innovate unless a positive rule of international law forbade, and the burden of proving the existence of the rule fell to the objecting party. The net effect was to increase greatly the formally unfettered area of state discretion and to rely predominantly upon informal, or political, checks to its abuse. This was not an unmixed blessing. The need for norms was met, somewhat clumsily, by increasing the number and scope of formal agreements, or treaties, and by a general deference to "customary" practices and ways of doing things without formal acknowledgment of their "binding" natures.

The techniques employed and the sources invoked are strikingly parallel in the domestic and international systems. The difference lies largely, as we have noted, in the difficulty of developing a system of legislation comparable to that developed by domestic governments, and of segregating, as a result, governmental functions structurally in the manner characteristic of domestic societies. The international process remains relatively undeveloped as a governmental system.

The sources of law are considered below. The use of sources to support reasoning concerning the state of international law restricts international decision makers to claims that have foundations in past agreement or conduct. Yet these sources do not restrict the decision maker to a single position. The use of sources involves technique and method, and conclusions reached are related to values and objectives. The technique is not purely mechanical and cannot be understood properly until related to the context in which it is used.

Treaties. Except for decisions by the Security Council and (perhaps) some recommendations by the General Assembly, the closest international analogue to legislation is international agreement. In a legal system that adopts a theoretically consensual approach and finds law in the agreement of states, the formal agreements embodied in treaties are obviously the prime sources of legal obligation. They are superior to other "sources" in several respects. The existence of the rule, and the acquiescence of the signatory states to be bound by it, are established without difficulty or cavil; in general, the language is carefully drafted and subject to no more ambiguity in its interpretation than the typical legislative enactment; the utility of the treaty process and the value of keeping agreements are appreciated by all states. The "scrap of paper" attitude toward treaties and agreements is rare indeed. In short, there is a strong predisposition to honor treaties faithfully and to comply with their terms. As a result, they add considerable certainty and stability to the conduct of international affairs.

There are several forms of intergovernmental agreement and several virtually interchangeable names for the documents customarily used: charter, convention, agreement, treaty, exchange of notes, and so forth. Such differences do not have, in intention or interpretation, any international significance. What is important is simply the fact of agreement, indicated in any appropriate form, by a head of state or by a properly authorized representative. Usually this is clear enough. International relations are normally attended by abundant formality. Controversy usually focusses on the interpretation of various provisions, or on whether or not an agreement has been terminated or suspended, not on whether it is initially in force. But the growing personal diplomacy by heads of state, during and since the Second World War, may be productive of new problems in this connection, especially since the agreements entered into may, like Yalta or Potsdam, have especially volatile political contents.

Such difficulties are to some extent compounded by the lack of any doctrinal requirement that the binding quality of an agreement

depends upon the use of a particular form.   In fact, the Permanent
Court of International Justice held that an oral statement by the
Norwegian foreign minister in a controversy with Denmark to the
effect that his government would not press any claims to Greenland
was legally binding on Norway, at least after Denmark had relied on
it to its detriment.   In the circumstances the decision may well have
been the fair one, but it is difficult to derive from the decision a rule
which is not too extreme for practical purposes.

In the course of conducting international relations, a vast number
of informal understandings are arrived at by officials at all levels.
Sometimes these are tacit assumptions, sometimes express agreements.
It is also clear that honoring these agreements is important to political
processes and that, generally, self-interest is promoted by a reputation
for honesty and integrity.   Comparable processes exist in business
relations and in domestic politics.   The businessman who does not
honor his word, irrespective of his legal obligations, usually loses
customers; the Senator who is unreliable is not admitted to the "Club"
and usually loses prestige, influence, and power.   A vast variety of
such agreements occur in society and are not regarded as legally binding; that is to say, a complainant cannot go into court and secure performance or compensation for the breach of such an agreement.
Sanctions exist, but they are not the formal ones of the governmental
process.

All domestic legal systems have difficulty in verbalizing the distinction between agreements that are legally enforceable and those
that are not.   Several different but complementary criteria are employed: the degree of explicitness, the formalities attendant, the
relationship of the parties, the subject matter of the agreement, the
seriousness of detrimental action in reliance, and so forth.   Courts
will not enforce "political" agreements, nor (for the most part) inter-
familial arrangements, or social obligations unconnected with profit.
To a degree courts are balancing the expectations of the community
as to the category of agreement involved and the social utility of
permitting recourse to governmental force to secure compliance.   Not
all promises are backed up by the government.

Despite a wholly different context, analogous considerations are
present in the international arena, and there is wide appreciation in
practice that many political understandings are not to be elevated to
the formal status of legally binding international agreements.   Despite
the judgment of the Permanent Court, it would be rare to find in-

formal arrangements treated as treaties. This is not to say that there is no expectation that they will be honored; the contrary is true. The understanding is simply that a failure to do so will not ordinarily be claimed to be a breach of an international obligation; the ponderous channels of formal protest will not be employed.

In the practice of states distinctions of this kind are made, and normally a good deal of formality attends the legally binding arrangements. But, in the international arena, the mechanisms for resolution and enforcement are not altogether similar to those of the domestic one, and, as a consequence, the two situations shade into one another. Resolution and remedy in both instances are likely to be accomplished through political channels—negotiation, compromise, threat, and (ultimately) self-help. Such sanctions may be real enough; it is unrealistic to talk of a lack of sanctions. Nor is it always a question of "power" in any easily measurable sense; disparity in size and military potential may make for peculiar difficulties for the "stronger" party, as Fidel Castro has discovered. In both cases, the most important sanction is usually the simple one of preserving the reputation for keeping agreements. The efforts to which states go in order to preserve this reputation is some indication of its efficacy. Yet it is clearly not always effective.

It is common practice for both statesmen and scholars (perhaps with differing conclusions) to resolve questions as to the existence of, or proper interpretation of, international agreements, by hypothesizing an impartial arbiter. The techniques of argumentation are thus associated with processes that rarely are actually available to the disputants, with the invocation of legal principles and the elaboration of relevant provisions in their application to facts. This fiction serves a useful function in promoting rational argument and discussion, in discouraging extreme positions, and, to the extent it is convincing to relevant audiences, in preserving a reputation for disciplined and lawful behavior. As a technique, it is familiar to all of us, for, in any argument, it is usually alleged that an unbiased observer would side with the proponent. Substantively it further moderates extreme positions by the practice of using formal arguments as precedent for future argument. Nonetheless, to talk in such fashion and actually to submit the dispute to an impartial arbiter are different decisions. A claimant may be convinced as to the merits of his position without feeling assured that a third person will accept it, particularly where the claimant is putting forth an argument that contains an element of novelty. And the fact that a dispute will not normally be resolved by such reference is clearly relevant to understanding the process.

The position that states are bound by law as they interpret the law is clearly different from the position that states are bound by law as an impartial observer interprets it. The first position leaves open the theoretical possibility that states will interpret treaties wholly arbitrarily and unreasonably. But extreme behaviour is in fact relatively rare. And it is at least possible, in the present state of world politics, that a counter-principle, subjecting agreements to impartial adjudication, would be more likely to discourage agreements than to promote reference to impartial tribunals. Until processes of evaluation, amendment, and enactment of law are improved, this possibility should be kept in mind. Making international law more "legal" might, without qualification, simply destroy the treaty as a workable tool of order.

In the view of legal scholars, the "law of treaties" is largely derived from general principles of contract common to the various domestic legal systems. The consensual approach to international law promotes this analytical method. So, too, does the fact that most treaties are formally bilateral arrangements between two states, rather than general "legislation" for the international community. Many such arrangements are cast in the form, and perhaps even have the substance, of mutual advantage and reciprocal rights, thus promoting a "bargain" concept characteristic of a contractual prototype. But it is sobering to remember, too, that the parties to these "contracts" are political entities, represented by governments subject to the vicissitudes of politics, and that they double as international legislators. The contract analysis can be overdone, for there may be overriding considerations which demonstrate that it is no longer in the interest of the community as a whole to insist on literal compliance with a particular agreement, or situations where it is not possible politically for a government to honor its international commitments. It is certainly unrealistic now, and even yesterday, to think of the international community as little more than a series of bilateral arrangements among various participants. Almost always it is and has been something more. Diplomats act with the awareness that other governments, like their own, have domestic political problems. They know, too, that arrangements between their government and others are watched carefully by still others, that States C and D are interested in what States A and B agree to.

For these reasons treaties are almost always something more than, or different from, a contractual arrangement. And the legislative analogy helps us to see why this is true.

On matters of common concern there have developed a variety of practices that tend to promote uniformity, thus approaching "legislation" for the community as a whole. The most straightforward and direct is the multilateral convention with a number of signatories and provisions for the adherence of still others. Such an approach to problems of general concern has become increasingly more common; it has the obvious advantage of a uniform arrangement (far more simple to implement in a bureaucracy) and the obvious disadvantage of accepting, in each case, the lowest common denominator at which it is possible to secure agreement. The search for unanimity tends, in some cases, to result in compromises that are really not satisfactory to anyone or that, in many instances, are difficult to "sell" to domestic politicians upon whom treaty ratification depends. It is, for example, often difficult for the United States government to persuade two-thirds of the Senators, answerable to a local electorate, that something less than the U.S. view is the best of all possible treaties.

Despite doctrine that treaties are only binding on signatory states, law-making treaties, such as the Hague Conventions on the rules of war, may have much wider effect. A treaty may, in fact, bind not only the states that sign it, but others as well. It cannot bind such other states as parties to the contract, but it may nonetheless be effective. Some multilateral agreements fall into this category and others do not. Let us examine why.

An agreement by South American nations to apply the vector principle to land claims in Antarctica may be binding on these nations but is certainly not binding on other nations. The failure to bind other nations does not stem from the fact that less than a majority of the nations of the world agree to the vector principle or even that less than a majority of the most powerful nations agree. There is no rule of the international society that an agreement becomes binding because a majority either of all or of the most important nations agree to it. The agreement fails to bind because the vector principle —apart from producing inconsistent claims—would exclude claims by important nations having a strong interest in Antarctic claims. It is not clear that nations have an interest in regulating claims to Antarctica but it is clear that many important nations have an interest in not accepting the vector principle. A principle that cannot reconcile the interests of all the important nations so that any momentary disadvantage arising from its application is outweighed by the the long-term advantages of the rule cannot gain recognition as a rule of law in a society structured like the international society. Judges or textbook writers may attempt to ignore this consideration. But an unenforceable normative structure is wishful thinking, not law.

The situation is quite different with respect to conventions on the treatment of prisoners of war. In a European society in which the objectives of war are limited and in which the enemy of today may be the friend of tomorrow, there is a clear interest in such regulation. And in societies in which a high value is placed on the individual, protection of nationals—even during war—is an important goal. In such circumstances all nations have an interest in a set of rules governing the treatment of prisoners. Obviously, many quite different sets of rules might be consistent with this interest. But the interest in a workable set of rules is much greater than is the interest in any particular set of rules (within some limits, of course).

The first enunciation of rules by a substantial body of nations is bound to be taken seriously because renegotiation, particularly during war but also during peace, is very difficult. It is usually much easier to secure agreement on well-delineated standards, than to agree on changes in those standards, for the attempt to change the agreement will often fragment the proponents into many sharply opposed camps. It is almost always easier to remain where you are, if that is fairly satisfactory, than to agree to any particular change.

But for this very reason, even nations that have not signed a convention on prisoners of war are likely to be forced to regard the rules as binding on them, at least within broad limits. They are likely to impose these obligations on themselves because of their interest in such regulations and because of the opportunity for reprisal by the other nations and the undesirable consequence of such reprisals.

For the reasons given, multilateral agreement between nations will not bind them unless the agreement regulates some aspect of behavior the international community (or its most important members) has an interest in enforcing. If the agreement is so specific that its particular form involves just the signatory nations, it is binding upon them only. Some conventions on the use of tributary rivers, for instance, may be related to local conditions; generalization from such an agreement may serve no useful purpose. In this case, the rules worked out may be enforceable with respect to the parties to the treaty because there is an international interest in enforcement but not applicable elsewhere because there is no international interest in extending the particular rule.

In other cases, agreements specify rules that are of general interest and which it is not possible or desirable to vary. Almost any nation may go to war with any other nation, for instance. Therefore it would be undesirable to have different sets of rules for every possible combination of belligerents. The pattern of international intercourse is too complex for anything but a single set of rules to prove workable. In this case, the accession of a sizable number of nations to a convention governing some aspect of waging war will have great weight. It may not prove desirable to attempt to extend the rules universally down to the smallest or up to the most general details. But the convention will set a general standard for practice from which permissible deviations will tend to be small even for non-signatories.

To the extent that a multilateral convention is itself claimed by the signatories to represent a codification of existing customary law, or general principles of jurisprudence, the universal effect is increased. For signatories it may be simply a formal restatement of the law, akin to domestic codes; for non-signatories it represents an impressive consensus of what "customary" law is, and puts upon them the difficult burden of justifying conflicting practices. They may not be legally bound by the treaty *qua* international agreement, but they are bound by the "customary" law that is here codified.

Even without this prop of "custom," the mere fact of substantial agreement among many weakens the case of the lone deviationist. Cautious institutionalization of this substantial majority "legislation" may be found in recent efforts, under UN auspices, to negotiate treaties of wide import and application. The four Geneva conventions on maritime matters, for example, were negotiated under a practice that required a two-thirds majority approval of each provision. What two-thirds of the nations approve is persuasive in most instances to the remaining dissenters, even if it cannot be said to constitute a formal legislative majority.

Although there is an increasing tendency towards formal multilateral resolution of common problems, something of the same effect has been achieved in the past by other devices. It has always been difficult, in matters of common concern, to negotiate separate and differing bilateral agreements. The United States, for example, has often proposed substantially the same language to many states on matters, such as those encompassed within the standard "Friendship, Navigation, and Commerce" treaties, which are of widespread interest. A concession made to one state must, without special circumstances, be extended to others who ask it. In any event the pressures of bureaucracy argue for the simplicity of common language and substance. Formal acknowledgment of this truism may be found in "most favored nation" clauses, in economic matters, where the parties agree to automatic extension to signatories of any future concessions made to others. At a less formal level, it is equally apparent that interpretations of language common to many treaties is persuasive with regard to others identically worded. In such fashion a process and rules that are formally bilateral, become, in most respects, of far wider effect and application. The result may fall short of universality, but it does produce principles of general, and potentially universal, relevance.

Although it is said that states have the widest latitude in their international arrangements vis-a-vis each other, it scarcely requires much argument to demonstrate that informal restraints are ubiquitous. States are hesitant to make arrangements with one another that are offensive to others or that will require renegotiation of existing agreements in order to accord equality of treatment to all. The "international interest," always present, is much more pervasive than formal doctrine acknowledges, just as, in domestic politics, the formal restraints on legislation are minimal and the informal restraints considerable. To some extent the international interest is formally acknowledged, as are constitutional restraints in domestic affairs. The UN Charter is a formal restraint upon bilateral arrangements which conflict with it. In this respect it resembles a constitution capable of invalidating inconsistent bilateral agreements, prior or subsequent, which impugn its provisions.

We cannot predict, in tumultuous times, the scope of this capacity to find treaties "unconstitutional" in an international sense. But it is possible and perhaps probable that prior or subsequent bilateral arrangements must comply with the terms of the Charter as interpreted by both the Security Council in its decisions (which must be "binding" despite conflicting interstate arrangements if they are to have the meaning attached to them by the Charter) and perhaps also even by recommendations of the General Assembly. Depending, of course, on the viability of Charter processes, the door is thus wide open for formalizing important international interests heretofore left to the realm of political restraints. It is, as a matter of technique, relatively simple to postulate for all agreements an implied condition that they comply with the Charter and actions taken thereunder by its component parts. The possibility that bilateral arrangements found inconsistent with the larger international interest may be thus invalidated formally, as a matter of law, or interpreted in a manner consistent with Charter obligations, is greatly increased by Charter arrangements that expand and channel the informal considerations that previously influenced the treaty process.

As we noted in Chapter 1, the difficulty with the treaty process is not with the basic concept that treaties should be faithfully honored, but with the processes for appraisal, modification and termination. Agreements in which there is and continues to be mutual advantage, and which are terminable by either party on short notice, generally work well enough, for the capacity to terminate is a pressure to discuss and modify oppressive provisions. Agreements of long duration, or agreements that are the result of coercion or superior bargaining power rather than negotiation (Versailles would be the obvious example) are far less satisfactory unless political conditions continue unchanged. Generally, circumstances do change, and agreements that are too burdensome to one party will not endure under circumstances favorable to denunciation. Doctrine neither prohibits, despite talk about a consensual base, long-term commitments (the Panama Canal Zone was granted in perpetuity) nor does it reprehend coerced agreements. But such commitments and agreements seldom work well, and the Versailles experience was not lost on the victors in the Second World War, despite the "unconditional" surrender of the Fascist states.

Attempts to freeze the future in terms of present advantages is really inconsistent with the role of states as legislative participants in the international community and with the fact that governments must answer to domestic constituencies. There are times when it is genuinely impossible for a government to honor an international agreement and to stay in power; and intervention by another state to secure its "rights" may well be contrary to the interests felt by international society and by other major states. There may be for most states a greater interest in preserving international order and dissuading violence in most situations than in preserving the provisions of any particular treaties, or even the principle of the sanctity of treaty obligations. United Nations Charter provisions reprehending any use of force give some evidence for this judgment.

In comparing the treaty process to domestic law making, we are struck by the fact that a law, or even a constitutional provision, is subject to the possibility of more liberal amendment than a treaty. When treaties have considerable flexibility, and when as a result there is willingness to reconsider, review, amend, or terminate in an orderly way, they work best.

The doctrine that treaties are no longer binding when conditions have so changed as to defeat their purpose (*rebus sic stantibus*) is an inadequate effort to invent doctrine to serve a real need. But conditions always change somewhat, and it is difficult to articulate an objective test to measure when they have changed sufficiently to invoke this escape. Some situations are relatively common and manageable, and a good deal of practice and precedent exists as to what treaties are suspended or terminated by hostilities between the signatories, and as to the right of one party to withhold performance, or terminate, in the event of non-performance by the other. But the need to improve processes of amendment and termination to meet new conditions remains, and it seems incapable of doctrinal solution. More workable processes are likely to be found in the pressures that can be organized and made effective in supranational forums.

The shift from the "balance of power" political system to the loose bipolar one has had several consequences for the treaty process. A few of the more important should be noted.

First, as between members of opposing blocs, and particularly between the U.S.A. and U.S.S.R., there is awareness that the opposing bloc will seize immediate political advantages whenever they arise, and little confidence in good faith execution of treaties in which there does not continue to be at all times a close balance of benefit and burden. At the same time, each is prone to accuse the other, on the slightest provocation, of failure to live up to its international obligations. These attitudes are scarcely conducive to a proliferation of new treaties. Indeed, a good argument can be made that the very formality of the treaty inhibits both from employing it for fear also of their own future inability to comply, and that less formal, even tacit, understandings work better.

The second major change has been touched on already in several places. A shift in internal politics that aligns a state with an opposing bloc may have considerable impact on the desirability of preserving many treaty arrangements that had tacitly assumed at least a neutral status. In many instances there may be mutual incentive to discontinue such treaties, but each may be reluctant to propose to the other that such a treaty be formally terminated. More likely, the treaty will simply pass tacitly into disuse in many cases, and in others be terminated by mutual agreement or, perhaps, unilaterally without serious protest.

Finally, among bloc members and between blocs and uncommitted nations there is (in sharp contrast to interbloc relations) great
reluctance to press treaty rights if to do so would be politically un-
wise, and consequently considerable willingness to renegotiate, amend,
and even terminate agreements that are unpopular or that, if pressed,
would lead to crises internally or internationally. The United States,
for example, has shown a restraint that in times past would have
been unbelievable in dealing with Castro's Cuba (even after it
became obvious that nothing could quickly be salvaged by dealing
patiently with Castro) because of considerable Latin American
sympathy with many of his reforms. And the British-French effort
at Suez in 1956 does not give us confidence that treaty rights are, in
the face of intransigeance, capable of vindication today on grounds of
law enforcement through self-help.

In a competing and divided world, there is maximum opportunity
within blocs and even between blocs and uncommitted nations to
improve the legislative process by acting within supranational organizations, and to modify treaty arrangements and "customary" rules to
take account of new political developments. Since such modifications are "voluntary," just as smaller nations once "voluntarily" accepted the rules of the major states, the modifications can be fitted
into the existing law of treaties. But to do so is to ignore the fact
that the treaty process today is very changed from what it was half
a century ago. We may look to less use of treaties to lay down substantive rules, and to more use of treaties to set up common constitutional procedures according to which such rules will be established
within the limits of competence set by the treaty itself. The treaty
process is simply too ponderous, without further mechanisms for joint
action, to deal with international legislative needs.

Custom as a source of law. In simple traditional communities custom is the major "source of law. It obliges not because of habit
but because such communities are tradition-oriented. Moreover,
such communities are the focus of solidary sentiments and loyalties.
Custom is binding because it is part of a pattern of mutual rights and
obligations—because it is right and not because it is expedient. The
violator of custom upsets the order of the world for such traditional
communities. The response of the community to the violation is
necessary to re-establish this order without which the individual
members of the community cannot have faith in the world or carry
out daily tasks necessary to the life of the community. It is of the

essence of customary law that it does not change rapidly and that it is relatively unresponsive to demands for change.

Attempts to invoke custom as international law inevitably run into the difficulties stemming from the differences between modern international society and custom-oriented traditional communities. The tradition-oriented community in which real custom plays a major role is largely a primary society; it is slowly changing; it is particularistic and ascriptive in its value orientations. The international society is a secondary society. It is subject to rapid change both in terms of developments internal to the nation and relations between nations. The relatively small number of nations in the international society means that there seldom are impartial bystanders or impersonal judicial organs to whom one can apply in case of dispute. The nations that are bystanders often have more to gain from taking sides than from maintaining a particular customary norm. The individual receives support from his national society and not from the international society. Indeed, he hardly ever participates in international activities until they affect him personally, by means of draft or taxation. International practice is largely instrumental.

It is commonly assumed that international customs do exist and to a considerable extent international law is assimilated to customary law. This assumption, however, deserves to be tested. It is clear that many decisions of law courts refer to putative customary international law. But do they refer to something more than habit or usage? Does it really prove anything to look at diplomatic correspondence, official instructions to diplomats or to military commanders, acts of national legislation and court decisions? Does practice alone create that obligatory character which raises the action from the level of mere habit? Even if one accepts general practice rather than the more difficult test of universal practice, what does this prove?

It is necessary at least briefly to examine the arguments for customary international law and to discover whether courts do accept the expediential character of practice or the binding character of custom. The difference is radically important, for in one case the obligatory character is independent of expediency and in the other case the obligation to observe the practice stems from and is no stronger than the expediency that gives rise to it. In the latter case, the "custom" will be changed as rapidly as expediency dictates.

The case of *The Scotia*, settled before the United States Supreme Court in 1871, is often cited as one of the strongest cases demonstrating the existence of customary international law. *The Berkshire,* an American sailing ship, carrying white lights, contrary to American and British law, was rammed and sunk by *The Scotia,* a British steamship operating under similar legislation. The owners of *The Berkshire* claimed that the steamship did not take the proper precautions to avoid collision and therefore was liable. The court examined the practice of nations and discovered that over thirty nations, "almost every commercial nation in existence," had adopted the same law with respect to lights. The court held therefore against the owners of *The Berkshire* on the ground that the violation of the law by *The Berkshire* was the cause of the collision.

Suppose for a moment, however, that over thirty nations had not adopted similar legislation. Would *The Berkshire* have been vindicated? Or would the court then have held that, since Great Britain and the United States had adopted similar legislation, and since these maritime routes were traversed primarily by British and American ships, *The Berkshire* had still caused the collision by, in effect, "signal[ling] to *The Scotia* that she was a steamer, and [thus] direct[ing] to *The Scotia* to do exactly what she did"? The court held that the law of the place, the maritime law, and not the law of the United States or Great Britain governed the case. But would it really have reached the outrageous decision that *The Berkshire* was not at fault if only the two countries had adopted the new regulations governing lights carried on ships?

It is difficult to believe that the court would have held that way. The concurrence of so many nations gave the court an easy solution but it is almost certain that the court's decision would not have been different under changed circumstances. Every nation has an obvious interest in avoiding maritime accidents. If nations can agree concurrently or independently upon the same rules for ships and vessels, the matter is simplified. In this case, even the ships of non-complying nations would be expected to comply because such a course is common prudence in view of the general practice. A vessel that did not comply or take precautions would be liable, not because it violated the law but because it was negligent.

In the same way, if only the United States and Great Britain had adopted the rules, *The Berkshire* would still have been guilty of negligence on those particular lanes. Suppose, however, that over thirty nations including Great Britain had adopted the new legislation, but that American legislation required *The Berkshire* to carry white lights. Suppose further that this particular lane were heavily traversed by British and American shipping, but not by the vessels of other nations. There is a high probability that the steamship would have been held liable for the collision. It would be in possession of information that the lanes were heavily traversed by American sailing vessels carrying white lights. It would then have no reason to assume from the lights that the ship was a steamer and that she was four or five miles away rather than near at hand. Being the sturdier and faster vessel, *The Scotia* would then be under an obligation in these circumstances to undertake due precautions. On the other hand, if the lane were one which an American sailing vessel almost never entered, an impartial tribunal would be likely to hold that *The Scotia* was not at fault and that *The Berkshire* would be expected to signal according to practice despite the American law or to take the consequences.

If this interpretation is correct, "customary" rights and obligations rest upon expediency and are no stronger than the expedients that lead to their adoption.[1] The need for regulation of the maritime traffic does establish a general obligation to be prudent. But this obligation does not arise from custom. It arises from the interests of nations in maritime commerce and rests upon expediency. But this is quite different from customary law, which must necessarily rest upon clear and traditional distinctions.

The distinction between custom and expediency can be illustrated even better by a brief glance at the "customary" law of neutrality. Reference is made to the treatment of neutral shipping and the changes in the law that occurred during the First World War. The law of neutrality was treated in Chapter 8 and need not be repeated in detail. It was permissible to stop neutral shipping on the high seas and to look at the manifest. Unless the manifest were suspicious or directly indicated that contraband was being shipped, the vessel was permitted to proceed. The British instituted the practice of challenging the manifest even though no evidence of a suspicious nature were present. The British either inspected the vessel on the high seas or took the vessel to a British port.

The great importance of the economy to the prosecution of war during the First World War led to this change. The Germans found it necessary to engage in deceitful practices in getting goods, and

---

[1] In point of fact, the decision was expedient in another sense. The court was forced to find a rule of law, rather than a practice, not because the difference was significant on the negligence issue, but because the custom had not been proved as a "fact," and indirect notice is limited to "international law."

made use of manifests that were misleading either with respect to the kind of goods or the source. U-boat warfare made it desirable to search ships under safe conditions. Therefore it became necessary to bring goods to British ports. This clearly violated the old law and often did damage to the shippers. On the other hand, the warring maritime nations no longer had an interest in maintaining the old rules, and these rules could not be enforced against their interests. In the same way, the doctrine of continuous voyage was reshaped during the First World War.

"Customary" law with respect to bombing also changed after the First World War. In that war, courts held that damage to neutral goods by bombing made the attacking nation liable for damages. The importance of air power in the Second World War made it impractical to enforce such law. It was not realistic to demand precise bombing of military targets when raids upon the civilian economy constituted one of the most effective military means of waging war. No nation was willing to deprive itself of this means of attack in order to defend some abstract right of private property. Thus the burden of risk was shifted to neutral property. If such property was located within the nation at war, it became subject to all the risks of war without any right of compensation.

It is less than intellectually clear to claim that customary law established the original practice and that new customary law governed the changed practice. Rather, the changed practice determined a new state of law not because the change was in any way customary but because the change represented the standards of behavior that powerful nations of the world were willing to support. Practice this might be, but custom it was not.

The relationship of the three illustrative cases deserves comment. In the case of *The Scotia*, there is a need for the regulation of shipping that is recognized by many important nations. This may occur as a consequence of general agreement among nations. If so, one may regard the matter as one of law but not a consequence of custom. If, on the other hand, most nations adopt relatively uniform legislation, this creates a condition to which others must pay attention. Because of the general practice, those who follow variant rules are placed under a special obligation to be prudent and will be held accountable by the maritime nations. To show that in this case it is the factual condition and not customary law that governs the case, an illustration will suffice. For instance, suppose there were a cave in a field known to be used by young children every Friday for meetings. Suppose now that a farmer decided to block off the entrance to the cave on Friday and the children were suffocated to death. Even if it is assumed that the cave was on the farmer's land and that he had full right to block it off, and even if it is further assumed that he had no knowledge that the children were in the cave at the time he blocked it off, the fact that he knew the children were in the habit of using the cave at that time would be sufficient to establish culpable negligence. The children have no customary right to use the cave but the farmer is guilty of negligence nevertheless. The generality of the rule in the case of shipping rules does not change the fact that it is negligence rather than custom which is at the root of the matter. There is law, namely, that law which makes the negligent party culpable. This law has nothing to do with custom.

In the case of the shipping and the bombing something of a different order is involved. In both cases, international law recognized the common interest that all nations had in protecting private property. By agreement and practice certain procedures were established toward this end. What happens in cases of this kind is that certain procedures that prove satisfactory are adopted by virtually all nations. It is easier to accept a satisfactory rule that has been adopted than to haggle over the details. When, however, changed conditions make the rule unsatisfactory to an important nation, that nation changes its practice. This may constitute a violation of the law if the violating nation believes that its conduct reflected only an unfortunate concession to momentary necessity and that such conduct will not be necessary in the future or if the nation engaging in the practice has been defeated in war and is forced to pay obeisance to the old rule as the price of its defeat. But if instead it is recognized that the conditions necessitating the conduct are likely to become the rule rather than the exception or if several nations are likely, for similar reasons, to be forced to adopt the practices of the defeated nation, the law will change. But the belief that the rule binds because of its customary qualities is untenable.

Statements about "custom" as a source of international law are more readily comprehended by lawyers than laymen. Most municipal systems, however, have analogous rules holding individuals to standards which prevail within particular groups, when others rely upon this practice. It is virtually impossible to give a meaningful answer to the question "When does a practice become or cease to be a custom?" and "What customs become law?" But perhaps one can identify the most important variables in this process.

In the first place, a practice usually becomes binding only when it induces some reliance by others, and this reliance either must be knowingly induced or at least reasonably anticipated. In addition, there must be some socially useful purpose served by the activity that makes enforcement of the practice socially justifiable; something of consequence must be thought to be involved, some importance attached to the conduct. For an individual to do things in an invariable pattern in a social context is bound to create expectations on the part of others that the pattern will be continued unless and until disclaimed, or until there is such a change in general conditions as to make that expectation no longer reasonable.

In the case of an individualized pattern of activity courts often say that people dealing with this person are entitled to assume that he will act as he has acted in the past if his activities have been of that order which is generally likely to induce reliance upon them, and if the total activities of the two parties are of a nature to be encouraged as socially desirable. We may say that he impliedly agrees to continue, or that he is "estopped" to deny the inference that he will continue to do so, or that a contract is to be interpreted in the light of past practice, and so forth. Normally courts require for redress that the party who relies upon this practice has done so to his detriment, and that he has been honestly misled.

We could loosely refer to this individualized pattern as the individual's "custom." Usually, however, lawyers reserve the term "custom" for a more general pattern of activity that predominantly characterizes the activities of a group of which the individual is a member. The pattern of conduct that characterizes activities of the group may then be attributed to its members by persons aware of the "custom." By merely identifying himself with the group—or being in a position where others would normally do so—such a member is saddled with group standards in the same way he would have been had this been his individual pattern of activity. Ordinarily he can relieve himself of these duties only by expressly disclaiming them or by otherwise informing those who deal with him that they may not rely upon his adherence to the particular practice. The stronger the "custom" and the greater the likelihood of reliance upon it, the more clear and unequivocal must be this disclaimer. A disclaimer of "custom" in a formal way may not be effective if, in practice, the member continues to conform to it—on the theory, apparently, that actions speak louder than words. If, of course, the reason for the "custom" disappears—if conditions change gradually or abruptly— other persons may no longer rely upon its existence, that is, it is no longer regarded as a "custom."

Now these ideas are fundamental to any system of order. We continuously depend upon—structure our expectations upon—conformity to "customary" norms. Not all of these take on the status of law. We do not enforce in law a requirement that husbands telephone their wives when they miss their usual bus or train. Expectations have been frustrated—the supper is burned—but we leave the parties to their own remedial devices. There must be some social purpose, some general significance to the society, before it attains the status of law. Let similar conduct take place in a commercial situation, and there may well be legal consequences. Obviously this requires some sort of policy judgment.

There is no reason to except international relations from these general principles. The way in which a state has acted in the past, or the way states habitually act in like situations, will be relied upon by other states. Whenever the expectations are frustrated, the frustrated party will react as does the wife with the burned dinner. If the issue has general significance, a state may argue persuasively that there has been a violation of law and may secure the agreement of the important nations of the system. Thus, as in individual social situations, deterrents exist at both the legal and the non-legal level. The United States would, for example, react angrily to a failure on the part of its NATO partners to consult with it on various political matters that would have an impact on the Organization. But the United States would be unlikely, save in the extreme situation, to claim that failure to consult was a breach of the Treaty obligation itself.

We have to this point been discussing "custom" only in the context of reliance. It most frequently is invoked in this situation—to supplement the provisions of an international agreement or to provide a norm where no more explicit agreement has been made. In both domestic and international cases it is used primarily to interpret the explicit provisions of an existing arrangement or to fill in the blanks. Just as states are free not to enter into such arrangements, they may specify the particular conditions. They may usually, as to prospective arrangements, disclaim past practices or common "customs." The merchant can say that he refuses to be bound by common mercantile understanding, and those who deal with him must do so on other terms. Since they do not rely on "custom" they may not be heard to invoke it as the appropriate standard for subsequent deeds. But this result is not invariable.

So is the case with states. As we have seen in the case of treaties, they are usually free *inter se* to change common understanding—to vary "customary" international law by explicit arrangements. In many cases they may do so unilaterally. For example, although diplomats are "customarily" immune from all local process of law, a state may unilaterally say that henceforth they will be subject to various laws or, perhaps, the entire civil and criminal codes. Similarly, the common practice of granting foreign sovereigns immunity from municipal legal process may be varied prospectively, though not retroactively, by any state. Presumably other states who continued to send diplomats or hold property within the enacting state would be deemed to have acquiesced in the change. A more likely reaction to drastic revision would be diplomatic objection and negotiation for terms more generally acceptable. Unilateral change of "custom," however "legal," is not necessarily politically acceptable to others and is unlikely to change existing obligations.

A series of unilateral changes, acquiesced in (or not objected to) by other nations is likely to change the "custom" itself. The more these changes are "reasonable" in the light of changed physical or social conditions, the more acceptable they may be to others, and the more quickly the "custom" itself will be changed.

It is often said that states must "consent" to a "custom" before it becomes binding upon them, but, more often than not, "consent" is implied from failure to disclaim or object to what is prevailing. Obviously "consent" here, as throughout so much of the law, is a fiction used to square practice with theory. If the practice is thought by the decision maker to be reasonable in the light of the needs of the international community, if there is some evidence that it has been followed (or would, in like circumstances, be followed) by a substantial number of states (and particularly those of most political importance) other states are likely to be held to the same standard. Thus, to take an extreme case, one act by one state in a non-recurring or unique situation may create a binding "custom" in the absence of precedent to the contrary or changed conditions.

Now not all practice or "custom" can be unilaterally disclaimed or changed. In the first place, we have already seen that a radical disclaimer is likely to run into political difficulty; it may be easier to change by a process of gradualism the practice itself, to adjust and modify the practice rather than to disclaim it. In the second place, in at least two types of situations, this technique is virtually mandatory. The first of these, and the most common, is where the "custom" is incorporated into existing formal agreements. A state cannot modify the agreement without the concurrence of the other party, and to the extent its language inferentially or explicitly incorporates common practices they cannot be unilaterally changed either; to do so would be to change the agreement itself. For example, by agreeing to play host to the UN the United States has (in addition to explicit agreements) inferentially agreed that it will not subject UN personnel or UN delegates to local regulations that would prevent the UN from performing its functions. Although the U.S. may be able unilaterally to modify to some extent the immunity "customarily" granted foreign diplomats, it cannot deviate to the point where it interferes with the UN's carrying out its mission. In addition, practice and the purposes of the UN would continue to set limits to unilateral U.S. action.

The third respect in which unilateral disclaimer of "custom" will not be legally acceptable is where the international community has an important stake in the practice itself that goes beyond reliance on past practice. Some practices become mandatory prospectively as well as retroactively. This is the area in which we have existing rules based upon practices that serve important needs of the community as a whole and that are binding upon all states and that cannot be varied save through agreement. A great many rules fall into this category: the law of the sea, many rules of warfare, and many rules providing protection to individuals—what may be referred to as "constitutional" principles protecting rights of foreigners. Whether or not they are codified in treaties, rules so generally supported are mandatory.

What must be emphasized here is not the rigidity of these rules derived from past practices or "custom," or even the conceptual difficulty in unilateral change or renunciation. The point here is that modification must gain the acceptance or acquiescence of the community in general; that is, important international decision makers must agree to any changes. We are here within the orbit of legislative change that gravely affects the interests of the community as a whole. The process requires moderation, the exercise of self-restraint, proposals that take into account the known interests of other states, interpretations that are politically reasonable and that are based upon contemporary conditions. Here we are positing an international interest in common norms—norms as universal as is politically possible. Thus each unilateral change must either be outside the orbit of the purpose served by uniformity—within the area conceded to national discretion—or must be couched in terms of that purpose, as an "interpretation" of existing norms, in a way that other states will approve, or at least tolerate. The more radical the innovation by both legal and political criteria, the more likely it will be claimed by others to be a violation of existing norms.

Thus, the use of "custom" in the international community is the predominant method of obtaining order and of deterring acts that frustrate the expectations of others. Since frustration is in any event an irritant that disturbs friendly relations, there is usually a common interest in avoiding the sort of crisis that may be provoked by abrupt change.

To say that "custom" is a source of law is only to say that decision makers invoke past practices to legitimize present decisions. Such a statement tells us very little that is helpful in predicting what practices will be asserted in what contexts as binding norms. It includes nothing of the "why," without which the statement is useless as a tool for predicting the actions of decision makers. A "custom" is not claimed to be law because it is a "custom." We need something more, some useful purpose or policy which is served by so regarding it. We need another dimension—a relationship between the "custom" asserted, the facts of the controversy and the issues raised, and the contemporary needs of international society as they are likely to be viewed by important policy-makers. Only when we add these dimensions can we predict what "customs" are likely to be asserted with regard to what fact situations by what decision makers with what results.

Reference to past practices is useful as a technique and is probably indispensable to any decision-making process. In the first place it provides the decision maker with some guide to the probable expectations of others. A decision that does not break too abruptly with expectation is more likely to gain acceptance, or at least tolerance from others, and is less likely to create political tensions. In the second place, it may reflect a past experience which is valuable in itself as a source of knowledge about social behavior. Finally, it promotes an aura of objectivity and impartiality if the decision maker can point out that his action is supported by evidence of like judgments by others. In this way he can focus attention on the quality of the general norm rather than on the consequences of the immediate dispute.

We do not, therefore, suggest that "custom" is merely a technique to justify decisions arrived at wholly on other grounds. We merely affirm the need for another dimension. Without it myth and technique are hopelessly confused.

Judicial precedents as a source of law. A third source by which international decisions are legitimized consists of the prior decisions of international and national tribunals that have expressed international norms. For the reason that they are more clearly independent, prior decisions by international courts stand on a higher footing, but the widespread independence of national judiciaries gives them a similar objectivity whenever they are not bound by particular national laws. Such decisions are not, however, regarded as "binding"; even the decisions of the International Court of Justice are not regarded as limitations on its authority to decide future controversies differently, though the fear of being attacked as politically motivated or biased is an effective restriction on doing so.

Regarding precedents as "sources," rather than formal limitations, in part reflects the jurisprudence of the civil law, where a code, rather than its interpretation, is the law; and in part the pluralistic political structure of international society and the difficulty of setting up a hierarchical structure. Article 38 of the Statute of the International Court of Justice makes precedent only a subsidiary means of determining the law and is evidence of the verbal (though not the practical) triumph of civil over common law juridical theory. Article 59, making precedent binding only on the parties to the dispute, is a recognition of a political structure that includes many policy makers, the absence of an international legislature, and the need for general acceptance of a rule before it can be generally applied. Other states with a stake in determining international norms have no procedural means of putting their views before the Court in particular disputes, and there is no formal way of securing a legislative reversal of norms adopted by the Court.

Differences between civil and common law treatment of precedent are less significant in practice than in theory. The reasons why prior judicial decisions are considered binding in common law (and why they are important, though secondary, sources in civil law) are principally three: First, decisions themselves are based on what some prior decision maker believed was a social consensus that it was in the interest of society to maintain. If he is clearly incorrect, he is likely to be reversed by other judges on appeal, by the legislature through the enactment of new norms, or, at least, heavily criticized by various political elites. If this does not occur, then the decision is valuable as a statement of that consensus and the institutional process values it as such by making it precedent; that is, by conceding its authority, or presuming it, the system feeds upon itself and in a way helps to preserve norm stability and maximum consistency of application. Secondly, this use of precedent operates as a sign of impartiality and objectivity in the legal system, and helps to lift the adjudicative process above the immediate controversy. Any legal system requires that the judge be neutral as to litigants; this can be assured in several ways, one of which is to require him to square his decision with past decisions by invoking common norms. He not merely uses precedent but creates it as well; objectivity is built upon objectivity; source upon source. Thirdly, it helps to protect the policy-making function of the legislature by limiting judicial discretion to modify existing norms in the creation of new ones.

These reasons are all present in international practice, though with different emphasis and institutional coloration. Both national and international judicial decisions are moderately good sources, particularly as they accumulate and represent the views of many over a period of time, of a social and political consensus. Other sources are always available to test or qualify such judgments. The fact that all courts use similar techniques, similar sources, and similar methodology and reasoning, helps to create consistency and stability internationally as it does domestically. Most important, the bulk of international law matters that arise in national courts or that the interested states are willing to submit to impartial decision do not involve policies involving serious disagreement or issues that directly threaten a state's political objectives. In view of this narrowing of the scope of the issues presented—their relative unimportance by political standards—the situation is far more comparable to municipal practice than it would otherwise be. If the issue is one that the parties are willing to submit to an international court, it means, too, that they have already assessed the state of the precedent that such a court will invoke, and are willing to accept it as the proper standard of decision. The same result is arrived at domestically when national courts are left free to invoke international precedent, for, if the issue were politically important, the foreign office would see to it that national courts got political guidance in the form of national law.

One must differentiate the use of precedent in municipal and international law on grounds already suggested. The fact that there are many decision makers operating in different social and political contexts means that the variances are somewhat greater than would be found in a municipal system, and the area of consensus is likely to be smaller. Secondly, even international tribunals purporting to use universal criteria cannot help but be influenced by what the parties urge and this, as we have already pointed out, has already been politically screened. States A and B may be willing to frame an issue and invoke rules that States A and C could not possibly agree upon; A and B may share views as to policy, despite a difference as to its applicability to a given situation, that C would find intolerable. The Court is likely to take a position that reflects the consensus of A and B as the applicable rule of international law. What purport in this context to be universal rules may in fact be something less.

Finally, if judicial precedent is invoked by a foreign office in a dispute negotiated through diplomatic channels, it may merely mean that this particular rule is favorable to the party invoking it, and that this party would like to keep the rule's status as law. The second state may seek to modify the rule, or even change it drastically or abrogate it, and justify its position by using other sources of law, other criteria of legitimacy, or other rules of law. If there is a real conflict in terms of underlying views as to the norms desirable it is difficult to see the utility of international adjudication. The judicial process requires some consensus as to applicable standards, or some way of achieving that consensus through political channels. It is not always easy to adapt the judicial process to the political technique of compromising claims.

Textbook writers as a source of law. The Statute of the International Court, codifying prior practice, permits reference to the writing of scholars for subsidiary evidence of what the law is, but not for speculations concerning what the law ought to be. However difficult the line between "is" and "ought," the mythology does not acknowledge the difficulty. The exception here excludes only clear speculations—those conceded to have no present authority, and it reflects the understandable unwillingness of politicians to delegate to scholars formal legislative authority. This refusal does not mean that scholars are ineffective in influencing the course of the law or in playing, like judges, a modest legislative role. They, too, can intermingle a touch of "ought" with the "is" through the way in which they analyze facts and issues, organize formal authority, relate sources to each other, and thus order conflicting precedent. Although they lack the formal status of judges they have the advantage of being free from particular controversies, and can range farther into the stuff of the law. Insofar as their views are persuasive to formal decision makers, scholars help to shape the course of the law.

Several reasons for using the work of scholars are apparent; the apolitical objectivity of scholars as a group; the extent to which their work is constrained by the critical comment of others; the ethics of scholarship in accurate statement and citation of authorities, including those that do not support their conclusions; and the extent to which scholars are above political pressures and enjoy academic freedom. To the extent that these conditions are not present in their work, they lose status as scholars. Hence what the scholar states to be prevailing doctrine ought to have considerable foundation, ought to be capable of verification by others, and ought to employ the same sources acknowledged by formal decision makers. What he says is both based upon, and inevitably an addition to, what went before.

It would make relatively little difference to the process if the views of writers were not formally permissible as sources, for they would be consulted by formal decision makers in any event as convenient collections of authority, analyses of material, syntheses of past practices and precedents, and expressions of relatively apolitical conclusions. Their inclusion as formal sources helps, of course, to prove the decision makers' objectivity by the normal law practice of showing that someone else said it first. More important, they constitute a convenient short-hand reference and, by the prestige it gives the authority cited, an encouragement of a useful activity. Scholarship often helps to establish an informed consensus on norms that is beyond the pressure of the immediate case. Unlimited by the facts of a particular controversy and potential political pressures, scholars can interrelate material with a freer hand than can judges. Scholars can indicate broad trends, can clarify the extent of both agreement and disagreement, and can point to social, political and economic factors to which decision makers must respond. Thus, they are often able to clarify the direction of change before it has become clear to the participants in the process and before a case arises. This is a creative task, and it is precisely in this area of limited creation that scholars play their most important role. Since scholars are likely to reflect the basic social and political values of their particular national societies, political elites have more to gain than lose by acknowledging the status of scholarly writings as a source of law.

Using the work of scholars to legitimize decisions is common in all national law institutions. Although in some systems the scholar plays a more important and more direct role than in others, most systems give him a significant role. It is not surprising to see this national role transferred to an international context on much the same terms—particularly since the conception of international law itself is a scholarly creation.

The general principles of law as a source of law. Another source of international law which may be used in the absence of more specific authority consists of the "general principles of law common to civilized nations." That such principles do exist cannot be doubted. After all, a large part—until recently the politically effective part—of the world has a common cultural heritage with large areas of common ethical and moral beliefs, similar political and economic institutions, and similar social problems. More specifically, the legal system of much of the world is derived from Roman law, and much of this passed over, via Scotland and the Scottish judges into the "competing" Common Law system. Although the same doctrine has not always developed in its particular applications in the same way—we must always beware of too easy a transposition of verbal equivalents—nevertheless, there is much that is common.

Even if these general principles were not formally recognized as sources of international law, they would still creep into the process. It is virtually impossible for anyone trained in the techniques of law not to resort to basic principles that are so clear as not to require argument. Recognizing them as "sources" is really a limitation on the judge, for he must now at least satisfy himself that they are not merely obvious to him but also generally applied; his own experience must be internationalized. They are invoked only when some direct international precedent is not available or persuasive, where no practice beyond that represented by the general principle itself can be found. In such areas there is a resulting freedom to the decision maker, which, in effect, is limited by requiring him to decide according to general principles. An existing rule shared by many has a quality of objectivity and impartiality that free judicial creativity cannot have. A norm invented for a case may be challenged on grounds of partiality or political expediency. What right does a judge have to create a new rule that favors one side rather than the other? But an existing norm, even where it may be possible on the particular facts to choose an equally general conflicting norm, at least seems to have the quality of "givenness," of not being arbitrary. From this fact stems the great pursuit of analogous situations by the judiciaries of all nations in all legal systems.

By the same token it is easier to agree on an existing standard, in most life situations, than to agree on any particular modification of that standard. And in circumstances in which continual disagreement is much more vexing than the use of any reasonable standard, there is a temptation to prefer the lesser evil to the higher but unobtainable good.

The arbitration between Russia and Turkey in 1912, before the Permanent Court of Arbitration, over interest on payment for damage suffered by Russian citizens during the Crimean War, was settled by a principle of Roman law. Actually the reasoning behind the use of the particular principle chosen is something less than compelling. But the fact that it was possible to find a rule for the case was much more satisfactory from the standpoint of both Russia and Turkey than if the same decision had been reached as a consequence of free judicial creation.

In some areas of international practice, general principles tend to merge with what might be called common national practices. There is considerable international law that we have described as incorporating a "constitutional" standard, and that requires a common measure. What, for example, constitutes a "fair trial"? Criteria for narrowing such general language must be taken from the jurisprudence of various nations, from what states explicitly or implicitly regard as its essentials. The Nuernberg trials forced the prosecution to search for a common international denominator, or measure, of rules of procedure and of "crimes against humanity." What conduct was universally proscribed; what constituted a legitimate excuse; what defenses, how proved, were open to the defendants?

Perhaps analogous to these uses of comparative method to arrive at general principles comprising an international standard are the "internal affairs" decisions of international agencies. Without applicable "international law" and reluctant to employ a particular national law to decide many disputes, the judicial-administrative arms of these agencies, such as the International Labor Organization, have drawn upon "general principles" as the guide and measure of adjudication. The apolitical nature of these disputes, not involving states, gives the decision maker a freer hand to use such principles than would be the case if states were directly involved.

Finally, in those areas that touch on international law without being a part of it as formally defined—not immediately involving states as parties—national courts frequently invoke such general principles as the measure of decision in cases involving a foreign element. In international commercial matters, in admiralty, and elsewhere, there is a general license and injunction to use "general principles" when more specific statutory criteria are not at hand.

As vague and discretionary as the injunction to use "general principles of law" may be, it is a limitation upon, rather than an extension of, the capacity of courts and other decision makers applying international law. We can see that this is true if we review the long and inconclusive debate about whether or not international arbitrators are free to decide *ex aequo et bono*—according to concepts of "justice and fairness." Prevailing doctrine is that they are not free to do so unless specifically authorized by the parties, which rarely occurs. The phrasing suggests an absence of objective standards required by the judicial function. Although we suspect that it makes little difference to the decision arrived at, preference for "general principles of law" is a preference for principles that are as definite as possible. It reflects consensus that agreement would be impossible if nations had to agree on new rules or if judges were free to create new norms unrestrained by recorded common experience.

Reason in the law. Little is added by the inclusion of "reason" as a source of law. Clearly lawyers must reason, but this reasoning is not strictly a deductive logical process by which conclusions follow from agreed premises as in the theories of mechanical jurisprudence. In point of fact, legal reasoning is one wherein the major premise keeps shifting. This is most clearly seen where the argument is by analogy. The judge, in deciding Case A, does not say that it is exactly like Case B and, accordingly, must be decided in the same way. What he does is to say that Case A is more like Case B than it is like Case C, and, hence, should be decided in the same way as was Case B. Obviously, the problem of "likeness" or "unlikeness" is what connects the legal process with other objectives. It is in using this criterion of "likeness" or "unlikeness" that the judge performs his creative function.

Judicial reasoning is more difficult in many areas of international law than it is in domestic matters for the reason that there are fewer cases and fewer recurring fact situations. Hence much of the law is largely skeletal and the gap between the cases much broader than that which exists in a more developed legal system.

CONCLUSION

The difficulty with most writing about international law is that it does not differentiate between myth and technique, and does not provide the student with any basis for judging the policy considerations that constrain the decisions of the legal system. There is a sense of frustration in discussion of the sources of law that brings the student no closer to understanding the process. In fact, we are talking here merely of technique, the mechanics of the process, and this provides no clue for answering the question of what the legal norm is in any given situation.

In emphasizing the extent to which technique can be used to reach any of the alternative conclusions possible in an international law case—as indeed in most municipal law cases—we do not intend to imply that the process of adjudication is unconstrained either procedurally or substantively. Clearly some assertions of what is legally acceptable violate the normative structure of the law so radically that they are not really taken seriously even by those who assert them. Some aspects of the Russian position with respect to a separate peace treaty with East Germany clearly violate the law. And the Egyptian interpretation of the Convention of 1888 concerning its right to halt Israeli shipping through the Canal is so thin that one has difficulty in taking it seriously. There are rules that govern the process even if they are broad. If one does not understand the constraints that influence the process of reaching juridical conclusions, then much of the substance and interest of the study of the law is lost.

10

THE INSTITUTIONS
OF INTERNATIONAL
DECISION MAKING

IN the previous chapter our emphasis was upon the techniques of the international legal process and the limitations upon the discretion of officials imposed by legal methodology—at least whenever the decision maker is concerned with providing a convincing legal justification for action taken or protested. Here we wish to pursue another facet of the process: Who invokes international law, in what arenas, and with what effects? Our points of attention in this chapter are, then, the ways in which the decision-making process is organized and the roles of the various participants.

In general theory and broad outline, the organization of the international legal process is underdeveloped and uncomplicated. As we have seen, international law is viewed as a body of rules binding upon states as entities, or "subjects." States are legally obligated, by whatever means they elect, to insure that state officials comply with international norms, but (at least, up until the Nuernberg trials) the obligation is not conceived as being imposed directly upon the officials themselves. Acts taken by state officials that violate international norms may be protested, through diplomatic channels, by an injured state, the protest being accompanied by a demand that the wrong be righted in some appropriate way. Diplomatic correspondence cast in terms of legal argumentation ordinarily follows such a protest. If disagreement persists at any level—as to the facts, the relevant norms, or the application of the norms to facts—the matter may be settled by the parties, mediated by a disinterested party, referred to an arbitrator or international tribunal, put before an international or supranational body, or simply left unresolved.

The offended state may, if other means of resolution are frustrated, resort to appropriate sanctions by way of reprisal if this possibility is technically feasible and politically possible.

Relatively few disputes are resolved by impartial judges. If the states involved desire adjudication, either of existing disputes or prospectively with regard to categories of questions, there is no difficulty in securing the services of objective and impartial observers who can employ the techniques described in the previous chapter to resolve the dispute. The services of the International Court of Justice are, of course, always available to states. The failure of states generally to resort to judicial resolution is attributable not to the lack of a mechanism for handling the dispute, but, rather, to a preference, in most instances, not to use this method of dispute settlement.

Our primary concern here is not with the reasons that underlie this preference, but rather with the fact of its existence. Nonetheless, it may be helpful to suggest at least some of the considerations that lead states to reject a judicial method of dispute resolution.

We must, first, bear in mind that, although all disputes involving normative standards can be decided by impartial reference to authoritative declarations and past practices, even a developed and comprehensive legal system does not attempt to resolve all disputes in this fashion. Although authoritative norms may be and are derived and abstracted from past experience, not all norms are created in this way. We would not ordinarily claim that a disagreement among interest groups as to a desirable general rule could best be resolved by reference to a referee who would determine which proposal more nearly complied with precedent and past practice; yet each group might, as part of its effort to gain political support, invoke precedent from sources analogous to those discussed in the prior chapter.

One factor, then, which influences states to refrain from any comprehensive acquiescence to adjudication is the belief that adjudication is inappropriate, at least until a more satisfactory international legislative system is evolved. The present system of international legislation, whether by multilateral treaty, United Nations vote, or otherwise, requires formal assent by others, and is, to say the least, a tedious process, the more so because the individuals involved operate under limited instructions from the states they represent. The clumsiness of this arrangement is compensated for within the system of international law by a looser technique of doctrinal innovation than exists in a more developed governmental system, by a failure to resolve definitively doctrinal issues, and by legitimizing retroactively, in a variety of ways, a great amount of unilateral policy, including the application of national laws to transnational events and interests. The reliance is upon informal—or political—restraints as well as the doctrine that has existed to enforce moderation. So long as prescribing and adjudicating functions are not embedded in separate institutional structures in the international system, reference to impartial adjudication will be limited.

Not all disputes are best resolved by the judicial process. We may agree that the Constitutional power of the President of the United States to send troops to participate in the UN action in Korea is a legal question. Yet we may doubt that the question would be best resolved by reference to the Supreme Court. Similarly, there are questions of law that courts decline to resolve on the grounds that the issue is "non-justiciable," or "political"; and these are better resolved in other arenas.

Also, disputes that affect the security or continued existence of a state cannot easily be put in the hands of a third party, however impartial, if any alternative is feasible. Even if the risk of unfavorable adjudication is slight, states are understandably reluctant to take any unnecessary risk on fundamental questions.

But basic to these reasons, and to others, is the simple fact that national identification still dominates, and there are no widespread ties of sentiment to the international community, or, though we are in a state of transition, to supranational entities. An important conviction as to the importance of preserving the group and a sense of group solidarity is a necessary condition to the establishment of comprehensive dispute-resolving mechanisms in the present period. Although we can see the growth of this identification in many areas, both geographical and functional, there is no indication that such supranational communities presently exist in any comprehensive way.

As a result of these conditions and of this organizational scheme, the international legal process, unlike its municipal counterpart, is not designed to operate primarily by means of judicial settlement; and international law is typically invoked in arenas other than international judicial arenas. The techniques described in the previous chapter may be employed by an impartial arbiter to decide a dispute, and sometimes are; but they are customarily employed in other contexts by persons who, in various degrees, have partisan political roles. This circumstance is of the utmost importance in understanding the process.

It does not by any means defeat the existence of an operative normative order; it does, however, mean that the international process differs importantly from one that includes the operations of an impartial judiciary. State officials may both act differently and conceive their roles differently with respect to international matters from the ways they act or conceive their roles with respect to national matters.

Let us consider the traditional arenas in which international law has been invoked—national courts and diplomatic intercourse—and proceed thereafter to the important institutional modifications resulting from the growth of international procedures and organizations.

National courts. In traditional theory, national courts apply national law—even when they apply international standards. National courts, it is said, apply international law only because the latter has been received into, or incorporated within, national law. There is a reason for this otherwise awkward theory, and that lies in the relationship of the judiciary to other branches of the municipal government. There is international law doctrine which requires a state to adhere to rules of international law, but there is no international requirement that a state take its judiciary's view of what the international norm is or how it applies. The international obligation is that of the state, and it may implement it internally in any way that it sees fit.

Issues of international law arise in national courts indirectly, and not as disputes between states; they are at one remove from diplomatic representation. For example, state officials may attach property and be faced with a claim that the property belongs to another sovereign entitled, under international law, to immunity from local process; a seaman may be apprehended for a minor crime committed on a foreign flagship in a local port and claim that he is immune from prosecution under customary international law; goods may be seized during wartime as contraband and the owner may claim the seizure is in violation of his rights as a neutral; property may be nationalized and the owner may claim that the compensation offered is inadequate under international standards; and so forth.

One primary function of courts, and the *raison d'etre* of an independent judiciary, is to insure that government officials do not exceed their lawful authority. A decision of the executive to take certain action does not automatically establish its lawfulness, and may be tested by impartial judicial review. If international law is a part of the national law, the court is acting on questions raising international standards exactly as it would if only local issues and local law (in a restricted sense) were involved. International law, for a national court, does not assume priority over national law; in fact, the latter almost always supersedes the former if there is unavoidable conflict. A statute in conflict with a prior treaty provision or customary international law will be applied nonetheless in most countries by national courts.

The result of this theory, then, is that the national judiciary must take the views of the political branches as to what international law requires whenever these views are enacted as formal municipal law; otherwise, courts determine independently what the international standard is and what it requires in the case at hand. Thus although national courts, in performing this latter function, develop a good many international standards, they cannot be regarded as independent and faithful custodians of international law doctrine. They may, in this respect, be contrasted rather sharply with state courts in our federal system which do have an independent obligation to uphold the federal Constitution. It hardly requires argument that this difference of role has considerable impact upon the development of the international law process.

The task of developing international law norms on the one hand and deferring to formal national policy on the other can make for awkward situations. A court in State X determines that international law prohibits a certain act, or requires a certain procedure; once this determination is made it is extremely difficult for the state's foreign office, or legislature, to arrive at a different formulation of the international rule without the considerable embarrassment of having its own judiciary cited to the contrary. For this reason, the state may be forced to reverse its judiciary by the tedious process of international agreement, even though, for local purposes, it could do so by simple legislative act.

This same difficulty—in part due to a semantic confusion and failure to clarify issues—often follows from the fact that a number of countries, including the United States, have taken the view that questions of law (what the international standard is) are questions for the judiciary, and that as a result the courts are not bound by foreign office views unless formally a part of municipal law. In the United States, the Constitution specifically describes treaties as "supreme law," and inferentially assigns courts the task of their interpretation. There is, of course, some justification for judicial supremacy where the issue has arisen and the interpretations could retroactively affect private parties in an existing suit. But, at least prospectively, it is difficult to justify anything but the greatest deference of municipal courts to their respective foreign offices.

In practice, courts are extremely sensitive to political involvement, particularly in recent years when it has been increasingly obvious that much traditional doctrine needs modification. Though troubled by the seeming intrusion on independence, courts have been desirous of getting political guidance on policy matters. In the United States, at least, it is not uncommon to see courts and State Department playing Alphonse and Gaston roles, the one saying a question of policy has arisen on which the court should have political guidance, and the other maintaining a discreet silence on the same issue, characterizing it as one of law. In this regard, we are conscious of a change of attitude over time. A century or more ago, courts played far more important roles in law development than they do in the present day. In the early nineteenth century, there was great confidence in a process of law development by the judiciary. As law has come to be thought of more and more in terms of a conscious community policy, initiative has shifted to political bodies. Norms previously conceived as derived from universal reason or practice or custom are now thought of as conscious community policy. With this in mind, courts have lost their confidence to prescribe in the international area, becoming sensitive to both the policy and political issues which may be involved. Often in cases where international law is invoked, American courts, at least, have tended to test the contention as much against foreign policy objectives—the norms the United States would like to see universally established—as against anything that could fairly be said to be derived wholly from any universal practice.

Thus, in the world today, there is relatively little effort by national courts to play what seems to be an overcomplex and difficult task of creating universal norms. This task is left to political officials, whose leads courts are desirous to follow. We might almost say that the theory which led national courts to be subservient to formal national policy has been greatly extended, and that courts are today subservient to even a whisper of national policy. Therefore, rather than playing important creative roles in determining common international standards, national courts have more and more become apologists for national policies determined by political arms of government.

This does not mean that national courts do not continue to play an important moderating role and to invoke international law to assist them in this function. But it suggests that national courts are less important to the performance of this task than in the past, and that the creative use of method and technique to establish new norms has passed to other branches of the government, and to supranational bodies.

Foreign office: diplomatic intercourse. The traditional method of maintaining the integrity of international norms has been through diplomatic protest by the offended state, or states, of action that in its view was incompatible with existing law.

But before a state reaches the point of formal protest, it is subjected to the moderating influence that arises from the self-restraint most states exercise in order to encourage self-restraint on the part of others. As we stated above, the incorporation of international norms into national law permits recourse to legal action by private citizens to insure the compatibility with international law of administrative actions taken by state officials. Municipal officials are thus subjected to judicial restraint in matters litigable in local courts. In addition, all govenments go to considerable lengths to make sure that administrative and military officers respect international norms, at least as set forth by the state involved. In the United States we find manuals prepared for the Armed Services setting forth what is permitted and prohibited in all likely situations, and this is supplemented by a network of competent legal officers whose advice can be sought to clarify close cases. In the Department of State, personnel trained in law check and coordinate policies and programs to insure that they do not violate treaties or customary law. In all aspects of government, and in all governments, there exist similar internal checks on official action to ascertain that it is consistent with international law at least as exposited by the state involved.

The fact that there may be different formulations of rules and different interpretations of doctrine does not invalidate the broad area of agreement thus achieved. Further, many differences are of marginal significance and well within a discretion which other states can tolerate. The important point is that before a state departs consciously and abruptly from norms strongly supported by others, there must be an authorization at a quite high level of government, a policy decision near the top echelon. There is a question of both timing and substance involved and of willingness to take political risks.

A similar judgment must be made by other states in a position to protest, or at least dissent from, the suggested departure. Among friendly nations there is caution. Clarification of the change is often requested, and typically there is an effort to explore and expand points of agreement and narrow as far as possible the area of dispute. Formal protests as to illegality are relatively rare, and are becoming much rarer today among bloc members though perhaps more frequent between blocs. There is, after all, little service to bloc interests in accusing bloc partners of disrespect for international law, although such accusations between blocs may actually help create a politically desired image.

Now, diplomatic negotiation involves techniques which are flexible and range widely in the process of accommodation. Legal doctrine and methods of argumentation may help to clarify issues, but the diplomat is by no means confined, as is the judge, to rendering an opinion based exclusively upon existing doctrine. He employs law more in the fashion of advocate and legislator, with the important qualification that he has to be circumspect in statements which enter into the law process as future sources. He is desirous to preserve certain norms and support them as strongly as he is able. Yet he must weigh the consequences of the immediate controversy in terms of other objectives as well. Finally, of course, he has a domestic public to satisfy.

The diplomat, then, is not using law to decide cases, as is the judge, but to support policies. Although his method may be similar, he is subject to different constraints and has different objectives.

Let us reflect for a minute on the considerations we discussed at the outset. If the decision makers of two states feel that the norm each state espouses involves a really important issue of principle, at least one state, and perhaps both, will refuse adjudication by an impartial tribunal. Each will present its case as strongly as possible and then, almost by an unspoken mutual assent, leave it undecided. If, however, the controversy has to be compromised, each will prefer a non-doctrinal horse-trade to a solution that in any way weakens its doctrinal claim. Yugoslavia and the United States were quite unable to agree on the right of a state to nationalize property of foreigners without compensation, but were able to agree on a lump sum settlement in which neither sacrificed its position. If the controversy is one in which only a doctrinal compromise will suffice because it will apply frequently in like situations affecting both states, then the basic question of whether the doctrine or the relationship is more important must be asked.

INTERNATIONAL PROCEDURES

Good offices, mediation, and conciliation. Good offices, mediation, and conciliation techniques, which make use of "third parties" not directly concerned in the dispute, are, like diplomacy, intended primarily to compose differences. Intervention by a third party, even if not in the form of a court or arbitral tribunal, usually compels the disputing parties, in order to appeal to the third party, to phrase their demands in terms of rules that could be applied universally to all similar cases. It must be added that this fact does not automatically guarantee the success of third-party efforts. Each party to a dispute may enunciate a seemingly reasonable general rule to support its position. The parties to a dispute may differ on the facts, the interpretation of the facts, or the rule to be applied to a particular case.

Nonetheless, the fact that reference to universal standards is facilitated explains in part the usefulness of third-party efforts. Good offices, mediation, and conciliation are variant forms of a common technique. Technically good offices are restricted to interceding with the parties to get them to use diplomacy to settle their quarrel; mediation occurs when the mediator aids in the discussion of the substantive issues; and conciliation occurs when the conciliator proposes for the consideration of the parties either the rules that ought to govern the settlement or the actual terms of the settlement. Despite the seeming distinctions, the lines between good offices, mediation, and conciliation are rather difficult to draw. The use of good offices may founder if completely unresponsive to the substantive issues that led to the quarrel, for the willingness of the parties to accede to the services of those performing the good offices role depends in part upon the relationship of negotiation to an acceptable settlement of the substantive issues.

For instance, in the Franco-Tunisian dispute of 1958, France would have been willing to discuss the question of indemnities for the bombing, but not the question of the right of French troops to remain in Tunisia, and particularly not any aspect of Algerian hostilities. Yet some extension of the discussion was necessary from the Tunisian point of view both for reasons of public demand and because Tunisia believed the issues to be inextricably related. Therefore it was not really possible for the United States to use its good offices to bring about discussions unless it used its influence to affect the agenda of the discussions. Yet it could hardly have done this without some discussion of whether the issues were in fact related.

The American representative, Mr. Murphy, was presumably able to discuss whether the issues were related and whether it was advisable to link them in these particular negotiations without prescribing the outcomes of the negotiations on the issues or even the rules that were to govern the settlements. But Mr. Murphy's intervention nonetheless affected the substantive issues. Persuasion of France to discuss Algeria inevitably would have affected the position of France in Algeria.

The use of good offices occurs when the negotiator meets with the contending states separately. The mediator or conciliator may meet with the parties either separately or jointly. In the past, it was generally regarded as a friendly act for a state to offer its services in one of the three roles. Today, it is extremely dubious that such an offer would be regarded as friendly unless the circumstances made it appropriate for that particular state to offer its services. For instance, an offer by the Soviet Union to mediate between France and Tunisia would be regarded—and rightly so—as an effort further to injure relations rather than to ease them. The United States offer of good offices (although made inadvertently) was acceptable to both sides because the United States had a real interest in finding some way to ease the problem. The French could not afford to allow conditions to deteriorate further and therefore welcomed the good offices of a friendly state. The Tunisians desired to remain friendly to the West and hoped that the United States would be forced to link the Algerian and Tunisian situations to prevent the North African position of the NATO states from crumbling.

The peculiarly long-term character of bloc alignment during the loose bipolar period, therefore, specializes the role of negotiator. In the "balance of power" system a state not directly involved in the controversy usually was sufficiently neutral to serve as a mediator. In the loose bipolar system, most conflicts indirectly affect bloc affairs and the blocs have an interest in influencing their course. Finding an appropriate mediator for a dispute becomes enormously difficult under these circumstances. The leading member of a bloc may be the appropriate mediator between two other members of the bloc. But who can mediate between the leading member and another member of the bloc? Even in the first case, less formal diplomacy may be more appropriate than formal good offices or mediation. Who can mediate between the leading members of the two blocs? A single uncommitted state would not have sufficient strength or prestige. Moreover, on any number of issues, many uncommitted states would not genuinely be neutral—for instance, on any issue involving colonialism or thermonuclear tests. If no single uncommitted state is likely to be an acceptable mediator in bloc disputes, large numbers of uncommitted states may have to play such a role through the United Nations or by means of joint political influence exercised informally. Conflicts between uncommitted states can probably be mediated by still other uncommitted states in an effort to keep the dispute from becoming involved in the bloc conflicts. These are not, however, exclusively techniques for law resolution, although their effective use may be responsive to precedent and norms and may, in turn, serve as precedent for future cases.

International arbitration and international courts. International arbitration and judicial settlement are virtually identical procedures. In neither procedure may the judge or arbitrator decide the case with a view primarily to the accommodation or compromise of the conflicting interests, although decisions that fail to take such conflicts of interest into account are unlikely to prove effective. In each case, the settlement must be made according to rules that could be applied with equal validity to all other cases involving the same issues of law and of fact. There is an important difference, however. In arbitration, the arbitration agreement (or special submission to an International Court) may specify the issues that are to be decided and the facts that are to be taken into account. The contending parties may, if they wish, instruct the tribunal to accept an interpretation of the law to which the parties agree or a special rule that is to be applied to the particular case. For these reasons, the norm-creating power of the decision is somewhat limited.

Arbitration may proceed by means of *ad hoc* tribunals or individual arbitrators may be used. Finally, the parties involved may establish a continuing panel to arbitrate specific or general issues between them or recourse may be had to a tribunal open to all parties, such as the Permanent Court of Arbitration created by the Hague Convention of 1899. Arbitration agreements that are general usually exclude the vital interests of the nation, matters of honor, and matters that affect the interests of third parties. Although these limitations are sometimes viewed as defects of the arbitral systems, they actually are necessary if the systems are to be workable. Any system must have political methods for settling important conflicts of interest as well as juridical methods. In the present state of the international society direct negotiations between the disputants, the intervention of third parties, the application of the political machinery of international organizations, or perhaps the use of force constitute political techniques open to the parties.

Ad hoc tribunals, as a general rule, have their members selected by the parties to the dispute. Two disputants, for instance, may each select an arbitrator, and the two arbitrators may then select a third, in order to avoid the possibility of a tie vote. It is usually easier for the two arbitrators to agree upon the third than for the parties to the dispute to select directly an individual whom they can agree will apply the law impartially to the points at issue. The arbitrators selected by the parties usually find for the party who selected them. This somewhat diminishes the impartiality of these arbitrators. But it remains true that the arbitral award must be couched in normative language and not in the language of political negotiations.

The Permanent Court of International Justice, established by the Statute of the Court in 1921, and associated with the League of Nations, has now been replaced by the International Court of Justice as part of the general framework or organization established by the Charter of the United Nations. The judges are appointed to the International Court of Justice by a complicated procedure. Each of the national groups represented on the Permanent Court of Arbitration, and still functioning under the Charter, may nominate up to four judges not more than two of whom may come from their own nation. From this list the General Assembly and the Security Council each choose fifteen persons. Each person receiving a majority vote in both organs is elected, except that if two or more are elected from the same nation, only the elder receives the position. If a deadlock occurs, the sitting judges are empowered, as a last resort, to elect the remaining members of the bench. Five judges are elected every three years for nine-year terms. Judges cannot be dismissed unless their colleagues unanimously agree that they have ceased to satisfy the requirements of the position. Nine judges constitute a quorum, although a smaller bench is provided for when the parties desire a summary decision. If no judge of the nationality of one of the disputing parties is sitting, that party may nominate a judge for the case.

The judges of the International Court of Justice occupy a role of greater impartiality than do the judges of arbitral tribunals despite the provision in the Statute of the International Court of Justice for judges who are nationals of the parties to the dispute. Disputes may be submitted to the Court by all states which have signed its statute and to other states under conditions established by the Security Council. The Court may hear any matter submitted to it by states party to a dispute, and may hear all matters arising from the provisions of treaties or conventions that provide for compulsory jurisdiction. Whether the Court has jurisdiction is determined by the Court. Theoretically, therefore, in the areas where the parties have accepted compulsory jurisdiction, either by acceding to the Court Statute under the "Optional Clause," or by entering into bilateral or multilateral agreements to this effect, one party to the dispute may bring the matter before the Court without the agreement of the other party.

The "Optional Clause" of the Statute of the International Court of Justice provides for compulsory jurisdiction between states that have accepted the clause in all legal disputes over the interpretation of a treaty, questions of international law, the existence of facts that, if established, would constitute a breach of an international obligation, or the kind or extent of reparation to be made for a breach of an international obligation. Although most signers of the Court Statute have also accepted the "Optional Clause," most of these have made reservations that diminish the significance of that action. The United States has excluded from the jurisdiction of the Court matters essentially with its domestic jurisdiction, as determined by the United States rather than by the Court, and disputes arising under a multilateral treaty unless either all the parties to the agreement affected by the dispute are parties to the action or the United States agrees to jurisdiction.

The idea of expanding the jurisdiction of the World Court is currently a very popular one in the United States. As a first step, the highest political circles have come to support a broader form of United States submission, although considerable Senate opposition appears to remain. To date, the Court has been very little used by Members, and there are few submissions to compulsory jurisdiction that are not qualified heavily. The reasons for this refusal to make use of the Court are worth examination.

It has already been noted that disputes about treaty interpretation or the application of rules of customary law are often a means of asserting what is really a desire for legislative reform; that is, for changing the content of the rules. To the extent that this is true disputes about the law are not *bona fide* legal disputes, but rather an aspect of political maneuver. In such cases at least one party does not want resolution by any third party institution, and particularly one employing the relatively narrow legal procedures of a court. A basic precondition to any voluntary submission to judicial resolution would seem to be agreement about the rules that will be applied. This is particularly true when there is no ready alternative to modify the rules except diplomatic negotiation. The unresolved dispute has a legislative impact, for the contentions of both parties enter into the stream of available precedent for others in like situations and for future decision makers to draw upon. This potential legislative power is important to states, and they are hesitant to entrust it to third parties, particularly if they believe, as do the smaller states, that their voice in world affairs is becoming more powerful.

Related to the foregoing is the fact that many disputes which appear to be disputes about the correct interpretation of a treaty or customary law have hidden motivation. Judicial resolution in terms of the legal issues presented would not touch the real source of difficulty, the real problems and policies that are involved. The recent dispute between Iceland and the United Kingdom as to the permissible breadth of the territorial sea is an example in point. Iceland wished to extend her sea to a breadth of twelve miles in order to protect her local fishing industry from foreign, particularly British, competition. Fishing is one of Iceland's most important industries, and the greater efficiency of British trawlers resulted in great loss of income to Icelandic fisherman. The government was under heavy pressure to protect the industry against more efficient foreign competition.

Great Britain wanted to protect its fishing industry from exclusion from Icelandic fishing grounds merely because it was more efficient. But, in addition, the three-mile limit to territorial waters was (and is) an extremely important principle to maintain for any country with extensive maritime interests throughout the world. For Great Britain, then, far more than Icelandic fish were in issue. If this question were submitted to the Court, as, surprisingly, the United Kingdom proposed, the Court could have decided either way, but it could not (unless specially empowered by the parties) have explored any other means of resolution, such as a subsidy to Icelandic fisherman. Its decision would have left unresolved basic problems for one party or the other, and would have been operative not to resolve the dispute but merely to change the bargaining positions of the parties.

Furthermore, for the Court to have decided this dispute would have had worldwide repercussions affecting the interests of other countries. The breadth of the territorial sea has been hotly debated by many countries; the International Law Commission failed to resolve the problem; it was not possible to find a two-thirds majority from among the eighty nations represented at the Geneva Conference on the Law of the High Seas for any specific proposal governing the width of territorial seas. Would the Court's imprimatur on one breadth or another have been the end of dispute? Indeed, could it have risked such a decision? A good guess is that it would have been forced to say that the matter was in such doubt that it could not find any rule of international law prohibiting a state from claiming as much as twelve miles. Yet, even this decision would have been, as decisions cannot avoid being, favorable to one party at the expense of the other. More importantly, it could not have overtly weighed, because neither its method nor its prestige would permit, the better rule from the viewpoint of the international community.

This controversy illustrates two other shortcomings of reference to the ICJ that should be noted. First, the Court, in deciding a particular dispute must almost inevitably lay down general principles of international law that are of considerable interest and concern to states not parties to the particular dispute. The Court is, after all, the highest existing authority on international law, and any statements it makes in clarification of existing doctrine must be taken accordingly as authoritative. It is no answer to say—as does the Charter—that decisions of the Court have no precedential authority. They cannot help but have, whatever the theories of precedent may be. The Court must pay deference to its prior decisions if it is to avoid attack on grounds of partisanship among litigants. In addition, the opinions of the Court are taken most seriously, by scholars and by foreign offices alike, and treated as authoritative on the points decided and, indeed, on those merely discussed. Given this situation, we should ask whether or not it is really desirable to use the Court as the most important instrumentality for restating general principles of international law. Even if we concede the wisdom of clarifying rules (and this should not invariably be conceded), is the litigated case preferable to other alternatives? Examples of other alternatives are the International Law Commission, and various forms of multilateral treaty. It may be easier and more generally satisfactory to negotiate treaties restating and codifying general principles of international law if the rules themselves are still moot rather than after the Court has ruled on disputed points.

A second major shortcoming rests with the underdeveloped state of international law. When the Court deals with "customary" rules, it adopts the position that states are free to take unilateral action in the absence of a clear rule prohibiting the action taken. To a lesser extent, the Court takes the same view of treaty interpretation, allowing either party to interpret its obligations within the bounds of reason. Although those who profess a fear of too much interference by the Court with "sovereign" prerogatives might take comfort from this traditional judicial conservatism, we should also be aware that the basic causes of disputes remain relatively untouched. In almost every case, the complainant is seeking to formulate a rule that suggests that matters of mutual concern should be subject to joint regulation, not unilateral decision. Yet the state of international law doctrine, and the Court's jurisprudence, tends to leave the dispute where it was by declining to curb unilateral action. Indeed, those who point with pride to the fact that the Court's judgments have almost invariably been complied with should not neglect to point out that with very few exceptions the present Court has left the parties precisely where they were when they came to Court.

These observations should not be taken as criticisms of the Court. Quite the contrary, for judicial institutions must essentially preserve the status quo. Neither the methodology nor the function really permits otherwise. Courts must make new rules slowly, conservatively, and, of necessity, interstitially; a court is ill-equipped to rewrite a whole area of law within the limits of a single narrow controversy. For these reasons the ICJ cannot really contribute greatly to relieving international tensions even should its jurisdiction be expanded; it can seldom get at the basic causes of which the particular dispute is merely symptomatic. Today, for example there is considerable controversy over whether or not a state can confiscate, without compensation, foreign-owned enterprises on a non-discriminatory basis. Would a decision on this issue by the Court be helpful? Would it reduce international tensions, whichever way it was decided?

Both the geographical composition and mode of selection of judges create some problems. It is difficult to do much about giving the Communist countries and Afro-Asia more representation without offending other nations, particularly Europe and Latin America at whose expense the seats would probably shift. Furthermore, contentions that the present distribution of seats is unfair does not represent, as it might in this country when geographical areas or minority groups demand Supreme Court representation, merely a local pride and desire for status. It is founded on the notion that the Court does play a political role and is not really non-partisan. To acknowledge these demands might be to destroy the tradition of impartial role that the Court, with great difficulty, is seeking to build. That the Court, with seven members from the Western bloc, plus three Latin Americans, a Russian, a Pole, a Pakistani, and an Egyptian, is not a suitable mechanism for determining inter-bloc disputes is obvious. Shift the seven from West to East and envision the United States' attitude toward it. The tradition of impartial administration is by all evidence far stronger in the Western world, and in those areas of Afro-Asia which have preserved the British common law, than it is among the members of the Communist bloc. A major shift in its composition would greatly affect the attitude of Americans and Europeans toward the Court.

The Court is a useful and probably necessary, though not yet very important or powerful, part of the UN organizational complex. It can offer advisory opinions on the Charter. In addition, it can provide opinions on other basic UN documents to other UN agencies and help to clarify the growing area of international administrative law. These latter functions seldom raise very hot political questions, and the present composition of the Court reflects reasonably well the membership of specialized UN agencies, although slight modifications might not affect this consideration.

But the utility of the Court, by reason of its pretension to universality, to decide disputes between Member states is more questionable. Quite apart from the difficulties of any third-party adjudication in many disputes, adjudication by the highest judicial authority raises further difficulties. We have already noted that clarification of a theoretically universal "customary" law by virtue of pronouncement in two-party litigation is problematic, and that decision by this Court cannot help but freeze rules at a time when new problems require a more flexible approach. In addition, there is some doubt of the utility of an interbloc court to resolve intrabloc differences, of the need for fifteen judges and an expensive litigation process to clarify minor technical differences of interpretation, and of the wisdom of selecting to interpret a particular bilateral arrangement a Court that, because of its composition and prestige, must look to the impact of its decision on a variety of other agreements among other parties using similar language. Although any impartial decision maker would take these considerations into account, the authority of other decision makers and the impact of their decisions on non-litigating states would be less than that of the Court, and their decisions would consequently be more responsive to the problems raised by the litigating states.

Many of these difficulties could be met by having the Court sit in smaller panels (as the Charter permits) in a more convenient location. Decisions rendered by panels composed of judges whose impartiality between the litigants would be less subject to attack, and whose opinions would be less finally determinative of the general rule of international law are a feasible alternative. But even here it is difficult to envision extensive resort to the adjudicative process. Insofar as the process of adjudication also involves the restatement and clarification of rules that have future impact on the participants, the process has a "political" element, and it is by no means clear that the participants really wish to delegate this kind of authority to third parties, no matter how impartial, at least in the absence of an alternative mechanism to which appeal can be made. This is particularly true today because the classical rules and processes of international law are strongly tinted by Western jurisprudence and by rules derived from a period of laissez-faire economics. Many were in effect legislated by the great nations of yesteryear. Recognition of these difficulties is conceded by those who propose a Court of Equity and review of its decisions by the General Assembly. But again, the clarification of important rules in the context of particular disputes is a questionable device. It has the difficulties of an interstitial approach, and lacks the moderating influence that can come from more flexible institutions capable of broadening the area of negotiation and compromise, and of recommending more comprehensive solutions.

Finally, it should be added that none of what has been said above is particularly relevant to the proposal current in the United States to remove the Connally amendment to the United States reservation with regard to compulsory jurisdiction of the World Court. The reservation states that the U.S. will not submit disputes "essentially within the domestic jurisdiction of the United States of America *as determined by the United States of America.*" (The italicized words are the so-called Connally Amendment.) Obviously, this submission, as qualified above, is a fraud, and on that ground alone should be withdrawn. The United States should be the more embarrassed that this form of submission has been widely copied by others.

There is little danger to the United States in submitting to compulsory jurisdiction of the Court reciprocally with all other states who are willing to do so. The United States has infinitely more to gain than to lose from such a submission. It is consistent with the faith professed by the United States in peaceful and legal means of settlement of disputes, and with the image that the U.S. has of itself and wishes to project into the world community. The existing state of international "customary" law, and the treaties the United States is party to, seem generally favorable to the values that the United States is trying to promote in the world today and to the position of the United States in the international system, although it would require much more prevision than any of us have to know this with certainty. And, finally, the composition of the Court could not be more favorable to the American position on virtually any important issue.

11

SUPRANATIONAL ORGANIZATION OF THE UNIVERSAL TYPE

UNIVERSAL organizations like the League of Nations and the United Nations represent attempts within the international system to modify its unstable tendencies. In the case of the League, the rigidities of the "balance of power" system necessitated some form of mediation other than the no-longer functioning "balancing" process. The United Nations, on the other hand, performs a mediatory role which is an inherent element of the loose bipolar system rather than a compensation for the rigidities of a system that would not normally possess such a role function. An effort will be made to sketch briefly the organs and jurisdictions of the two universal organizations and the consequences for international law of their existence.

THE LEAGUE OF NATIONS

The League of Nations possessed two major organs: the Council and the Assembly. The Council had two classes of members: the permanent members and the elected members. Permanent representation was ostensibly given to the major nations. The United States refused to accept its seat; Germany was not admitted until 1926; the Soviet Union was admitted only in 1934, just a few short years before Italy, Germany, and Japan withdrew, and barely five years before the League collapsed. Also, Poland and Spain, in effect, were given permanent seats by being made eligible for re-election. The Council, as a smaller body, was the organ designed to handle the most pressing political problems, although the Assembly had the constitutional right to consider exactly the same sort of question and although a party to the dispute had the right to shift the dispute from the Council to the Assembly. The ability of the Council to act was severely restricted by the requirement for unanimous voting, excluding only the votes of the parties to the dispute.

The Assembly was not restricted to unanimity with respect to questions affecting the settlement of disputes (although with respect to most other measures, excepting certain procedural matters, the rule of unanimity did apply); but the actual arrangements were almost as restrictive as if that had been the case. The settlement of disputes coming under the crucial articles, 12, 13, 15, and 16, of the Covenant required the unanimous vote of the Council members, except for parties to the dispute, and a majority of the remaining members of the Assembly. The only consequence of this loosening of the rules was to prevent one or two minor states from interfering with recommendations. Clearly there could be few cases in which the Council members would be unanimous in which the great majority of the remaining members of the League would be unwilling to go along.

The Covenant also provided for a Permanent Court of International Justice to supplement the Permanent Court of Arbitration established by the Hague Conventions. The primary purpose of the Court was to decide disputes involving the interpretation of treaties, questions of international law, the existence of facts that, if established, would constitute breaches of international obligations, and the extent and nature of the reparations to be made in the case of such breaches. The Court did not exercise compulsory jurisdiction over states, unless such jurisdiction was accepted under the "Optional Clause" by the states in question, although the Covenant sought to encourage such reference. The Court of Justice was also supposed to advise the League on matters affecting the jurisdiction and constitutional operations of the League of Nations. These provisions are virtually identical with those adopted after the Second World War as the Statute of the present International Court.

Although the League of Nations could hardly have been called a government in any rigorous sense, the Covenant did establish institutions designed to regulate aspects of international behavior. The test of government is its ability to regulate activity within a territory or over functional areas. Whether the constitutional law that establishes this government becomes part of the law of the society—in this case the international society—depends upon whether the constitutional law is by and large effectively enforced. The League was unable to meet this test.

In examining the status of international law following the adoption of the Covenant, two things must be kept in mind. First, the Covenant could apply to non-Members without, and even against, their consent, provided only that the League was powerful enough to make its applications stick. Second, the failure of the League does not imply that the law of the League is entirely discredited. Some aspects of law espoused by the League may survive as a consequence of support from international society, even though the League itself passed away. This would be true, even had the League not been replaced by the United Nations. The factors which led to the formation of the League, but were not strong enough to sustain it through its period of trial, may none the less be sufficiently strong to sustain some aspects of the law of the League of Nations.

The League of Nations did not have legislative authority to change the status quo. On the contrary, Article 10 of the Covenant specifically obligated the League of Nations to maintain the territorial status quo established by the peace treaties. According to Article 10 the "Members of the League undertake to respect and preserve as against external aggression the territorial integrity and existing political independence of all Members of the League." Thus, in the absence of mutual consent, the League bound its members to the maintenance of a juridical status quo against forcible change, without establishing political organs that had the authority to legislate peaceful changes. The founders of the Organization thus made the *wrong* concession to the French point of view and thereby attempted to establish an order resistant to the changes that are produced by the ordinary, as well as by the extraordinary, workings of social and political systems.

As early as 1920, the fundamental validity of this norm was questionable. Although the norm was applied successfully in the Aaland Islands dispute, the League recognized Poland's forcible change of the Lithuanian border, primarily because France had a decided interest in a strong Poland as a counter-weight to Germany. A seizure of territory by a large state from a small and weak state rarely involves the threat of war—particularly if the large state is in a position to terminate the matter before anything can be done to interfere.

Consequently, the first practical reinterpretation of Article 10 was to restrict its effective application to those cases that, by affecting the interests of major states, create a threat of war. With the Balkan Wars preceding the First World War still fresh in mind, wars between minor states also fell under the rubric because of their propensity to affect the interests of major states. But forcible seizures of territory from states too small and weak to resist were not effectively prohibited by Article 10. The matter can be clarified further by examination of Articles 11, 12, 13, 15 and 16.

Article 11 states that "Any war or threat of war, whether immediately affecting any of the members of the League or not, is hereby declared a matter of concern to the whole League, and the League shall take any action that may be deemed wise and effectual to safeguard the peace of nations." The problem of justice clearly appears to be subordinated to the need for peace. We may ask whether "wise and effectual" means which conflict with Article 10 could have been contemplated with propriety. Where alternative wise and effectual means (one consonant with Article 10 and the other not) were available, no real problem would have existed. But, if the only wise and effectual means were not consonant with Article 10, which provision was to be preferred? Undoubtedly, a jurist would have posited a new rule that permitted him to assign priority to Article 10 or to Article 11 in the existing circumstances. This at least would have maintained the normative character of the system. But can there be any doubt that political considerations would have been uppermost in "discovering" this new rule?

In case of war or the threat of war, the Secretary-General of the League was obligated on the request of any member of the League to summon forthwith a meeting of the Council. Thus the procedure for getting the matter before an appropriate organ of the League was both clear and efficacious. It was also the right of any Member of the League to call to the attention of the Assembly or the Council "any circumstance whatever affecting international relations which threatens to disturb international peace or the good understanding between nations upon which peace depends." This provision of Article 11 is considerably broader than the preceding one but less efficacious, since no procedure for summoning a meeting was provided.

Article 12 required parties to a dispute to submit the dispute to arbitration, to judicial settlement, or to enquiry by the Council. It did not rule out war, however, but merely required the parties to agree not to go to war until three months after the award, decision, or report. Moreover, it required the arbitrators or judges to make their awards or decisions within a reasonable time and specified a limit of six months for the report of the Council if the case went before that body. Thus Article 12 established a "cooling-off" period, while ensuring the parties to the dispute against a "stall." Thus far, therefore, war was not outlawed, but certain procedures had to be followed before the resort to war rightly could be made. Article 13 introduced further qualifications that appear to restore, to some extent, the old distinction between "just" and "unjust" war that, for reasons already noted, had no place in a "balance of power" system. It thus gave additional evidence for the breakdown of that system. If the process of "balancing" and flexibility of alignment cannot be depended upon to limit wars and to maintain the independent existence of the major states, some additional criterion, other than the immediate self-interest of the major states must be discovered to prevent the overturn of the system. The trouble with the proposed solution the League represented is that it did not really provide a workable mechanism to replace the self-interest of states. Study of the succeeding articles will show what a weak reed the League of Nations leaned upon.

The important modification of the right to war in Article 13 reads: "The Members of the League agree that they will carry out in full good faith any award *or decision* [of an arbitral or judicial tribunal respectively] that may be rendered, and that they will not resort to war against a member of the League which complies therewith. In the event of any failure to carry out such an award *or decision,* the Council shall propose what steps should be taken to give effect thereto." Thus the party that failed to carry out the award or decision lost the right to wage war against the other party. The aggrieved state theoretically had to depend upon the action of the Council, but there was a loophole that would have permitted it to wage war in support of its claims and would have prevented League members from coming to the aid of the other party. Presumably, however, the right of the attacked state to defend itself would have been recognized, even though the state was at fault, unless the Council itself should have agreed to strong measures against it. Article 13, however, is not as practically important as Article 15, for states that would refuse to carry out the award or decision, are most unlikely to agree to arbitration or to judicial process in the first place.

Article 15 deals with disputes that are not submitted to arbitration or to judicial settlement and provides for submitting them to the

Council for consideration. The Council was to endeavor to settle the dispute but, failing settlement, either unanimously or by majority vote, to "make and publish a report containing a statement of the facts of the dispute and of the recommendations that are deemed proper in regard thereto." If the report was unanimous, except for the states party to the dispute, the members of the League were obligated not to go to war with the state that complied with the recommendations. If the report was not unanimous, however, the members of the League reserved the right individually to take whatever measures appeared right and just. Clearly, under such conditions, war was permitted. The League Covenant therefore was not written in such a way that its members would have been bound legally to inaction in the event of disagreement. And the obligation to support the aggrieved state was weak, since an expansionist state was likely to find at least one supporter.

Article 16 represented an attempt to implement the concept of collective security by declaring that any state that "resort(s) to war in disregard of its convenants under Articles 12, 13, or 15 . . . shall *ipso facto* be deemed to have committed an act of war against all other members of the League, which hereby undertake immediately to subject it to the severance of all trade or financial relations, the prohibition of all intercourse between their nationals and the nationals of the covenant-breaking State and the prevention of all financial, commercial or personal intercourse between the nationals of the covenant-breaking State and the nationals of any other State, whether a Member of the League or not." These actions, although obligatory, were dependent upon the individual actions of the states. The obligation included that of bringing non-members of the League within the framework of the sanctions. No effective machinery was provided for this objective, although the use of diplomacy toward this end during the Ethiopian crisis was partly effective.

The use of armed forces against the offending state was related to a recommendation of the Council, although it could be contended that the failure of the Council to respond to its duty did not relieve individual League members of their individual obligation to take effective action against the offender. Article 16 also provided for the possible expulsion of the offender, a procedure employed only against the Soviet Union in 1939 for its attack against Finland. Germany, Italy, and Japan, however, gave the League no opportunity to use expulsion; each renounced its League membership with disdain. By the time expulsion was employed, the Second World War had already commenced and the League, for all practical purposes, had been relegated to history.

In principle, the League Covenant outlawed wars designed to change the territorial status quo and specified procedures designed to discourage and punish states engaging in such wars. However, there must be institutions—or at least interests—ready to implement procedures. Like Banquo's ghost, disembodied procedures may stalk the international stage to haunt the players, but their import is more symbolic than real. Legal norms do not spring from words on documents or from abstract systems of thought. They must be filled out with institutional flesh and warmed into action by interests. Futile efforts were made to provide the skeleton of the League with flesh; all were brought to naught by the myth of collective security, and particularly by British unwillingness to be committed to military action on the Continent.

The French strongly advocated institutional modifications designed to insure the purposes for which the League was organized. Apart from the rather unrealistic discussions on disarmament, the Temporary Mixed Commission formulated the ill-fated Draft Treaty of Mutual Assistance in 1923, which, if it had been adopted, might have created an adequate instrument to maintain the peace. The Draft Treaty introduced an essential modification in Lord Cecil's concept of a general treaty of assistance by providing for special defensive arrangements, which would have come into operation automatically upon a finding by the Council of aggressive war, while placing upon the Council the obligation to make the finding of aggression within four days of the outbreak of hostilities. Aggressive war was specified as an international crime. It is quite true that the finding of aggressive war might have been difficult to make and for many reasons the Temporary Mixed Commission refused to define aggression. However, in most of the actual cases that were to arise, this theoretical difficulty would not have proved important. Given the instruments of warfare of the time, defensive forces would have had sufficient time, during the four-day period, to be mobilized, particularly since they would have been based upon special arrangements entered into previously. The Draft Treaty, however, foundered on British objection.

The Geneva Protocol (Protocol for the Pacific Settlement of Disputes) was endorsed in 1925 by the League Assembly but never implemented by the League members. The failure to implement the Protocol was unimportant. It is true that the Geneva Protocol specified the refusal to arbitrate as the test of aggression, provided for compulsory jurisdiction of the International Court of Justice in matters coming within the "Optional Clause" of the Court Statute, and provided that the Council would appoint compulsory arbitrators if the parties refused to arbitrate or to go to the Court, thus closing a gap in the verbal provisions of the Covenant. The last provision eliminated the case under Article 15 where, in the absence of a unanimous vote, the parties remained free to take any action they saw fit. The Geneva Protocol, however, was a pious legalism that did nothing to provide an institutional structure for action. It closed the gap in the Covenant but left the Covenant as lifeless as before. Without defensive alliances ready to act, the Geneva Protocol was as defective as the original League Covenant and added nothing to it save words.

The Locarno treaties of 1925 made some progress—if not very much—toward providing potentially effective procedures. In addition to providing for arbitration, they guaranteed the French and Belgian borders with Germany, with England and Italy as additional guarantors. The difficulty was that these borders were unlikely to constitute the point of immediate difficulty; by the time they were at issue, matters would have got beyond the point of repair. The General Act of 1928, which provided for general accessions to regional pacts similar to the Locarno Pacts, and the Pact of Paris (Kellogg-Briand Pact) of 1928, providing for the renunciation of war as an instrument of national policy (with understandings), were also unimportant because they provided no effective institutional procedures, even though, as an ironic afterthought, the violation of the latter was the gravamen of war crimes at the Nuernberg trials.

The presence or absence of institutional means of enforcement of legal principles determines whether a system of law exists or not. Municipal courts are able to call upon the assistance of sheriffs, or, if necessary, the total armed force of the state, to aid in the execution of sentence. The political arm of government is obligated to sustain legal process. And a municipal system of law that is not sustained by the cooperation of the body politic will not persist. The assertion that the Covenant and the Pact of Paris outlawed wars of aggression seems excessive when measured against the realities of the international society of the time. These were statements of wishful thinking, not law. The norms of the nineteenth century with respect to the limitations of aims in war or the restoration of defeated major states were not enforced by formal international government.

But they were enforced by an international society, which was organized in a manner that permitted it to respond in an appropriate manner. The times were out of joint for the League, and its announced principles represented ideals rather than rules; no alliances existed to enforce them.

The experiences of the League demonstrate the lack of political wisdom—at least with respect to international politics—of the leaders of the time. But the aims to which they gave voice were not without foundation in the hopes of the people they represented. And there can be little doubt that the use of war as an instrument of policy was becoming increasingly less desirable with the difficulty of limiting aims that was a consequence of the breakdown of the "balance of power" system. The new technology emphasizes this fact. States now do possess some common interest in avoiding war and in finding mechanisms toward this end where no path to quick and cheap victory exists. The experiences of the post-Second World War period demonstrate the emergence of a new institutional form—the bloc—designed to prevent cheap victory and the difficult search for ways to prevent the outbreak of war. The law is still in the process of evolution.

The United Nations

The way in which the conceptions of the organizers of the United Nations failed to correspond with the realities of international politics has already been described and need not be repeated. But the Organization deserves a close scrutiny with respect to its formal structure and its actual functioning.

Security council. The United Nations has two major political organs: the Security Council and the Assembly. The original functions and importance of the two organs differed sharply as contrasted with the rather similar functions of the corresponding organs of the League. Even the term "Security Council" as contrasted with the plain "Council" of the League was intended to emphasize the responsibility of the UN organ for the maintenance of peace and security. The Security Council has eleven seats,[1] five of which are

---

[1] There is considerable pressure, with the admission of large numbers of African states to the UN, to enlarge the Security Council or to give the African nations representation on the Security Council at the expense of European and Latin

held by the permanent members of the Council. When these five are agreed upon a course of action, they have to sway only two additional votes—presumably a very easy task—in order to authorize measures including the use of armed force. Since the five permanent members of the Council virtually monopolize the possession of military capabilities, they clearly are capable of maintaining peace and security as long as they are in agreement. But the fact that they monopolize military force has proved sufficient to insure that their interests would almost always conflict. Wartime harmony had been based upon the existence of a powerful and hostile Axis coalition. It should have been obvious that the defeated Axis nations would constitute prizes that would divide them and that the task of destroying the military potentialities of the Axis states was not sufficient to maintain long the wartime harmony.

Both Chapter VI and Chapter VII of the Charter of the United Nations call upon the Security Council of the United Nations to take action when disputes threaten the maintenance of international peace and security. Chapter VI also may be employed by the General Assembly. Chapter VI concerns the pacific settlement of disputes, and Chapter VII authorizes the use of force.

Article 33 of Chapter VI calls upon the parties to any dispute that, if continued, is likely to endanger international peace and security to seek solution by "negotiation, enquiry, mediation, conciliation, arbitration, judicial settlement, resort to regional agencies or arrangements, or other peaceful means of their own choice." If the parties to the dispute do not agree to such means voluntarily, the Security Council has the right, if it thinks it necessary, to require the parties to settle their dispute by the aforementioned means. Article 33 gives recognition to the consideration that less formal procedures than those of the Security Council are desirable, for the procedures of the Security Council bring the full glare of publicity upon the parties and are likely to inflame passions and to produce rigid positions. However, the knowledge that the matter will be brought before the Security Council if the participants do not agree voluntarily to other procedures puts pressure upon them to make use of other procedures for peaceful settlement. Thus, for instance, the Tunisian complaint to the Security Council in February, 1958,

---

American states. The West favors expansion of the Security Council but is unwilling to agree that Communist China take the Chinese seat on the Security Council. The Soviet Union insists that it will veto any expansion of the Security Council unless Communist China is given the Chinese seat.

over the French bombing of Sakiet-Sidi-Youssef made the French more amenable to American good offices than if the Tunisians had been unable to resort to Security Council procedures.

Article 34 gives the Security Council the right to consider disputes or situations likely to produce international friction and to determine whether their continuance is likely to endanger international peace and security. It differs from Article 39 of Chapter VII in two important respects. Article 39 deals with threats to the peace, breaches of the peace, and acts of aggression. It is technically mandatory upon the Security Council, rather than permissive, to consider such situations. But, in addition, the use of Article 39 contemplates the use of force if the recommendations of the Security Council are not adopted. In fact, many of the same situations could be considered either under Chapter VI or VII. However, the employment of Chapter VI indicates that force will not be used and therefore permits the parties to withdraw from a challenged position with more grace than if the use of force were threatened from the outset.

Article 35 provides that any member of the United Nations may bring a dispute before either the Security Council or the General Assembly; states that are not members of the United Nations may also bring such matters to the attention of the United Nations provided that such states accept the obligations of pacific settlement provided in the Charter. There is nothing in the article to prevent Members from bringing to the attention of the United Nations a dispute or situation involving non-Members; and, in this case, the parties would be obliged to accept the procedures for pacific settlement or to reckon with the possibility that Chapter VII would be employed. Thus, it is doubtful that obligation to use the methods of peaceful settlement flows only from the use of the procedures of the organization. It would appear rather that the privilege of bringing the matter before the United Nations is dependent upon the recognition of an obligation that is already present in any case. The priority of the Security Council with respect to disputes was asserted by the provisions of Article 12 which prevent the General Assembly from considering matters that are on the agenda of the Security Council. (By subsequent practice, removal from the agenda has become a procedural matter, not subject to veto.)

Article 36 empowers the Security Council to recommend procedures for the settlement of a dispute, but it is to take into consideration procedures already adopted by the parties or the desirability, as a general rule, of referring legal disputes to the International Court of Justice. Article 37 extends to the Council the power to "recommend" appropriate terms of settlement if it feels the continuation of the dispute will threaten international peace and security. This is the first substantive power which Chapter VI provides and it is hedged by "recommend" rather than the more compelling "call upon." This dilution of authority is, of course, necessary if the United Nations is not to become an international government. Yet, the power to legislate political change is potentially present.

Chapter VII, which provides for action in cases of threats to the peace, breaches of the peace, or acts of aggression, was intended by the drafters of the Charter to contain the teeth of the organization. Consequently all action provided for under this Chapter was to be taken by the Security Council alone. Article 39 of Chapter VII called for the Security Council to act where the peace was threatened or already breached and to make recommendations, or to take measures in accordance with Articles 41 and 42, to restore international peace and security. It was recognized, however, that events might transpire in a manner not favorable to the implementation of recommendations unless immediate steps to prevent the aggravation of the situation could be taken. Therefore, Article 40 permits the Security Council to call upon the parties to "comply with such additional measures as it deems necessary or desirable." It was asserted that these provisional measures were not to prejudice the rights or claims of the parties. Finally the Security Council "shall duly take account of failure to comply with such provisional measures."

Article 40, which was employed at the outbreak of the Korean War, had the important function of stopping hostilities in order to prevent a forcible solution of the problem. Obviously, this intention would be frustrated if the continued use of force, contrary to the determination of the Security Council, were not to involve penalties for the offending state. On the other hand, the assertion that these provisional measures were not to prejudice the rights or claims of the parties must be viewed as an intention rather than an indication of the necessary development of the controversy. The preoccupation of the Charter with calling hostilities to a halt is quite likely to prejudice the claims of one of the parties. Thus, for instance,—although this action involved the General Assembly rather than the Security Council—Israel was unable to enforce her claims to the use of the Gulf of Aquaba until she employed force. Moreover, in this case, the tacit recognition of Israel's right to such use stemmed primarily not from a recognition of the legality and justice of the claim, although the claim may have considerable legal merit, but rather from a desire to secure the withdrawal of Israeli forces from the Sinai peninsula. Perhaps this only emphasizes the fact that the United Nations proceedings are more political than juridical.

Article 41 provides for the use of means short of military force. It leaves the means employed to the discretion of the Security Council but permits that body to "call upon" other members of the United Nations to apply the measures it finds necessary to give effect to its decisions. "These [measures] may include complete or partial interruption of economic relations and of rail, sea, air, postal, telegraphic, radio, and other means of communication, and the severance of diplomatic relations." If the Security Council considers such measures inadequate or if they have been demonstrated to be inadequate, it may order, according to Article 42, action by land, sea, or air to maintain or to restore international peace and security. "Such action may include demonstrations, blockade, and other operations by air, sea, or land forces of Members of the United Nations." Articles 39 to 42, therefore, document the intention to prevent forcible political change.

Although the finite means available to the Security Council may be used at its discretion, its decision to employ appropriate means was not intended to be a matter for discretion. The power of the Security Council to recommend meant that the United Nations was not tied to the status quo as the League of Nations was tied to the regime established by the peace treaties concluding the First World War. Priority given to the maintenance of peace and security, and the very title of Chapter VII, which calls it into play only if there is a breach of the peace, threat of a breach of peace, or act of aggression, indicate that recommended changes in the status quo must themselves play a role in the maintenance of peace and security.

The subordination of the requirement of justice, or of political change, to that of peace and security indicated that the United Nations was not expected to take the initiative in changing the status quo, even though, unlike the League of Nations, the UN was not obligated to preserve the status quo. As a consequence, the more intransigent a claimant, and the more it rattles the sabre and threatens the peace, the more likely are its claims to receive consideration. This applies not only to attempts to change the status quo but also to attempts to enforce claims under the existing status quo. The United Nations system is still a system that may prove exasperating to nations whose claims are clear and important, yet ignored. Conceivably, this system could drive such nations to resort to force, or to the threat of force, to bring into play the United Nations' power of recommendation. Once recommendations are made, they are likely to have considerable political importance and to be supported by active national and supranational policies.

With respect to the possibility of military enforcement action, however, the United States and the Soviet Union were never able to reach agreement on the composition of United Nations forces and a Military Staff Committee under Articles 43 to 47 of the Charter. And, in any event, such forces could never have functioned adequately in the event of serious disagreement between the United States and the Soviet Union. Technically, this still permits individual nations to supply military forces for United Nations operations on an *ad hoc* basis, if the Security Council calls for them. But the fundamental cleavage of interests that prevented the establishment of the Military Staff Committee also prevents Security Council action in those cases where the interests of the United States and the Soviet Union are opposed, for any permanent member can veto such action. The concatenation of circumstances, including Soviet absence from the Council, that permitted initial United Nations action in Korea is not likely to recur often.

The general assembly. The General Assembly of the United Nations has come to perform functions that previously came within the jurisdiction of the Security Council. Chapter IV of the Charter, which deals with the General Assembly, can be interpreted to include these added jurisdictional functions. There can be no doubt, however, that the framers of the Charter did not anticipate the ways in which their words would be interpreted. Neither did the drafters of the American Constitution!

When the Charter was drafted, there was a strong conflict between the Soviet Union and most of the small states over the powers of the General Assembly. The United States, like the Soviet Union, desired to keep the Security Council as the effective enforcement agency of the United Nations within the foreseeable future. Nonetheless, the United States did not want to preclude entirely the possibility of developments in the future that might transform the organization from one based on the monopolization of force to one based on consent and justice. The United States was not so indifferent to the hopes and aspirations of the small states in the present era that it wanted to restrict the General Assembly to the status of a functionless forum in which ideas could be expressed but no action taken. As a consequence, the United States stage-managed a compromise in which the General Assembly was given the appearance of powers that very few thought would ever be exercised effectively.

Article 10 gave the General Assembly the right to discuss any question or matters within the scope of the Charter or relating to the powers and functions of any organ of the United Nations, except as provided in Article 12, and also gave the General Assembly the right to make recommendations on these matters. This grant is broad, but Article 11 immediately seems to delimit the powers of the General Assembly and casts its recommendations in a different light from those of the Security Council. The General Assembly is given the right to consider "general principles" for the maintenance of peace and security, disarmament, and the regulation of armaments. It may make recommendations on these subjects. It may also discuss and make recommendations concerning any question related to the maintenance of international peace and security, except that any "question on which action is necessary shall be referred to the Security Council by the General Assembly either before or after discussion." This would seem to preclude recommendations for any sort of enforcement action. However, Article 11 also states that "The powers of the General Assembly set forth in this Article shall not limit the general scope of Article 10."

Article 14 gives the General Assembly the right to "recommend measures for the peaceful adjustment of any situation, regardless of the origin of the situation, that it deems likely to impair the general welfare or friendly relations among nations, including situations resulting from a violation of the principles of the present Charter setting forth the Purposes and Principles of the United Nations." This might seem to imply authority to take enforcement action. However, the careful reference in Article 14 to powers of peaceful settlement, and the absence of any reference to the power even to recommend enforcement action would lead one to believe that such powers were not intended, despite the wide grant of authority in Article 10. And, indeed, apart from interpretations of the wording of the Charter and despite the compromises that were made at San Francisco, this was the intention of the states which cooperated in the establishment of the United Nations before the San Francisco meeting and without whose participation the organization could not exist as an effective body. The constitutional development of the United Nations, like most constitutional developments, is a product of the political situation—in this case, that existing in the postwar period.

The democratic states were continually frustrated in the Security Council on measures where they had a constitutional majority except for the veto of the Soviet Union.   The annual meetings of the General Assembly, as an alternative, did not provide a continuous forum in which pressing issues could be discussed.   In an effort to provide such an alternate forum when the Security Council ceased to function effectively, the Interim Committee of the General Assembly, sometimes known as the "Little Assembly," was organized in 1947, and was made permanent in 1949.   The Interim Committee was to remain in continuous session and to have the same membership as the General Assembly.   Its mandate included the consideration of and the right to make recommendations to the General Assembly concerning matters referred to it by the Assembly, disputes or situations proposed for the agenda of the Assembly or brought before the General Assembly by the Security Council, or methods useful for the consideration of the general principles of cooperation in the maintenance of international peace and security, including the regulation of armaments.   The Interim Committee was also authorized to conduct investigations and to appoint commissions of inquiry by the same two-thirds majority which applies to important matters considered by the General Assembly, and to advise the Secretary-General if a special session is desired to consider a matter under discussion.

The Soviet Union viewed the Interim Committee as an illegal body and refused to participate in its sessions.   Although the Interim Committee has considered procedures for the peaceful settlement of disputes and did interpret the mandate of the Temporary Commission on Korea, it has never considered any situation or dispute directly nor has it ever appointed a commission of inquiry.   As a consequence, efforts to consider many matters of importance in this subsidiary organ of the General Assembly, rather than in the Security Council, were not successful.   In general, resort to the device of the special session has occurred when urgent sessions were required, when the annual meeting was not in progress, and when the usual difficulties were stalling Security Council procedures.

The first important formal effort to treat the General Assembly as if it possessed formal enforcement powers—powers lodged by the Charter in the Security Council—rather than merely to use it as the major forum for discussion and peaceful settlement procedures, occurred during the Korean War.

When the Soviet Union returned to the Security Council after the initial resolutions authorizing United Nations military action in Korea, the United States came to the conclusion that effective action against aggression was unlikely to be taken by that organ of the United Nations. Shortly after Secretary of State Dean Acheson's speech to the General Assembly on this subject, a joint resolution—the "Uniting for Peace" Resolution—to guard against this contingency was introduced and passed by a large majority. The resolution stated that if the Security Council, because of any action by its permanent members, failed to exercise its primary role in the maintenance of peace and security where there was a threat to the peace, breach of the peace, or act of aggression, the General Assembly should consider the matter immediately with a view to making recommendations. If there was an actual breach of the peace or act of aggression, the recommendations might include the use of armed force in order to maintain or to restore international peace and security. If the General Assembly was not in session, an emergency session could be called within twenty-four hours by any seven members of the Security Council or by a majority of the Assembly.

The resolution also called for the establishment of a Peace Observation Commission which could observe and report on any situation producing international tension likely to endanger the maintenance of international peace and security. If the Security Council is not properly exercising its functions, and if the Assembly were not in session, the Interim Committee could make use of the Peace Observation Commission. Each member of the United Nations was instructed to survey its resources in order to determine the assistance it would be able to give to the Security Council or the General Assembly in maintaining international peace and security, and to maintain within its territory elements of its armed forces trained, organized, and equipped in such a way that they could be made available promptly for service as United Nations forces. The Secretary-General was advised to appoint a panel of military experts who could give the member states technical advice on the organization, training, and equipment of forces that could be used as United Nations forces. It was also recommended that a Collective Measures Committee be established to report to the Security Council and the General Assembly on methods of maintaining international peace and security, including the use of armed forces.

This "Uniting for Peace" Resolution was intended, in effect, to provide the General Assembly with enforcement powers the Charter had lodged in the Security Council. But other powers of the Security

Council—and perhaps some it did not possess—were also taken over by the General Assembly during the Korean War. It authorized the crossing of the thirty-eighth parallel (though in fact Washington had given General MacArthur permission before the matter was considered by the General Assembly), called for the unification of Korea, and condemned the Communist Chinese regime as an "aggressor." However, the "Uniting for Peace" Resolution has remained virtually a dead letter despite the effective usurpation of Security Council powers by the General Assembly. The General Assembly and Secretary-General Hammarskjold have subsequently preferred *ad hoc* solutions to standing procedures for the use of international forces. Thus, the United Nations Emergency Forces employed during the Suez crisis of 1956 and the forces provided during the Congo crisis of 1960 were not provided under the provisions of the "Uniting for Peace" resolution. Their use is normally dependent upon the consent of the local states, although this consent, if not absent, may be questionable in the Congo crisis. Such forces, provided on an *ad hoc* basis, rather than the Korean type of forces, would seem to provide the model for the future.

In fact, although particular expedients may have become moribund the assumption of new powers by the United Nations—and, in particular, by the General Assembly—has been part of a continual process of constitutional development within the United Nations since its early days. Important political powers were exercised by the General Assembly in the Palestine dispute as early as the 1947-1948 period. In this case, the General Assembly "legislated" the broad lines of a settlement, and the Security Council used its powers to halt the subsequent armed conflict.

It may be asked from where the General Assembly acquired the power to make a recommendation, in effect, disposing of territory and authorizing the formation of two states, only one of which, Israel, had the practical requirements for existence. Britain, the mandatory state, brought the matter before the General Assembly in 1947, under the provisions of Article 10 of the Charter, after it had been unable to find any solution acceptable to both Arabs and Jews. The Arabs challenged the competence of both Britain and the Assembly to adopt a solution inconsistent with the terms of the Covenant of the League of Nations referring to former areas of the Turkish Empire, whose existence as independent nations could be provisionally recognized, and which should be placed under a mandatory state responsive to the wishes of the people. The Covenant, however, was not binding in this respect. Britain's authority came from the peace treaty with Turkey; and Palestine became a League mandate only after the League accepted Britain's terms, which included the ambiguous Jewish "home" in Palestine. This consideration, however, only disposed of the obligation to create an Arab state of Palestine; it did not establish United Nations authority to create any states, whether Jewish or Arab, in Palestine.

Nevertheless, the United Nations voted for the partition plan. The United States began to have second thoughts about the wisdom of the partition early in 1948 and questioned whether the Security Council could act to enforce a political settlement rather than merely to remove a threat to the peace. The Council referred the matter back to a special meeting of the General Assembly, which refused to retreat from its previous position. But we may question whether the General Assembly did create the state of Israel or whether the existence of the state of Israel is only indirectly related to the Assembly's decision. After all, the Arab state, which the Assembly recommended, never did come into being. When the British withdrew, the Israeli state came into being as a consequence of the existence of a people occupying a territory and possessing both a government and an army. It might have been possible to destroy this state with sufficient force, but the state was not created by an Assembly resolution. Nor did the Security Council really help to preserve Israel by calling a halt to the fighting. There is little doubt that the Arab armies were in serious trouble at the time of the cease-fire, and it is known that only a British ultimatum prevented the Israelis from chasing the Egyptian armies across the Nile.

On the other hand, it would be going too far to say that Assembly and Council action had no subsequent effect. The existence of the Assembly resolution is a factor adding to the legitimacy of the Israeli state. Moreover, there may be circumstances in which substantive decisions of the Assembly to halt fighting are the decisive factors in stabilizing a situation and in giving it legal effect.

The shift in responsibility, during the past fifteen years, from the Security Council to the General Assembly makes it important to examine more specifically the conditions under which General Assembly resolutions embodying political recommendations or concerning peace and security are likely to prove effective. General Assembly resolutions, despite occasional ineffectiveness, cannot be taken lightly. When, for instance, the General Assembly enacts a recommendation by a majority of two-thirds or more, it is likely to have considerable political and moral appeal for a number of reasons. It is quite likely to be a proposal that takes into account the positions defended by the leading adversaries and some of their unstated political problems as well—for example, their domestic political situations, the personalities of government officials, and estimates of what, despite conflicting claims, might be an acceptable compromise. By leaving some latitude to the parties to accept or reject, it does not put the integrity of the UN itself directly in issue. However, not all two-thirds majorities are of equal effectiveness. To understand why some resolutions are more effective than others, we must examine the composition and circumstances of the votes.

During the Suez crisis of 1956, effective General Assembly procedures could be employed to bring about the withdrawal of Israeli, French, and British forces from Egyptian territory, because the Soviet Union found it expedient to pose as the friend of the "downtrodden" Arab and President Eisenhower disapproved the use of force to accomplish political objectives. Although the British and French had vetoed Security Council resolutions, a firm two-thirds majority was established in the Assembly. Dependent upon the United States for oil—once the mideast lines were cut—and seeing the NATO security system at stake, Britain and France were quite vulnerable to United States pressure. Moreover, in Great Britain, large sections of the Labour Party and some elements within the Conservative Party disapproved of the actions of the Eden government.

The Israelis, however, resisted the pressure to withdraw unless they were compensated in some way for the strategic disabilities to which withdrawal would condemn them. In this situation, the decision of the General Assembly to send United Nations forces to the area to supervise the withdrawal and to serve as a buffer at the points of greatest tension provided an opportunity for the Israelis to bow before the pressure exerted upon them. Although the Secretary General stated that these United Nations forces would remain only at the pleasure of the local states, they did not interfere with Israeli use of the Gulf of Aquaba. Thus there was de facto recognition of the Israeli breach of the Arab blockade of the Gulf and this constituted a kind of compensation for Israeli withdrawal. The fact that effective Israeli use of the Gulf occurred while United Nations forces controlled the key points along the Egyptian shore of the Gulf permitted the Egyptians to accept this change in the status quo more gracefully than if they had had to submit directly to Israeli force.

Despite the resolutions passed by the General Assembly in the case of Hungary, it was not possible to affect the course of events against the will of the Soviet Union unless the United States had been willing to go to war to achieve that objective. The Eisenhower administration was unwilling to run the risks involved, even in order to destroy the Soviet satellite system. As a consequence, the international position of the Soviet-imposed regime, despite occasional harassing moves in the United Nations, has been consolidated.

In the Korean War, the United Nations placed itself in the unfortunate position of being a party to, rather than a mediator of, the dispute. In direct clashes between leading bloc states, the United Nations cannot expect to play an enforcement role successfully, and the attempt to do so may possibly have untoward consequences for the prestige of the organization.

Where, however, the interests of the Soviet Union and the United States are not directly involved—where both support the United Nations action, or one supports it and the other remains indifferent, the United Nations can play an effective political role in composing conflicting national interests. Thus, in the Suez case, the Assembly took a stand—perhaps unwisely—against the use of force to bring about political change, while at the same time giving recognition to some of the grievances of Israel. The *status quo ante* was changed, even if this change occurred as a consequence of actions not officially designed to change them. And in the process certain rules of procedure were at least temporarily enforced upon the parties to the dispute.

How effective the procedures of the United Nations become in building a more secure and peaceful, and a better world depends upon the wisdom with which they are used and upon the kind of opportunities presented to the organization. If the decision makers in the organization recognize its practical limitations where it does not have the force to act effectively, and if they recognize that the outlawry of force, where the organization is able to act effectively, is not a full substitute for doing something about the conditions that lead to the use of force, the organization may make decisions that have a cumulative impact upon world conditions. If the decision makers pass resolutions that are impracticable—as were the resolutions on Palestine that called for the creation of two states (Jewish and Arab) without taking account of the requirements for their future viability—or if they close their eyes to problems (again Palestine is an example) until the parties resort to force in either desperation or exasperation, its procedures may become increasingly ineffective. In the few limited areas in which it can act effectively, the organization has an opportunity to temper the outlawry of force with the creation of political conditions necessary for stability. The task is not an easy one. If political complacency or "do-nothingism" is one danger, its equally dangerous counterpart is the search for abstract and absolute justice. The proper mixture of justice and prudence is difficult to determine. One can only hope for a policy requiring both vision and courage. Unfortunately the large number of Asian, African, and Arab states in the General Assembly seem more concerned with righting the real or imagined wrongs of the last century, and with trading off votes, than with supporting policies capable of universal application or with making substantial contributions to the amelioration of the political problems of our times.

In a sense, however, the General Assembly suffers from a defect common among parliamentary bodies. It hesitates to act until matters are urgent, and, in these instances, resorts to patchwork artifices in lieu of acting. Indeed, the present composition of the General Assembly makes it most difficult to force a constructive solution of such problems as the one in Palestine. The United States must share the blame, since a more forceful policy in 1948, when the Soviet Union was complaisant (and, in any event, could not have asserted major influence in the Middle East), might have averted many of the problems now producing tension in the area. Whatever we may think of the cease-fire and withdrawal recommendations in the Suez crisis of 1956, we must consider the possibility that minimizing the resort to force, or curbing the use of force, although not really adequate, may be the most satisfactory general policy that the General Assembly can agree to impose—and succeed in enforcing—under present political conditions. If this be so, we may hope that the passions of the new Member nations will at least permit the universal and impartial application of this minimal standard. If this comes to pass, under more favorable political conditions, the United Nations may be able to play a substantial and constructive role in peaceful settlement of world problems.

Authority of United Nations Organs

"Decisions" of the Security Council (at least under Chapter VII) are regarded as legally binding, since the Charter explicitly obliges states to regard them as such, and to carry them out. "Recommendations" (under Chapter VI) are not generally regarded as legally binding, but a good argument can be made that, where it is found that a Member has failed to fulfill an obligation undertaken under the Charter itself, a "recommendation" calling upon it to implement the Charter is legally binding simply as an authoritative interpretation of the Charter. What is the legal status of a purportedly binding decision or recommendation? What organ, if any, of the United Nations possesses the authority to decide questions of jurisdiction?

The provisions of the Charter, like other constitutional mandates, are important in determining what the organs of the United Nations can consider and what action they can lawfully take. Although these provisions are broadly phrased, there is no question that they set limits to the discretion of decision makers at any given time. Within the limits of reasonable interpretation, the question is not what the Charter provides, but who can make authoritative decisions concerning the application of its terms in specific situations. The Charter, like the American Constitution, provides no conclusive answer, though the discussions of this problem at San Francisco suggest that the draftsmen intended each body to determine its own competence, at least initially. Whether each organ should conclusively determine its own jurisdiction, whether there should be judicial review of that determination by the World Court, or whether the Members may each interpose their own interpretation has not yet been finally decided. The problem will be resolved by practice, and by the precedential value of prior practice.

Various checks presently exist on the "abuse" of authority; that is, on interpretations that cannot be supported by arguments that are within the expectations of the participants. For the most part, these checks are embodied in the necessity of a two-thirds majority for recommendations, the reluctance of the major nations to give too much authority to the smaller states via the General Assembly, and the possibility of the Security Council taking jurisdiction. At present, no system, other than that of the advisory opinion, has yet been adopted for the purpose of referring jurisdictional questions to the World Court—although such a system is possible. In addition, it is still maintained in some quarters that the Members themselves may review jurisdictional findings and need not comply with action that is beyond the power of the UN organ under the Charter.

The position that an interested party can determine for itself the "lawfulness" of UN action would, in principle, seem unsupportable, particularly to those familiar with the American system. It is probably not so unworkable as it appears at first glance, for if there is in fact general interest and support for the UN as a decision-making body the doctrine of interposition will seldom be invoked. The fact that the argument is available will tend to moderate any extremes of UN decision, since the UN itself will be reluctant to test its authority. Furthermore, the doctrine can operate effectively only if the particular state is invoking it against some form of decision or binding recommendation; it cannot be effectively used to prevent discussion and lesser forms of persuasion. As the UN gains in prestige and power, and if the practice develops of accepting its decisions, then support for the theory of interposition will gradually dissipate and disappear. It may, therefore, even serve a useful interim function insofar as it serves to encourage responsible decisions that do not prematurely test constitutional questions.

The theory of interposition—no obligation to comply with "unlawful" decisions of UN—could apply to Charter interpretations by any UN body, including the International Court. There is nothing in the Charter that explicitly, or inferentially beyond reasonable argument, says that interpretations by the Court are absolutely binding on other organs of the UN or on Members individually. Clearly they should be given great weight if the Court is to perform a useful function, and one could argue quite persuasively, but not conclusively, that when a UN organ asks for an advisory opinion those who vote for judicial decision impliedly agree to be bound by it. It is somewhat more difficult to make the argument that a Member is bound unless it agrees to be bound, or concurs in the reference to the Court. A state taking interposition to its fullest would say that there is no more authority in the Court to make an "unlawful" interpretation of the Charter than in any other organ.

Ultimately, of course, the power of authoritative decision must rest somewhere, and it is somewhat discouraging to think that so little progress has been made in organizing international society that such power may still rest formally only with "sovereign" states. It is not the opinion of the authors that it does. But it may, should the UN not act with caution in asserting compulsory authority.

Some observers seem to believe that a Member need not obey a UN mandate if the Member contends the mandate to be unlawful, so long as the Court has not passed on its legality; that is, some believe that the General Assembly is not itself competent to determine with finality its own jurisdiction vis-a-vis Members, but that the Court may do so. Such a view reflects a preference for the Court and the judicial method for determining a variety of Charter questions. It apparently rests on the assumption that the Court will "better" resolve disputes about jurisdiction than the Assembly or the Security Council, because the Court is more impartial, because judicial techniques are better suited to the task, or because it would (for these reasons or others) be more acceptable to the disputing parties than other alternatives.

The difficulties of distinguishing "legal" and "political" questions, save in terms of the institution best suited to resolve them, have already been commented upon. Where questions are regarded as important by political participants in terms of their political ramifications, political organs are generally best suited to resolve them. Where, as in domestic law-government, both a legislative and judicial arena are available, with the latter generally subordinate to the former in terms of policy formulation, no great problems are raised. But if courts must decide these disputes as an alternative to legislative resolution, serious questions as to the propriety of the judicial methodology are raised, and courts may well jeopardize their status as impartial, non-political decision makers.

The advisory opinion is a potentially dangerous mechanism for thrusting the World Court into the midst of hotly disputed questions with obvious political overtones. The Court itself has recognized this danger by refusing to render an advisory opinion where it believes the effect would be to resolve an existing dispute between states who have not consented to its jurisdiction. Neither the Security Council nor the General Assembly has submitted questions of Charter interpretation where these were the source of major dispute, either because they wished to save the Court from politics or because they already believed it was partisan.

Although the same considerations are raised, it is possible that a system of judicial review, garbed as an advisory opinion, would be more workable and less dangerous. If the role of the Court could be conceived as one of curbing flagrant abuses of their competence by other organs, rather than an initial decision of competence, it might serve a useful function. Under this conception, the General Assembly or Security Council would initially determine, without judicial advice, its own competence. If an affected Member objected to any decision or binding recommendation as going beyond the Charter, it could ask that the opinion of the Court be requested. This would permit the Court to develop a jurisprudence that gave a very strong presumption of legality to the decisions of other organs as to their jurisdiction and as to the meaning of Charter provisions, although permitting it to find, in exceptional cases, that the other organ had acted in flagrant disregard of Charter limitations. Under this system, the original decision maker would bear the brunt of political attack, yet the consciousness of potential judicial review would tone down excesses.

CONCLUSIONS

In the loose bipolar system, the principal roles of the United Nations are those of mediation, of conciliation, and of providing a forum. These functions are of great importance in moderating extreme actions and thus in helping to ease international tensions. There is understandable impatience at times with the difficulty which exists in arriving quickly at definitive solutions, and an occasional tendency to disparage the organization as little more than a debating club. But, even if the UN must defer to the blocs in major questions of war or peace, impatience should not cause us to underestimate the real and valuable functions that the UN can and does perform.

Efforts to strengthen the UN should be aimed at improving its capacity to perform the roles it can perform and should not assign to it roles that it cannot possibly perform in the present political structure. There are risks in overreaching. To put the situation in blunt terms, the resolution of disputes within the UN framework must depend largely upon its capacity to persuade the parties to a solution— to mediate differences—and to refrain from making binding decisions that the UN cannot possibly enforce against opposition. And the UN is unlikely to be able to coerce acceptance by use of force.

This is not to say the UN is without influence; far from it. In the West and in Afro-Asia it can make important appeals to populations that look to the UN as an important political institution. Governments cannot afford to ignore these appeals to their own populace, nor to that of other states. By and large it is in their interest to promote the prestige and authority of the United Nations. Particularly is this true of the smaller nations, most especially the uncommitted ones, because it is through this institution, in this forum where votes are equal, that their political voice in world affairs carries the heaviest weight. Nor, so long as these areas have potential importance to the two blocs, can demands voiced in the General Assembly be ignored or disparaged.

By and large the UN has sufficient formal powers to accomplish the only roles it can perform today. The Security Council has diminished in importance, not merely because of the veto, but because its structure tends to oppose the blocs too directly with insufficient forces for moderation—though the Secretary General and the temporary Members, if dissociated from a bloc, do help in achieving moderation. The veto merely symbolizes the underlying realities, at least insofar as the U.S.A. and U.S.S.R. are concerned; admittedly a veto for Nationalist China is unrealistic. As a result, political power has passed to the hands of the General Assembly.

The Assembly, however, is an unwieldy body at best, and both its composition and the desire of Members to use it as a propaganda platform create doubts as to whether it is really a fit body to make responsible recommendations. Too often the exuberances of short-term politics have mooted efforts to secure more meaningful and rational standards of long-range policy. If it is difficult to get a two-thirds majority for extreme positions in the General Assembly, that organ too often resorts to compromises unlikely to resolve the issue or to proposals that cannot be implemented with the means available. The inexperience, the impatience, and the ideological fervor of many of the new Members often leads to ill-considered action or to passionate judgment, particularly with respect to issues involving colonialism or disarmament. The Security Council, which might have toned down irresponsible politics, and which was conceived to be more fit for sober contemplation by its size and the importance of the permanent Members, has rather tended to encourage Assembly irresponsibility by its own incapacity to act and by the temptations of the two blocs to make excessive accusations and counter-accusations.

A possibility of improving UN processes, particularly in the Assembly, may lie in building up the office and the role of the Secretary General. A framework of impartially determined facts and impartially presented alternatives may help to moderate Assembly politics. This requires creating and bolstering non-partisan roles in the political processes. And it requires improving administrative, fact-finding and intelligence functions.

The Office of the Secretary General has accomplished a quite remarkable tradition of impartial civil service—remarkable because this is such a difficult world in which to appear non-partisan. At least, prior to the Congo crisis, there was amazing trust, in view of bipolarity, in the present Secretary General. To some extent this was personal with him, perhaps too much so. The task is to depersonalize and further institutionalize the office. If the office could be expanded, assigned more tasks by the Assembly, and recapture its reputation for non-partisan fact finding and statement of issues, it could do much to curb irrational Assembly debate.

This task is not an easy one, for the Secretary General, no more than the Court, can afford to have every hot potato dumped in his lap. There are disputes which simply have to remain disputes because there is no present possibility of solution. In the present world the tendencies of the blocs to attempt to subordinate all agencies to bloc politics would not automatically stop with the Secretary General's office any more than it would with the Court. Prior to the Congo crisis, the present Secretary General had not been confronted with problems so big and involving so many conflicting bloc interests that his assumption of a positive role in helping to meet the problems would involve enormous difficulties. The general consensus is that he performed ably in meeting these problems and the pressures arising from them.[2]

The Congo crisis, however, may have placed a burden upon the Secretary General and the United Nations that the organization is not equipped to handle successfully. It is still too early to assess accurately the probable outcome of this crisis or the impact it will have upon the structure and functioning of the United Nations, particularly with respect to the office of the Secretary General. The original decisions to intervene in the Congo were made in the Security Council at a time of temporary concordance between the policies of the United States and the Soviet Union, although since then the focus of attention has shifted to the General Assembly.

[2] There are some critics who were unhappy with the actions of the Secretary General at the time of the 1956 Suez crisis. These critics viewed the Suez venture as a means of forcing the Egyptians to abide by recognized principles of law. They therefore viewed its partial failure as an event reducing the constraining force of norms they regarded as desirable. In addition they felt that the Secretary General was too ready to accept the Egyptian dictator's assurances concerning his intentions and were afraid that the UN force established during the Suez affair might merely provide a cover under which Nasser might reorganize his forces and gather his strength for some future test. Although this position is moot, it is difficult to see that the Secretary General could have taken a different position, even had he wanted to, in view of the position of the United States government. If there was a miscalculation of the situation, the most drastic miscalculation must have occurred in Washington, for the Suez campaign could not have been continued against the opposition of the United States, considering the dependence of Great Britain and France upon American support.

The Secretary General, under directives from the United Nations, acted boldly and effectively in an attempt to restore some order in an anarchic situation while attempting to maintain an impartial attitude concerning the contestants for political power in the Congo—an attempt that, in the nature of the case, could not satisfy everyone, since the Secretary General's intervention necessarily must help one side or the other.

Soviet attempts to intervene outside the framework of the United Nations in favor of a seemingly demagogic and irresponsible Patrice Lumumba in the hope of securing political influence in the Congo were successfully resisted by the Secretary General. Many African states gave support to these efforts of the Secretary General. Others, such as Ghana and Guinea, imposed obstacles in the path of the Secretary General. Perhaps they were hopeful of gaining political influence themselves in a quest for African hegemony; perhaps they were influenced by leftist ties; or perhaps they responded to Lumumba because they desired a centralized and unitary state in the Congo or because he was anti-Western.

The anarchic disorders in the Congo, the unpreparedness of the Congolese to govern themselves, and the danger that the United States and the Soviet Union might intervene, and that the Congo might become another Korea, forced United Nations intervention. However, this intervention was of a political magnitude previously unemcompassed by United Nations operations. To a considerable extent the United Nations assumed responsibility for governmental functions in the Congo; presently it virtually plays the role of trustee. The magnitude of the task the United Nations has assumed almost necessarily brings it into conflict with the interests either of the Soviet Union or of the United States and therefore gives one of the leading bloc nations a strong reason to undercut its effectiveness.

The United Nations has little real choice except to work for stability in the Congo. But stability is essentially opposed to present Soviet interests. The Soviet Union prefers stability only if it is a Communist stability. Otherwise it prefers regimes sympathetic toward it or regimes whose activities will spread the type of disorder that in the long run will favor the growth of Communism. If the United Nations helps to produce stability by positive political intervention and thus helps to prevent the spread of Communism—unless this helps to deter some greater danger facing the Soviet Union—it is only natural that the Soviet Union will attempt to immobilize the organization.

The immediate attempt by the Russians to force the Secretary General to give up his efforts to restore stability in the Congo, or to resign, were overwhelmingly rejected by the United Nations. Khrushchev's proposal to create three Secretaries General, operating under a veto principle, and representing the West, the Communists, and the neutrals failed to achieve substantial support. However, as a consequence of Soviet attacks, the Secretary General now can maintain his position only by keeping the support of the Asian and African nations in the General Assembly. The degree to which he must be responsive to the demands of the African and Asian nations represents a major curtailment of his independence and of his ability to act impartially and effectively, particularly since some of these nations are dissatisfied with and profess suspicion of his efforts.

Thus the immediate Soviet effort has not been a complete failure by any means. In addition, the incumbent Secretary General, if he is to be reappointed, cannot gain reappointment over Soviet objections. Nor can other potential Secretaries General secure the office except with Soviet approval. The strong manifestations of Soviet displeasure during the UN meeting on the Congo may influence the behavior of the incumbent or of his replacement. Indeed the organization may be partly paralyzed by a Soviet refusal to permit any replacement at the expiry of the present incumbent's term; alternatively great concessions may be made to secure Soviet approval of a candidate. Although the United Nations may yet survive the present crisis with its structure and functions unimpaired and the Secretary General may yet resume the strong role he played before the Congo crisis, a prognosis to this effect at the present time would represent a hopeful estimate rather than one firmly grounded on substantial evidence. Much may depend upon whether the United Nations faces great crises bringing into substantial conflict interests of the United States and Soviet Union and perhaps also of major groups of "uncommitted" nations.

Developments in the functioning of the United Nations will have obvious consequences for the norms enforced in international politics. Paralysis of the United Nations is likely to loosen the reins on the resort to force. Capture of the organization by revolutionary nations is likely to increase intervention in the internal affairs of other nations and to decrease normative constraints on that kind of activity. Restoration of the organization's effectiveness and strengthening of the office of the Secretary General is likely to have the consequences elaborated earlier in this chapter.

12

SUPRANATIONAL ORGANIZATION OF THE BLOC TYPE.

In the loose bipolar system, we find, in addition to universal organizations such as the United Nations, other supranational entities such as blocs. Although the simplified models employed in Chapter 2 are concerned primarily with two major blocs—NATO and the Communist bloc—this form of international organization is in fact much more varied in the real world.

Bloc organization exists when there are governmental bodies that exercise exclusive and ultimate authority within the territory of more than one state, over functional areas of activity that otherwise would be subject to the exclusive and ultimate authority of the several states. The bloc form of supranational organization may be distinguished from mere alliances or cooperative agreements by the fact that decision-making authority in some functional area of government—sometimes in extremely important military or economic areas—is in fact transferred from national centers of authority to bloc centers of authority. Blocs do not merely implement specific policy decisions arrived at independently by national governments. With respect to some matters, the bloc is the agency within which the decision is made. (In the Communist bloc, however, the authority is informal and is exercised largely through party channels.)

Although some bloc members may support the policies of the leading member of an opposed bloc in particular cases, this should not be confused with the flexibility of alignment of the "balance of power" system. Transfers of support across bloc lines are inhibited by the amalgamation of interests and destinies that the blocs represent. Such transfers of support are most unlikely to occur in the specific areas where the blocs exercise authority, and it is these areas that are likely to be the most important, if not vital, areas of modern international activity.[1]

Blocs differ also from the rigid alignments that occurred during the breakdown of the "balance of power" system. These rigid alignments occurred in important areas of activity. But they were designed to implement specific and limited agreements entered into by the governments concerned. They also lacked exclusive or ultimate authority of a functional nature. The rigid alliances of the "balance of power" period were manifestations of an abnormal condition of international politics. They did not represent new organizational forms, and they did not give rise to new frameworks within which law developed.

The blocs of the loose bipolar system, on the other hand, are new organizational forms that have appropriate places within the organization and normative structure of the new international system, whether the system remains bipolar or becomes somewhat more complex. They are a response to bipolarity. But, inasmuch as they may overlap territorially because membership may vary with function, a complex form of international system has arisen.

There is the additional possibility that more than two major blocs of great military significance may arise, although there seems no immediate prospect of this. In such a case, there might be a return to some "balance of power" characteristics between blocs if not between nations. On the other hand, if each bloc of a multi-bloc system were to have protected second-strike nuclear forces, there might instead be a unit veto international system in which alliances between blocs had only minor significance. In either case, the existence of additional functional blocs exercising authority in important economic or political areas, whose memberships cut across the memberships of the military blocs, would make for considerable complexity in the political and normative behavior of the international system. In any event, the rise of the bloc form of organization is

---

[1] A member of NATO might support a Soviet resolution advocating the seating of the Chinese Communist delegates as the representatives of China in the UN, although even this kind of support for the leading member of the opposed bloc is unlikely in view of NATO membership. It is almost inconceivable that a NATO member would support a UN resolution demanding the removal of U.S. military forces from Western Germany. Such support would almost surely indicate the decay of NATO as a viable international organization or the imminent departure of the state so voting from the organization.

an event of major significance. And it heralds the decline in importance of the nation state.

Several factors account for this decline of the nation state—at least in Europe. Some of these have already been mentioned. The most important, of course, is the rise of a huge Communist state and the relative weakening of the Western European states after the Second World War. France was newly liberated, and Italy was defeated, Germany was defeated and divided, and Great Britain was impoverished and shorn of its Empire as a consequence of the magnitude of its contribution to ultimate victory. Europe was thrust out of Asia and Africa for the most part and reduced to a peripheral land mass on the edge of the Eurasian continent; it still possessed important resources in trained manpower and technical facilities but was tired and divided. Within the Communist sphere, organizational party ties permitted a degree of unity and consistency not present in the democratic nations. Within the democratic nations, political parties received support from electors whose demands focussed attention on local rather than general or supranational considerations. Without supranational forms of organization, these wider interests could not secure recognition, and even with supranational organization, it would be difficult to offset the pulls of national politics.

Still other factors militated against the division of Europe into isolated nation-states. Economically this division made no sense and had harmful effects upon the economies of the individual nations. Moreover, modern technological warfare meant that the small independent nation-state could not play a major or even an important secondary role in world politics. Not only was it necessary for Europe to unite to offset Soviet armed capabilities, but European security also required the military support of the United States. Europe did not have sufficient space to be fully defensible, either against Soviet conventional capabilities in the jet age, or against Soviet nuclear capabilities (even if Europe had had its own nuclear resources) unless the weight of the United States were thrown into the balance.[2]

---

[2] Problems of military defense in the nuclear age have raised serious questions concerning the viability of the nation-state as an independent unit. Even the larger NATO states such as Great Britain and France cannot economically support nuclear forces sufficient to make irrational a nuclear attack by the Soviet Union. The so-called triggering value of such forces according to which they could do sufficient damage to an attacker to make that attacker excessively

Regardless, however, of the reasons for this development at the midpoint of the twentieth century, the fact of its occurrence merits attention. From the standpoint of international law, the supranational entity constitutes an additional subject. The existence of this new subject is bound to influence both the procedures and substance of the international legal process.

NATO. From the standpoint of international law, as well as from that of international politics, the North Atlantic Treaty Organization is extremely important. NATO was brought into being in 1949 in response to the military threat from the Soviet bloc as perceived by the members of the Brussels Pact, by the United States, and by other North Atlantic states. It was later acceded to by Greece and Turkey, although these two hardly belong to the North Atlantic area, and by Western Germany. The signators legitimized the organization by a reference to Articles 51 and 52 of the United Nations Charter. However, it seems clear that NATO is not the kind of regional organization the drafters of the Charter had in mind, and that its organization gave recognition to a change in the conception of the role of the United Nations and possibly to a change in the conception of its importance.

The possibility of regional organizations was included in the Charter as a concession to the Organization of American States and, to some extent, to the Arab League. Regional organizations were recognized for the purpose of dealing with problems arising within the region—not with problems arising between one region and another or between one group of states and another. Moreover, the right of collective self-defense had not been clearly understood to

---

vulnerable to American counter-attack has probably been overstated. Moreover, the land masses of both Great Britain and France are so small, they can be saturated in a first strike. Only Polaris submarine forces would be relatively invulnerable to a Soviet first strike. But such forces can be obtained only in cooperation with the United States, and, as independent forces, would still be subject to blackmail that might well be effective. That even the United States alone is capable of sufficient military preparedness for security purposes in the nuclear age is doubtful, and, in any event, NATO is probably essential to American security for political and economic as well as military reasons. It is not impossible that technological and political developments will invalidate these statements. But it would appear that nationalism is a dying phenomenon despite its ideological value and the popular support given that ideology in the new nations. Perhaps this nationalism is only another example of the bulb that flares brighter just before it burns out.

include anything as formal as an organization of limited membership ready-and-waiting to assume this function even before an overt "breach of the peace."

Generally, NATO was regarded as an intergovernmental rather than a supranational form of organization. It was pointed out that NATO operated only in terms of unanimous agreement and that NATO, as an organization, lacked any jurisdiction within the territories of its members that was not derived from unanimous consent of its members. This view was, at least partly, mistaken even for the early phases of NATO. On the other hand, there is no doubt that the treaty establishing NATO placed serious restrictions on its functions. The crucial Article 5 was particularly hedged with language that appeared to take back as much as it promised: "The parties agree that an armed attack against one or more of them in Europe or North America shall be considered an attack against them all; and consequently . . . will assist the Party or Parties so attacked by taking forthwith . . . such action as it deems necessary . . . ." In principle, therefore, commitments were restricted regionally (primarily to satisfy the Senate that the United States would not be dragged into war for colonial possessions or to defend unimportant areas of the world) and institutionally, so that the measures to be taken, if any, depended upon the decisions of the parties to the treaty rather than upon the decision of the organization established by the treaty. These limitations, however, are more restrictive verbally than practically.

It is quite true that the balanced forces concept, according to which members would make the contribution to NATO military forces that took greatest advantage of their resources—for instance, the United States might have supplied strategic airpower but not ground forces, Great Britain, naval forces, and France and Germany, armed troops— was not adopted, and that the major states each contributed elements from their armies, navies, and air forces. Apart possibly from the very important annual review, this further emphasized the national-component aspect of organization rather than the functional interdependence that would be most characteristic of supranational organization. But it also is true that NATO used common supply dumps, service installations, communication networks, and headquarters staffs. Even from a physical point of view, national forces cannot be removed from NATO unilaterally without serious consequences both for NATO and for the national forces themselves. Even though the balanced forces concept was not adopted, each of the NATO nations has based its military policy upon the existence of NATO and has developed its armed forces in ways that permit the forces to fit into NATO. Although Great Britain, France, and the United States have armed forces that are responsible for global policies as well as for NATO area policies, the portions of the forces designed to meet NATO area responsibilities depend upon the existence of NATO. Defense of the democracies of Western Europe requires, in terms of bases and land area, resources that can be provided only in combination.

The matter extends, moreover, from the physical aspects of organization to the political aspects of organization. The North Atlantic Council, composed of the foreign ministers of the NATO states, and the Defense Committee, composed of the defense ministers, might properly be viewed as intergovernmental. But the Military Committee, designed to establish policy, and the Standing Group, which has executive functions, are supranational in scope. The Standing Committee included only England, France, and the United States. Although all NATO members are represented in the Council of Military Representatives, with headquarters in Washington, its functions are purely consultative. Thus the executive functions vested in the three states represented on the Standing Group originally included the Supreme Allied Command in Europe, the Supreme Allied Command Atlantic, the Canada-United States Regional Planning Group, the Channel Committee, and the Allied Maritime Air Command Channel. The Mediterranean and the Near East are now handled as part of the European Command.

NATO planning extends to a very large and important area of the globe. Its importance might seem therefore primarily to derive from its scope. However, joint planning and, in particular, joint military organization were unknown in Europe during time of peace until after the Second World War. Moreover, it is not possible to divorce NATO planning from other aspects of the military and political planning of the members. The existence of the organization is a fact that governs the military plans of the members, even with respect to activities that technically are unrelated to NATO, for instance, diplomatic action. France may pull troops out of NATO (technically with permission from that organization) for use in Algeria, and Great Britain may decide to reduce its commitments either because of internal financial difficulties or because Western Germany will not continue its financial contributions to the British forces in Germany, but the organization remains interdependent. Even decisions that are, to a considerable extent, unilateral, feed back into the central organism and require complex adjustments and counter-adjustments.

The most important innovation in NATO occurred in 1950, during the Korean War, with the appointment of the Supreme Commander. This, plus the allocation of American infantry divisions to the continent of Europe in peacetime, constituted the price that secured at least temporary French consent to German rearmament within the framework of the ill-fated European Defense Community. The Supreme Commander might have to depend upon the members of NATO to supply him with troops and equipment—certainly he lacks the authority to requisition troops or supplies—but he has command of these forces as a supranational and not as a national officer.

Integration was still limited. Units of the forces remained national and also remained under national command at the unit level. Status-of-forces agreements were necessary to regulate their behavior and their treatment in their assigned areas. But the top military command was integrated and remains integrated. Today French troops in Europe serve under General Speidel of Germany, who, in turn, serves under the French Deputy Chief of Staff. Command over armed forces, even if limited, is one of the most important forms of jurisdiction a political entity can possess.

But the matter does not rest there. NATO must have access to its dumps and must be able to secure its communications. Arrangements for these purposes must be worked out with the states in which the dumps, supplies, and bases are located; arrangements for use of roads, railroad systems, air lanes, and telephone and telegraph facilities must be made. Once arrangements are made, NATO must have at least limited jurisdictional and police powers to maintain these rights and facilities. Unlike agreements with private companies, which may be appealed to and reviewed by the courts, disputes between NATO and the host state must be negotiated. Since these matters often cannot be referred back to the intergovernmental Council of Foreign Ministers, they must be negotiated by NATO with the states that provide facilities for NATO. NATO, therefore, is a governmental body with at least limited powers.

But the actual powers of NATO go even farther. NATO has the right to defend the NATO area without reference to the governments of the members of NATO. Technically, NATO cannot decide to use any nuclear capacity assigned to it without such reference. However, a moment's reflection will establish that this limitation is designed more to allay the apprehensions of populaces and political representatives than it is to dictate the actual conduct of the organization should war break out. It is no reflection on the motives of the officers commanding NATO to assert that the outbreak of war in Europe would discover NATO asserting the functions of a supranational government and making the most vital decisions that any government can be called upon to make.

In the missile age, warning of attack upon the United States may come only minutes before missiles hit. Europe would have virtually no warning. For this reason, SAC Europe in particular would not have the luxury of referring matters to Washington in the event of nuclear attack. It also seems clear that even in the event of conventional attack, the military forces of the European NATO Command will necessarily assume command of major aspects of the transportation and communication facilities in Western Europe upon notice of the attack. The phrase stating that each member nation will take "such action as it deems necessary" will lose substantive merit; since this clause applies only to conditions of war, the virtually complete inapplicability of the stipulation is preordained in fact.

NATO therefore lacks only authority for direct acquisition of manpower and supplies, and may even acquire the latter in war. In fact, we can imagine a situation in which civilian government could not be carried on in Europe and in which NATO would directly assume all governmental functions. It may be suspected that NATO already possesses plans that specify the performance of such functions but that are hedged with statements making the assumption of the functions technically dependent upon delegation by the existing political governments in order to avoid injury to the susceptibilities of those who would resist a bald statement of the powers NATO must have to function effectively under conditions of modern war.

Even the peacetime requirement which channels troops and supplies to NATO through the member states may be subject to some re-interpretation. To a major extent, allocations are made either by intergovernmental negotiation or by the decisions of national governments. But it is sometimes overlooked that NATO—in the guise of the headquarters staff—negotiates either with the member states in a body or with their governments individually. The Supreme Allied Commander Europe in particular presents his recommendations for forces to the Foreign and Defense Ministers and to Committees of the American Congress. The Secretary General of NATO conducts important political negotiations with NATO members. This may be, and usually is, regarded as a mere information function similar to the performance of the Joint Chiefs before Congress. This understates the role, however. The Joint Chiefs exercise governmental functions in making their budget recommendations although their positions are subordinate to higher civilian officials. Although in testifying before Congress the Joint Chiefs are primarily suppliers of information rather than negotiators, even here they may negotiate privately with influential members of Congress. The Supreme Commander of NATO and the Secretary General also negotiate before recommendations are made and there is a sense in which they represent an independent organization. Their bargaining power is limited in that they cannot withhold anything in return as a threat against the other negotiators. But the fact that they represent all the member states rather than any of them individually insulates them and permits them to represent NATO rather than the member states. They thus can be and often are effective independent negotiators. They may even take a strong initiative in negotiations. And these are governmental functions.

SEATO and Baghdad Pacts.   Neither SEATO, or the Baghdad Pact possesses supranational characteristics to the same extent as does NATO. No effective military forces-in-being or joint commands exist, and the only military forces capable of responding to alarms in Southeast Asia would necessarily come from remote areas of the world. Indeed, the United States entered a stipulation with respect to SEATO that only Communist armed attack would constitute a danger that would invoke automatically United States aid. Under other circumstances, the United States would be willing only to "consult" over measures to be taken. The United States is not formally a member of the Baghdad Pact, although it participates on its defense and finance committees. Some joint military planning operations do take place. But the Baghdad Pact is subject to such internal strains and has such tenuous support in the Near East, that it can hardly be viewed as an effective supranational organization.

French, German, Italian Weapons Development Center.   One of the supranational developments taking place at the present time is the joint French, German, Italian Weapons Development Center which is being established. Such an organization does not have direct governmental authority, but it is functional rather than geographical in structure and operates in one of the most sensitive areas of national jurisdiction. Particularly, should the center extend its activities to the area of nuclear weapons and missiles, it might produce a military interdependence that would have profound consequences for national political decisions. Development of nuclear capability by these three states would both increase their influence on the international scene and tend to require their cooperation in the formulation of policy. In one sense, since the cooperation extends only to weapons development rather than to possession and use, it might appear that interdependence of policy could be avoided. But it is altogether unlikely that the development center can be anything but a precursor to weapons production and possession, for the very same factors and national limitations which make joint research desirable will also extend later to weapons production, possession, and use. Since this will have still additional consequences, the potential beginnings of an important supranational tendency are already present in this project.

The European Communities. By far the most remarkable development among the democratic states is the European Economic Community, which has common institutions with the Coal and Steel Community and Euratom. Only the briefest note can be taken of the antecedents of the revolutionary Common Market. Readers will undoubtedly be familiar with the Organization for European Economic Cooperation (OEEC), formed by the European nations to establish plans which would enable them to take advantage of Marshall Plan appropriations by the United States. Indeed, it is worthy of notice that the impetus for European unity gained considerable momentum as a consequence of the efforts of the United States, even though the United States desired to remain aloof from any direct participation in the organizations established as a consequence of its efforts. The OEEC was charged with preparing and carrying out measures of economic cooperation and with reviewing the programs of its member states in implementing the recovery program stemming from Marshall Plan efforts. To aid the operations of the OEEC, a European Payments Union was established and a Commercial Code was drawn up. In particular, the power of the EPU to facilitate trade within the OEEC grouping, and to arrange for deferred meeting of balances, did extend to a supranational authority some jurisdiction in the delicate financial area.

The Coal and Steel Authority established by Treaty among the "European Six"—West Germany, France, Italy, Belgium, the Netherlands, and Luxembourg—finally began to operate in 1952, after long negotiations. Equipped with both a court and executive organ, the

Coal and Steel Community established effective operations over policy with respect to production and sales of these two basic industrial resources. Control, even if only partial, over production, pricing, transportation, and sales policy concerning coal and steel represents supranational jurisdiction in an exceptionally important area. The establishment of a court to decide matters under dispute represents the crucial jurisdictional element in government. It is only necessary to remember that the right to appeal from state courts to the Supreme Court in the United States was one of the critical factors in establishing uniform policy and in consolidating federal predominance.

The Coal and Steel Community has a High Authority, an Assembly, a Council, and a Court. The High Authority performs executive functions. It is composed of nine members, eight chosen by the member states. The ninth member is co-opted. The members of the High Authority serve for six years and are not responsible to the states that appoint them. The High Authority may consult the Consultative Committee on any matter and must do so in relation to matters affecting the principal objects of the treaty, such as production, marketing, pricing, and employment. The Assembly, by a vote of two thirds of those present and voting, may censure and force the resignation of the High Authority. The Court may nullify the actions of the other organs for constitutional reasons.

The European Economic Community or Common Market, a later development of the same six nations, has common institutions with Euratom and the Coal and Steel Community in the Court of Justice and the Assembly. It has its own Executive: the European Commission. The Assembly initially is to consist of delegates chosen by the parliaments of the member states. West Germany, France, and Italy have thirty-six delegates each, Belgium and The Netherlands, fourteen each, and Luxembourg, six. The treaty directs the Assembly to draft a plan for its election by universal direct suffrage. This indeed would be a remarkable development, even though any plan of the Assembly toward this end would have to be ratified by member states before taking effect. But if such direct elections occur, they may have interesting consequences for the structure of political parties and electoral alliances. If well-disciplined supranational parties or party coalitions should develop, there may be conflicts between the Community Assembly and the National Assemblies. Too much stress, however, should not yet be put upon this possibility. The only substantial task of the Assembly—and even this constitutes only a minor responsibility—is to discuss the report of the "Commission, whose resignation it can compel by a two-thirds vote of censure."

The Council has power of decision with respect to the Common Market. The Council has a single representative from each of the member states. Some of its decisions are made by majority vote and some are made unanimously. In the case of majority vote, the representatives of France, Germany, and Italy cast four votes each, the representatives of Belgium and The Netherlands cast two votes each, and the representative of Luxembourg casts a single vote. Twelve votes constitute a majority, except that in some cases the twelve votes must come from at least four states. The unanimity requirement is less restrictive than it might seem on the surface. The procedures by which the Common Market are to come into being are automatic unless disapproved by unanimous vote and, in any case, must be implemented within a maximum period of fifteen years. Thus the Council has the authority to delay but not to negate with respect to exceptionally important aspects of supranational jurisdiction.

The tasks of the Commission include the application of the treaty, making recommendations to the Council, and the exercise of powers conferred upon it by the Council. The Commission has nine members, not more than two of whom may come from any one state. The Court of Justice, which has seven members named by the member states, has the authority to interpret the treaty, "to decide disputes between member states and to determine violations of the treaty." Its powers are, therefore, very close to those of the United States Supreme Court.

An Economic and Social Committee, composed of various functional groupings, such as, industry, farmers, workers, and tradesmen is to be established to advise the Community. The costs of the Community are proportioned by treaty among the members and the treaty has an unlimited duration.

The jurisdiction of the Community is of remarkable importance even though only its general outlines are set by the treaty which becomes its constitution. A customs union is to be established by stages. With the exception of agriculture, where some quantitative and other restrictions may continue to apply, goods are to have free movement within the community without hindrance of tariffs or of quantitative restrictions. Moreover, the Community is establishing a common tariff affecting imports from states or areas outside the Economic Community. In itself, this is a radical program. But, in addition, the treaty provides for the free movement of persons and of capital within the Community after a transitional period. Common rules for transportation within the Community are to be established and eventually rules or rates that discriminate against any of the states of the Community or that protect specific industries are to be abolished.

With some general exceptions, the treaty establishes a policy designed to prohibit all agreements to restrain competition, to fix prices, or to control and divide markets. Monopolies are to be checked, practices such as dumping to be halted, and abusive practices by dominant industries that affect trade between the member states are to be halted. Aid to producers, except for the development of backward areas, that interferes with free competition and trade within the Common Market is forbidden. Discriminatory taxes are not permitted and the Commission is to study the fiscal legislation of the member states in an effort to make their legislation more nearly uniform. Each state agrees to follow policies designed to secure its "global balance of payments and confidence in its currency at the same time as a high degree of employment and price stability." An Advisory Monetary Committee is to be established to watch over this coordination of policy. Unrestricted payments across the frontiers of the member states are to be permitted. If balance-of-payment difficulties arise, the Commission immediately must examine the situation and recommend remedies. The Commission is to negotiate tariffs for the Common Market with states outside the arrangement. Thus the European Economic Community becomes an actor on the international scene and engages in direct negotiations with states outside the Community.

The six states belonging to the Community agree to coordinate industrial conditions including conditions of employment, social security, and negotiations between trade unions and employers. Equal pay for men and women is provided for and a European Social Fund to be created to facilitate employment within the Community and to provide for the retraining of employees whose jobs are lost as a consequence of the operations of the Community. A European Investment Bank is to be created to promote a common investment policy and especially to stimulate investment in underdeveloped areas of the Community. The overseas territories of member states are to be associated with the Community and investment opportunities developed in these areas.

Many of the directives of the treaty obviously cannot be implemented automatically and will require future cooperation of the member states. But the potential jurisdiction of the Community includes the most important aspects of economic policy, apart from tax powers. Yet even the tax powers of the national governments are limited by the terms of the treaty to measures compatible with the Common Market and alleged incompatibilities are appealable to the Court of Justice. It is hardly necessary to note that this circumscription of the jurisdiction of the member states with respect to economic policy will both influence strongly most other aspects of political and social policy—since these cannot be divorced from economic policy—and lead to an interdependence among the members of the Community which is bound to have still further consequences of a supranational character.

Because of the tremendous impact of the Common Market on all European trade, the Community and the most affected countries have been negotiating for an expanded "Free Trade Area." This would include some of the other members of the OEEC. These states are not yet willing, however, to join in all the provisions of European Community, but, rather, are seeking a simple Customs Union.

At the same time the treaty for the Economic Community was signed in 1957, the treaty that created the European Atomic Energy Authority, or Euratom, was also signed. Euratom, like the ECSC, touches a vital interest of the same six Western European nations that signed the treaty—that interest being energy resources. Western European energy requirements are going to expand rapidly over the next generation and must be met unless the nations of Western Europe are to fade into international insignificance. In addition, dependence upon the oil supplies of the Middle East is hazardous. Therefore, the six nations decided to cooperate both in research designed to exploit the use of atomic energy and in the development of facilities to produce that energy. The Council may decide (unanimously) upon investment policies and upon whether facilities shall be produced jointly or, possibly, with the participation of outside states or agencies. The Council may even place these enterprises in the category of public utility and permit the right of expropriation and exemption from taxes. There is common policy of supply with all member states having equal access to materials. An agency of the Community has the exclusive right to contract for supplies produced within the Community and to supply such materials whether produced inside or outside the Community. This agency is under the supervision of the Commission. If the Commission cannot supply these materials at reasonable prices, member states may contract for material outside the Community for a period of one year, but the contracts must be transmitted to the Commission.

Security controls will be maintained and patents affecting defense will be kept secret. The Commission may order the deposit of fissionable materials in its safekeeping and has powers of control and inspection within the Community. The Commission may even replace, temporarily, the management of an enterprise offending the rules of the Community, and may order the member states to comply with its security regulations.

Other technical provisions are of importance but would not add appreciably to this account. However, one provision of substantial importance from the standpoint of international law should be noted. Agreements with outside states, citizens of those states, or international organizations may be negotiated by the Commission on the basis of directives from the Council, which must then approve the agreement by majority vote. Individual member states must inform the Commission of agreements they intend to make. The Commission has the right of objection, but the state may appeal to the Court of Justice if the Commission rejects a proposed treaty.

Euratom has only limited jurisdiction over its member states, but, again, the jurisdiction it has is important. And it has the right to enter into treaties on behalf of its members with states outside Euratom. Moreover, it must be remembered that the Economic Community, the Coal and Steel Community, and Euratom all share the same Council, Commission, Assembly, and Court of Justice and that they therefore constitute a single supranational organization with several functional subdivisions. Seen in this light, the projected jurisdiction of the Community within the territory of its member states and over the relationships of the Community with the outside world become extraordinarily impressive.

Nation-states will continue to exist in Western Europe, to engage unilaterally in negotiations with other states, to serve as members of international organizations, to participate jointly in wider supranational organizations like NATO and the Free Market. But, clearly, the exclusive territorial jurisdiction of the nation-state is passing into history. Functional as well as territorial distribution and sharing of authority and jurisdiction may well become facts of international life. Nation-states may be bound by agreements negotiated by supranational bodies, and it is possible that agreements negotiated by national-states may be subject to the veto of supranational bodies.

Council of Europe. Unlike the Communities, the Council of Europe does not exercise directly governmental functions but is, rather, designed to promote European cooperation through promoting intergovernmental agreements. Established by the Statute of the Council of Europe in 1949, it is composed of Germany, Austria, Belgium, Eire, France, Great Britain, Greece, Italy, Luxembourg, the Netherlands, Norway, Sweden, and Turkey. The Foreign Ministers of the member states meet in a Council. In addition, a Consultative Assembly, purely advisory in function, is elected by national parliaments with representation roughly based on population.

Two interesting Conventions have been produced by the Council. The first, signed in Rome in 1950, is the Convention for the Protection of Human Rights and Fundamental Freedoms, providing for protection of such basic human rights as life, liberty and security of person, freedom from slavery and servitude, freedom of thought, conscience and religion, and freedom of expression and association. A protocol in 1952 added the right to education, property rights, and free and secret elections to its provisions. A European Commission of Human Rights was established to implement its provisions; any party to the Convention may refer to the Commission a complaint that another party has violated the Convention. In addition, and of significance to the role of the individual with regard to supranational institutions, nine states have agreed to permit individuals to submit petitions to the Commission. The Commission may investigate the facts and is bound to publish its findings, along with its opinion as to whether or not the Convention has been breached. Finally, eight states have agreed to submit disputes under the Convention to a European Court of Human Rights, established in 1959. The Court may hear cases brought before it by a state party to the Convention and agreeing to the Court's jurisdiction, or by the Commission. The Court has yet to decide a case, but the Commission has heard over three hundred petitions, the great bulk of which were dismissed for want of exhaustion of remedies available to petitioners within the state alleged to have breached the Convention.

The second Convention promoted by the Council is the European Convention for the Peaceful Settlement of Disputes of 1957. Modeled on the Geneva General Act for the Pacific Settlement of

International Disputes of 1928, it provides for reference of all international legal disputes among signatories to the International Court of Justice. By February, 1960, the Convention had been ratified by six states.

Organization of American States. The Organization of American States was created in 1948 as a result of a reorganization of a number of inter-American institutions that preceded it. A separate American Treaty on Pacific Settlement (the Pact of Bogota) was signed at the same time establishing various procedures for settlement of disputes between American states (principally good offices, mediation, conciliation), and further provisions that are relevant to peaceful settlement are contained in the Inter-American Treaty of Reciprocal Assistance of 1947 (the Rio Pact). Only eight states, not including the United States, have ratified the Pact of Bogota, but some eight different treaties signed in the 1920's and 1930's among various states of Latin America are still in effect, and many of these also provide for Commissions of Inquiry, Commissions of Conciliation, and so forth. On top of this hodge-podge of different, overlapping, and sometimes conflicting agreements, sits the Council of the Organization of American States. As a secretariat the Organization uses the older Pan-American Union. This provides it necessary professional expertise, but there is little in the way of supranationalism. The Organization remains largely an intergovernmental organization.

Acting through procedures of intergovernmental consultation the Organization is useful in promoting international cooperation in the Americas but has little real power. There is great sensitivity among the Latin Americans toward giving up any power of decision to an agency such as the OAS, particularly because it cannot help, in the nature of things, being dominated by the United States, or giving that appearance. The OAS has concentrated on conciliation and mediation procedures for the purpose of keeping peace in the Americas, and to some extent for promoting economic assistance. The Council approved the Statutes of the Inter-American Peace Committee in 1956 as a semi-autonomous Committee, with rotating membership, and, under a 1959 amendment, the Committee was authorized to examine various possible causes of tension and to take action on its own initiative. It cannot, however, make investigations in the territory of a state without that state's permission. The new powers of the Committee were given it only temporarily, and await final decision at the Eleventh Inter-American Conference.

The relationship between the OAS and the UN, with regard to peaceful settlement of disputes between states, was raised in the Guatemalan case of 1954. The leftist government of Guatemala wished to bypass the OAS in order to embarass the United States. It did not follow regional procedures but rather complained directly to the Security Council that it had been invaded by rebel forces operating from bases in Honduras and Nicaragua, and requested the Council to send an observation mission to Guatemala and call upon the other two states to apprehend Guatemalan exiles operating to overthrow the Guatemalan government. The United States, supported by the Latin American members of the Security Council (Brazil and Colombia) suggested that the Council refer the difficulty to the OAS for urgent consideration. This proposal was vetoed by the Soviet Union. The Council then adopted a vague resolution calling "for the immediate termination of any action likely to cause bloodshed."

Guatemala contended that, by passing this resolution, the Security Council had fully assumed jurisdiction, that a "dispute" under the Charter existed, and that obligations under the Charter took precedence over those toward the OAS. The United States continued to insist the matter was one for the OAS, which was prepared to send a Commission of Enquiry to Guatemala, and that for the Council not to recognize the right of the OAS to achieve pacific settlement would be a "catastrophe of such dimensions as will gravely impair the future effectiveness of the United Nations itself and of regional organizations." By a narrow vote of 5–4, with two abstentions, this view prevailed over arguments that the UN should not abdicate its responsibilities, and that every Member had a right to be heard if it so desired. The interpretation of the interrelated paragraphs of Article 52 of the Charter dealing with Regional Organizations was thus left in doubt. The Guatemalan question itself was made moot by overthrow of the government before an OAS Commission arrived there.

The importance of the question to United States efforts to consolidate Latin America and prevent intrusions from the other bloc scarcely needs to be emphasized. Whether the essentially weak nature of the OAS will permit it to prevail in future cases, such as Cuba, remains to be seen.

The Communist bloc. Not long after it came into power the new Communist government of the Soviet Union held a Congress for Communist and allied parties. Out of this, the Communist International, or Comintern, was developed. It was organized by Lenin according to the principles of democratic centralism, which meant that the member parties were bound by disciplinary rules to accept the principles and policies of the organization. Its headquarters was located in Moscow and its rules insured the dominance of the Communist Party Soviet Union (Bolshevik). Although the sixth Congress met in 1928, the seventh and last Congress of the Comintern did not meet until 1935. The organization was reduced to a mere administrative apparatus subordinate to the Politburo of the Communist Party Soviet Union (CPSU), and was dissolved in 1943 to make relationships with wartime allies of the Soviet Union easier. Although questions have been raised concerning the genuineness of the dissolution, there is little reason to doubt the Soviet claim. The organization had already become moribund, with all international activities being supervised by regular and special sections of the Soviet Communist Party.

Whether the Comintern should be viewed as a transnational or as a supranational organization raises interesting questions. The discipline it imposed and the loyalty it demanded from its agents added up to a kind of jurisdictional control that few states have ever asserted. It was a government within a government operating at least partly contrary to the laws of the "bourgeois" states in which the Communist Parties carried on their activities and providing a center from which the policies of those states could be influenced or opposed. It seems accurate to conclude that it was supranational in a factual but not a formal sense that international law would be able to recognize. It constituted a revolutionary shadow government and shadow state within the fabric of the international system. It was inconsistent with the orderly operations of the international system and existed to frustrate and overthrow that system. For this reason, it could not be regarded as legitimate any more than any revolutionary activity can be regarded as legitimate within the framework of any existing municipal legal order.

The Comintern was supplemented by functional groupings such as the Profintern (the Communist international labor organization) and also maintained an international press service that kept the movement informed, and through which it was possible to convey policy directives. The functional divisions of the Communist movement permitted the Communists to infiltrate all sorts of organizations on a worldwide scale and to carry out their activities in all areas of economic, political, and social life.

Even with the dissolution of the Comintern, these organizational advantages were not entirely lost. At the close of the Second World War, individual national Communist Parties still existed legally in most states. Very large Communist Parties in Italy and France participated in the governments of those nations and had the distinct possibility of becoming the main governmental force. These national parties assumed the task of organizing front groups and social and political alliances. In Western Europe, discipline was maintained by the fact that the great strength of the Communist Parties stemmed from their association with the Soviet Union. In the absence of this source of strength, they would have been as futile as the various leftwing splinter groupings. The leaders of the Western Communist Parties desired to cooperate with the Soviet Union and, moreover, could be replaced at any time by manipulations originating in the Soviet Union.

In the satellites, occupation by the Soviet Army maintained one important lever of control. Stalin's manipulations between the resistance Communists and those who sojourned in Moscow during the war constituted another method of control. A third important control stemmed from the fact that virtually all important leaders of the Communist Parties in these countries recognized the need for unity until the front governments were replaced by governments completely controlled by the Communist Party. At least as long as power was shared with other parties, unity within the Communist party was a desideratum of policy. Moreover, the minority position of the Communist Parties—at least with respect to popular favor—made for a certain dependence upon the Soviet Union. Finally the Leninist organization of the party operated in the same direction. Even so, there was a tendency on the part of nationalist leaderships in Yugoslavia, Bulgaria, and Poland, in particular, to follow policies that diverged from those of the Soviet Union or to attempt to influence Soviet policy in a manner unacceptable to Stalin. This may have at least one of the factors leading to the formation of the Cominform.

In the last analysis, however, the reasons for the formation of the Communist Information Bureau, or Cominform, in the autumn of 1947 must remain a matter of conjecture. The first meeting in Poland was secret, but many details of the meeting were published in the organ established by the Cominform—*For A Lasting Peace: For A People's Democracy*. Representatives attended from the Soviet Party, from the satellite parties with the exception of East Germany and

Albania, and from the French and Italian parties. The representation was restricted to Europe, unlike the worldwide Comintern—and even within Europe, membership was restricted in such a way that governmental aspects could not be ignored. With the exception of Czechoslovakia, the satellite parties were in almost full control of the government, and within Czechoslovakia the Communist Party held effective levers that were to be used during the coup in February 1948. The insignificant Albanian party, which, for the moment, was within the sphere of Yugoslavia, was not represented, and the East German Party, which did not yet represent a state and which may have been expendable in this period, was not represented either. On the other hand, the Communist Parties of France and Italy, which had been in the governments of their respective states until the spring and mid-summer, respectively, of 1947, and which still seemed to have the opportunity to take over by electoral means, were represented, while the minuscule and unimportant British party was not.

The mode of representation adopted by the Cominform gives rise to the distinct suspicion that the Cominform, unlike the Comintern, was established, not to give central direction to Communist Party activity everywhere, but to facilitate the coordination of Communist government policy in Europe. There is at least some evidence to support the view that two major and closely related objectives of the meeting were to constrain nationalist economic tendencies and to stimulate industrial plans that placed emphasis on the growth of heavy industry.

Although the Cominform journal, in its esoteric language, signalled shifts in world Communist policy that were faithfully followed by all Communist parties, including those not represented in the Cominform, there is little reason to believe that the Cominform amounted to more than the claims made for it by its sponsors—that it was a forum for the exchange of views and information. An attempt was made to haul the dissident Yugoslav leaders before a meeting of the Cominform. But even this demand was not put in the form of a summons to trial but rather as a proposal that the matter be discussed at the Bucharest meeting. The Cominform never claimed any formal jurisdiction over Yugoslav policy, whatever private thoughts Josef Stalin may have had about Tito.

After the Yugoslav episode, the Cominform passed into a moribund condition although its house organ continued to engage in propaganda warfare and to blister the capitalist "warmongers" as well as the Titoist "deviationists." The organization became increasingly ineffective. As the Soviet regime under Khrushchev moved toward a *rapprochement* with Tito, the organization became an embarrassing relic of the unsavory past and was dissolved. During its existence, the work of the Cominform was supplemented by various functional and special organizations some of which have survived its demise. Among these were the World Federation of Trade Unions, the World Congress of the Partisans of Peace, the World Peace Council, the International Economic Conference, the World Federation of Democratic Youth, and the International Union of Students. The names give some indication of their activities.

In 1949, the Soviet Union formed the Council for Mutual Economic Assistance as a counter-weight within the Communist sphere to the Marshall Plan, and in 1955, plans were laid for a unified military command among the European Communist states. These plans were later formalized in the Warsaw Pact. Some of the same supranational features operating in the NATO commands also come into play in the Warsaw arrangement. The arrangements incidental to the cooperation of the Communist states were complicated, however, with the rise of China after 1949 as a major Communist state. There is some substantial evidence that China has begun to play a leading role in the Asiatic Communist movement. The Asian Peace Conference held in Peiping in 1952 gives further support to this point of view. These relationships, however, are so informal—at least at the public level—and so difficult to disentangle, that interpretations are hazardous.

From a formal point of view, supranational aspects of Communist state organization would seem to be minimal. Yet events in the Soviet Union cast their shadow on the European satellites. The fall of Beria, for instance, led to important changes in the hierarchy of the East German Communist Party. The degree of economic cooperation is very great. Some evidence seems to be accumulating that a major economic change is underway, according to which the satellites will specialize in those forms of production in which they have the greatest comparative advantage rather than continuing to emphasize heavy industry. This, of course, would increase interdependence within the Communist bloc.

It would seem that supranational aspects, formally at least, are less important within the Communist sphere than in Western Europe, and, therefore, that the nation-state continues to play a larger role in their relationships. Certainly this is true with respect to China, which, after a successful revolution based primarily on internal strength and waged partly at least against the advice of Stalin, has little reason to kow-tow to Moscow. This remains true despite

China's dependence upon the Soviet Union within the Communist bloc.[3] In Eastern Europe however, the Soviet Union does not need formal supranational organs to insure virtual uniformity of policy. The influence of the Soviet party within the satellite parties, and the ability to support those satellite leaders who are loyal to it, constitute two important methods of control. In addition, the Soviet Army lurks in the background ready to crush any revolt by a European satellite against the leadership of the Soviet Union. Events in Hungary in the autumn of 1956 gave striking evidence of this, and Gomulka in Poland never loses sight of this possibility. Technically, therefore the satellites are independent nations with exclusive jurisdiction within their own territory and free to contract out of any arrangements with the Soviet Union. In fact this will not be permitted; nor can these technical rights be enforced without support from NATO and at a price the NATO bloc seems quite unwilling to pay. Moreover, maintenance of the present situation accords with the requirements of the Soviet Union, which finds it useful, in view of its efforts to win over other nation states, not to remove the facade of national independence. Therefore legal recognition of the factual supranational aspects of the Communist bloc are likely to be delayed or postponed indefinitely.

Conclusions

In the present political context regional organizations are efforts to consolidate blocs. It is embarrassing to the major bloc leaders to

[3] In 1960, there was considerable evidence of a doctrinal clash between Moscow and Peiping concerning the use of war, the ability of the Communist states to survive nuclear war, and the means of achieving Communism. The pointed failure of the Chinese Communist delegation to arrive at the World Orientalist Congress held in Moscow in the summer of 1960 caused much comment concerning a potential split. In addition, the apparent commitment of Albania, the sole European Communist state that lacked a land frontier with either the Soviet Union or a satellite state, to the Peiping "line" stirred much speculation. However, despite the obvious conflicts of interest between the Soviet Union and China, any "break" between them comparable to the Yugoslav affair seems unlikely as long as the United States survives as a major nation. China is much too dependent on Soviet support to break with Moscow, and, ideologically, China is committed to a more radical domestic and international policy in any case. Although the Soviet Union may have an interest in moderating China's policies, or in rejecting the corollaries of the "leading role" in the Communist bloc that China wants to thrust upon it, it is difficult to see the Soviet interest in forcing a split.

have intrabloc disputes aired in an arena where the opposing bloc participates and, understandably, not always helpfully. Examples are well-known: Hungary, Suez, Cyprus, and Guatemala. The Soviet Union prefers to remove tensions in the Communist bloc by intra-Party resolution. The United States has used NATO and the OAS for the same purposes, and it has given every encouragement to European union (in its many related forms) as a method of resolving and settling problems that might otherwise lead to dispute.

To say that these organizations are a means of bloc consolidation is not to be either critical or cynical, but is merely to point out their obvious advantages and growth potential. If the United States desires to secure peace, then encouraging intrabloc settlement is a fruitful alternative to UN disposition for the very reason that the opposing bloc is not represented and has no effective means of exploiting existing tensions to its advantage. We must always keep in mind that the pressure to weaken the other bloc by causing internal dissension is difficult to resist.

The success of law-government institutions in Europe has been far greater, and has resulted in much more extensive cooperation there, than in Latin America. United States relations with European countries, and their relations among themselves, are predominantly through multilateral organizations. The European Communities, the OEEC, and the EPU, as well, of course, as NATO, are more closely integrated in terms of planning, dispute avoidance and settlement, and make infinitely more use of common staff and supranational authority, than does the OAS with its complex intergovernmental and treaty basis. The latter has been successful in dousing brush fires (except for Guatemala) and encouraging some hesitant and strictly minor league economic and social cooperation. But unlike Europe, Latin America remains torn by centrifugal forces. This is reflected in the emphasis within the OAS upon formal intergovernmental techniques.

There are a number of reasons why this tends to be so. The most important are worth recalling briefly.

European political leaders, in contrast with those of Latin America, felt after the Second World War a need to unify (or at least to increase the mechanisms of continual cooperation) in the face of what was regarded as a serious internal and external Communist threat, and as a means for recovery from war devastation. The European democracies possessed a common outlook, highly similar political views within a welfare-oriented democratic framework, and a wealth of educated and skilled leadership. In addition, many perceived that future greatness and future leadership in world affairs could exist only in terms of cooperation and integration. Thus, Western Union preceded NATO; and OEEC, EPU and the ECSC preceded the more extensive forms of economic and political integration of the Common Market.

Political difficulties have been persistently present, but always seem to be surmounted. Former colonial powers have created difficulties for the United States, and the West generally, in Afro-Asia; and the United States has not always foreseen the difficulties that it would face with independence as clearly as it did the need for an end to European political domination of these areas. There have been forces making for dissonance in Europe: the ambivalence of the United Kingdom, born of conflict between its need for Europe and its pride in the Commonwealth; the Swiss tradition of neutrality, and that of Sweden, with two Scandinavian partners in NATO; the remnants of four score years of Franco-German mistrust and hostility. But throughout, the inability to turn inward to "sovereignty" has overcome bias, prejudice, and even preference. The realities of intra-European defense and economic interdependence were understood by an educated and skilled political elite, and the result has been the most effective and durable forms of partial supranational government yet devised.

The United States has been the beneficiary of European functional unification, not its originator or moving force. It has aided and assisted the movement and created formal ties, especially at the military level. And it has helped greatly to build the Western bloc by providing economic assistance without which it would have been extremely difficult politically for the European countries to have resolved conflicting economic interests. It is almost no exaggeration to say that today it is more complicated for Europe to break apart than it was to bring it together. Indeed, the Free Trade Area, despite immense difficulties, will come into being for just this reason. The fundamental precondition to peaceful resolution of differences exists once groups are convinced that their unity is more important to preserve than any dispute which arises among them.

The road to supranational unity may be paved with ambiguity and overlapping organization rather than with clear-cut legal rules and orderly structure. In this respect, the evolution of constitutional forms of European cooperation are instructive. They have ranged from quite traditional inter-governmental arrangements, formalized

by treaties stating general purposes, pledging assistance and cooperation, but preserving all the formal prerogatives of the signatories; to
continuing forms of cooperative endeavor with joint staffs; to supranational communities with formalized common decision-making institutions binding national governments. The key, in each case, to
successful intergovernmental arrangements has been the joint staff
at the working level. Although these staffs have been composed of
national officials, they have characteristically been quite independent
of formal governmental instructions and have not been closely supervised or controlled by national bureaucracies. Actually they have
been playing simultaneously national and supranational roles, presenting national problems and views informally, more often than
formally, transmitted, in order to work out, rather than negotiate, a
common position that they have then supported to their national
governments. By first digging out jointly relevant facts and preparing analyses, they have greatly speeded up, improved, and de-
politicized the process of intergovernmental agreement at the formal
level. Indeed, the official of ambiguous role—national and supranational—may be the most important contribution to international law
government in this century.

Although European unity is only partly achieved, although it is
only functional in nature, and although different states participate
in different organizations, it is nonetheless effective in its capacity
to avoid and resolve disputes of a serious nature among participants.

In Latin America centrifugal forces predominate and make far more
difficult the creation of effective governmental institutions above the
national level. Great emphasis is given to national sovereignty and
independence. The dominating position of the United States tends
to increase rather than mitigate this feeling. From the economic
viewpoint, economies tend to be competitive rather than complementary, and too greatly dependent on one basic resource that is far
too sensitive to international trade fluctuations. From the political
viewpoint governments run the spectrum from right to left in every
possible sense. Cooperation, for these reasons, is most difficult save
on strongly national intergovernmental lines—and even here there is
mistrust and hostility. Furthermore, the ranks of trained and efficient civil servants and technical experts in various fields is in Latin
America, unlike the situation in Europe, quite thin. By and large
there remains, in Latin America, a strong hostility to foreign interference which sometimes includes and sometimes excludes the United
States; that is, the Latin Americans appreciate that the United States

has historically been their protector against European domination and that they must turn to it for help in this respect when threats exist, but they fear United States domination of their domestic affairs.

Although the bloc type of organization is not presently appropriate in all regional areas, it does represent a major trend of the international politics of the present age. Bloc organization—whether the bloc has primarily a military orientation as in the case of NATO or primarily an economic orientation as in the case of the Common Market—is a new kind of political structure within which law is developed. These blocs exercise exclusive and ultimate authority in areas that previously were considered to be within the exclusive competence of "sovereign" states. Their existence forces us to reconsider our notions concerning sovereignty. They also help to stabilize the bipolar international system and thus help to maintain important norms of that system. These bloc organizational forms are revolutionary in nature. Never before have actors of such a kind participated to an important degree in international politics. They are still in early stages of development. We do not yet thoroughly understand their natures, their functioning, their probable development, or their impact on international law. The authors do predict, however, that such organizations are more likely to proliferate than not and that their impact on the law is likely to be profound.

13

THE ROLE OF NORMS
IN INTERNATIONAL
POLITICS

AMONG the cynical reasons for discounting the influence of norms in international politics is the claim that states are interested only in increasing their power,[1] or, more modestly, that unless states strive for power they will fail to survive. The authors think that both formulations are unsound; the first descriptively and the second theoretically. States do observe norms because their leaders want to live in a lawful world and also that states ought to observe norms because they have an interest in doing so. The latter conclusion is less obvious in present-day bipolarity than it was during the "balance of power" period, but we believe that this interest is present to some extent even today.

No state has yet adopted the Gandhian philosophy of non-violence. Even India arms heavily to protect its Kashmir interests. As long as this is true, we will continue to have superficial demonstrations that states are interested only in power. That formulation, however, ignores differences between power as an instrumental goal and power as an intrinsic goal. In the sense that, to achieve any goal, it is necessary to have the "power" to gain the goal, power may be the goal of states. But, in this sense, the term "power" is misleading, for the power to maintain free institutions may be incompatible with the power to rule others. The two kinds of powers are qualitatively different. States have many objectives and these are determined by their cultural values. Alternative international actions are available

[1] This position is widely held among laymen and students, particularly among foreign students. The position is stated in generic form and is not intended to be precisely descriptive of any particular academic position.

to states and these implement or interfere with these values in different ways. It is the differences in values and in actions that make the study of international politics interesting. The assertion that all states are the same because all seek power obscures and confuses the important issues. According to such a formulation, Christ and Hitler, the Rotary Club and the Communist Party, Great Britain and Nazi Germany all would be the same because they all have sought power.

The important questions of international politics and law concern the values states seek, the risks they are willing to run to protect given values, and the policies that are appropriate in pursuing and implementing the values they hold. Some states have defined their interests to include conquest and others to include the protection of still other states from conquest. Some are willing to wage preventive war at the slightest indication that other states at some future time might be powerful enough to attack them and others to fight only when physically attacked. Some states at war are willing to impose total controls on the populace to secure victory, whereas others will impose only controls that are not inconsistent with the restoration of free institutions at the end of the war.

For some time after the conclusion of the Second World War, it would have been within the power of the United States to lay waste the Soviet Union, without suffering armed reprisal, or to forbid other nations to test nuclear weapons under penalty of nuclear attack. In, part, the failure of the United States to employ such a policy may have been a consequence of its inability to visualize at that time the consequences of future Soviet possession of nuclear weapons. But, even had the United States foreseen the future with greater clarity, even had it foreseen the hazards of Soviet possession of nuclear weapons, preventive war—particularly preventive nuclear war —was not a possible policy for a nation possessing the institutions and values that characterized the United States.

It might, however, be conceded that the values of nations differ and that their international behavior also differs. A more sophisticated version of the cynical position still might contend that in the last analysis nations would implement only national and not international values. We think that this position undervalues the extent to which it is important to strengthen rules that serve to restrain all nations. It is true that almost every norm of international law has been broken at one time or another and that some states are less constrained by a recognition of the importance of normative behavior than others. We do not deny this. We believe, however, that many writers fail to distinguish between frequent efforts to change rules and relatively rare rule-less behavior.

In the nineteenth century, for instance, many nations might on specific situations have derived gains from violating the rules concerning the conduct of war or the treatment of property in occupied territory that would have outweighed reprisals possible in the particular case. They would, however, have weakened the general rule and this would have been to their disadvantage. Once a rule is weakened, it is not always easy to renegotiate a new rule. A new bargaining situation develops; there are competing alternatives; and, even if all parties to a dispute prefer some agreement to none, the inability to find some clear rule that naturally secures agreement may result in no agreement. This explains, in part, the durability of recognized "customary" rules and the self-restraint of nations where the potential injured party is helpless to withstand demands made upon him. Even where the norm itself has become undesirable to some of the important actors on the international scene, they may be cautious about violating it, lest the general rule of law be weakened. And, even where they break the old norm because they can no longer abide by it, they may attempt to justify this in terms of other norms or by a reinterpretation of the old norm. This should not be viewed as mere hypocrisy, for it plays an important role in maintaining the rule of law in international affairs. It is one way of "legislating" change; and, precisely because of its irregular nature, may in fact be used more sparingly than legislative change in municipal politics.

Nor should we underestimate the extent to which law-abiding behavior is strongly protective of a nation's interests. A reputation for principled behavior is an asset for nations as well as for individuals despite the factors in international politics that make it somewhat more difficult to remain virtuous than in ordinary civil life. One obvious instance is that it is important to be dependable. In effect this is a modification of the previous statement, for there may also be some advantage in being dependably wicked. It is a mistake to believe that Germany and Japan left the League of Nations because they did not possess a veto and that the Soviet Union remains in the United Nations because it does have a veto. The Security Council took effective action in Korea during Russia's absence by a strained interpretation of the rule on abstention; the General Assembly authorized United Nations action north of the thirty-eighth parallel. Yet the Soviet Union remained in the UN. The League of Nations' action at the time of the China incidents was, if anything, even less effective than General Assembly action at the time of the Hungarian revolution in 1956. Yet Japan left the League.

Germany and Japan left the League deliberately to shock and frighten other nations into accepting their aggressive aims whereas the Soviet Union—reluctant to engage in overt military conquest—makes use of the United Nations in an attempt to influence the uncommitted nations. The Soviet Union may use its United Nations forum to threaten or to cajole other nations. But, unless it intends to resort to force to resolve its international claims, it is most unlikely to quit the United Nations merely because of adverse votes. The forum provided by the United Nations is too important for influencing other nations and world opinion. And the veto is not the major bar to effective enforcement action, although it may be useful to the Soviet Union in preventing legal condemnation by the Security Council or enforcement action by that body under Chapter VII of the Charter. In any event, Mr. Khrushchev blustered mightily at the 1960 session of the General Assembly. This would seem to indicate that he thought it an advantage to be considered aggressive or demanding and he may well be correct.

On the other hand, Churchill understood better than most—and apparently better than the then Chief of the Imperial General Staff understands to this day—the importance of the reputation of virtuous behavior. A splendid instance of this understanding occurred when scarce British forces were removed from the desperate struggle for Egypt to the hopeless defense of Greece. Churchill understood, however, in this dark hour that Great Britain's reputation for honoring its commitments was an important asset that had to be preserved even at great cost under conditions of high risk.

A reputation for principled behavior is highly advantageous for a nation. Its agreements are respected and its offers more acceptable because they can be counted on. Forcible efforts to protect its interests will be recognized as such and are unlikely to be confused with more unlimited objectives that stir the antagonism or opposition of others. These are generalities of course; the heritage of colonialism has done much to create suspicions that principled behavior can do little to diminish. And the United States is still bearing the cross of "dollar diplomacy" with respect to Latin American affairs. We do not deny that contingencies of this sort modify general principles, but we think they still hold. Particularly as we move from the response of the masses to those of professional diplomats do the differences in behavior become important. Whatever reasons some may have had to oppose the American actions in Lebanon—and there were in many cases important political reasons—few professional diplomats thought the United States was attempting to institute colonial rule and therefore that they had to oppose it as urgently as otherwise might have been the case. This is an important consideration for the United States, which is unable or unwilling to use force in the same way as the Soviet Union.

But there is another side to the coin. A principled nation, with a reputation for being principled, is less subject to blackmail and hard bargaining techniques than a nation that continually trims corners to gain some advantage. No one thinks of asking Brooks Brothers to give a cash discount, or of asking Albert Schweitzer to pay graft to get his medicines. No one would have attempted to blackmail Gandhi.

If we move to the international realm, we can think of many cases in which the United States, for instance, is in a weakened bargaining position if it does not stand on principle. Egypt, for instance, can point out that it can hardly pay for the United States to force Egypt into a pro-Soviet position by actively supporting Israel on the Suez Canal issue with respect to the passage of Israeli cargoes. If, however, the United States establishes clear principles governing its policies and demonstrates that it intends to follow those principles, regardless of what that decision costs in any individual instance, the United States becomes a virtual force of nature with respect to its behavior pattern and other nations will be deterred from attempting to exploit the situation to their advantage. If the United States has committed itself to certain principles of action and is willing to lose Egypt rather than to renege on its principles, Egypt might hesitate before backing itself into a corner.

Commitment to principle is not an advantage if it is engaged in mechanically. A nation ought to commit itself only to principles with which it can live—and with which others can also live. Principles that do not give promise of a durable and acceptable international order are likely to stir only rigid opposition rather than acceptance. Moreover, principles cannot be asserted merely as a bluff, for the bluff may be called. To be effective the commitment to principle must be credible in terms of a nation's institutions, its values, and its character. A weak and flabby nation, subject to the political pressures of a satisfied and cowardly public, will not be convincing if it attempts to take a strong international stand. Moreover, even under the best circumstances, the commitment to principle will involve costs, for often other nations will remain unconvinced or, for reasons of their own, will feel that they cannot agree to the solution for which the principles call. We do not assert that commitment to principle always works, but we do feel that we have explained one of the reasons why some nations have committed themselves to principle in the past and why others may do so in the future. And this, in turn, helps, in part, to explain the strength of the normative structure of international law.

In non-zero-sum games like international politics an important part of the play involves influencing the alternatives open to other players, their expectations, and, thus, their future behavior. The expectation that a nation will give way on its principles encourages demands that it give way, and may help to create a situation in which normative behavior breaks down if other nations do not exercise self-restraint. In such a case the international system is either transformed in an undesirable way or the rule of the jungle prevails. The strategy of a nation cannot be divorced from the kind of political order it desires to establish.

Every time the United States compromises its obligations—as in the failure to enforce the Security Council resolution on Israeli passage through the Suez Canal—in order to avoid some immediate undesirable consequence, it demonstrates its susceptibility to blackmail and encourages further blackmail attempts. The moment principles are blurred, without being replaced by new principles, there is no longer a clear standard to guide policy. Most concessions are defended on the basis of the immediate or short-run alternatives, without sufficient consideration being given to the possibility that they may open up a process the costs of which are large and indefinite.

This is not an argument for absolute inflexibility or for refusal to bargain. If each nation stood inflexibly on principle, all negotiations and international intercourse would break down. But there are some principles that are of great importance and that can be made generally effective. To acquiesce in or to condone violations of these principles is to surrender a long-term interest for temporary advantage. On the other hand, the principle need not be enforced in each instance. For example, the United States may not be in a position where it is practicable to enforce the Israeli right under the Convention of 1888 and Security Council resolution to passage through the Suez Canal. To attempt to enforce that right quixotically would impair American prestige, and to enforce the right at great cost to other important political interests might be imprudent.

However, to condone Egyptian violation of the law by, for instance, resuming economic aid or supporting Egypt's bid for a Security Council seat, is to surrender a long-term interest for a temporary advantage. The Egyptians view such actions as evidence of an American surrender to their political strength, lose respect for the United States, and resolve to engage in additional blackmail, thereby serving notice to others that blackmail pays. Patience and moderation undoubtedly are admirable qualities in dealing with the suspicious and rebellious leaders of the new nations. But it is a disservice to them also to lead them to anticipate rewards for their lawless behavior when they do not understand the long-term costs they also will have to pay if the normative standards of international law are weakened. And, when the United States stains its honor by fearing the costs of forthright behavior, it undermines its most important permanent interests and betrays those of the free and democratic world for which it bears responsibility in the present bipolar period.

We have already seen how a wide area of agreement on normative standards existed during the "balance of power" period. The general political constraints flowed from the political patterns of activity of the period, in particular, the need for a system of flexible alliances. The institutions of private property and the economic system of capitalism structured still other norms of the system, while the need for markets, sources of materials, and peaceful trading also played a role. Technology influenced many of the rules, particularly with respect to warfare—for instance, rules concerning the submarine and airplane. There is no need to dwell on these rules, for they have been covered in the previous chapters, and they were reinforced by the necessary universalism of the system. They represented a generally common interest of the then European world system.

In the present day world, norm stability is weakened by bipolarity, by the hierarchical organization of the Communist Party and the close organizational ties within the Communist bloc, by the revolutionary and hegemonic goals of Communism, by the rapid emergence of so many new and inexperienced nations, by their revolutionary economic, political, and social goals, sometimes by their instability in organizational and policy senses, and sometimes by sheer destructive drives on their part to destroy the existing order.

In the new bipolar system, the interests uniting members of blocs are easy to perceive. The extent to which opposing blocs have common interests is much more limited. That there are some matters on which it is possible for opposing blocs to agree is scarcely to be questioned (the example of the Antarctic Treaty, and perhaps some matters with regard to Outer Space, here join with more traditional areas of international law such as diplomatic immunity). The extent to which uncommitted nations will be able to support effectively universal standards of international conduct is less obvious. We are left with a legal system in which some norms will receive widespread support, others less extensive support, and still others support only within allied blocs. This would seem to present an argument for at least some universal interests, and others which may be common to many, or some, but not to all.

Short of major thermonuclear war, however, both the United States and the Soviet Union have a joint interest in maintaining those minimal normative standards that permit each to live tolerably in a world in which the other is powerful. Such standards might govern the exploitation of the Antarctic and of outer space, the control of satellites, the degree of permissible interference within blocs and in uncommitted areas, the regulation of air routes, radio and television channels, the control of commercial transactions, the treatment of foreign nationals, the restriction of the spread of nuclear weapons, and so forth. The interest of the two blocs in these rules might be weaker than the interest of a major nation in the normative rules of the "balance of power" period because any sudden technological development might permit one or the other of the blocs to establish a world system under its control. Since the Soviet Union is both more revolutionary than the United States and more able, politically, to take the measures necessary to exploit the consequences of technological development, either in terms of hard political bargaining or the waging of war, its attitude toward the normative rules is naturally more instrumental than that of the United States. This places a harsh burden upon the United States, for it must now bear most of the costs and much of the burden of maintaining desirable normative rules of international law. The burden can be neither shifted elsewhere nor broadly shared.

If we return to the analogy of the non-zero-sum cooperative game, the bipolar situation is one in which both the United States and the Soviet Union have a joint interest in one of the possible cooperative solutions (unless military developments permit victory for one of the nations at an acceptable cost). However, the Soviet Union has a better threat position because of its internal political system; and the

United States can maintain its position best if it stands on principle and thus forces the Soviet Union to treat it more or less as an inflexible force of nature, unresponsive to bargaining pressures. It is worth noting that the United States—despite accusations of rigidity —has failed to make proper use of a rigid position, whereas the Soviet Union—already in a superior bargaining position—has been permitted to appear as a force of nature.

Thus, the Soviet Union makes ever increasing demands that the Western publics regard as justified because "one cannot expect the Soviet Union to accept any other position." Although the Soviet Union denounces bourgeois democracy and capitalism, the allied occupation of Berlin, American arms and arms-testing policies, the United States and NATO have failed either to establish a line of principle from which no retreat will be permitted or to point out that the Soviet regime by its nature is responsible for the danger of war. Under the present conditions of development of political and economic forces, any erosion of existing normative standards will work to the disadvantage of the NATO nations. Although the Soviet Union has an interest in supporting these standards, provided the United States follows policies that will raise the costs of contrary policies, there is a non-cooperative solution that is advantageous to the Soviet Union if the United States and its allies do not find the right strategies. Thus, although it would be false to state that existing normative standards are not supported in terms of the present interests of the Soviet Union and the United States, it is true to state that the present equilibrium is precarious.

An example may help to make this clear—particularly if the example is fairly obvious. Given the potential dangers of present military technology and the condition that either a relatively unpredictable technological jump or the exploitation of surprise may permit either the United States or the Soviet Union to gain a decisive advantage, each nation has an interest in an arms control agreement that minimizes the possibility that either will gain an unpredictable decisive advantage and maximizes the possibility that each can maintain its present relative position. Thus, norms governing the use and development of arms, and even possibly the development of scientific technology, are negotiable in principle, if difficult to negotiate in fact. If, however, these norms are not supervised under appropriate institutional arrangements, the Soviet Union will then find an interest in utilizing its advantage in maintaining secrecy to break the agreement. In short, the Soviet Union may prefer agreement on such norms to no agreement; weak supervision to strong supervision; and breaking the agreement to keeping it if the supervision is weak, or if it believes that for domestic political reasons the democratic governments will be unable to respond to a Soviet breach of agreement by breaking the agreements themselves.

The relationship of the normative structure of international law to the social structure of the international system is affected by the fact that the international system is a subsystem-dominant system. A system is subsystem dominant to the extent that an actor in the system can influence the important or characteristic behavior of the system—in the case of law, the norm structure—and system dominant to the extent that the characteristic behavior operates as a parametric given, to which the actor must conform or suffer the penalties. In the "balance of power" international system, each major nation had a great influence upon the normative structure of the system. But if a given nation deviated from the norms tolerated by the other nations, it usually was forced to conform. This is equivalent to an oligopolistic situation in industry, where the pricing policies of a small number of major producers obviously result in a price-level different from a perfect—or system-dominant—market, in which each producer must treat prices as given. Yet the influence of the oligopolistic producer upon price is limited by the countervailing actions which his competitors may take. The influence of the oligopolistic producer is there; it results in a different price level from the perfect market; there is greater latitude in determining price and production levels; and yet the freedom is limited.

In the extreme subsystem dominant case—monopoly—except for the influence of products that are different but may displace the product of the monopolist in the market, the producer may choose the particular relationship of price and production he wants. A political example is provided by the Soviet Union—an example in which the Communist Party has a virtual monopoly of political control. Thus, the system is toward the subsystem-dominant end of the political scale and the dictatorship may impose collective farms or *agorogrods* or new forms of production almost at will, taking into account only such factors as political response (which may be treated as equivalent to the price of the raw material and elasticities of demand for the monopolist).

The bipolar system—perhaps similar to duopoly—is closer to the subsystem-dominant end of the scale than is the "balance of power" system (oligopoly). In the bipolar system, the United States and the

Soviet Union obviously exert more influence on the normative structure of the system than did individual nations in the "balance of power" system.   Since the influence exerted is the product not only of mechanical factors but also, in part at least, of the strategies that the United States and the Soviet Union choose in order to implement their goals, a trend analysis of the normative structure of international law is dependent not merely upon technological, economic, or political events that may change the situation but also upon the rationality of the United States and of the Soviet Union in choosing their strategies and their steadiness and resolution in implementing them.

More than one normative structure may be consistent with the present facts of international politics, although the different normative structures may themselves play roles in determining future trends in political, economic, and political international relations, as well as in determining the values that are implemented both nationally and internationally.   For instance, an American armaments drive of huge potential, coupled with a standing offer to negotiate arms controls that minimized the danger of surprise attack, might strain the Russian economy and make the idea of arms control acceptable to the Russians even though rigorous inspection were involved, whereas otherwise the Russians might prefer the arms race to controls that interfered somewhat with their domestic political system.   Clearly, such an American effort does not appear presently to be in prospect.   Yet, if such a move were made, the resulting agreement—supposing that agreement were the outcome—would have a major influence on national authority over military bases, and might establish new international law concerning the use of satellites and missiles, the production and distribution of weapons and personnel, and the access by inspection groups to national facilities.

Perhaps these agreements might have long-term consequences for the institutions of the Soviet Union and for the values implemented by Soviet institutions—consequences that would be desirable from the standpoint of American values.   Failure to reach such an agreement might increase the danger of war, result in a greater militarization of the American society, undercut the present liberal values of American society, possibly increase the resistance of nations in an intermediate period to the exercise of jurisdiction by international or mixed commissions within national territory, and possibly increase the likelihood of Soviet domination of the world in the long run. These alternatives obviously have important and different consequences for both international and domestic law.

Any number of factors might play roles in this respect. The uncommitted nations might slide into Communism for internal reasons. Conversely, they might be able to solve their economic problems and stabilize their present position—perhaps to become genuinely neutral. The NATO alliance might fall apart under both internal and external pressure. The Communist regimes might collapse from internal conflicts. Unforeseen changes in weapons systems might give one bloc or the other a decisive military advantage or might make inspection easy to evade or much more practicable than at present. The spread of nuclear weapons might have unforeseen effects. Possibly the world will become so dangerous a place in which to live, that a preventive war will be launched or a universal government formed.

The range of possibilities is large and efforts at exact prediction would be unscientific. We can, however, analyze the trends as they presently appear, as we have done, and emphasize the range within which conscious strategic choice may play an important role in shaping the normative pattern of the developing bipolar world. Cooperative solutions are not necessarily more likely than uncooperative solutions. And among the possible alternative (cooperative or uncooperative) solutions, the choice may depend upon the intelligence and skill with which the United States and the Soviet Union employ the resources available to them.

A normative pattern of behavior will emerge in the new bipolar system because nations and supranational entities must in some way regulate their activities, whether by explicit or implicit agreement. The numbers, resources, and dispositions of the actors will set some limit upon the number of normative patterns consistent with the facts of international relations. But, within those limits, the norms that are finally imposed will depend upon the choices made by human and social agencies. Once chosen, the norms will themselves influence the patterns of the future, for they will set constraints on future behavior and affect institutional structure in both gross and subtle ways. Our choices then have grave consequences from the standpoint of our values. Law is not morality but, even in the international area, the choice of law depends upon moral standards and is itself a test of those standards.

It is interesting that game theory may help to explain how some issues become arbitrable, although the United States and Soviet Union are not able to reach agreement in bilateral negotiations. To explain this possibility, we will discuss an oversimplified case. Suppose, on an issue such as the control of outer space satellites, there were three possible positions: no control, very restricted employment of satellites without supervision, and less restricted employment of satellites under supervision. Suppose both the United States and the Soviet Union preferred some form of control to no control but that each had a strong preference for a different one of the remaining alternatives. Neither would see any reason to concede to the other and the least-preferred alternative, no control, might result. If, on the other hand, an arbiter were chosen—a state whose position was neutral, at least in the sense of being unknown—then the U.S. and the U.S.S.R. would each have a chance of gaining its position and might be willing to accept this chance in preference to no control. The game thus becomes a bargaining problem in which the participants attempt to control the odds that determine where the outcome occurs within the negotiation set. Since, however it would be unpalatable to admit that a random device was used (the arbiter may in fact be viewed as a random device) the arbiter picks from among alternative norms to justify his choice. This indeed performs a social and ritual function in buttressing the decision he makes.

We pass over the real difficulties of agreeing upon an arbiter. These difficulties, however, can be solved when agreement is desired. It is worthwhile to note the device that has been employed historically of each party to the dispute picking an arbiter and the two arbiters choosing a third. This is simply another example of the employment of random devices where agreement cannot be reached. Each party to the dispute might insist on an arbiter reasonably certain to decide in its favor if a single arbiter were chosen. So each picks an arbiter, who, in turn, will pick a tie-breaking arbiter. The first two arbiters, however, are chance devices, even if those devices are loaded in favor of the parties who pick them. Thus, not being identical with the original parties in terms of outlook, they have a greater capacity to agree on a third party. Perhaps they evaluate the unknown elements in his choice pattern differently from each other. In any event, the randomness is carried to a second level by the choice of the third arbiter. By this process, the parties escape the domestic political difficulties involved in giving way to the other and yet provide themselves with a "fair" opportunity to get their way. Other tribunals, such as international courts and the United Nations, may be viewed as partly—

although obviously not completely—random devices, and their decisions may be acceptable in some cases partly for this reason and partly for other political and psycho-sociological reasons.

In a work of this type it is not possible to use analogies from game theory to carry the technical analysis of the problem further; and at this level of analysis game theory simply reinforces insights that might be obtained from more discursive analysis. But it is interesting to repeat that the norms of international law are enforcible and are also enforced; however, it is necessary to look at the structure of the situation to determine when this is or is not likely to be the case. Thus, although no international government may be said to exist, in the sense of a concrete institution, that can coerce nation-states, there is international government and international law. States are not free to violate norms without real costs or, in many circumstances, without being coerced or penalized by other states that have interests in maintaining the norms. Thus, the sanctions of international law may stem either from internal motivation or from external action. In either case, these sanctions are real. And, in either case, the life of the state is a life governed, in part at least, by law, rather than merely by appetite.

BIBLIOGRAPHICAL NOTES

GENERAL REFERENCES

The literature on international law and international politics is vast. Anything save a short reference to principal sources we have used has seemed to us unnecessary. These references should suffice to give the interested reader further sources in the literature, without, at the same time, overwhelming him with choice. They also serve, with regard to each chapter, to document statements contained therein without cluttering the text with footnotes and specific references.

Standard treatises on international law are:

Oppenheim, *International Law* (vol. 1, rev. 8th ed., 1955) H. Lauterpacht, ed.; (vol. 2, 7th ed., 1952).

Edited and revised by the late Sir Hirsch Lauterpacht, a judge on the International Court of Justice and a distinguished professor at Cambridge, this is the best of the treatises.

Hyde, *International Law, Chiefly as Interpreted and Applied by the United States* (2nd ed., 3 vols., 1945).

Comprehensive and, as the title indicates, particularly complete on United States practices and positions on matters where international opinion is variant.

Fenwick, *International Law* (3rd ed., 1948).

A good one-volume treatise, widely used in the United States.

More readable works of interest on the processes of international law, but ones not attempting comprehensive coverage of all problems of international law are:

Brierly, *The Law of Nations* (5th ed., 1955).

The best short introduction to the study of international law. Well-written and traditional in its view of international law.

Brierly, *Outlook for International Law* (1944).

Less comprehensive in its coverage than *The Law of Nations*.

Jessup, *Modern Law of Nations* (1948).

An American counter-part to Brierly, and somewhat more compatible with the views expressed in this book, though with much less emphasis on the political aspects of international law.

355

REFERENCES FOR CHAPTER 2

A detailed study of states as national actors in the international political system, grounded on the systems analysis summarized in this chapter, has been attempted by one of the authors. See Kaplan, *System and Process in International Politics* (1957). See also Kaplan, Burns, and Quandt, "Theoretical Analysis of the 'Balance of Power'," 5 *Behavioral Science* 240 (1960).

Other useful studies are Hartmann, *The Relations of Nations* (1957); Haas and Whiting, *Dynamics of International Relations* (1956); Schwarzenberger, *Power Politics* (2nd rev. ed., 1951); Schuman, *International Politics*, (6th ed., 1958); Van Dyck, *International Politics* (1957); Strauz-Hupe and Possony, *International Relations* (2nd ed., 1954); Organski, *World Politics* (1958).

A comprehensive study of American Foreign Policy after the Second World War is contained in Reitzel, Kaplan and Coblenz, *United States Foreign Policy, 1945–1955* (1956).

On the impact of the bipolar political system on international law, see Fox, *The Super-Powers* (1944), a brilliant prediction; Stone, *Legal Controls of International Conflict* (1954); Smith, *The Crisis in the Law of Nations* (1947); Schwarzenberger, "The Impact of the East-West Rift on International Law," 36 *Transactions of the Grotius Society* 229 (1950); Wilk, "International Law and Global Ideological Conflict: Reflections on the Universality of International Law," 45 *American Journal of International Law* 648 (1951).

For further references to the theory of games and of decision making, see Von Neumann and Morganstern, *Theory of Games and Economic Behaviour* (3rd ed., 1953); Luce and Raiffa, *Games and Decisions* (1957); Kaplan, *op. cit.;* Kaplan, *Some Problems in the Strategic Analysis of International Politics* (1959); Schelling, *The Strategy of Conflict* (1960).

REFERENCES FOR CHAPTER 3

On the evolution of the "law of nations" into international law, and the problems of universality, see especially Nussbaum, *A Concise History of the Law of Nations* (1947); Jenks, *The Common Law of Mankind* (1958), especially Chapters I and II; Wheaton, *History of the Law of Nations* (1845). In addition, most of the works cited in the General Bibliography contain relevant materials.

On Grotius, see Lauterpacht, "The Grotian Tradition in International Law," 1946 *British Year Book of International Law* 1; Dumbauld, "Hugo Grotius: The Father of International Law," 1 *Journal of Public Law* 117 (1952).

For a provocative approach to some of the current problems of interdependence see Jessup, *Transnational Law* (1956), and his "The Subjects of a Modern Law of Nations," 45 *Michigan Law Review* 383 (1947); McDougal and Leighton, "The Rights of Man in the World Community: Constitutional Illusions versus Rational Action," 14 *Law and Contemporary Problems* 490 (1949).

REFERENCES FOR CHAPTER 4

On the nature of a "state" see Laski, *The State in Theory and Practice* (1935); MacIver, *The Modern State* (1926). On the "equality" of states consult Dickinson, *Equality of States in International Law* (1920). For discussion of theory with regard to "states" as "subjects" see Kelsen, *General Theory of Law and State* (1945); Jones, "The 'Pure' Theory of International Law," 16 *British Year Book of International Law* 5 (1935); Hurst, "The Nature of International Law and the Reason Why It Is Binding On States," 30 *Transactions of the Grotius Society* 119 (1945); Humphrey, "On the Foundations of International Law," 39 *American Journal of International Law* 231 (1945).

For scholarly criticism of attempts to state "the rights and duties of states" see Kelsen, "The Draft Declaration on Rights and Duties of States," 44 *American Journal of International Law* 259 (1950).

On the "personality" of international organizations see Jenks, "The Legal Personality of International Organizations," 22 *British Year Book of International Law* 267 (1945); Liang, "The Legal Status of the United Nations in the United States," 2 *International Law Quarterly* 577 (1949); Lauterpacht, "The Subjects of the Law of Nations," 63 *Law Quarterly Review* 438 (1947) and 64 *ibid.* 97 (1948).

On the "place" of the individual, see especially Jessup, *A Modern Law of Nations* (1948) and Lauterpacht, *International Law and Human Rights* (1950).

REFERENCES FOR CHAPTER 5

Exhaustive works on problems of "recognition" are Chen, *The International Law of Recognition* (1951) and Lauterpacht, *Recognition in International Law* (1947). The Lauterpacht view is criticized in Kunz, "Critical Remarks on Lauterpacht's Recognition in International Law," 44 *American Journal of International Law* 713 (1950). Kelsen's views are found in his *General Theory of Law and State* (1954), and in "Recognition in International Law: Theoretical Observations," 35 *American Journal of International Law* 605 (1941). On "collective recognition" see Briggs, "Recognition of States: Some Reflections on Doctrine and Practice," 43 *American Journal of International Law* 113 (1949) and "Community Interest in the Emergence of New States: The Problem of Recognition," 1950 *Proceedings of the American Society of International Law* 169. On "admission to the United Nations" see the Secretariat Memorandum on "Legal Aspects of Problems of Representation in the United Nations," *U.N. Document S/1466* (9 March 1950), reprinted in 4 *International Organization* 356 (1950).

Problems of state succession can get extremely complex. See Feilchenfeld, *Public Debts and State Succession* (1931); Jones, "State Succession in the Matter of Treaties," 1947 *British Year Book of International Law* 360; O'Connell, "Economic Concessions in the Law of State Succession," 1950 *British Year Book of International Law* 93.

REFERENCES FOR CHAPTER 6

On "sovereignty" see Merriam, *History of the Theory of Sovereignty Since Rousseau* (1900); Laski, *Studies in the Problem of Sovereignty* (1917) and *Foundations of Sovereignty* (1921); Keeton, *National Sovereignty and International Order* (1939); Friedmann, *The Crisis of the National State* (1943).

On the various modes of acquiring territory, settling boundary problems, and so forth the literature is too vast to make selection. The reader may consult any of the standard treaties for authority. The classic case is *The Island of Palmas Case* (United States v. The Netherlands), decided by The Permanent Court of Arbitration in 1928, and reported in 2 *U.N. Reports of International Arbitration Awards* 829.

On territorial waters, continental shelf, and other maritime problems see Jessup, *Law of Territorial Waters and Maritime Jurisdiction* (1927); Higgins and Colombos, *International Law of the Sea* (4th ed., by Colombos, 1959); Reiff, *The United States and the Treaty Law of the Sea* (1959); United Nations, *Laws and Regulations on the Regime of the High Seas* (U.N. Legislative Series, 1952); McDougal and Burke, "Crisis in the Law of the Sea," 67 *Yale Law Journal* 539 (1958). Texts of the treaties negotiated in 1958 at the U.N. Conference on the Law of the Sea are reprinted in (1959) *Department of State Bulletin* 1110.

Problems of Antarctica and Outer Space, as well as a useful study of forms of international and joint national administration, are discussed in Jessup and Taubenfeld, *Control of Outer Space* (1959). See also McDougal and Lipson, "Perspectives for a Law of Outer Space," 52 *American Journal of International Law* 407 (1958) and for the lighter side of current activities by "space lawyers," Katzenbach, "Law and Lawyers in Space," *Bulletin of Atomic Scientists* (June 15, 1958) 220. Some of the text of this chapter is based on a study and report done for the American Bar Foundation in 1959 by Katzenbach and Professor Leon Lipson of Yale.

REFERENCES FOR CHAPTER 7

The analysis of jurisdiction in this chapter, particularly as it relates to the work of national courts, is more fully developed for lawyers in Katzenbach, "Conflicts on an Unruly Horse: Reciprocal Claims and Tolerances in Interstate and International Law," 65 *Yale Law Journal* 1087 (1956). See also Jessup, *Transnational Law* (1956) and the *Hague Lectures* by McDougal cited in the general bibliography.

The process through which states give protection to nationals through diplomatic channels is fully discussed in Dunn, *The Protection of Nationals* (1932); Eagleton, *The Responsibility of States in International Law* (1928); and Freeman, *The International Responsibility of States for Denial of Justice* (1938).

Exhaustive citations to further authority are contained in The Harvard Research in International Law, "Jurisdiction with Respect to Crime," 29 *American Journal of International Law* (Supplement 1935) 519; *ibid.*, "Competence of Courts in Regard to Foreign States," 26 *American Journal of International Law* (Supplement 1932) 451; *ibid.*, "Diplomatic Privileges and Immunities," 26 *American Journal of International Law* 15 (1932) and (on consular immunities) 189. On more recent practice see Fensterwald, "Sovereign Immunity and Soviet State Trading," 63 *Harvard Law Review* 614 (1950); Bishop, "New United States Policy Limiting Sovereign Immunity," 47 *American Journal of International Law* 93 (1953).

Maritime immunities are discussed in the treatises cited in the previous chapter. On the Latin American practice of extensive asylum consult Morganstern, "Extraterritorial Asylum," 1948 *British Year Book of International Law* 236 and "The Right of Asylum," 1949 *ibid.*, 327. The *Haya de la Torre case* (Colombia v. Peru) is reported in 1951 *International Court of Justice Reports* 71.

REFERENCES FOR CHAPTER 8

Again the literature is vast. On current problems of "limited war," and on the conception of "economy of force," see Osgood, *Limited War: The Challenge to American Strategy* (1957); Kissinger, *Nuclear Weapons and Foreign Policy* (1957); Kaplan, *The Strategy of Limited Retaliation* (1959). A monumental prenuclear study is Wright, *A Study of War* (1942).

The most interesting general studies of law and war are McDougal and Feliciano, "International Coercion and World Public Order: The General Principles of the Law of War," 67 *Yale Law Journal* 771 (1958), with which contrast Stone, *Legal Controls of International Conflict* (1959).

On the history of the "just war" concept see Von Elbe, "The Evolution of the Concept of the Just War in International Law," 33 *American Journal of International Law* 665 (1939) and Waldock, "The Regulation of the Use of Force by Individual States in International Law," 81 *Hague Receuil* 455 (1952).

On the Kellogg-Briand Pact see Shotwell, *War as an Instrument of National Policy* (1929). On the League Covenant consult the analysis of Lauterpacht, "Resort to War and the Interpretation of the Covenant During the Manchurian Dispute," 28 *American Journal of International Law* 43 (1934); Williams, *Some Aspects of the Covenant of the League of Nations* (1934).

On the difficulties of dividing "war" from "peace" see Grob, *The Relativity of War and Peace* (1949); McDougal and Feliciano, "The Initiation of Coercion: A Multi-Temporal Analysis," 52 *American Journal of International Law* 241 (1958). See also McNair, "The Legal Meaning of War and the Relation of War to Reprisals," 11 *Grotius Society Transactions* 29 (1925); Brierly, "International Law and Resort to Armed Force," 4 *Cambridge Law Journal* 308 (1932).

On the impact and interpretation of the Charter see Goodrich and Simons, *The United Nations and the Maintenance of International Peace and Security* (1955); Wright, "The Prevention of Aggression," 50 *American Journal of International Law* 514 (1956); Kelsen, "Collective Security and Collective Self-Defense under the Charter of the United Nations," 42 *ibid.*, 783 (1948); Green, "The Double Standard of the United Nations," 11 *Year Book of World Affairs* 104 (1957).

The definitive study of neutrality before the Second World War is the four-volume study published by Columbia University and consisting of: Jessup and Deak, *The Origins* (1935); Phillips, Allison, and Reade, *The Napoleonic Period* (1936); Turlington, *The World War Period* (1936); and Jessup, *Today and Tomorrow* (1936). The last volume is of the most general interest today. On contemporary problems see Castren, *The Present Law of War and Neutrality* (1954); Tucker, *The Law of War and Neutrality at Sea* (1957); Komarnicki,

"The Problem of Neutrality under the United Nations Charter" 38 *Transactions of the Grotius Society* 77 (1952).

In addition, on the laws of war, consult Baxter, "The Role of Law in Modern War," 47 *Proceedings of the American Society of International Law* 90 (1953); Kunz, "The Law of War," 50 *American Journal of International Law* 313 (1956); Wright, "The Outlawry of War and the Law of War," 47 *American Journal of International Law* 365 (1953); Lauterpacht, "The Problem of the Revision of the Law of War," 29 *British Year Book of International Law* 360 (1952).

REFERENCES FOR CHAPTER 9

Generally see Finch, *Sources of Modern International Law* (1937), and the discussion in the treatises cited in the general bibliography.

On treaties see McNair, *Law of Treaties* (1938); Harvard Research in International Law, "Treaties," 29 *American Journal of International Law* 698 (1935); International Law Commission, *Report on the Law of Treaties* (Fitzmaurice, Rapporteur, in process of drafting and discussion).

On reservations to treaties, especially multipartite ones, see Malkin, "Reservations to Multilateral Conventions," 1926 *British Year Book of International Law* 141; Owen, "Reservations to Multilateral Treaties," 38 *Yale Law Journal* 1086 (1929).

On treaties as "sources" consult Starke, "Treaties as a Source of International Law," 1946 *British Year Book of International Law* 341; McNair, "International Legislation," 19 *Iowa Law Review* 177 (1934).

On "custom" see Kopelmanas, "Custom as a Means of the Creation of International Law," 1937 *British Year Book of International Law* 127; Schwarzenberger, "The Inductive Approach to International Law," 60 *Harvard Law Review* 539 (1947). On "judicial decisions" see Lauterpacht, *Development of International Law by the Permanent Court of International Justice* (1934) and *The Development of International Law by the International Court* (1958). On "general principles" see Cheng, "General Principles of Law as a Subject for International Codification," 3 *Current Legal Problems* 35 (1951); Lauterpacht, *Private Law Sources and Analogies of International Law* (1927).

There is considerable agitation for codification today, and this is one of the principle functions of the International Law Commission.

REFERENCES FOR CHAPTER 10

On the role of national courts and international law, as to which there is some variance in both practice and theory, see Borchard, "The Relation between International Law and Municipal Law," *Proceedings, 8th American Scientific Congress,* Washington, 1940, X (1943) 77; Hyde, "The Supreme Court of the United States as an Expositor of International Law," 1937 *British Year Book of International Law* 1; Lauterpacht, "Is International Law a Part of the Law of England?," 25 *Transactions of the Grotius Society* 51 (1940); Masters, *Inter-*

national Law in National Courts (1932) (surveying various countries and now out of date on some).

On diplomatic negotiation as affected by the United Nations complex see the interesting study by Jessup, "Parliamentary Diplomacy," 89 *Receuil des Cours* 181 (1956).

Standard treatises describe the functions of "good offices," "mediation," "conciliation," and so forth in adequate detail. On international arbitration and adjudication consult the definitive work of Hudson, *International Tribunals* (1944). The work of the International Court of Justice is analyzed by Fitzmaurice in eight articles under the heading "Law and Procedure of the International Court of Justice," 1950–1958 *British Year Books of International Law;* and see Jessup, *The Use of International Law* (1959) and Lauterpacht, *The Development of International Law by the International Court* (1958). Problems of procedure and jurisdiction are dealt with comprehensively in Lissitzyn, *The International Court of Justice* (1951).

On reservations to the Court's jurisdiction see Briggs, "Reservations to the Acceptance of Compulsory Jurisdiction of the International Court of Justice," 93 *Receuils des Cours* 223 (1958).

REFERENCES FOR CHAPTER 11

On the League of Nations consult Walters, *A History of the League of Nations* (2 vols., 1952); Schwarzenberger, *The League of Nations and World Order* (1936); Zimmern, *The League of Nations and the Rule of Law* (1941).

On the general development of international organization see Eagleton, *International Government* (3rd ed., 1957) (a comprehensive one-volume study).

On the United Nations the indispensable work is Goodrich and Hambro, *Charter of the United Nations. Commentary and Documents* (2nd ed., 1949). Valuable also are Kelsen, *The Law of the United Nations: A Critical Analysis of its Fundamental Problems* (1950); Potter, *An Introduction to the Study of International Organization* (5th ed., 1948); Jenks, "Some Constitutional Problems of International Organizations," 1945 *British Year Book of International Law* 11.

An excellent symposium (although now somewhat out of date) appears in 55 *Yale Law Journal* 886 (August 1946), in which note especially Lasswell, "The Interrelations of World Organization and Society" (at page 889).

On converting the United Nations into a limited world government see the exhaustive analysis of the Charter in Clark and Sohn, *World Peace through World Law* (1958).

A great deal of periodical literature on particular problems exists and can be located by reference to the bibliographical section of *International Organization*.

REFERENCES FOR CHAPTER 12

On NATO see Deutsch and others, *Political Community and the North Atlantic Area; International Organization in the Light of Historical Experience*

(1957); Patterson and Furniss, *NATO, A Critical Appraisal* (1957); Salvadori, *NATO, A Twentieth Century Community of Nations* (1957); Knorr, *NATO and American Security* (1960). The periodical literature is too numerous for citation. Useful bibliographies are collected each year in *International Organization*.

European integration and its significance are discussed in Beloff, *Europe and the Europeans* (1957); Bowie and Friedrich, *Studies in Federalism* (1954); Haas, *The Uniting of Europe* (1958); Robertson, *European Institutions, Cooperation, Integration, Unification* (1959); Zurcher, *The Struggle to Unite Europe, 1940–58* (1958). The *European Yearbook*, published each year since 1955 under the auspices of the Council of Europe, contains useful bibliographical and documentary sections.

On the difficulties of inter-American regionalism see Ball, *The Problem of Inter-American Organization* (1944); U.S. Senate, Committee on Foreign Relations (86th Cong., 1st. Sess., 1959) *The Organization of American States* (prepared by Northwestern University). On the Guatemalan incident, see Fenwick, "Jurisdictional Questions Involved in the Guatemalan Revolution," 48 *American Journal of International Law* 597 (1954).

INDEX